The planetary interest

The planetary interest:

A new concept for the global age

Kennedy Graham

(Editor)

First published in 1999 by UCL Press

UCL Press Limited
1 Gunpowder Square
London EC4A 3DE
UK

The name of University College London (UCL) is a registered trade mark
used by UCL Press with the consent of the owner.

British Library Cataloguing-in-Publication Data
A CIP catalogue record for this book is available from the British Library.

Library of Congress Cataloging-in-Publication Data are available

ISBN: 1–85728–892–0 HB
        1–85728–893–9 PB

Typeset by Graphicraft Limited, Hong Kong
Printed by T.J. International, Padstow, UK

There are worlds on which life has never arisen.
There are worlds that have been charred and ruined by cosmic catastrophes.
We are fortunate we are alive; we are powerful;
the welfare of our civilization and our species is in our hands.
If we do not speak for Earth, who will?

Carl Sagan, *Cosmos*, 1980

Contents

List of tables and figures   ix
Notes on authors   xi
Acknowledgements   xviii
Glossary   xx
Foreword
Kofi A. Annan   xxiii
Preface
Kennedy Graham   xxv

Part 1   Introduction   1

1   The planetary interest
    Kennedy Graham   3

2   Legitimacy in twenty-first century politics
    Gwyn Prins   15

3   The legitimate national interest and legitimate global power
    Kennedy Graham   21

Part 2   The vital planetary interest and the legitimate national interest   29

Section I   Global strategic security   31

4   Nuclear disarmament   39
    4.1   Introduction   39
    4.2   New Zealand
           David Lange   48
    4.3   The Russian Federation
           Andrei Kozyrev   54

5   Chemical and biological disarmament   63
    5.1   Introduction   63
    5.2   Jordan
           Toujan Faisal   67
    5.3   Israel
           Naomi Chazan   74

Section II   Global environmental integrity   81

6   Ozone protection   87
    6.1   Introduction   87
    6.2   Argentina
           Dante Caputo   92
    6.3   Japan
           Koji Kakizawa   99

7 Climate stabilization   105
   7.1   Introduction   105
   7.2   The Maldives
       Ibrahim Hussain Zaki   115
   7.3   China
       Qian Yi   122

Section III   Global sustainability   129

8 Population stabilization   139
   8.1   Introduction   139
   8.2   India
       Margaret Alva   144
   8.3   Australia
       Margaret Reynolds   151

9 Development   159
   9.1   Introduction   159
   9.2   Bangladesh
       Abdul Moyeen Khan   168
   9.3   Kenya
       Charity Kaluki Ngilu   176

10 Forest management   185
   10.1   Introduction   185
   10.2   Indonesia
       Theo Sambuaga   189
   10.3   Brazil
       Fabio Feldmann   196

11 Consumption   203
   11.1   Introduction   203
   11.2   United States
       Claudine Schneider   208
   11.3   Sweden
       Lena Klevenås   217

Part 3   The vital planetary interest and legitimate global power   227

12 Global powers: Earth's planetary interest
   Shridath Ramphal   229

13 Global and regional powers: Europe's regional interest
   Emma Bonino   241

14 Global and national powers: Britain's national interest
   Michael Marshall   247

15 Global and local powers: Rome's municipal interest
   Francesco Rutelli   257

Part 4   Conclusion   267

16 The planetary interest: thoughts for the future
   Kennedy Graham   269

Bibliography   275
Index   282

List of tables and figures

TABLES

Table 4.3.1	Strategic forces reduction plans: United States	56
Table 5.1.1	Political commitment to eliminating weapons of mass destruction in the Middle East	65
Table 5.3.1	Air-to-surface missile launching capabilities in the Middle East	76
Table 5.3.2	Surface-to-surface missile launching capabilities in the Middle East	76
Table II.1	Opinion survey on the environment: selected countries	84
Table 6.1.1	Phase-out regime of ozone-depleting substances	89
Table 6.1.2	Contributions to the ozone multilateral fund	89
Table 6.2.1	Argentina: consumption of ozone-depleting substances, 1986–92	94
Table 6.2.2	Argentina: phase-out regime, 1996–2006	95
Table 7.1.1	Greenhouse gases: anthropogenic emissions and concentrations	106
Table 7.1.2	Carbon dioxide: annual average anthropogenic carbon budget, 1980–89	106
Table 7.1.3	Atmospheric concentration of carbon dioxide	107
Table 7.1.4	GHG emission performance of the Climate Change Convention reporting parties, 1990–2000	110
Table 7.1.5	Global carbon dioxide emissions from fossil fuel burning	111
Table 7.1.6	Kyoto Protocol: differentiated obligations for GHG reductions by 2012	111
Table 7.1.7	GHG anthropogenic emissions: major countries	111
Table 7.1.8	Negotiating proposals at UNFCCC-COP3 (Kyoto): proposals for CO_2 reductions	113
Table 7.3.1	Simulated changes in China's climate with a doubling of CO_2	122
Table 7.3.2	Carbon emissions from fossil fuel burning (1995): selected countries	128
Table III.1	Earth's land surface	131
Table III.2	Ecological footprint analysis: selected nations	133–4
Table III.3	Selected countries: basic lifestyle indicators	135
Table 8.1.1	Global population projection: 2000–2150	139
Table 8.1.2	Global population programme: estimated annual cost of implementation	141
Table 8.2.1	Population assistance (ODA) to India: 1985–94	149
Table 8.2.2	Population assistance (ODA) to India: 1995–6	149
Table 9.1.1	Estimated annual costs of basic human needs: 1993–2000	163
Table 9.1.2	ODA performance of DAC countries: selected years	165
Table 9.3.1	Kenya: official development assistance: 1984–96	181
Table 10.1.1	Forest coverage and roundwood production: 1980–89	185
Table 10.1.2	Sustainable forests: the annual global cost: 1993–2000	187
Table 11.1.1	Consumption and consumption-related levels: the North–South divide	205
Table 11.1.2	Consumption-adjusted population: selected countries, 1990	205
Table 11.1.3	Waste generated by the North: late 1980s	206
Table 15.1	City development index: ranking for 236 cities	259

FIGURES

Figure 1.1   "Today, states must be prepared to accommodate the concept of a common – global or planetary – interest", says Secretary-General Boutros Boutros-Ghali.   8

Figure 2.1   The voting lights flash on at the UN General Assembly.   20

Figure 3.1   Some of the 185 flags flying outside UN headquarters, New York.   24

Figure 4.2.1   Citizens of New Zealand take to their boats to block the entry of a US nuclear attack submarine into their harbour.   52

Figure 4.3.1   Military officials and journalists view the remains of a former Soviet nuclear missile silo, Pervomaisk, Ukraine, January 1995.   60

Figure 5.2.1   A Palestinian confronts Israeli soldiers at the entrance to the Aidi refugee camp, November 1997.   70

Figure 5.3.1   A Patriot anti-missile missile streaks towards an incoming Iraqi Scud over Tel Aviv, February 1991.   78

Figure 6.2.1   NASA satellite imagery showing the ozone hole over Antarctica, October 1996.   93

Figure 6.3.1   A Japanese scientist prepares measuring equipment in Antarctica.   102

Figure 7.1.1   Economic cleanliness; energy profligacy: Annex I parties.   112

Figure 7.2.1   One of the atolls of the Maldives, 1 to 2 metres above sea level.   120

Figure 7.3.1   Chinese lorries dump the last truckload of rock into the Yangtze River during construction of the huge Three Gorges Dam.   127

Figure 8.2.1   A woman doctor distributes free contraceptives to women, New Delhi.   148

Figure 8.3.1   Immigrants commence a new life in Australia in the 1960s.   156

Figure 9.2.1   Women staging a torch-light march on International Protest Day against the Repression of Women, Dhaka, November 1997.   173

Figure 9.3.1   Riot police break up a political rally in Kamukunji, Kenya, October 1997.   182

Figure 10.2.1   A Malaysian fire-fighter battles the Indonesian forest fires of October 1997, along with Indonesian servicemen.   194

Figure 10.3.1   The result of a clearing fire in the Amazon region, Brazil, 1988.   199

Figure 11.2.1   The lights of New York's World Trade Center burn through the night, using more electricity than an Asian village would in a year.   214

Figure 11.3.1   Mayor Mats Hulth drinks a glass of water from Lake Mälaren, outside City Hall, Stockholm.   219

Figure 12.1   The UN Security Council at its historic summit meeting, January 1992.   236

Figure 13.1   Sky-diving over Europe.   244

Figure 14.1   Former British Foreign Secretary Malcolm Rifkind leads his national delegation to the 5lst Session of the General Assembly, 1996.   252

Figure 15.1   "Anyone who has visited Rome", says Francesco Rutelli, "carries lifelong memories of the city's glorious chaos of cars and mopeds."   262

Figure 16.1   Earthrise, from lunar orbit, Apollo 8, 24th December 1968 (Courtesy NASA).   273

Notes on authors

EDITOR

Kennedy Graham, a national of New Zealand, is Director of the Project for the Planetary Interest, a project supported by The Rockefeller Foundation and located in 1996–7 in the Global Security Programme, Cambridge University, England. He studied at Victoria University (Wellington) and Fletcher School of Law and Diplomacy (Boston), and in 1995 was a Visiting Fellow at Emmanuel College, Cambridge. Dr Graham served in the NZ foreign service for 16 years, taught international relations at Victoria University, and was for seven years Secretary-General of Parliamentarians for Global Action, New York. He is currently Director of Planning and Co-ordination at International IDEA (the International Institute for Democracy and Electoral Assistance), Stockholm. His earlier book was *National security concepts of states: New Zealand* (1989), and he has written extensively on issues of arms control and global security.

CONTRIBUTORS

Margaret Alva was India's Minister for Human Resource Development in charge of women, children, youth and sports in the mid-1980s under Prime Minister Rajiv Gandhi. She was subsequently Minister for Personnel, Public Administration and Pensions. She remains a member of the upper chamber of the Indian parliament, the *Rajya Sabha*, serving her fourth six-year term. She represents the Congress (I) Party for which she is a member of the National Co-ordination Committee. Ms Alva has been deeply involved in population planning and women's rights issues, and has served on several UN and national committees.

Emma Bonino is European Commissioner for Humanitarian Aid, Consumer Policy and Fisheries. A national of Italy, she was elected three times to the European Parliament, and six times to the Italian parliament, the *Camera dei Deputati*, representing the *Partito Radicale*.

Dante Caputo was Foreign Minister of Argentina in the Alfonsin Government, 1983–9. He was a member of the *Camara de Diputados*, the lower chamber of the parliament of Argentina, representing the Radical Civic Union Party. Dr Caputo served in the early 1990s as Special UN Representative for Haiti, being responsible for the negotiations with the military junta for the return of President Bertrand Aristide to office. He was re-elected to the parliament in 1997.

Naomi Chazan is a Deputy Speaker of the Israeli parliament, the *Knesset*, representing the Meretz-Democratic Party. She is a member of the Education Committee, the Immigration Committee and the Committee on the Status of Women, where she chairs the Sub-Committee on the Personal Status of Women. Professor Chazan is Vice President of the International Political Science Association and the Israel chapter of the Society for International Development. She is active in a variety of professional, human rights and peace organizations, having co-founded the Israel Women's Network, the Israel Women's Peace Net, and the Jerusalem Link: A Women's Joint Venture for Peace.

Toujan Faisal is the only woman member to have been elected to the lower house, the Chamber of Deputies, of the *Majlis al-'Umma*, the National Assembly of Jordan, where she represented the Circassian seat, 1993–7. Graduating in English from the University of Jordan, she has been a political columnist, presenter on Jordan Television, an adviser to the Ministry for Social Development, and Director of Cultural Programmes at the Noor Al-Hussayn Foundation. She has also been a member of the Executive Committee of the Inter-Parliamentary Union, Geneva.

Fabio Feldmann is a member of Brazil's parliament, the *Camara dos Deputados*, representing the Party of Brazilian Social Democracy (PSDB). Mr Feldmann was a practising lawyer in São Paulo and a leading environmentalist. As a member of the parliament he played a major role in drafting the environmental sections of the new Brazilian constitution. He is also currently Secretary for the Environment of the State of São Paulo City.

Koji Kakizawa was Japan's Foreign Minister in the Hata cabinet and before that Parliamentary Vice-Minister for Foreign Affairs in the Miyazawa cabinet. In the early 1990s he was Chairman of the Foreign Affairs Committee. He was first elected to the Japanese *Diet* in 1977, representing the Liberal Democratic Party, and in October 1996 was re-elected to the House of Representatives for a sixth consecutive term.

Abdul Moyeen Khan was Bangladesh's Minister of State for Planning, 1993–6, and is currently a member of the opposition Nationalist Party in the *Jatiya Sangsad*, the parliament, having been elected first in 1991. He was a Professor of Physics at Dhaka University, having studied at the University of Dhaka (Bangladesh), University of Stockholm (Sweden) and Oxford University (UK). Dr Khan was founding Director of the Bangladesh Centre for Advanced Studies, and editor of the *Bangladesh Environment Newsletter*. He was a member of the Dhaka University Senate, 1991–5.

Lena Klevenås has been a member of the Swedish parliament since 1991, representing the Social Democrat Party. She served on the Foreign Affairs Committee, 1994–6, and is currently on the Committees on Agriculture and Cultural Affairs. She is also Chairman of the Parliamentary Human Rights Group, and is on the Swedish board of the Inter-Parliamentary Union. Before entering politics she was a teacher.

Andrei Vladimirovich Kozyrev was Foreign Minister of the democratic Russian Federation within the Soviet Union, 1990–91, and of the independent Russian Federation, 1991–6. He is currently a member of the Russian parliament, the state *Duma*, representing the northern Murmansk region. Before his political appointments, Dr Kozyrev served in the Soviet foreign service, his last position being Director of the International Organizations Department. He is the author of *Transfiguration*, advocating political and economic reform in Russia, and has written extensively on international affairs.

David Lange was Prime Minister of New Zealand, 1984–9. He qualified in law from the University of Auckland and practised as a barrister before entering the NZ House of Representatives in 1977, becoming Leader of the NZ Labour Party in opposition in 1981. Mr Lange has written several books, including *Nuclear-free, the New Zealand way* (1990). He remained a member of the NZ parliament until October 1996.

Michael Marshall was a Conservative Member of Parliament of the House of Commons in the United Kingdom, 1974–97. He was an industry minister in Mrs Thatcher's first administration. Sir Michael also served as President of the Inter-Parliamentary Union, Geneva, 1991–4.

Charity Kaluki Ngilu is a member of the National Assembly of Kenya, having first been elected in 1992 to represent the Democratic Party. Since 1989 she has been a leader of the *Maenbeleo ya Wanawake* organization, the national women's movement. Before entering politics she was managing director of a food-manufacturing company in Nairobi. Ms Ngilu, who is a mother of three, was the Social Democratic candidate for the presidency of Kenya in the 1997 elections.

Gwyn Prins, a national of the United Kingdom, was for 20 years a Fellow, and Director of Studies in History, at Emmanuel College, Cambridge. He was also founder and Director of the Global Security Programme at the University of Cambridge, 1989–97. He is currently Senior Research Fellow at the Royal Institute of International Affairs (Chatham House, London), Visiting Senior Fellow at the British Defence Evaluation and Research Agency (Farnborough) and Senior Fellow in the Office of the Special Adviser to the Secretary-General of NATO (Brussels). Dr Prins is editor of *Threats without enemies* (1993), and author of *Top guns and toxic whales* (1991).

Qian Yi is a member of China's Standing Committee of the National People's Congress. She serves on the Standing Committee's Natural Resources and Environment Commission. Dr Qian is Professor of Environmental Engineering at Tsinghua University, Beijing, China. She is a member of the China Academy of Engineering, Director of the State Key Joint Laboratory of Environmental Simulation and Pollution Control, and Vice President of the World Federation of Engineering Organizations.

Shridath (Sonny) Ramphal is co-chairman of the Commission on Global Governance. He was Commonwealth Secretary-General, 1975–90, having earlier served as Minister of Foreign Affairs of Guyana. Sir Shridath is chief negotiator for the Caribbean on regional economic issues. He is chairman of the International Steering Committee of LEAD (the international programme for Leadership in Environment and Development), of the Board of International IDEA (the International Institute for Democracy and Electoral Assistance), and of the International Advisory Board of the Future Generations Alliance Foundation. He is Chancellor of the University of the West Indies and of the University of Warwick in Britain. A member of the Commission on the Prevention of Deadly Conflict, Sir Shridath chaired the West Indian Commission and served on each of the international commissions that reported on global issues in the 1980s. He was President of the World Conservation Union (IUCN), 1990–93. Among his many books, *Our country, the planet* (1992) was written for the Rio Earth Summit.

Margaret Reynolds was Australia's Minister of Local Government, 1987–90, and Minister for the Status of Women, 1988–90. She is an elected member of the Australian Senate, representing the Australian Labor Party for Queensland since 1983. In 1992 she was appointed as Federal Government Representative on the Council for Aboriginal Reconciliation, in which capacity she was directly involved in the development of native title legislation following the landmark "Mabo" decision. Her book *The last bastion* (1995) chronicles the contribution by social democratic women to policy development in Australian parliaments during the twentieth century.

Francesco Rutelli is the first directly elected mayor of Rome (1993). In 1983 he entered the lower chamber of the Italian parliament, the *Camera dei Deputati*, representing the *Partito Radicale*. He was re-elected in 1987, and again in 1992 as leader of the Greens, serving in both terms as chairman of the Human Rights Committee. In 1993 he was appointed Minister for the Environment and Urban Areas in the Ciampi Government but resigned after one day in office in protest over a policy issue. Mr Rutelli is chairman of both the Commission for Urban Policies of the Committee for the Regions in Brussels and the National Council of the Association of Italian Municipalities. In December 1997 he was re-elected for a second term as mayor.

Theo Sambuaga is Indonesia's State Minister for Housing and Human Settlements in the Habibie cabinet, having recently been Chairman of the Golkar Faction (majority leader of the House). He was first elected to parliament in 1982, and has served on the Foreign Affairs and Defence Commission. He has also been chairman of the Committee for Political Matters, International Security and Disarmament of the Inter-Parliamentary Union, Geneva. Mr. Sambuaga graduated from the University of Indonesia and the Paul Nitze School of Advanced International Studies, Johns Hopkins University, Washington, DC.

Claudine Schneider served Rhode Island as US Congresswoman in the House of Representatives, 1980–90, and was Republican candidate in the congressional elections for the US Senate in 1994. After her congressional career Ms Schneider was Director of the Artemis Project in Washington, DC, devoted to the relationship between modern lifestyles, sustainable development and the global environment. She has been a Fellow at Harvard University's Institute of Politics, teaching leadership and public policy. She is co-recipient of an Emmy Award for an ABC television series, has also co-anchored CNN, and made guest appearances on ABC, NBC and CBS television channels in the United States. She is currently employed with Land and Water Fund of the Rockies, Boulder, Colorado.

Ibrahim Hussain Zaki is Minister of Tourism and Deputy Foreign Minister of the Maldives. He has been a Member of Parliament, representing the Ari Atoll constituency since 1994. He served as Secretary-General of SAARC (the South Asian Association for Regional Co-operation), 1992–3. Before entering politics, Dr Zaki was his country's Secretary of Foreign Affairs.

Acknowledgements

This book owes much to many people. The idea of the "planetary interest", as a political concept, emerged in the course of the work done by inspiring politicians, members of Parliamentarians for Global Action, a worldwide network of national legislators committed to the broader global view in guiding policy in their own countries on international issues. Leading members of that non-governmental organization, one of the more effective and innovative examples of the emerging global civil society, included, in addition to most of the contributors to this book, George Foulkes, now Under-Secretary of State for Development Assistance in the United Kingdom; Olafur Ragnar Grímsson, now President of Iceland; Silvia Hernandez, recently Minister of Tourism in Mexico; A.N.R. Robinson, now President of Trinidad and Tobago; and Lloyd Axworthy, now Foreign Minister of Canada. Their dedication to the "higher good" combined with their political skills and personal dynamism made for a formidable team and it was a privilege to work for them and their colleagues for seven years.

The concept, inspired in a different context by Tissa Balasuriya's "Planetary Theology", was first explored during my tenure as a Visiting Fellow at Emmanuel College, Cambridge, in 1995. The result was an initial foray into this new and interdisciplinary enquiry, with *The planetary interest*, Occasional Paper No. 7, May 1995, translated into Spanish, French and Arabic. The collaboration of Gwyn Prins, Director of the Global Security Programme at the university, who has contributed a chapter to this book, was critical in stimulating thought and offering insight into what was a rather dimly perceived and inchoate set of thoughts at the time. A colleague in the programme, Chris Williams, provided invaluable support and a positive critique of the concept as it took form and substance, both then and in the course of the preparation of this book.

Similar support was extended by the Bangladesh Centre for Advanced Studies, in Dhaka, which offered a Guest Fellowship, also in 1995. Facilitated by Abdul Moyeen Khan, co-founder of the centre and at the time Minister of State for Planning, the fellowship allowed an opportunity to gain insight from the work of professionals such as Saleem ul Huq and Atiq Rahman, who promote the interests of the South as a legitimate part of the planetary interest in a manner that is perhaps without peer. They needed no elaboration on the meaning of the concept when it was first raised with them.

The intellectual sympathy and financial support of The Rockefeller Foundation made the rest of the work possible. An invitation to undertake a month's in-residence study at the foundation's Bellagio Centre in Italy in 1995 helped complete the initial work on the concept and exposed the ideas being developed to the first critical scrutiny from the academic world. A subsequent Special Initiatives Grant to "further define and develop the planetary interest and to promote it among policy-makers worldwide" provided the basis from which this book has sprung. Specifically, it allowed the convening of an Authors' Workshop at Cambridge University in August 1997, and associated travel and other costs in connection with the preparation of the book. Special acknowledgement must go to Stephen Sinding.

Appreciation is extended to all contributors for collaborating in the exploration of the planetary interest concept. Responsibility for the overall scope and content of the book, however, remains with the editor. Thanks also to Caroline Wintersgill of UCL Press, for a calculated step into the unknown. Let us hope this torch lights some of the path ahead.

Other experts who have helped with advice and other assistance are Marco de Andreis of the European Commission, Brussels; Roger Clark of Rutgers Law School, Camden, New Jersey; Tom Downing of the Environmental Change Unit, Oxford University; Hao Jimin, Head of Environmental Engineering, Tsinghua University, Beijing; Barry Kellman of De Paul University, Chicago; Taher Masri of Amman, Jordan; Habel Nyamu, member of the Kenyan Electoral Commission, Nairobi; Nick Rengger of St Andrews University, Scotland; David Mepham of Safer World, London; Kevin Sanders of War and Peace Foundation, New York; Rajendra Shende of OzonAction Programme, UNEP, Paris; Sarah Willen, parliamentary assistant, the Knesset, Jerusalem; and Ziauddin Sardar of Middlesex University, London.

Not least – and perhaps most – appreciation is extended to Marilyn Moir Graham, Elizabeth Sellwood and Alison Suter for unflagging support and assistance in proof-reading and other logistical work, and especially to Marilyn for her valued insights and an extraordinarily compassionate understanding of what is required in an odyssey of this nature.

Glossary

ABM	Anti-ballistic missile
AFDB	African Development Bank
AOX	Absorbable organic halide
ASEAN	Association of South East Asian Nations
AusAID	Australian Agency for International Development
BWC	Biological Weapons Convention
C.	Degrees Centigrade (or Celsius)
CBR	Crude Birth Rate
CCL_4	Carbon tetrachloride
CFC	Chlorofluorocarbon
CHC	Child health centres
CITES	Convention on International Trade in Endangered Species of Wild Fauna and Flora
CO_2	Carbon dioxide
CT	Carbon tetrachloride
CWC	Chemical Weapons Convention
ECSC	European Coal and Steel Community
EEC	European Economic Community
EU	European Union
GDP	Gross Domestic Product
GHG	Greenhouse gas
GNP	Gross National Product
Gt.	Gigatonnes
GWP	Global warming potential
Habitat	see UNCHS
HCFC	Hydro-chlorofluorocarbon
HDI	Human Development Indicator
HYV	High Yield Variety (rice)
IBRD	World Bank
ICBM	Inter-continental ballistic missile
IMF	International Monetary Fund
IMR	Infant Mortality Rate
IPCC	Inter-Governmental Panel on Climate Change
IPU	Inter-Parliamentary Union
MCF	Methyl chloroform
Meth. br.	Methyl bromide

NGO	Non-governmental organization
NOX	Nitrous oxide
NPT	Non-Proliferation Treaty
ODA	Official development assistance
ODP	Ozone Depleting Potential
ODS	Ozone Depleting Substances
OECD	Organization for Economic Co-operation and Development
OPCW	Organization for the Prohibition of Chemical Weapons
PGA	Parliamentarians for Global Action
PHC	Primary health centre
ppmv	parts per million volume
SLBM	Submarine-launched ballistic missile
SOX	Sulphur oxide
SSBN	Nuclear-fuelled ballistic missile submarine
TgN	Teragrams of nitrogen
UCL	University College London
UN	United Nations
UNCHS	United Nations Commission for Human Settlements (Habitat)
UNDH	United Nations Daily Highlights
UNDP	United Nations Development Programme
UNEP	United Nations Environment Programme
UNFCCC	United Nations Framework Convention on Climate Change
UNFCCC-COP	UNFCCC Conference of the Parties
UNGA	United Nations General Assembly
UNSC	United Nations Security Council
UV	Ultra-violet
WFP	World Food Programme
WMO	World Meterological Organization
WWF	World Wildlife Fund for Nature

appropriated carrying capacity is another name for the ecological footprint. "Appropriated" signifies captured, claimed or occupied. Ecological footprints demonstrate that we appropriate ecological capacity for food, fibres, energy and waste absorption. In industrial regions, a large part of these flows is imported.

ecological deficit of a country measures the amount by which their footprint exceeds the locally available ecological capacity.

ecological footprint is the land and water area that is required to support indefinitely the material standard of living of a given human population, using prevailing technology.

hectare is 10,000 square meters of 100 times 100 meters. One hectare contains 2.47 acres.

natural capital refers to the stock of natural assets that yield goods and services on a continuous basis. Main functions include resource production (such as fish, timber or cereals), waste assimilation (such as CO_2 absorption, sewerage decomposition) and life support services (UV protection, biodiversity, water cleansing, climate stability).

Foreword

I am very pleased to have been asked to write the foreword to this book. The "planetary interest" is the kind of forward-looking concept we need as the world goes through a period of profound transformation. Its central message – that in addition to personal, group and national interests we must think in terms of the interests of the entire planet – is of special significance to the United Nations, an organization whose *raison d'être* is to advance the interest not of any one group but of humankind as a whole.

The world of today is not the world of 1945 when the United Nations was founded, nor even the world of 1985. The international environment has become more complex and more dynamic. Fundamental forces are at work reshaping the globe, presenting unparalleled opportunities as well as unforeseen dangers. We do not yet know whether the transformation underway is towards greater peace, prosperity, justice and freedom – the founding vision of the Charter of the United Nations – or whether in fact it is pushing us in the opposite direction, towards war, economic collapse, social breakdown and repression.

Fortunately, it is not beyond the powers of political volition to tip the scale. We can influence the course of history and shape the world we shall inhabit in the twenty-first century. Culturally, the world is configured into civilizational groupings, with all their richness and diversity. Politically, it is configured into nation-states, each pursuing perceived national interests. The international community is struggling to devise new ways of coping with the challenges it is facing, many of our own making and many of them potentially divisive. With the world configured as it is, this divisiveness can all too easily descend into violent conflict. It is incumbent upon us all to resist this danger. We can, by our actions and by our example, provide a resounding answer to those who say war is inevitable.

The planetary interest provokes us to think anew about how we must share this fragile planet. These insights of eminent figures from around the world offer hope that the principles of tolerance and co-operation will survive in a world in which intolerance and unilateralism have too many adherents. And because these figures have vast and varied experience in the political life of this transitional era, it offers practical suggestions on how we can move from goals to policies and action.

Kofi A. Annan

Preface

The purpose of this book is to develop the concept of the "planetary interest" and to promote the concept among policy-makers, and the citizenry whom they represent, around the world.

The rationale for the book rests on five propositions:

1 The world is in a state of transition to a new age in which nation-states are compelled to address certain problems of a global nature.
2 Some global problems now threaten the viability and integrity of the planet, and place in jeopardy the wellbeing of humanity and other species.
3 These problems are beyond the capacity of any country, no matter how large and powerful, to solve alone.
4 Contemporary political norms and institutions, based on national sovereignty as a principle and the nation-state as the decision-making unit, are not able to handle such problems adequately.
5 New concepts and methods of decision-making are therefore needed to augment existing ones in dealing with the challenges of the twenty-first century.

The fundamental premise of the book is that the planetary interest is a concept that is now necessary to assist humanity address and resolve the global problems of our time. Humankind has left behind the age when all international problems could be adequately handled simply through the resolution of conflicting national interests of nation-states. Today, a qualitatively new approach to policy and politics at the global level is required. In this new paradigm, the method by which certain global problems are resolved needs to involve, first, an assessment of the planetary interest and, secondly, a reconciliation of all national interests with it. This will be an essential method of reasoning for our collective wellbeing, and perhaps even our common survival, to be secured.

In the ensuing chapters, twenty-two authors contribute to the development and promotion of the planetary interest concept. Twenty hold or held elective political office in their country. The other two have in varying ways been involved in seeking to develop new global concepts for political discourse and action. The idea is to have political figures around the world address the major global problems which humanity will face in the early twenty-first century from the vantage point of the planetary interest.

The insight and views offered by the authors in this book make it clear that public opinion will tend towards the introduction of new concepts of this kind as the twenty-first century opens. This, it is believed, is critical to the development of a more unified and harmonious global society and a more rational and enlightened approach to the future of humanity.

The reader may not necessarily agree with everything which the authors have said in their chapters. The contributions in Parts II and III are essentially political, expressing personal judgements. The point of the book is not to postulate unanimity of opinion and harmony of view among every individual in the face of complex global problems. There is much scope for individual opinion, and it is important that any differences are articulated openly and transparently. The point is rather to develop a new conceptual construct for approaching global problems in the future that can accommodate variety yet facilitate action – a new political paradigm for a new age. That construct does not presume a philosophical or cultural unity among humanity in the late twentieth century. But it does offer a conceptual means of perceiving, within a rational framework, those interests that are common to us all.

One intended author of the book is absent from the list of contributors. Professor Carl Sagan of Cornell University had agreed to contribute the final chapter, drawing together conclusions from the content and views expressed. Among our generation Carl was gifted in imparting a planetary and cosmic perspective to our human existence on Earth, in a way that was at the same time rational and fearless yet positive and inspiring. The world is impoverished by his passing, and this book is dedicated to him.

Kennedy Graham
June 1998

(email address: graham@tpi.pp.se)
(website: http://home8.swipnet.se/~w-89119)

PART ONE

Introduction

In Part I, the basic concepts that govern the contributions to this book are introduced, viz., the *planetary interest*, the *vital planetary interest*, the *legitimate national interest* and *legitimate global power*.

The planetary interest is the fundamental concept of the book. Everything turns on an acceptance of the concept – its definition and application – and a recognition of its relevance to the times of the late twentieth and early twenty-first centuries. The distinction between the vital planetary interest and the normative planetary interest is also critical. The subsequent parts of the book focus exclusively upon the vital planetary interest and the problems and challenges to humanity which might be perceived as directly confronting that interest.

From the vital planetary interest is derived the conceptual distinction that structures the two major parts of the book, the legitimate national interest (in Part II) and legitimate global powers (in Part III).

Because of the central role which the notion of "legitimacy" plays in politics, particular attention is devoted to the role it might be expected to play in the critical transition from domestic legitimacy within the nation-state to a higher level in two areas: the "international legitimacy" attending national policy towards global problems and "global legitimacy" pertaining to enforcement power.

CHAPTER ONE

The planetary interest

Kennedy Graham

The world of today is experiencing a paradigmatic shift as profound as any before. Through space exploration and the transport, communications and information revolutions, we are in a turbulent transition to a new age. It is best described as the "global age", and it is captured most simply and eloquently in the breathtakingly beautiful image of Earth from lunar orbit on Christmas Eve 1968. The *Apollo 8* photograph has become the icon of the global age, symbolic of its portent and evoking a new and nurturing attitude towards the planet that had not been present in the popular mind before. In the words of the UN secretary-general in 1993, "the first truly global era has begun".[1]

From the earlier industrial age, however, humanity has inherited problems which, in the new age, have themselves become global. As it prepares to enter the twenty-first century, the international community faces problems that demonstrably threaten the planet. There was general agreement among the experts in the Ward-Dubos Report commissioned for the UN Environment Conference of 1972, that "environmental problems are becoming increasingly worldwide and therefore demand a global approach".[2] The existence of nuclear weapons, said the *Final document* of the 1978 Special Session on Disarmament, poses an "unprecedented threat to the very survival of mankind".[3] Global questions, said the independent Brandt Report on development, require global answers: "since there is now a risk of mankind destroying itself, this risk must be met by new methods".[4]

The new paradigm is the growing realization, a new awareness, of the vulnerability of humanity – a "cosmic" vulnerability that has a spiritual dimension, threading its way through to secular political thought and action. Not only are we no longer the centre of the universe, but we might, as a species, be dispensable, and then, perhaps, even by our own hand. Henceforth we must plan for our own survival, albeit, in the view of some of us, with providential guidance. It is a sobering thought, and it denotes the maturation of the species. There is no alternative: we must address the global problems of our time.[5]

Grappling with those global problems today is the recognized task of some two hundred nation-states, each claiming independent and sovereign powers.[6] Thus is portrayed the dysfunctionality of our age: the scale of policy-making in the world today, on certain critical issues, falls short of the scale of the problem by an order of magnitude. The interests of humanity suffer accordingly.

Excepting violent revolution or cataclysm, political change in the world proceeds at an evolutionary pace. The formation of political units and the bestowal of legitimate authority on leaders proceed slowly, and for good reason. The civilized state rests on a thin veneer of law and order built up through millennia of human effort and sacrifice, and it is essential to keep secured the good that has been won. Organized political society is some ten millennia old. The nation-state, the main political unit of the modern age, is some four centuries old. International organization, in an institutional sense, is some eight decades old.[7] But sovereignty remains with the nation-state. And the nation-state has become universal, the planet a closed political system, a worldwide grid of sovereign states, only a few decades ago. Humanity has yet to agree upon a system of governance for the planet as a whole. The political evolution of the world is not complete, even in the simplest, most basic sense of a self-governing unit.

The world polity is thus not a single entity. There is no single sovereign assembly of the global commonwealth with legitimate authority and enforcement power. Were this so, it could conceive of a single interest on behalf of all humankind whom it would represent and for whom it would formulate strategy and execute policy in pursuit of such an interest. But this is not the case. The present General Assembly of the United Nations is not itself sovereign but rather a body of sovereign states, a "centre for harmonizing the actions of nations in the attainment of [the] common ends".[8] That is a different thing – harmonizing several hundred common "ends" – from conceiving and articulating a single "end". And in truth, the sovereign member states perceive the United Nations, and judge the utility of membership, in terms of how well it advances their national interests.[9]

Thus the reason for, and the subject of, this book: the compelling need for a facilitating concept that can trigger action in a time of transition – a single interest of a magnitude commensurate with the scale of the problems faced. And the concept, while rooted in abstraction, must be capable of being operationalized for political action.

THE NATIONAL INTEREST

It is axiomatic that every socio-political unit has an "interest". There is the individual and the family interest, expressed at the municipal and national levels through electoral and other civic activity. There is the local interest, expressed through municipal activity and parliamentary activity at the national level. There is the national interest, expressed at the international level in UN voting, diplomatic negotiations and other forms of nation-state activity. There is a regional and a transnational interest, expressed by nation-states co-operating or integrating within a region or along lines of a particular concern. And there is the planetary interest, which as yet is hardly expressed at all. The concept of interest validly attends any such identifiable unit. The strength or weakness of that concept correlates closely with the importance and vigour of the unit.

At present, the national interest commands the overwhelming focus of political attention in global affairs. Other influences are at play – most notably transnational business and non-governmental organizations involving both professional and citizen activity. But the national interest, as conceived and formulated by the governments of nation-states, remains the well-established concept driving political decisions and policies in the modern world. Constitutionally and politically, each nation is bound to look after its own interests, to make its own way in the world and seek its own fortune. Leaders are expected to exercise power to serve the nation alone, and when they take office they formally swear under oath to do so. Citizens are bound to acknowledge and give obeisance to the national sovereign, and to defend the nation with arms and with their life. The law of treason, the act of betraying one's country, remains the highest crime in domestic law, carrying severe political odium and generally earning the highest penalty. Nations carry all the trappings of group identity: the flag, the armed forces, the airline, the currency, the postage stamp and, not least, the sports team. Government officials sign secrecy oaths to protect information acquired on a "need-to-know" basis. Risks to national security, real or perceived, are treated with the utmost seriousness, and can fundamentally alter lives. And in what may become known as one of the greatest anomalies of all, the first humans on the moon planted a national flag.

Above all, the value system of the *polis* – the citizens and their leaders – remains, in the 1990s, principally national. In a recent State of the Union address, the US president declares: "As we embark on a new course, let us put our country first, remembering that regardless of our party beliefs, we are all Americans. Let the final test of any action be a simple one: is it good for the American people? . . . The New Covenant unites us behind a common vision of what's best for our country."[10]

As with values, so with policy. Memoranda prepared by the bureaucracy for ministers of government present analysis and argumentation in the name of the national interest. The national interest remains the most entrenched political concept in the world today. It is the principal criterion by which political leaders – heads of government and ministerial colleagues – make their decisions. In the conduct of "external affairs", the foreign policy of one state towards others, the national interest is explicitly invoked; in domestic issues, it is assumed.[11] At international conferences and negotiations such as those at the United Nations, the national interest forms the basis of the perceptions and policies of member states. The official briefs which diplomats carry to these meetings specify their national objectives, with instructions to the delegations on how to achieve them. The diplomats are tightly constrained, and usually can diverge from their briefs only upon new instructions from capitals.

As with so many political concepts that are rooted in values, a definition of the national interest is relatively simple for the practical purposes of political action, relatively complex for the refined rigour of academic enquiry. The concept is invoked on the basis of what is "best for the country", as the American president's appeal cited above demonstrates and the *International Encyclopaedia of Social Sciences* confirms.[12] Although Italy and England first started using the concept three centuries ago, it is only the twentieth-century international community that has used it as the standard referent for political action as the nation-state system became universal and the public stake in international affairs and foreign policy grew.

In the real world, people strive for the national interest as they subjectively perceive it. The relationship between the objective and subjective versions of the concept is inevitably problematic. Is there an objective national interest that exists for a country whether or not citizens and leaders correctly perceive it, or is the national interest comprised of whatever the nation-state, through its ever-evolving values and political process, determines it to be at any one time? The answer invites epistemological enquiry beyond the scope of this book. But whatever the insights might be, it is generally accepted that Morgenthau's dictum of the 1940s still holds, that "the objectives of a foreign policy must be defined in terms of the national interest" and the application of national power is the medium through which nation-states follow "but one guiding star, one standard for thought, one rule for action: the national interest".[13]

Since the mid-twentieth century, the concept has been treated as the bedrock criterion of decision-making in international relations, and a number of authoritative works have focused on its meaning and use.[14] Reflecting these insights, *the national interest* may be defined as:

> the interests of a nation-state, including the integrity of its territory and the welfare of its people, based on its particular national values, formulated through its particular political process, and articulated by its leaders in terms of national aspirations, goals and policies.

Defining and identifying the national interest of a state, as opposed to analyzing the means by which states pursue them, has received little attention within the academic community.[15] Among policy-makers, the level of attention given to the concept of the national interest by the major powers has fluctuated with the degree of concern over their clarity of thinking in foreign policy at any one time – in the US in the 1970s, the USSR in the 1980s, and the US again in the 1990s. In the 1980s, for example, the "new thinking" that characterized Soviet foreign policy ushered in the concept of a "national interest" for the USSR in a formally stated preference over the traditional interests of the international proletariat, linking it however to Gorbachev's vision of universal "common human values".[16] The debate over what comprises the national interest continues in the new Russia.[17] In the 1990s, the loss of the "Cold-War compass" in US foreign policy has resulted in the concept returning to the centre of academic attention, with several studies seeking to clarify US national interests in a changing and uncertain world.[18]

In the context of political action, two levels of national interest are generally cited. The higher level is the "vital" national interest of a nation-state. It is cited as justification for threatening or undertaking military action, or applying non-violent but severe measures such as economic sanctions, whether lawfully through the UN or extra-legally in a unilateral move.[19] Vital national interests traditionally concern the defence of national territory, access to energy sources, security of transport and communication lines, and control of key industrial assets.[20] They are the issues for which leaders will call upon their citizens to pay the ultimate sacrifice. The *vital national interest* has been defined in the following way:

> An interest is vital when the highest policy-makers in the sovereign state conclude that the issue at stake in an international dispute is so fundamental to the political, economic and social well-being of their country that it should not be compromised further, even if this results in the use of economic and military force.[21]

The lower level is the normal national interest. This traditionally concerns two objectives: peaceful competition for the largest slice of the global economic cake; and the peaceful promotion of national values that form the consensual basis for the national society and which the country may wish to see emulated around the world. Some major powers are more concerned than others to see their national values, generally their version of political truth and human rights, so promoted. But the normal national interest falls short of resorting to force.

The process of globalization of the 1990s has blurred the boundaries delineating the nation-state and thus the national interest. As Robert Cox has put it, "States can no longer be thought of as the hard billiard balls of classical international relations theory ... [They] can no longer be conceived meaningfully as fully autonomous entities pursuing self-defined national interests."[22] The regional interest is being asserted more forcefully than before, as the principles of integration and subsidiarity become painstakingly reconciled. As the international community of states transforms into a global community of states and people, it is clear that something higher than the national interest is emerging.

THE "COMMON INTEREST": A PRECURSOR

Philosophically, the notion of an interest higher than the national interest is millennia old. The early civilizations all had their worldview, and the major religious faiths that underpin contemporary civilization have their vision of human unity as well. But the idea of a political interest higher than the national is quite new. Barbara Ward's pioneering work of the mid-1960s spoke of "Spaceship Earth":

> The most rational way of seeing the whole human race today is to see it as the ship's crew of a single space ship on which all of us, with a remarkable combination of security and vulnerability, are making our pilgrimage through infinity. Our planet is not much more than the capsule within which we have to live as human beings if we are to survive the vast space voyage upon which we have been engaged for hundreds of millennia, but without yet noticing our condition. This space voyage is totally precarious. We depend on a little envelope of soil and a rather larger envelope of atmosphere for life itself ... We are a ship's company on a small ship. Rational behaviour is the condition of survival.[23]

The independent commissions established over the 1980s and 1990s have promoted the political concept of a "common interest" of humanity. The 1982 Palme Commission concluded that "our discussions over almost two years ... convinced us of the urgency of working together for common interests".[24] Our inability to promote the "common interest in sustainable development", said the 1987 Brundtland Commission on Environment and Development, was often the product of a relative neglect of economic and social justice.[25] The 1995 Carlsson–Ramphal Commission on Global Governance was of the view that "the idea that people have common interests irrespective of their national or other identities and that they are coming together in an organized way across borders to address these is of increasing relevance to global governance".[26]

The nearest thing to a global conscience, as distinct from a global sovereign, is the voice of the UN secretary-general. Successive incumbents have consistently referred to a "common" or a "higher" interest. As early as 1950, Trygve Lie spoke of the "true interests of the world at large".[27] In 1960, Dag Hammarskjöld believed that UN member states would find it "increasingly necessary to maintain [the UN's] strength as an instrument for the world community ... in efforts to resolve problems ... in a spirit reflecting the common overriding interests".[28] U Thant contended that "all governments have an overriding, long-term, common interest in protecting and preserving the framework of peaceful international communications and the simple rules of responsible behaviour on which human society is necessarily based".[29] And in the early post-Cold War era in 1991, Javier Perez de Cuellar noted that "the unique opportunity that is now being presented to the world should be the subject of reasoned discussion and negotiation in the best interests of the world community ... The way we treat the new generation of global problems that now confront humanity may very well determine the quality of life for all peoples living on the planet."[30]

At the UN General Assembly, nation-states are giving rhetorical voice to the global concept. In 1993 the US president refers to the need to "take stock of where we are as common shareholders in the progress of humankind and the preservation of the planet".[31] One of his cabinet ministers asserts that "we all have to bring a global vision to the decisions we make; and we have to feel a sense of personal responsibility for all the people and all the countries with which we share this beautiful planet".[32] A foreign minister advances his country's draft resolution on the grounds that it "is intended to advance global interests".[33] The president of another sees the UN as "the most privileged forum for harmonizing the global interests of all peoples of the world ...".[34] The Group of Sixteen working on UN reform urges all nations "to rise from immediate concerns [and] focus on their long-term common interests".[35] And the president of the 1996–7 General Assembly observes that "the United Nations is best when it serves States coming together to make the United Nations a global vehicle to serve the interests of all and the welfare of the planet".[36]

Juridical thought has reflected this political trend in acknowledging the "higher interest". The UN Charter states that "We the peoples of the United Nations [are] determined . . . that armed force shall not be used save in the common interest". The Antarctic Treaty of 1959 refers to the "interest of all mankind" in the exclusively peaceful use of the continent. The Outer Space Treaty of 1967 claims, with a sublime anthropocentrism that could yet come to haunt us, that all celestial bodies shall be the "province of all mankind". The Moon Treaty of 1979 introduced the seminal concept of the "common heritage of mankind", and the Law of the Sea Convention of 1982 applied it to the seabed and ocean floor. And the climate change and biodiversity conventions of 1992 perceive their subject areas as matters of a "common concern of humankind". Clearly, the concept of the common interest, in various terminology, has entered the establishment of twentieth-century legal theory.

THE PLANETARY INTEREST

It is on this basis that the "planetary interest" has recently begun to be articulated. In the political world, a parliamentarian group, Parliamentarians for Global Action, articulated the concept of the planetary interest in the early 1990s. "The hallmark of our organization," said its President, Senator Silvia Hernandez of Mexico in 1993, "is the *planetary interest* – perceiving the world as a single whole, and responding, politically, with global solutions that reflect an enlightened national interest, not one that is narrowly conceived and competitively pursued."[37] And in March 1994, UN Secretary-General Boutros Boutros-Ghali contended that "States have always defined their national interests. Today, States must be prepared to accommodate the concept of a common – global or planetary – interest".[38]

The question must then arise, what substantive meaning does this phrase have? To consider this it is necessary first to develop a definition of the planetary interest. This is new territory, and any first attempt at a definition of so all-embracing a concept can only be tentative. But a preliminary definition is necessary in order to begin to delineate the subject matter more clearly and develop different levels of the planetary interest for more detailed analysis.

The *planetary interest* is defined here as:

> the interests of the planet, comprising: (1)   the survival and viability of humanity, contingent on main-tenance of the physical integrity of Earth and the protection of its ecological systems and biosphere from major anthropogenic change; and (2)   the universal improvement in the human condition in terms of basic human needs and fundamental human rights.

Use of the word "planet" here signifies more than the physical properties of Earth. It denotes a political construct comparable in kind to, but different in scale from, the nation-state. No institutional reality currently reflects this; that is the problem identified in the preface. But the absence of the institutional reality does not preclude the introduction of the political construct – indeed, it necessitates it.

The definition is, inevitably, anthropocentric insofar as it focuses on the survival and viability of humanity and improvement of the human condition. Yet, without according an "interest" to an inanimate object such as the planet, it concomitantly incorporates both a human interest in, and responsibility for, planetary stewardship. Obversely, the planet can be accepted as having a claim on humanity for that stewardship.[39]

Nothing contained in the definition is not already on the agenda of the international community. Its potential lies in capturing the fundamental aims of humanity in one operational concept.

What criteria can be developed for knowing when the planetary interest is applicable? Three are most obviously relevant: spatial scale, time-period and magnitude. These combine to determine the potential severity of a threat. Something concerns the planetary interest if it materially affects, not necessarily uniformly, the planet as opposed to the region or the nation-state alone, and humanity as opposed to the national community. The planetary interest is involved whether or not that threat is confined to, or extends beyond, the current generation. Finally, and as a result, it concerns the planetary interest if it threatens to fundamentally and adversely affect the integrity of the planet, that is to say, its natural equilibrium and/or the human condition. Because such threats are generally slow to materialize, the planetary interest is usually more readily recognized over a longer time-period. Normally the national interest is prevalent over the planetary interest in the shorter period. But with the passage of time, the national interest and the planetary interest are seen to have a closer fit.

The planet has been affected already by human behaviour. The global temperature, for example, has risen significantly since the Industrial Revolution. While a term such as "major anthropogenic change" begs the question of what is an absolute or accurate quantification of effect, it is judged here that the changes to the planet to date have not yet caused unacceptable damage. Yet the prospect exists in the future of major anthropogenic change which could result in such damage.

Figure 1.1   "States have always defined their national interests," said former UN Secretary-General Boutros Boutros-Ghali in 1994. "Today, States must be prepared to accommodate the concept of a common – global or planetary – interest." The secretary-general confers with PGA president, Silvia Hernandez, and the editor at a parliamentarian workshop, The Hague, January 1994. (Courtesy PGA)

Having regard to the taxonomy used over many decades for the national interest, the question arises whether the planetary interest can be assessed in a similar manner. Are there vital planetary interests, as opposed to less compelling planetary interests, that can be identified to help clarify the perceptions and judgements of nation-states as they grapple with global problems in the 1990s?

Two levels of the planetary interest might be identified, inherent in the general definition already advanced:

- The "vital planetary interest" would have to do with the survival and viability of humanity, contingent on maintenance of the physical integrity of Earth and the protection of its ecological systems and biosphere from major anthropogenic change. It would be applied to issues relating to the "fundamental health" of the planet, that is to say, the continuation of the planet in its state of natural equilibrium.
- The "normative planetary interest" would have to do with the universal improvement in the human condition in terms of meeting the basic human needs of each individual and observance of the fundamental human rights of each. It would be applied to issues concerning the quality of life of all peoples around the world, and implicitly invoke a set of values attributable to the global referent.

The distinction here is between survival and viability on the one hand, and wellbeing on the other. As the Group of Sixteen put it, "Global co-operation is critical to the survival of humanity".[40] In a Hobbesian world, the only issues around which disparate human individuals or groups can rationally unite for political action without dispute or dissent are those concerning their common survival. Virtually all peoples of the world today and all nation-states, it is contended, can agree that the physical integrity of the planet and the continuation of the human species are in the vital planetary interest.

This premise does, however, require rationality and soundness of mind as these are normally understood, eschewing extreme views such as any cult belief in the collective suicide of the human species. More difficult is the belief held by some that certain human values are so essential to all humanity that their absence might justify the risk of collective obliteration of the species.[41] The judgement entered in this book is that the survival and viability of the species is the absolute value of humanity. The way of life of a particular society is of importance to that society, but it must not undermine the absolute value of survival and viability of the species.

In contrast to survival or viability, basic human needs and fundamental human rights are universal but normative. Their violation against individuals around the world, however reprehensible on moral grounds, invokes a normative dimension of the human condition, one not vital to the continuation of the planet and the species.

The meaning of "survival" and "viability" needs to be explored. "Survival" is formally defined as the continuation of life after some event, and "viability" as the ability to live under certain conditions.[42] There is clearly a close inter-relationship between the two concepts but they do have different meanings. The former carries the eschatological implication of a threat to the whole human species; the latter of a longer-term strain on the human condition that could jeopardize its survival. For the purposes of this book, "survival" of humanity is taken to mean the continuation of some human life, whatever the decimation of its numbers. "Viability" of humanity is taken to mean the continuation of human life under conditions, both natural and anthropogenic, that provide a credible prospect of its indefinite existence. It would be an artificial precision to specify any greater exactitude in numbers or condition than this, but the above terminology does facilitate application of the definition of the "planetary interest".

What, then, might these "vital" and "normative" planetary interests be? The United Nations today handles some hundred and seventy items on its annual General Assembly agenda. They range from the truly global to the subnational. Yet they are all treated as if they are of similar or comparable scale. Only one – the maintenance of peace – evokes enforcement power. Yet in the half-century since the charter was framed, new issues of global import have come onto the agenda. Which are they, and what is their distinctive status? To quote the president of the 1996–7 General Assembly, "Environmental degradation and pollution, the spread of infectious disease, the international trafficking of drugs and weapons, the spread of organized crime, the mass movements of peoples, and the crisis of social sustainability are survival issues requiring global solutions . . . The multiplicity of these challenges underscores the need for effective global institutions".[43] Biological diversity is also referred to as an "urgent global problem".[44] Everyone today has their list of global problems. What is needed is some differentiation among these items that would allow the international community to distinguish, in terms both of analysis and power, the global issues from the international. The planetary interest concept can serve as a clarifying tool in this respect.

It is contended here, as a fundamental premise of this book, that the three vital planetary interests politically recognized by the international community in the 1990s are global strategic security, global environmental integrity and global sustainability. Avoiding self-destruction, protecting Earth and meeting humanity's basic needs on an enduring, intergenerational basis rank as the three priority global issues of our age. No other is, at present, recognized as of the same "vital" nature. Many others concern humanity as a whole, but they do not threaten its survival or viability. These three need to be treated separately from all others – *sui generis* – in terms of how nation-states determine their national policies and how humanity constructs global powers of policy-making and enforcement. This is not to say that other issues may not arise in the future that threaten the vital planetary interest; or, indeed, that some might be discernible today as potentially of that kind – it often takes time before emerging threats recognized by some are accepted as such by a majority. But for such problems to be accepted as threatening the vital planetary interest, it would need to be demonstrated that they do indeed threaten the very existence, or viability, of the species, as opposed to adversely affecting the human condition, however severely and reprehensibly.

Cases involving the normative planetary interest are, by definition, the totality of the remaining issues of a magnitude that concern the planet and humanity. They would comprise, in short, a minimum global standard of living for all individuals in terms of the basic human needs of shelter, food and health; and the development of a common global ethic that would underpin observance of universal human rights.[45]

Two of the above objectives, global strategic security and global environmental integrity, are self-evidently "vital". Threats to these address either the survival itself of humanity or its viability. Even if the damage caused in the event such threats are realized does not wipe us off the planet immediately, it is likely to undermine the viability of humankind over the longer term, given the interlocking nature of our national economies and societies today.

The third issue, global sustainability, needs careful consideration. What is the relationship between the carrying capacity of the planet and the basic human needs of all humanity? At the global level, it is axiomatic that global sustainability is in the vital planetary interest, since humanity cannot afford that the planet become degraded simply in order to meet the basic needs of an infinitely large population. What is in the vital planetary interest is global optimality – an optimal balance between the planet's resources, its carrying capacity and the human population. There is an optimal range of global population, whatever it might be, that is sustainable by the planet. Meeting the basic human needs of that number of people is in the vital planetary interest. But meeting the basic human needs of a particular individual is in the normative planetary interest. The distinction is subtle but important.

Similar subtleties attend the relationship between global and national sustainability. Must a nation-state, for example, live within the constraints of nationally sustainable development? Countries have vastly disparate resource bases; and international trade continues to grow exponentially. Must every nation-state live within its own national carrying capacity in the name of global sustainable development? This is a complex issue. Global sustainable development, it would seem, is in the vital planetary interest, while nation-states are, at present, free in international law to engage in nationally unsustainable development, which is, for better or worse, partially compensated for by the actions of other states. That is to say, some nation-states effectively subsidize others through lower consumption patterns, drawing down less upon the planet's natural resource capital, while others "overconsume" disproportionately to their populations. While, therefore, notions of economic and social justice of such skewed production and consumption patterns may be seen as in the normative planetary interest, the related question of whether the overall global consumption pattern is sustainable in the context of the planet's carrying capacity, whatever that might quantitatively be, is in the vital planetary interest. These considerations are explored further in later chapters.

Clearly there is not, and never will be, any satisfying intellectual precision in delineating the distinction between the vital and the normative planetary interests. In the world of politics, intellectual precision is not a common luxury. Such lack of clarity, however, does not preclude use of the distinction by leaders who employ the vital national interest concept in emergency situations confronting their countries. And at the global level, the international community itself is already using the concept: at its First Special Session on Disarmament, the UN General Assembly identified the elimination of the danger of nuclear war as "reflecting the vital interest of all the peoples of the world".[46]

These three issues, then, global strategic security, global environmental integrity and global sustainability are taken here as the vital planetary interests. The specific issues that currently threaten each of these interests are explored in Part II. Henceforth, the book focuses on these three issues alone, leaving unexamined all other issues that are in the normative planetary interest. This is not to say that these latter issues are unimportant. But the distinction is critical since once an issue is seen, by consensus, as affecting the integrity of the planet or the survival of the species, far-reaching consequences are set in train. Rationally, it is in the interests of humanity to act together, to accept curbs and constraints on excessive behaviour, to acknowledge a single interest that both meets and yet transcends national interests at the same time. In the case of other issues, the common interest does not exist or it concedes to disputation, reflecting the stronger pull of divisive interests. It is for this reason that the book focuses on the three issues that are in the vital planetary interest.

A METHODOLOGICAL FRAMEWORK

The methodological framework used in this book conforms to the reasoning process employed in contemporary national security analysis. Traditionally, four categories of analysis for the pursuit of the national interest are used: threat, objective, strategy and policy. Fundamentally, a country's national interest lies in protection from national security threats. In traditional security thinking, a nation perceives a problem or a threat, real or imagined. It identifies a national objective – essentially, means by which it can resolve the problem or secure protection from the threat. It devises a national strategy for the attainment of the objective, and policies (foreign policy and defence policy) in accordance with the strategy.

At the global level, the analysis is compellingly similar in the late twentieth century. Humankind today has a planetary interest in protection from any problem confronting it or threat posed to it as a single collective. It perceives problems and threats that are global in scale. In response, the international community of nation-states has, in varying degrees of clarity and formality, identified and articulated a "global objective", generally in a declaration or the preamble or first articles of a treaty. It then has devised a "global strategy" – a plan or programme of action – in response to the objective, and a certain set of policies, generally a set of national policies, in accordance with the global strategy.

The remaining issue is the nature of the power structure through which the international community implements that global strategy at the national level. The nature of sovereignty and political authority at the global, regional, national and local levels is undergoing profound change, and this explains the frustration felt by many over the inability of humankind to react quickly and effectively enough to the global problems and threats as they arise and are perceived.

This, then, is the reasoning process employed in this book: global problem or threat, global objective, global strategy, national policies and the changes in sovereign power to implement them.

NOTES

1. Boutros Boutros-Ghali, *United Nations chronicle* (March 1993), **XXX**(1), cover page. Three years later, Mr Boutros-Ghali spoke of the trend in "criminal globalization" such as the traffic in illegal drugs, terrorism and money laundering. Breaking these trends, he said, would require "global awareness, global commitment and global action". United Nations Daily Highlights, 31 May 1996 (hereafter UNDH).
2. B. Ward & R. Dubos, *Only one Earth: the care and maintenance of a small planet* (New York: Penguin, 1972), 28.
3. United Nations, *Final document: First Special Session of the General Assembly on Disarmament* (New York: UN Series 87-16283-10M, 1978), para. 11 (hereafter *Final document*).
4. Independent Commission on International Development Issues, *North–South: a programme for survival* (London: Pan, 1982), 27.
5. There is, as one national leader has observed, a need to distinguish between problems that occur globally and problems that demand global solutions. As an example of the latter, if environmental damage is not contained within national borders and if national institutions are undermined by non-compliance of others,

then global solutions "make sense". Address to UN General Assembly, New Zealand Minister of Environment Simon Upton, UNDH, 24 June 1997.

6. This book is not about "sovereignty" *per se*, but the concept underpins some of the reasoning throughout. It is taken here to comprise two elements, viz, full legislative, judicial and executive powers, and the status of not being answerable to any higher authority. The distinction between "internal sovereignty" (in the national sphere) and "international sovereignty" (on the international plane) is important – the latter dimension being the one pertinent to this book. The concept is subject to considerable reassessment in contemporary political and legal thought. See, for a recent authoritative analysis, E. Lauterpacht, "Sovereignty – myth or reality?", *International Affairs* **73**(1), 137–50, 1997.

7. The Universal Postal Union was created in 1874, but the birth of international organization in the sense of universal breadth of membership and mandate is generally taken to be the League of Nations in 1920.

8. United Nations Charter, Article 1.4.

9. See, for example: ". . . When the United States knew what it wanted from the United Nations and took the lead in getting it, the United Nations provided important assistance in advancing American interests". The right of the Security Council to authorise the use of force to maintain international peace and security was a "highly significant tool for the United States in promoting US security objectives". Commission on America's National Interests, *American national interest and the United Nations* (New York: Council on Foreign Relations, 1996), 5, 8. Also: E. Luck: "For many national officials, the UN is a functional and instrumental place, a place to carry out some portion of the nation's business, and a forum in which support can be gathered from other nations for one's own priorities or opposition can be generated to actions perceived to be antithetical to US interests." During the Cold War, the UN served as a vehicle "to promote [US] core values and principles in a strikingly successful and dynamic manner". E. Luck, in *US foreign policy and the United Nations system*, C.W. Maynes & R.S. Williamson (eds), 28, 53 (New York: Norton, 1996). See also, in a different context, comment by the foreign minister of Singapore:

    > Prospects for further progress in reforming the Security Council are not good. The reasons were embedded in the international system, which was still largely defined by the relations between sovereign states. No great power or even a power with aspirations to greatness had ever been willing to submit its own vital interests to United Nations jurisdiction. Although UN reform may be widely accepted, what the great powers want is not a strong United Nations *per se*. They want a United Nations just strong enough and credible enough to serve as an effective instrument of their will and policies. Small countries are more inclined to take the United Nations on its own terms and in its own right (UNDH, 29 September 1997).

10. President William J. Clinton, *State of the Union Address,* January 1995.

11. The Australian government, for example, has recently established a parliamentary mechanism which assesses Australian membership of international treaties and organizations by the criterion of the national interest:

    > Treaties will be tabled in Parliament with a National Interest Analysis (NIA) in order to facilitate scrutiny and to demonstrate the reasons for the Government's decision that Australia should enter into legally-binding obligations . . . The NIA is an important mechanism for the Committee to be able to assess, in the first instance, the implications of a proposed obligation and whether or not sufficient support exists for the proposed action (*Joint Standing Committee on Treaties, First Report* (Canberra: Parliament of the Commonwealth of Australia, 1996), 2).

12. *Encyclopaedia of Social Sciences* (section on "National Interest").

13. Ibid.

14. See, principally, C.A. Beard, *The idea of national interest* (New York: Macmillan, 1934); H.J. Morgenthau, *In defense of the national interest: a critical examination of American foreign policy* (New York: Knopf, 1951); J. Frankel, *National interest* (London: Pall Mall, 1970); D.E. Nuechterlein, *United States national interests in a changing world* (Lexington, Ky: University Press of Kentucky, 1973).

15. See, for example:

    > How do states know what they want? One might think this would be a central question for international relations scholars. After all, our major paradigms are all framed in terms of power and interest. The sources of state interests should matter to us. In fact, they have not – or not very much . . . We cannot understand what states want without understanding the international social structure of which they are a part. States are embedded in a dense network of transnational and international social relations that shape their perceptions of the world and their role in that world. States are *socialized* to want certain things by the international society in which they and the people in them live . . . Interests are not just "out there" waiting to be discovered; they are constructed through social interaction. States want to avoid invasion, extinction, and economic collapse, but for most of the time these

negative interests do not narrow the set of possible wants very much ... State interests are defined in terms of internationally held norms and understandings about what is good and appropriate. That normative context influences the behaviour of decision-makers and of mass publics ... (M. Finmore, *National interests in international society* (Ithaca, NY: Cornell University Press, 1996), 1–3).

16. See, for example: A. Kozyrev, "Trust and the balance of interests", in *Mezhdunarodnya Zhizn* (Oct. 1988); and S. Sestanovich, "Inventing the Soviet national interest", in the *National Interest* (Summer 1990), 16.

17. See, for example: G. Torfimenko, "The US national interests and Russia", in *International Affairs: A Russian Journal* **42**(5/6), 49–59, 1996; and "Moderation in the national idea", D. Baluev, in ibid., 105–15.

18. See, for example, *American national interest and the United Nations,* op. cit. Also, Commission on America's National Interests, *America's national interests* (Kennedy School of Government, Nixon Center for Peace & Freedom, The Rand Corporation, 1996); and *UN foreign policy and the United Nations system*, op. cit.

19. See, for example, former US Secretary of State Weinberger: "The United States should not commit forces to combat unless our vital interests are at stake ... Our vital interests can only be determined by ourselves and our definition of the threat." Cited by New Zealand Acting Prime Minister Palmer (New Zealand Ministry of Foreign Affairs Press Statements no. 12, 11 July 1986), 17–18.

20. An alternative version is the "supreme national interest" in arms control treaties, cited as the justification for withdrawal.

21. D. Nuechterlein, "The concept of 'national interest': a time for new approaches", *Orbis* **23**(1), Spring 1979, 85. Nuechterlein in fact uses four categories to distinguish national interest, viz., survival, vital, major and peripheral. See also Nuechterlein in "National interests and foreign policy: a conceptual framework for analysis and decision-making", *British Journal of International Studies*, 246–66, 1976; F. Kratochwil, "On the notion of 'interest' in international relations", *International Organization* **36**, 1982; and A. Tonelson, "The real national interest", *Foreign Policy*, 61–4, 1985–6.

22. R.E. Cox, "An alternative approach to multilateralism", *Global Governance* **3**(1), 106, January–April 1997.

23. B. Ward, *Spaceship Earth* (London: Hamish Hamilton, 1966), 3, 18.

24. Independent Commission on Disarmament and Security Issues, *Common security: a blueprint for survival* (New York: Simon & Schuster, 1982), xiii, 12 (hereafter *Common security*).

25. World Commission on Environment and Development, *Our common future* (Oxford: Oxford University Press, 1987), 49 (hereafter *Our common future*).

26. Commission on Global Governance, *Our global neighbourhood* (Oxford: Oxford University Press, 1995), 254 (hereafter *Our global neighbourhood*).

27. United Nations General Assembly. Official Records; 5th Session, Supplement. No. 1, A/1287, xiii.

28. UNGA. OR; 15th Session, Supplement. No. 1.a, A/4390/Addendum 1, 8.

29. UNGA, *Introduction to the Annual Report 1969* (New York: United Nations, OP/374-69-21161, September 1969), 17.

30. UNGA, *Report of the Secretary-General on the Work of the Organization 1991* (New York: United Nations DPI/1168, September 1991), 16–17.

31. President William J. Clinton, United States of America, 48th UNGA Session, 4th Plenary, 27 September 1993, A/48/PV.4, 7.

32. Secretary of Health and Human Services Donna Shalala, United States of America, 48th UNGA Session, 71st Plenary, 7 December 1993, A/48/PV.71, 5.

33. Foreign Minister of Papua New Guinea, John Kaputin, 48th UNGA Session, 55th Plenary, 15 November 1993, A/48/PV.55, 15.

34. President Joaquim Alberto Chissano, Mozambique, 48th UNGA Session, 27 September 1993, A/48/PV.5, 9.

35. Statement by the Sixteen Heads of State or Government in Support of Renewing Multilateralism, 25 September 1996 (Stockholm, Swedish Ministry of Foreign Affairs, 1996).

36. Razali Ismail, President of the United Nations General Assembly, address to the 23rd Annual Yale Model United Nations, New Haven, Connecticut, in UN doc. GA/9220, 6.

37. Parliamentarians for Global Action, *Annual Report 1993* (New York, 1993), 3. See also:

> Our members, who represent the people who elect them through the democratic process, are committed to solving global problems from a global perspective, with the interests of the planet foremost in mind. The organization approaches the problems of our time with a new political maxim: that the paramount value is no longer the national interest but rather the planetary interest (K. Graham, *Global Action* **III**(3), (New York, PGA, September 1991), 8).

38. United Nations Secretary-General, address to the Argentine Council for Foreign Relations, 14 March 1994, *UN Chronicle*, **XXXI**(2), June 1994, 3.

39. The distinction needs to be drawn here between legal and political theory, and also between "rights" and "interests". Strictly, the law in most cultures accords "rights" only to animate creatures and indeed only to

humans, although consideration has been given to extending that notion (see: C. Stone, "Should trees have standing?", *Southern California Law Review* **45**, 450 (1972), and C. Stone, *The gnat is older than man* (Princeton, N.J.: Princeton University Press, 1993); also Justice Douglas's dissent in *Sierra Club v. Morton* (1972). Islamic thought includes *amana*, literally "God's trust", which requires humans to care for all living and non-living things, including environmental objects such as wells, forests, grazing areas, mountains and deserts (see Z. Sardar, *The touch of Midas: knowledge and environment in Islam and the West* (Manchester: Manchester University Press, 1982). Generally, political thought allows for greater flexibility and creativity than the law. It is credible to postulate that it is in the interests of humanity to recognize that the planet, on which it depends for its survival, should be given ultimate respect, including the "right" to be left to future generations in a comparable natural state to that when humanity first made its imprint felt. This is but a step to the principle of intergenerational equity, enshrined at Rio. The right of the next generation to inherit an unaltered planet, and the "right" of the planet to remain unaltered, are essentially the same thing.

40. *Statement by Sixteen Heads of State or Government in Support of Global Co-operation*, 23 September 1995 (Stockholm: Swedish Ministry of Foreign Affairs, 1995).

41. See, for example:

> If one asks, "what is worth a billion lives (or the survival of the species)", it is natural to resist contemplating a positive answer. But suppose one asks "is it possible to imagine any threat to our civilisation and values that would justify raising the threat to a billion lives from one in ten thousand to one in a thousand for a specific period?" Then there are several plausible answers, including a democratic way of life and cherished freedoms that give meaning to life beyond mere survival . . . Survival is a necessary condition for the enjoyment of other values, but that does not make it sufficient . . . We can give survival of the species a very high priority without giving it the paralysing status of an absolute value. Some degree of risk is unavoidable if individuals or societies are to avoid paralysis and enhance the quality of life beyond mere survival. The degree of that risk is a justifiable topic of both prudential and moral reasoning (J. Nye, *Nuclear ethics* (New York: Free Press, 1986), 45–6).

42. The shorter Oxford English dictionary (Oxford: Clarendon Press, 1965), 2093, 2352.

43. Razali Ismail, address to the 23rd Yale Annual Model United Nations, GA/9220, 27 February 1997, 4.

44. UNDH, 4 April 1997.

45. That would even include issues critical to the character of humanity, such as human cloning which is rapidly becoming a focus of global concern. In March 1997, for example, the World Health Organization declared that it considered the use of cloning for the replication of human beings to be unethical since it would violate some of the basic principles which govern medically assisted procreation. In November, the Council of Europe adopted the first legally binding international instrument prohibiting "any intervention seeking to create a human being genetically identical to another human being, whether living or dead". See UNDH, 11 March 1997 and *International Herald Tribune*, 7 November 1997 (hereafter IHT). Such issues, of grave ethical import, are nonetheless seen as normative in their nature. By comparison, the prospect of Earth being impacted by an extra-terrestrial object, once dismissed as speculative but now accepted as a serious scientific issue, would be seen as addressing the vital planetary interest.

46. *Final document*, para. 8.

CHAPTER TWO

Legitimacy in twenty-first century politics

Gwyn Prins

The fundamental challenge of twenty-first century politics will be to ensure action, at the global level, which commands the understanding, support and involvement of all peoples of the world, acting together in the name of humanity. Action that will be both timely and legitimate. It is my purpose here to explore the ramifications of this dual requirement for politics on the threshold of the new century.

Necessarily, we must begin with first principles. Yet it is not long before such reasoning takes practical hold on our daily lives and our national politics. The stability of a Russian submarine commander, the judgements of an Australian immigration minister, the investment decisions of a Chinese coal-industry technocrat, the murder of a Brazilian environmentalist, all stand testimony to this, all have an impact on humanity acting together. Henceforth at the global level, every public political act will impinge upon the individual citizen on the planet. Conversely, decisions and actions by individuals will collectively affect the planet, in a manner inconceivable even half a century ago.

THREE FACTORS OF LEGITIMACY

Legitimation of any political act requires three factors working in concert: a cause, an actor and an underpinning political culture.

An action is legitimated when those acting and those experiencing the consequences of the action all agree that there is a cause – a reason to act. If consent is withheld, then the issue is forced if it is pursued. The ability to act is predicated upon the existence of the second requirement, namely, a defined and competent agent. This means that an actor, whose powers are appropriate and competent to address the problem, may be generally agreed to be an actor. Both these factors are imbedded in the third, which is the most fundamental requirement, namely, the existence of a self-conscious political culture. A political culture is the invisible energy which flows through and maintains the visible structure of any social contract.

The robustness of society at any level (family, tribe or municipality, nation or region) depends upon there being an alignment between the sentiments of individuals and the actuators of the levers of power. "Civil society" links private and public cultures. In Gellner's words, "civil society is that set of diverse non-governmental organizations which is strong enough to counterbalance the state and, while not preventing the state from fulfilling its role as keeper of the peace and arbitrator between major interests, can nevertheless prevent it from dominating and atomising the rest of society".[1]

Maintenance of that alignment is a dynamic process. It is not in some sense distant from or optional to the construction and maintenance of the instruments of power in a democratic society. As the legal philosopher Philip Allott writes, "The culture of a society . . . is the totality of all the processing of society's total social process, the imagination of its imagining, the reason of its reasoning".[2] To maintain this congruence between civil society and the structures of power is the difficult act of balance to which any form of democracy aspires. A well-ordered society is regulated by its public conception of justice, observes John Rawls[3]; and public affirmation of its existence in a political culture, in which justice is equated with fairness, is shown through the conferring of legitimacy by civil society upon actions emanating from superordinate power and affecting individuals.

At present, we see few such acts of affirmation at the level of global politics because, as yet, there is no self-conscious culture of global society.

At once a clarification must be made of which types of society principally concern the authors of the following chapters. This book is concerned with legitimation as it occurs in the third of Weber's ideal types, namely, rational, contract-framed social relations. The manner in which legitimation is achieved by charismatic power, or by the power of custom, is not unimportant, not least since part of humanity lives under that sway. But the task at hand is more specific than that, and it addresses the dominant global power structures at the turn of the millennium.

The kind of civil society which concerns us is one which, in Gellner's phrase, "... excludes both stifling communalism and centralised authoritarianism".[4] To accommodate, engage and legitimate the actions of a clear and competent agent from a wider civil society does not call for carbon-copied unanimity of view. In fact, the likelihood of global civil society in the twenty-first century being filled with incoherent violence is increased if we are unable to cultivate what John Keane has eloquently named "public spheres of controversy", in which the exercise of power is monitored non-violently by citizens. This, he rightly states, is a "culture of civility"; and it is the absence of such a culture in international society which makes it both important and difficult to render the concept of the planetary interest diplomatically and politically concrete.[5]

Invocation of the national interest is able in many contexts to mobilize all three of the requirements for legitimated action – cause, actor, political culture. The threat of invasion in war is the most obvious, clear-cut case. A national objective which overrides any substantial objection is self-evident: there is a clear and present danger. The agent is equally self-evident and uniquely competent, namely, a national government working through its armed forces. The political culture, focused through and stimulated by the speeches of eloquent leaders, vibrates with such unity of purpose that individuals willingly surrender a certain freedom of action for the manifest public good. They accept conscription, temporary restraints on freedom of expression, the internment of enemy aliens and the like. All this is in the expectation that the sacrifice, while considerable, will not last for ever and in the end will lead to a better future.

In contrast, problems with all three requirements are encountered with the planetary interest.

First, the cause. There is a difficulty in defining clear and present dangers which show symptoms that are incontrovertible. The threats associated with global warming are not as visible or as immediate as foreign troops on the border. Therefore, one important aspect of the chapters that follow is their exploration of ways in which the nature of risk and threat arising from global phenomena can be presented accurately, and yet simultaneously trigger an awareness of the need for action. The decidedly patchy history of the international political response to global environmental threats during the last 15 years is illuminating, for it shows both the difficulty of seeking immediate political action on the basis of an assessment of long-term possible threats, and the temptation of "short-circuiting" that frustration by exaggeration and oversimplification.[6]

Secondly, the actors. There are at present no clearly self-defined and competent actors able to defend the planetary interest in a transnational context. In fact, the evidence from fishing disputes is worrying; for the high seas provide what is possibly the most benign political environment in which to experiment with new regimes of international co-operative policing of the global commons. The same lesson is to be drawn from experience of "ozone diplomacy".[7]

Thirdly, the underpinning political culture. As noted, what causes the difficulties above is that there is, as yet, no self-conscious culture of global society. Allott captures the present situation in grimly memorable words:

> Contemporary international society has an unculture of its unsocial becoming. That vacuum is being filled by a culture of primitive capitalism, dominating an undemocratized and unsocialized international system. An international society which is at last a society will have as its ideal the word-idea-theory-value of eunomia, the good order of a self-ordering society.[8]

LEGITIMACY AND THE PLANETARY INTEREST: THREE OPTIONS

If the issues reviewed in the chapters of this book are as important as their authors believe, this is not an encouraging state of affairs. How can legitimated action in the planetary interest be achieved?

What are the options available to the international community? Three types can be identified: direct mandate, indirect mandate and mandate by extension.

Direct mandate

There are two ways of proceeding. Either one can ignore the "general will" or one can seek to shape it. In the first case, a decision will be taken that a situation is too serious, too complicated and too urgent to risk being taken to the process of public debate and, accordingly, by some form of diktat, actions will be taken in the planetary interest but not necessarily with public assent. This dictatorship would be more that of the philosopher-kings than of the mafia, for the source of legitimation offered would be that special knowledge gave special mandate.

Merely to write such a prescription is to underline its deep unattractiveness. Actions taken from the "aristocracy of knowledge" are brittle. They are usually accepted only in contexts of generally agreed clear and present danger. Yet one quality shared by many of the planetary threats is that, unaddressed at an early stage, they can reach a point where action is unavoidable and must be draconian. In order to avoid that unpalatable circumstance it is worth considering other options now.

There are three direct mandates which can be achieved through the general will.

Delegated authority

This method of achieving a mandate is, of course, often used already for some of the issues discussed in the chapters below. It is where a government acts on the international stage – the forum is the large international conference at which leaders claim to hear, or to articulate, a general will upon which they then act by treaty. Thus at the global level, the national programmes of action which were put in place in many countries after signature of the Climate Change Convention agreed at the Rio Earth Summit in 1992 followed this route. That example is in itself salutary for, while some countries have achieved reductions in carbon emissions, others manifestly have not and there is no superordinate power to ensure compliance. Another more familiar form of delegated authority is at the regional level, where nations routinely pool authority within, for example, the European Union. That, too, has demonstrable limits because of lack of powers to enforce compliance.

Public fear

The second form of direct mandate is the one which does produce political action more reliably. This is when public fear is inflamed and in consequence forces a traditional political reflex. Examples of this already exist at both regional and global levels. At the regional level, the management of the so-called "mad cow disease" problem in some European countries is illuminating, showing the limitations on the ability of traditional political mechanisms to alleviate public fears. Step-by-step, what appeared to be reluctant measures were introduced after the extent of the problem had become publicly apparent, and with each further revelation public confidence eroded. Also at the regional level, fear has produced a patchy, reactive international response to the uncontrolled forest fires that swept South East Asia in 1997. At the global level, fear has undoubtedly propelled AIDS research. Noteworthy in all these cases is the fact that public fear typically shows itself in concentrated bursts rather than continuously. When a reluctant response of the power structure is driven in this way, equally sporadic effort may result. The main problem, as noted earlier, is that most of today's global threats creep up upon us slowly and are pervasive. Consequently, they do not generate a lively, urgent fear in response.

Citizen activism

It is not far to cross to another type of mandate which has become increasingly important as the information technology revolution has empowered individuals. Confronted with traditional political structures in which they have lost confidence, or which they believe to be unable or unwilling to act in their interests, individuals take matters into their own hands. Clearly, each category is empowered in different ways, but, being empowered, has the means to construct new forms of global politics by fostering a political agenda. Such pressure-group politics follows in the footsteps of activists against slavery or for women's suffrage. Never a majority, such groups nonetheless change the norms of political culture. John Vidal has observed that while anti-road protesters, evicted from tunnels dug to frustrate the construction of a bypass in beautiful countryside in the south-west of England, appeared to be marginal to mainstream society, protest camps such as these were a first-class "finishing school" for individuals wanting to do active "citizen service".[9] Similarly, the millionaire philanthropist George Soros has been able to change the terms of public debate about the future of European politics by using his financial resources to support positions, through empowering local individuals, in ways which otherwise would not have occurred.[10]

In the second and third methods above, success in transforming the general will on particular issues from the outside is achieved when both ideas and actors "graduate" from the finishing school that Vidal describes.

Indirect mandate

A fundamentally different way of affecting the general will is indirect and does not operate in the formal political arena. This "stakeholding" can take two forms.

Consumer pressure

Delegated power to act on many of the issues pertinent to the planetary interest is given by individuals to agents not as voters but as consumers.

Clearly, the relationship between manufacturing and producing companies and their consumers is intricate. Consumers are not rational actors nor are multinational companies purely passive. In fact, as J.K. Galbraith has argued through many volumes, the central point to grasp about the modern multinational company is that, after a certain level of profit has been achieved, its prime concern is to maximize control over its environment – upstream and downstream – which it does through investment in advertising, sponsorship and the like.[11] However, as many environmental activists have come to realize, it may be more efficient to seek to influence the behaviour of large companies in nodal positions in the global economy obliquely, via consumer pressure, than to address them directly through the traditional mechanism of a political mandate translated into governmental regulation.

Accordingly, the later 1990s have seen the emergence of important new initiatives to build bridges between the environmental and business communities. An example is the Forum for the Future, launched in Britain in 1996 and grounded by environmentalists in the business community through the journal *Green Futures*.[12]

This manner of seeking to create a legitimate mandate for action, by the indirect approach, is close to one of the emerging strands of legitimation of political action that has become part of mainstream political discourse in the West in recent years, namely, the "stakeholder" approach to the reconstruction of national civil society. It has become widely accepted in both Eastern and Western Europe that, albeit for different reasons, alienation is on the increase in many sectors of society.

The stakeholder approach has in its favour the fact that it builds incrementally upon old-established roots. In common law, it is property and the possession of property that gives individuals standing. Indeed, some of the most creative new thinking about how to address the problems of the global commons approaches directly from that foundation; for, as Kevin Gray has argued, there is much in the existing laws of property which permits extension into the field of global commons.[13] The issue, however, becomes complex at the global level since consumer pressure is generally less clearly manifest or potent in many non-Western societies.

Informed consent

The second approach to stakeholding is through the generation of "informed consent". This is the only robust alternative to imposed direct mandates derived from the "aristocracy of knowledge". It means that tasks of communicating planetary threats and translating that analysis into calls for action cannot be avoided. In the case of the planetary interest concept, informed consent would have to be linked to supranational political mechanisms which, at the moment, do not exist, if the concept of stakeholding in the global commons is to become a viable route to legitimated political action. However, if successful, and in contrast to reaction to fear, sustained rather than sporadic effort becomes possible.

Many now follow the lead of the Second Report of the Inter-Governmental Panel on Climate Change in thinking that time is not on our side and that, therefore, interim measures – or further measures in the aftermath of Kyoto – must be taken in the nearer term to produce legitimated political action on global interests. This, therefore, makes the case for the third of the options which could be considered now.

Mandate by extension

A third alternative is mandate by extension. This is, I believe, at the heart of Dr Graham's ingenious concept of the planetary interest.

There is much to be said in support of this approach. It promises a more immediate mobilization of legitimated political action than other forms of mandate and it also offers a gradual pathway into the new agenda of global security from the familiar agenda of national security. In contrast to direct mandates given in international fora, to regional or global mandates responding to fear or to national action driven by citizen activism, a mandate by extension operates uncontroversially at the national

Figure 2.1 "How", asks Gwyn Prins, "can legitimated action in the planetary interest be achieved?" In the 1990s, he says, through a "mandate by extension": "it offers a gradual pathway into the new agenda of global security from the familiar agenda of national security". When a true global consciousness develops in the twenty-first century, effective global authority will develop, with legitimacy based on the "informed consent" of all humankind. Meanwhile, the voting lights flash on as the General Assembly expresses the views of the nation-states of the twentieth-century world. (Courtesy UN Photo)

level. It is quickly and easily effected through existing national institutions and is internally motivated within the elected and professional institutions of power. An example is in a recent official White Paper in the United Kingdom which states that, as an extension of British national interest, "this White Paper sets out the Government's policies to achieve the *sustainable development of this planet*" (emphasis added).[14] An example at the regional level is the creation of ECHO (the European Community Humanitarian Office) by the Council of Ministers under the responsibility of one of the contributors to this book, Commissioner Emma Bonino, with a mission to develop an integrated response to humanitarian crises, including means to analyze and provide early warning of future crises.[15] So "mandate by extension" is the extrapolation of forms of power and authority already legitimated by centuries of political thought and behaviour at the national level on to new planes of conduct.

This form of mandate is not the final state of political evolution necessary to respond to the challenges of the twenty-first century. It is no more – and no less – than a readily achievable position pro tem. Historically, the development of common law through precedent is the main example of an "extension" within the nation-state. In future, the planetary interest concept will no doubt operate in the same way. For, as noted earlier, the prerequisite to a self-sustaining mobilization of the planetary interest in global politics will only come from a transformation – indeed, an awakening – of a new form of global social consciousness. This global consciousness alone can ensure that new institutions and mechanisms, designed to protect the planetary interest, are granted the legitimacy they need in order to be effective, grounded in an informed consent of the people. As later chapters I think make clear, this will be the key requirement of politics in the twenty-first century.

NOTES

1. E. Gellner, *Conditions of liberty: civil society and its rivals* (Harmondsworth: Penguin, 1996), 5.
2. P. Allott, *Eunomia: new order for a new world* (Oxford: Oxford University Press, 1990), 376.
3. J. Rawls, *The theory of justice* (Oxford: Oxford University Press, 1973), 454.
4. Gellner, *Conditions of liberty*, 12.
5. J. Keane, *Reflections on violence* (London: Verso, 1996).
6. For further discussion on this, see G. Prins, "The curious recent history of environmental politics" in Environmental change and international security: proceedings of the International Workshop of the Royal Dutch Academy of Sciences, 20 January 1997 (Rijksuniversiteit, Groningen, 1998); and E. Sellwood, "The foreign policy implications of the Kyoto climate change conference", UK parliamentary brief, December 1997.
7. R. Benedick, *Ozone diplomacy: new directions in safeguarding the planet* (Cambridge, Mass.: Harvard University Press, 1991).
8. Allott, *Eunomia*, 419–20.
9. J. Vidal, "The scum also rises", *Guardian*, 29 January 1997.
10. G. Soros, *Opening the Soviet system* (London: Weidenfeld & Nicolson, 1990); "Capital crimes", *Guardian*, 18 January 1997.
11. J. Galbraith, *Economics and public purpose* (London: Vance Packard, 1974); and *The hidden persuaders* (Harmondsworth: Penguin, 1981).
12. In the magazine, the business sponsors (corporate partners) are given space in special "partners' pages" to express their own views.
13. K. Gray, "The ambivalence of property" in *Threats without enemies: facing environmental insecurity*, G. Prins (ed.). (London: Earthscan, 1993).
14. Department of International Development, *Eliminating world poverty: a challenge for the twenty-first century* (London: Department of International Development, November 1997).
15. ECHO was established by resolution 1257/96 of the Council of Ministers, adopted 20 June 1996.

CHAPTER THREE

The legitimate national interest and legitimate global power

Kennedy Graham

As Gwyn Prins has observed, at the global level the cause, the actor and the political culture are inchoate but discernible. Today, the threats and problems exist. Determining which are genuinely global, however, which are regional, which national and which local is a tough undertaking, intellectually imprecise yet politically essential. There is a degree of "blurring at the edges". The actors exist but with limited powers which, even in limited form, do not command complete consent around the world. A global political culture has only begun to emerge over the past decade as the televised and computer links wire the planet together, juxtaposing global images of virtual reality and nationalistic feelings of local identity in a potentially explosive mix. Complexity and uncertainty promise to be the norms of twenty-first century global politics.

In a situation where sovereign entities are responsible for issues that are of a magnitude one scale higher than the entities themselves, three challenges arise. There is the difficulty of conceptualizing a single vision that can serve as a lodestar for all the entities in negotiations. There is the problem of judging each other's policies objectively. And there is the need to establish new authority and power at that higher level for implementation of any agreement reached. These three factors – negotiating vision, objective judgements and effective enforcement – are the weak points in the way humanity is currently acting together.

Enduring progress in recognizing the causes, strengthening the actors and extending the enforcement power will not occur without a legitimizing consent that is genuinely worldwide. Whether the mandate is direct, indirect or by extension will depend upon the pace at which the global political culture takes root among the peoples of the world, and the degree of insight they bring to bear on those global problems, problems that are essentially of humanity's own making.

The notion of legitimacy advanced in Chapter 2 underpins the concept of the planetary interest when it is operationalized for the purposes of practical politics. Without a proper mandate from the people, governments cannot act. Without a proper mandate from all governments, the international community cannot act, at least not decisively and effectively. The struggle for credibility over judgements of executive policy at the national level and for legitimacy of institutional authority at the global level is the critical challenge of our time.[1]

Use of the vital planetary interest concept will assist policy-making at both the national and global levels with each of these three challenges. It evokes that single higher vision, and would guide intergovernmental negotiations with less of the chaos and brinkmanship that many international conferences exhibit today. It helps formulate the national policy of a country in approaching global problems and negotiating solutions, and enables a country better to judge the merit of another's. And it can act as a criterion for determining which issues justify enforcement power at the global level.

Three propositions can be derived from and advanced with respect to the application of the concept:

- the "planetary interest" must be acknowledged by all nation-states as the agreed vision reflecting their common interests;
- each country's "legitimate national interest" should be compatible with the planetary interest; and
- global "legitimate power", as recognized by the global community, should respond to the nature and severity of the global threat.

THE SINGLE NEGOTIATING VISION

The single negotiating vision is essentially the planetary interest itself. If it is accorded the highest priority, it will alter the way diplomatic negotiations are currently pursued. In addressing global problems today, a nation-state pursues a national brief that reflects the national interest formulated in the capital. Generally, an official delegation has an opening negotiating position and a fallback position. The opening position is generally the maximum that a nation-state believes it might conceivably aspire to secure in the negotiations. The fallback position is the minimum it is prepared to accept without walking out. The opening position is generally excessive and unduly demanding, at least as perceived by other states. Yet in alleging this, other states cannot avoid the criticism that they, too, are acting from the subjective perspective of their own national interests. Larger states generally attain an outcome closer to their opening position than smaller states. All states, however, formulate their policies with the interests of their own people only in mind, and with no more than a passing regard for the interests of others, or of the global commons, or even without due regard for the long-term consequences of their actions on their own national self-interest. The outcome of a negotiating session is almost always the haphazard and unplanned consequence of a competitively pursued set of excessive national interests.

The way to overcome this problem can be found in an alternative approach to international negotiations. Instead of the negotiations being the consequence of the competing claims of all national interests, the global objective and strategy would be identified first, and then negotiations would determine what national obligations arise from this. This was the approach advocated, for example, by UNEP's Executive Director in the context of global environmental negotiations over both ozone protection and climate stabilization.[2] The IPCC itself suggested that a framework convention should articulate a multilateral greenhouse gas control strategy, with global goals regarding future emissions of greenhouse gases, and simultaneously negotiated protocols establishing specific national requirements to ensure attainment of the global targets. It is only by identifying a single global vision first, and then subsequently recognizing equitable national obligations, obligations that are binding upon nation-states even if they are reluctant to assume them, that the planet will be rescued from global threats of this nature. The same holds true for weapons of mass destruction. But so long as nations refuse to accept an overarching interest – a superordinate power, to cite Gwyn Prins's phrase – a "rational, contract-framed" approach to global problems will not exist.

THE LEGITIMATE NATIONAL INTEREST

If the vital planetary interest is accepted, the way is clear for nation-states to assess one another's policies and actions with a greater objectivity and efficacy than has been the case hitherto. They will be able to determine more readily, with an agreed negotiating vision, what is reasonable in the common interest of the planet and of humanity.

An intrinsic link between the national interests of nation-states and the planetary interest of the world community has, in fact, been perceived by political leaders in the past. Addressing the British parliament in 1958, Dag Hammarskjöld observed that the United Nations is the natural development from lines of thought reaching back in time "since a few men first began to think about the decency and dignity of other men". Now, said Hammarskjöld, "the lines between national and international policy have begun to blur. What is in the national interest, when truly seen, merges naturally into the international interest".[3] Twenty-two years later the Brandt Report affirmed that its aim was to point out the immense risks threatening humankind and that "the legitimate self-interest of nations often merges into well-understood common interests".[4] In an effort at bilateral objectivity, in 1995 the French Prime Minister, Edouard Balladur, expressed the desire, following the American–French espionage dispute, that French–American relations would continue to be based on "mutual trust" and "mutual respect for each others' legitimate national interests".[5]

The idea that nation-states might be able to assess each other's policies with greater objectivity than in the past is a new one, and raises many questions. How might such judgements take place, in what fora, through what process, under whose authority and to what effect? In fact, the process and procedure of such behaviour would remain the same as today – articulated in present negotiating and deliberative fora, and claiming no more than political status. No nation-state, moreover, can ever validly claim to have ultimate objectivity in its views and policies. But the use of the vital planetary interest and the legitimate national interest concepts would assist in attaining greater objectivity than a pure expression of national self-interest without regard for broader consequences.

How might the legitimate national interest be identified and defined? As with certain other concepts, it is perhaps more instructive to define it by exclusion, through what might be perceived to be an "illegitimate national interest". It is an illegitimate national interest grossly to pollute a neighbouring state; to degrade the global commons; to engage in an act that would devastate the planet. Is this a valid way of defining the concept? Such an approach is similar to the perception of citizen responsibilities, which are defined more by circumscription of prohibited behaviour (murder, arson, theft, fraud) than by positive identification of rights or other lawful action. A citizen's freedom extends to the point beyond which it interferes with that of others. Anything not thus prohibited is lawful behaviour. Similarly, anything that is not illegitimate national behaviour may be undertaken as a "legitimate national interest".

This notion of a legitimate national interest is critical to the future of the planet. It can be seen as related to the "principle of good faith" of the UN Charter in which all member states "shall fulfill in good faith the obligations assumed by them in accordance with the present Charter".[6] That principle applies to every other part of the charter, including the requirement that the Security Council acts on behalf of all member states.[7] It follows, it has been advanced, that member states on the Security Council are obligated to have regard for an interest beyond their own national interest in their actions on the council.[8] This standard has, of course, not always been met, and the relationship between the larger interest which permanent council members must respect and the national interest which they tend to pursue is being increasingly critiqued in the context of the UN reform process, including by one permanent council member itself.[9] It is significant that the principle was reaffirmed in 1992 as one of the 27 principles in the Rio Declaration, and also in the UN Convention on the Law of the Sea (Article 300) which came into force in 1994.

In the course of this book, the legitimate national interest will be applied to national policies with a view to determining whether they are compatible with the planetary interest. Two criteria are relevant in this respect. First, having negotiated a global agreement, nation-states frequently enter a reservation or interpretation that establishes, in law, their particular national position on the provisions agreed. Secondly, the manner of the implementation of their national obligations under the global agreement subsequently reflects the national interest more vividly than their global rhetoric at the conclusion of the agreement. These criteria, reservations and compliance, largely though not exclusively reveal the "lack of fit" between the national interest of a state and the planetary interest which the community of states has painstakingly identified and negotiated.

The *legitimate national interest*, then, is a conceptual means, an objective criterion, for judging what is acceptable to all in the vital planetary interest. It may be defined as

> the national interest, and policies deriving from it, of a nation-state which are compatible with, and do not adversely affect, the interests of the planet and humanity as a species – both current and future generations.

LEGITIMATE GLOBAL POWER

"Legitimate power" has been defined as "power that is valid according to rules, and where the rules themselves are justifiable by and in conformity with the underlying beliefs".[10] Thus, the main way in which the powerful will maintain their legitimacy is by respecting the intrinsic limits set to their power by the rules and underlying principles on which they are grounded. Legitimate power, then, is limited power.

As noted, enforcement power at the global level remains, in the 1990s, inchoate and rudimentary. Powers at the national level have been developed in a gradual manner, primarily through evolution but on occasion revolution, through to a stage where the legitimacy of national power itself is not questioned. Nation-states claim different sources of legitimacy, for the most part in the people, in some cases in God. Whether the legitimacy is popular or divine – the political system democratic or theocratic – leaders and rivals compete for power in the name of that source of legitimacy, answering always to the national interest.[11]

Sovereignty and the bestowal of legitimate authority should not be treated lightly. As noted in Chapter 1, civilization is a thin veneer resting precariously upon the norms and institutions of human society. The thin fabric of socialized behaviour can tear with ease. Civility among the citizenry of a society can break down, the state collapse, and anarchy prevail. Two opposing tendencies – authority for the sake of stability which, if taken too far, runs the risk of repression of the people; and freedom for the sake of expression which, if taken too far, runs the risk of anarchy – are in constant mutual tension. Over the longer term, human society strives for a balance between authority and freedom.

Figure 3.1   The United Nations, said Dag Hammarskjöld in 1958, is the natural development from lines of thought reaching back in time "since a few men first began to think about the dignity and decency of other men". "Now," he said, "the lines between national and international policy have begun to blur. What is in the national interest, when truly seen, merges naturally into the international interest." When Hammarskjöld spoke, 82 nation-states comprised the UN membership. Today, 185 flags fly outside UN headquarters. Yet the single planetary interest embraces all their "legitimate self-interests" as the Brandt Report noted. (Courtesy UN Photo)

At the national level this has been developed through centuries of painstaking effort and sacrifice – from the early Icelandic *alting* through the Swiss confederation and the various political revolutions of recent centuries to the decolonization movement of the twentieth century. The source of sovereignty and the political structure of the state differ among societies, but the two fundamental conditions of political legitimacy – popular participation in public affairs and informed consent of the people in political decisions – are largely present in all. In the present age most nation-states have relatively stable governmental structures, even if they do not agree among themselves over the ideological underpinnings and even if regimes occasionally usurp the legitimacy of the leadership. To what extent can this legitimacy, invoking these two conditions, be extended at the global level?

At the global level, the situation is considerably less developed, reflecting incremental progress through the twentieth century. The Covenant of the League of Nations was concluded in the name of the "High Contracting Parties", being the grouping of sovereign nation-states of the world at the time – not all of them finally agreeing to participate. The legitimacy of the League thus lay in its voluntary membership, and indeed nation-states did choose to withdraw as time passed. The United Nations, however, represents a significant step forward, on three counts:

- The charter is proclaimed in the name of "the peoples of the United Nations", and it is "we" the people who "resolve to combine our efforts" to accomplish the aims of the UN. Accordingly, the peoples' respective governments agree to the "present Charter" and establish the UN organization.
- While application to join is voluntary and open to peace-loving states, once inside the organization there is no provision for unilateral withdrawal. Rather, the UN itself can temporarily suspend membership privileges of a state against which it has taken enforcement action, and it can expel a state which has persistently violated the charter's principles.
- The nation-states have, under the charter, surrendered national sovereignty to the Security Council's enforcement power in one area (the maintenance of international peace and security) through the provision of national armed forces and access to national territory by a UN force. In practice that concession to the planetary interest has been observed on only a few occasions and the political norm of the 1990s is in fact to preserve national discretion over contributing troops to a UN action. But the theory of conceding national sovereignty to the UN in an area of critical importance already has a precedent, established, moreover, 50 years ago. And the world has changed considerably since then, with new global challenges and threats confronting humankind.

Thus both the principle of a global popular sovereignty accorded by the peoples of the world, and the concession of national sovereignty in the name of the common UN interest are already established, and indeed half a century old. The challenge today is to determine which other areas of nation-state behaviour, areas that have arisen in recent decades and pose new challenges of a global kind, might justify a comparable surrender of legitimate sovereign powers to the UN.

In a world that is responding increasingly to global forces yet is increasingly nationalistic at the same time, the question of legislative and enforcement authority at the global level is a delicate and sensitive one. Some propose greater powers for the United Nations on the grounds that the international community is not acting fast enough in the face of certain global problems. Others oppose this on several grounds: some on philosophical judgements of individual and national freedoms, some in the political judgement that the global institutions as presently composed are not sufficiently representative of the world's people. Legitimate global power can only derive from competent authority as agreed by consensus of all nation-states. Legitimacy of the United Nations has become the focus of attention in recent years and the apparent criterion by which UN reform is going to be judged, as many states have made clear in the debate at the General Assembly in 1997.[12]

The planetary interest concept can help clarify this issue as well. Application of the principle of subsidiarity, in which jurisdictional competence is accorded to the lowest political entity commensurate with the scale of the problem or area of responsibility, is increasingly influencing political decision-making. No body should have jurisdictional authority on an issue if it can be adequately handled by a smaller body. This principle secures much of the regional politics of the European Union, as is shown in Chapter 13. But in recent years it has had an effect even upon the traditional primacy of the nation-state. Devolution of power and authority downward to sub-state level over certain issues such as health, education and justice, is established practice in federated states and is occurring now also in unitary states such as, for example, the United Kingdom.[13] A greater interaction between city, province, nation-state, regional organization and global organization is occurring as the involvement of all such levels in the global conferences of the 1990s demonstrated. But will this be accompanied by an evolution of power and authority upward to the global organization? Only in those issues involving the vital planetary interest, it is contended here, might greater global powers be seen as legitimate.

Legitimate global power, then, might be defined as

> Legislative, executive and judicial competence at the global level which is agreed by consensus of all nation-states as in the "vital planetary interest", involving those issues which threaten the survival and viability of humanity and the protection of the planet from major anthropogenic change.

In applying this definition to issues invoking the planetary interest, much turns on the meaning of "consensus". It is not intended here, and never has been accepted in state behaviour, that consensus means unanimity; were it so, the work and even the existence of the United Nations would be nullified by the absence of Switzerland and Tonga, and the efficacy of international treaties would be thwarted by the sovereign decision of a few states not to accede. Humanity cannot afford that a small group of "outliers" undermine the entire normative and legislative process. Legitimacy, whether applied to the legitimate national interest or to legitimate global power, must not be taken as unanimity of all nation-states, but rather as a set of generally recognized principles with the consensus of a significant majority of states from a representative range of regions and cultures.

PARTS II AND III: PREMISES AND STRUCTURE

The above considerations structure the remaining substantive parts of this book. The fundamental premise for Part II of this book, therefore, is the following:

- whatever is in the vital planetary interest requires that a nation-state pursue a legitimate national interest; and, as a corollary:
- any national policy which is not in the legitimate national interest violates the vital planetary interest.

The fundamental premise for Part III is:

- the sovereign powers attributed to the international community at the global level – legitimate global powers in any particular area – should be confined solely to those issues that are in the vital planetary interest.

Thus, Part II focuses on the legitimate national interest as it is derived from the vital planetary interest. Contributors, current or former parliamentarians in their countries, are asked whether their own country is pursuing a legitimate national interest in its policies on a particular global problem. If not, it is unreasonably living off, or posing a threat to, the rest of the world.

Part III focuses upon the notion of legitimate global power in the three areas of vital planetary interest. Contributors are asked whether binding enforcement power on the part of a global sovereign assembly is legitimate and justifiable in connection with a particular global, regional, national or municipal interest.

The method used in this book to elaborate these thoughts deriving from the methodology introduced in Chapter 1 involves an interaction between the editor and the contributing authors. In short, it responds to the following structure:

A.   Identification of the global objective, global strategy, and prescribed national policies

In introductory sections to the chapters in Part II, the editor undertakes to identify the following:

(i)   the global problem or threat in those areas which are taken to concern the vital planetary interest;
(ii)   what the international community, speaking officially with one voice has, to date, perceived as the global objective in response to the problem or threat;
(iii) the global strategy which the international community has devised in order to attain the objective;
(iv)   the national policies prescribed by the international community to implement the global strategy.

B.   Assessment of the global objective and strategy, current national policies and the legitimate national interest

Contributors of chapters in Part II undertake the following:

(i)   to assess the adequacy, in their political judgement, of the global objective and strategy, so identified;
(ii)   to identify their country's current national policy on the issue;

(iii)   to assess its compatibility with the vital planetary interest, employing for the purpose the concept of the legitimate national interest, and also the national interests of other relevant countries.

C.   Assessment of legitimate global power in relation to regional, national and municipal powers

Contributors of chapters in Part III undertake the following:

(i)   to consider the relationship between the planetary interest and the regional, national or municipal interest; and

(ii)   to assess the manner in which legitimate global power might impinge upon jurisdictional competence at the regional, national or municipal level.

NOTES

1.   Michael Barnett, for example, reviews the various independent commissions in the mid-1990s and their recommendations on what constitutes "legitimate state action" and a "legitimate international order": "In a series of intriguing observations and hypotheses concerning the legitimation process in global politics at this historical moment, they remind international relations scholars of the potential importance of the concept of legitimacy, a concept that once found a central place in the works of the classical realists but that has fallen out of favour in recent decades." And "... the reports offer an additional message – that international order is produced not only by force coupled with institutional aids but also by legitimacy". "Bringing in the new world order", *World Politics* **49**(4), 528–9, July 1997.
2.   Mostafa K. Tolba, *Saving our planet: challenges and hopes* (London: Chapman & Hall, 1992), 31.
3.   *Today's world and the United Nations: four addresses by Secretary-General Dag Hammarskjöld* (New York: United Nations, OPI 7448, April 1960), 12.
4.   Brandt Report, 25.
5.   *IHT*, 28 February 1995.
6.   UN Charter, Article 2 (2).
7.   Ibid., Article 24 (1).
8.   See, for example:

> For the Security Council to be effective, it needs, *inter alia*, to have authority within the international community. This authority must not be abused and its exercise will be regarded as legitimate only if the Security Council acts within a margin beyond which its use would be regarded as an abuse ... The members of the United Nations have agreed that the Security Council acts under Article 24 on their behalf. This means that Members, when acting as members of the Security Council, act not on their own behalf but on the behalf of all other Members of the United Nations. Consequently it follows that when performing their duties, their concern should be the interests of the Members of the United Nations and not their own self-interest (D.R. Browne, *Good faith and the Security Council: ensuring members of the Security Council act in good faith*. PhD thesis (George Washington University National Law Center, 1993), 8, 20–1. Professor Hans Kelsen also argues that the Security Council acts on behalf of the UN itself and not its members: H. Kelsen, *The law of the United Nations* (London: Stevens & Sons, 1951), 280. Also T.M. Franck, *Of gnats and camels: is there a double standard at the United Nations?* AJIL **78** 811 (1984); and J.F. O'Connor, *Good faith in international law* (1991).

9.   See, for example:

> In order to prepare itself for the demands of the next century, the United Nations should make an early departure from the outdated structures that serve only the interests of a few countries, allowing their privileges and high-handedness (Deputy Foreign Minister of Democratic Peoples' Republic of Korea, UNDH, 2 October 1997);
>   It is necessary to reconsider the composition and the role of the Security Council so that it may become an effective instrument which is not subjected to interests and considerations which are not consistent with the United Nations Charter. (Prime Minister of Morocco, UNDH, 25 September 1997);
>   Increase in membership must be based on the ultimate interests of the international community (Foreign Minister of Venezuela, UNDH 24 September 1997);
>   Member States must support the Secretary-General's reforms, as they will give the United Nations what it needs to respond rapidly to the new challenges of a new century. We must each stop measuring

> each proposal for reform in terms of narrow self-interest and instead recognize that we all have a greater interest in supporting reform . . . We all agree that what was appropriate in 1945 is not what is right in 1997 (Foreign Secretary of United Kingdom, UNDH, 23 September 1997).

10. D. Beetham, *The legitimation of power* (Atlantic Highlands, N.J.: Humanities Press, 1991), 35.
11. Dictatorships remain present in the nation-state age. But there is no authoritarian leader or single-party state that does not claim legitimacy for government rule. This is advanced in the name of the people or of God, however controversial such claims may be.
12. See, for example:

> In relation to this working group, we are looking at rectifying long-standing imbalances in the composition and decision-making process of the Security Council which will serve to enhance its credibility, legitimacy and authority in a rapidly changing and increasingly demanding world (Chairman of the Working Group on United Nations Reform, UNDH, 11 March 1997);
>
> Reform of the Security Council should not only make the Council more representative and legitimate, but should also make it transparent and more open towards non-members (Foreign Minister of Surinam, UNDH, 7 October 1997);
>
> It is necessary to make the Council more representative to enhance its legitimacy, to give it greater transparency, and to take the first steps towards abolishing the veto through strict limits on its use (Foreign Minister of Peru, UNDH, 25 September 1997);
>
> The time has come to agree on measures which will lead to the creation of a Security Council which is transparent, democratic, accountable and thus credible and legitimate (Foreign Minister of South Africa, UNDH, 22 September 1997);
>
> . . . we will succeed in restructuring the Security Council and modernising it by making it more democratic and giving it greater credibility, as well as greater legitimacy and transparency (Foreign Minister of Mali, UNDH, 2 October 1997).

13. The referendum of 11 September 1997 in Scotland recorded a 74% opinion in favour of such devolved powers for a Scottish Assembly, and a 64% opinion in favour of taxation powers for it.

PART TWO

The vital planetary interest and the legitimate national interest

In Part II, those global problems which threaten the vital planetary interest are addressed. In each case, the planetary interest itself is identified, in the form of goals already proclaimed by the international community through UN legal instruments or declarations and programmes of action. The vital planetary interest is identified as strategic security, environmental integrity, and sustainability. Global objectives for each are identified as is the global strategy for attaining those goals, and then the national policies prescribed in the global strategy. Contributors to each chapter are then asked to identify the national policies of their own countries in respect of the global issue, to determine the legitimate national interest of their country, and to compare it with the current national policy.

Strategic security is considered first since it has been the principal challenge to the international community in the twentieth century. Attaining stability among nation-states without having to threaten the planet in its name has preoccupied policy-makers since humankind first developed the capability of weapons of mass destruction. Yet while this was the first global problem to emerge in the nation-state age of the mid-twentieth century, or indeed perhaps because of that fact, the international community is probably the least clear in its formulation of how to respond to the threat. It is not easy to develop common security with traditional enemies. In contrast, the environmental threats have emerged in the early years of the global age when nation-states have developed a greater capacity and habit of co-operation. They also involve, to a large extent, the "global commons", and so more naturally evoke the vision of a common solution. They are, to use Gwyn Prins' phrase, threats without enemies. And the question of sustainability – or sustainable development – also naturally evokes a common theme at the global level.

SECTION I

Global strategic security

Security from the threat of aggression from other human groups remains the principal goal of nation-states. The distinction between the lawful use of weaponry within a society for the purpose of maintaining law and order and the retention of weapons as a deterrence or a defence against aggression from another society remains fundamental. When a global community emerges that maintains weapons exclusively for the sanctioned purpose of suppressing criminal acts, the species will have matured. So long as the peoples of the world are divided into sovereign groups, whether nation-states or regional blocs, the threat of "external" aggression remains and the inflationary push to possess weaponry with it.

Weapons of mass destruction were defined by the 1948 UN Commission for Conventional Armaments as "those which include atomic explosive weapons, radioactive material weapons, lethal chemical and biological weapons, and any weapon developed in the future which has characteristics comparable in destructive effect to those of the atomic bomb or other weapons mentioned above".[1] Four classes of weapons of mass destruction have been recognized to date by the international community: chemical, biological, nuclear and radiological. Chemical weapons were used in the First World War by both sides, and since then by only one nation-state in war (Iraq against Iran in the 1980s). Biological weapons have been used rarely and in very limited manner in warfare. There is evidence of attempted use by Germany to disrupt reindeer transportation lines in northern Norway in 1916–7, experimentation on humans by Japan in China in the 1930s, and deployment on missiles by Iraq during the Gulf War in 1991.[2] Nuclear weapons have been used only in one military operation (by the United States twice against Japan in 1945). Radiological weapons have never been manufactured, and the debate continues whether they should be classified as a weapon of mass destruction. With the exception of attacks on nuclear facilities, no agreement has been reached on what such weapons really are, and they remain a hypothetical possibility only. For all practical purposes, they need not be considered.

It is well recognized that humanity faces the risk of severe damage to the planet and the species, or even jeopardy to its survival, through the unrestrained use of weapons of mass destruction. There is, however, a close link between weapons of mass destruction and conventional weapons. Military strategists once sought to explain nuclear weapons as simply "a very large bomb", and some modern high explosive "smart" weapons and air-fuel explosive (AFE) weapons can cause havoc to an area of a size that rivals that threatened by any chemical weapon or low-yield tactical nuclear weapon. But the qualitative difference lies in the "escalation effect", namely, the recognized risk of escalation of use from one nuclear weapon to the global nuclear arsenal; and there is also a fundamental difference in the irreversible nature of the damage caused by weapons of mass destruction. It is these fears that prompt strategists to retain the "firebreak" between conventional weaponry and weapons of mass destruction in contemporary military doctrine. The distinction is as much politically as scientifically based. Yet on this basis, the international community has recognized a significant risk of global devastation from "weapons of mass destruction".

Such a fate is in the interest of no nation-state. Yet nation-states have traditionally claimed the right to engage in behaviour that can produce that fate, in the name of the national interest.

National sovereignty and weapons of mass destruction form a potentially catastrophic mix. Together they pose the risk of global destruction or degradation, in perpetuity. So long as nations retain the sovereign right to deploy such weapons, the challenge will be to preserve a level of strategic stability that minimizes the risk of their use. Non-possession is a greater guarantee of global safety than non-use. Whether non-possession is a realistic goal in an age of sovereign nation-states has always been fundamentally queried. Yet whether a policy of non-use of deployed weaponry is more realistic can also be queried. Non-possession is harder to attain; non-use may prove illusory. The choice between these alternative strategies will continue into the twenty-first century.

THE GLOBAL PROBLEM

The international community has recognized the threat of weapons of mass destruction since the beginning of the twentieth century. Its repugnance over chemical weapons early in the century prompted it to ban their use in warfare in 1925, such weapons being "justly condemned by the general opinion of the civilised world" and their proscription on use "binding alike the conscience and the practice of nations".[3] Such a ban, however, rested on a moral repudiation of an horrific weapon rather than a rational rejection of their destructive capacity. Biological weapons were perceived in similar manner.

A qualitative change occurred with the advent of nuclear weapons in the second half of the twentieth century, generating alarm over the threat they posed to the planet and humanity. In 1978, after two decades of the strategic arms race among the major powers, the UN General Assembly reflected that alarm in its first Special Session on Disarmament. The *Final document*, adopted by UNSSOD-I, was in two main parts. The declaration identified the global threat and the final objective. The programme of action sought to lay out a strategy.

In its declaration, the Assembly registered its deep concern over the nature of the global threat facing humanity:

> ... the continued arms race means a growing threat to international peace and security and even to the very survival of mankind. [It] threatens to ... hinder the solution of other vital problems facing mankind ... Mankind is confronted with an unprecedented threat of self-extinction arising from the massive and competitive accumulation of the most destructive weapons ever produced ... The vast stockpiles and tremendous build-up of arms and armed forces and the competition for qualitative refinement of weapons of all kinds, to which scientific resources and technological advances are diverted, poses incalculable threats to peace ... It is essential that not only Governments but also the peoples of the world recognise and understand the dangers of the present situation ... Mankind is faced with a choice: we must halt the arms race and proceed to disarmament or face annihilation.[4]

THE GLOBAL OBJECTIVE AND STRATEGY

The General Assembly saw the planetary interest clearly. It was nothing less than a qualitative break with the past, from the traditional perception of security through national defence to security through global co-operation:

> The attainment of the objective of security, which is an inseparable element of peace, has always been one of the most profound aspirations of humanity ... The ending of the arms race and the achievement of real disarmament are tasks of primary importance and urgency. To meet this historic challenge is in the political and economic interests of all the nations and peoples of the world, as well as in the interests of ensuring their genuine security and peaceful future ... All the peoples of the world have a vital interest in the success of disarmament negotiations.[5]

The global objective was perceived by the General Assembly as early as its first regular session in 1946, when, in its first resolution of 1946, it recommended that atomic weapons and all other weapons of mass destruction be eliminated from national arsenals.[6] But in its Programme of Action of 1978, it drew a dual time-frame for that attainment. In the short term, the "immediate goal" was the ending and the reversal of the arms race; in the long term, the "final objective" was general and complete disarmament:

> While the final objective of the efforts of all States should continue to be general and complete disarmament under effective international control, the immediate goal is that of the elimination of the danger of nuclear war and the implementation of measures to halt and reverse the arms race and clear the path towards lasting peace.[7]

The General Assembly had, in 1959, defined the concept of general and complete disarmament. It was "...a system of international security in which States will possess armed forces for the purposes only of (i) maintaining internal order, and (ii) providing agreed personnel for a UN Peace Force".[8]

The long-term goal of general and complete disarmament has, since then, become the philosophical lodestar of nation-states in arms control negotiations. It is referred to, somewhat canonically, as the ultimate goal of the international community in many arms control treaties for curbing weapons of mass destruction.[9]

The realism of attaining general and complete disarmament is open to query. Two alternative views compete. In one, it is unrealistic to expect the global power structure of the planet in the future to be reduced to "agreed levels of personnel for a UN peace force". The level of force in human affairs has, in the past, increased in response to two factors: technological advancement and the size of the social unit. It follows that the maximum level of force required for stability through law and order will be obtained, not at the national level, but the global level. Technology, it is contended, has progressed beyond the level of "agreed manpower for a UN peace force" and many assume that it will never return to it. It is more probable, perhaps, that the human species will extend its reach into the solar system in future centuries, and that the concomitant issues will be, not whether the global community will have an agreed manpower for a UN peace force, but whether and which exotic weaponry will be required in the outer reaches of space. In this view, global security thinking in the coming decades will benefit from focusing away from general and complete disarmament and on to more realistic goals.

In the other view, humanity is slowly but surely becoming civilized. Individuals and nation-states are learning to live with one another and tame their aggressive instincts. This is discernible in disarmament legislation of the international community and the growth of international jurisdiction generally. The idea of general and complete disarmament, of humans living harmoniously together without destructive weaponry, is the natural culmination of that evolutionary process. If and when humanity seriously reaches out into space – settling the solar system and exploring beyond it – enough time will have elapsed for it to have attained that higher state of being.

These are deeply philosophical issues concerning the human condition and its relationship to the Cosmos. They cannot be divined in the present era and are certainly beyond the scope of this book to explore. They are, however, relevant to current security thinking since the prospect of a world free of weapons of mass destruction evokes such considerations, while adumbrating national policies that reflect different judgements of the planetary interest, even in the contemporary world.

How is the international community to move towards these short-term and long-term objectives? Fundamentally, what is required is a psychological shift on the part of humankind. In fact a paradigmatic shift, by no means complete, is underway. The traditional belief has been that the safety of one's people rests on national security through military defence. The *Final Document* renounced that perception:

> States have for a long time sought to maintain their security through the possession of arms. Admittedly their survival has, in certain cases, effectively depended on whether they could count on appropriate means of defence ... [But] the time has come to put an end to this situation.[10]

There is, now, a philosophical acceptance that a population's safety is part of a "common security" of all the world's people. As the independent Palme Commission described it in 1982,

> States can no longer seek their security at each other's expense; it can only be attained through co-operative undertakings. Security in the nuclear age means common security. Even ideological opponents and political rivals must have a shared interest in survival ... International peace must rest on a commitment to joint survival rather than a threat of mutual destruction.[11]

This is a security, moreover, that depends on more than physical protection from immediate aggression, but also a "human security" that draws on long-term issues of economic and social justice and environmental integrity – the sustainability of the planet.

In its Programme of Action, the General Assembly sought to "lay the foundations" of an international disarmament strategy aimed, ultimately, at general and complete disarmament. The Action Programme focused principally on short-term priorities and measures that states should urgently undertake. These concerned nuclear weapons, other weapons of mass destruction, conventional weapons and the levels of armed forces.[12] The programme focused exclusively on such short-term measures, leaving aside the long-term goal. Progress towards general and complete disarmament, said the *Final document*, could only be achieved through the implementation of a separate programme of action on disarmament.

Taking its cue from the Action Programme, the Committee on Disarmament in 1979 adopted the "decalogue", a permanent agenda for its work consisting of ten areas which included nuclear and chemical weapons and other weapons of mass destruction.[13] In the event, however, the Committee on Disarmament has not pursued many of these issues systematically, and has on occasion failed even to agree on an annual work programme because of procedural deadlocks.

The three multilateral treaties dealing with weapons of mass destruction also identify their total elimination as the goal of the global strategy. The 1967 Non-Proliferation Treaty (NPT) envisages the "elimination of nuclear weapons from national arsenals" as the goal.[14] The subsequent Biological Weapons Convention (1972) and Chemical Weapons Convention (1993) identify the broader goal of the elimination of all weapons of mass destruction.[15] It was left unclear in the NPT whether the absence of nuclear weapons from national arsenals implies a nuclear-free world, or whether a stage will be reached, either temporary or permanent, in which a few nuclear weapons are retained under the collective ownership of the international community, perhaps through the UN Security Council. But the two subsequent treaties do make it clear: the world is to be free of all weapons of mass destruction, whether held in national arsenals or through multilateral ownership.

In 1992 the UN Security Council, in its only summit meeting to date, judged that "the proliferation of weapons of mass destruction constitutes a threat to international peace and security".[16] This effectively enables the council to use its enforcement powers under Chapter VII to prevent the acquisition of weapons of mass destruction by any other state. The council had already acted under enforcement powers to deprive one member state, Iraq, of possessing such weapons. Each nation-state has traditionally been free in its sovereign discretion to withdraw from arms control treaties such as the NPT or the Biological Weapons Convention provided extraordinary events, in its own judgement, jeopardize its "supreme interests".[17] It is unclear whether the council's 1992 determination has effectively nullified that right of withdrawal henceforth through making it clear that any further acquisition of weapons of mass destruction is a threat to the peace. But this would seem to be the case. If any country outside the nuclear weapons non-proliferation regime declares possession, this would trigger the Security Council's judgement of a threat to the peace.

The council, moreover, said nothing about the current possession of weapons of mass destruction by its own permanent members apart from "the need for all Member States to fulfil their obligations to arms control and disarmament". The implication is that these weapons do not constitute, in its judgement, a threat to the peace. But the normative goal of a world free of weapons of mass destruction enshrined in the chemical and biological weapons conventions still applies, including to the council's permanent members. And there is a binding legal obligation on the permanent members under the NPT's Article VI to negotiate nuclear disarmament measures in good faith. It would therefore seem that acquisition of weapons of mass destruction by any country except the council's permanent members constitutes a threat to the peace, whereas their possession by the permanent members is not a threat to the peace but imposes a legal obligation upon them to ensure their elimination.

The nuclear testing by India and Pakistan of May 1998 has put the council's judgement to the test. The UN Secretary-General was "deeply disturbed" by the tests and looked forward to an "unequivocal assurance" that the international community's norm on nuclear testing and non-proliferation would be adhered to, in order that progress towards nuclear disarmament – a "common desire of all States and peoples" – could be achieved as soon as possible. The "further dangerous and senseless escalation of tension" could lead to a nuclear arms race with "incalculable consequences". The president of the General Assembly recalled that during its current session the Assembly had reaffirmed its commitment to creating a nuclear-free world and had welcomed recent steps by states to promote the non-proliferation regime. The nuclear testing was contrary to that positive trend.[18]

For its part, the Security Council "strongly deplored" the testing and "strongly urged" the two countries to refrain from more. It viewed such testing as "contrary to the de facto moratorium on nuclear weapons tests and global efforts towards nuclear non-proliferation and disarmament". It appealed to them to adhere unconditionally to the NPT and CTBT without delay, and to participate in the proposed negotiations for a fissile material cut-off.[19] In terms of national policies, the council's permanent members appeared to perceive the problem differently, with the United States applying unilateral sanctions and France maintaining that in neither case had India or Pakistan violated any international commitment since neither had adhered to the non-proliferation regime. No reference was made to its Summit determination that any further acquisition of weapons of mass destruction is a threat to the peace nor any explanation as to why not. It appears that the Council has felt unable to measure up to the standard of its own strict, if discriminatory judgement, and that India and Pakistan have, indeed, tested its will and found it lacking.[20]

The global strategy then, as set out in the Action Programme and associated arms control treaties, is a set of measures that will lead to a world free of weapons of mass destruction. It was left unclear, however, whether that goal was feasible in the long term or the short term. Nation-states have different views on that, as is explored in the two chapters in this section.

The Action Programme was shaped two decades ago at the height of the Cold War. Yet despite the lessening of tensions since then, the programme remains relevant as a blueprint for the international community to proceed towards a stable global security system at a lower level of weaponry. Two subsequent Special Sessions on Disarmament have since been held, in 1982 and 1988. Both failed to produce a consensus document but both reaffirmed the 1978 Action Programme. In the late-1990s, calls have been made for a Fourth Special Session to consider afresh the global strategy for a world free of weapons of mass destruction in light of post-Cold War conditions. To date, such calls have not been heeded by the major powers.

PRESCRIBED NATIONAL POLICIES

The 1978 Action Programme enumerated the measures necessary "over the next few years", as well as other measures that would prepare the way for future negotiations and progress towards general and complete disarmament.[21] It identified a number of specific measures in each category of weapon: nuclear, biological, chemical, radiological, "other weapons of mass destruction", and conventional. Those pertaining to weapons of mass destruction are considered in more detail in Chapters 4.1 and 5.1 For nuclear weapons, they included bans on the production and refinement of further weapons, fissile material and testing, an effective non-proliferation regime including nuclear weapon-free zones, and a nuclear weapon elimination programme. Nation-states were called upon to consider adhering to the Biological Weapons Convention and to conclude both a chemical weapons and a radiological weapons convention. Finally, they were to take measures to avoid the emergence of any new weapon of mass destruction.

Since 1978, some progress has been made in implementing the above strategy through curbing weapons of mass destruction in line with the Action Programme. In brief, the numbers of nuclear weapons have been halved, their geographical deployment curtailed, nuclear-free zones introduced, a comprehensive test ban completed, the NPT extended indefinitely and a Chemical Weapons Convention completed and brought into force.

Two major problems, however, remain. First, the distinction remains as strong as before between two schools of thought over what constitutes global strategic stability. On the one hand, the existing nuclear powers, with the understanding and tacit support of their allies, accept the retention of nuclear weapons for themselves "into the indefinite future" that is to say, "well into the twenty-first century".[22] On the other hand non-allied states and particularly the threshold states – notably Israel, India and Pakistan – refuse to be part of the "discriminatory" non-proliferation regime, and retain the option of developing and deploying nuclear weapons.[23] They are now believed to have that capability, if not deployment status. Secondly, the collapse of the Soviet Union was followed by a deterioration in control of its nuclear weapons and there is a risk today of the acquisition of nuclear weapons or weapon material by other states or private groups.

LEGITIMATE NATIONAL INTERESTS

The conundrum underlying the goal of strategic stability is the freedom of nation-states to determine the level of destructive power in their arsenals which they deem necessary for their "national security". So long as they have this freedom, the threat of devastation from weapons of mass destruction will remain. In that situation, what criteria can be developed, on both a theoretical and a political level, for judging what a country's legitimate national interest might be in the possession of weaponry? What level of weaponry possessed by nation-states is above an acceptable limit to avoid devastation of the planet?

The UN Charter requires a system for the regulation of armaments in order to maintain international peace "with the least diversion for armaments of the world's human and economic resources".[24] The article makes it clear that there is a legally binding obligation on the Security Council to submit such a plan to the General Assembly. That obligation was reaffirmed in the 1967 Non-Proliferation Treaty.[25] But in the event, this charter objective has been effectively ignored. No such plans have yet been prepared by the Security Council. And no effort has been made, even on a theoretical level, to determine what quantitative limit this might be.[26] A related concept, however, was advanced by the UN secretary-general in 1994, viz., that the goal of the international community needed to be a level of armaments commensurate with the "genuine security needs" of states.[27]

These concepts, the "least diversion" and the "genuine security needs", are closely related to the legitimate national interest of nation-states in the area of weaponry. And the notion of legitimacy in the possession of all weaponry by nation-states is now being authoritatively developed. The independent Commission on Global Governance, for example, concluded that "weapons of mass destruction are not legitimate instruments of national defence".[28]

These criteria need to be developed further to assist in formulating more objective judgements over what is in the legitimate national interest of a nation-state in possessing a certain level of weaponry. Chapters 4 and 5 explore this question for four countries with very disparate security perceptions of the world – New Zealand and Russia, Israel and Jordan.

NOTES

1. United Nations Commission for Conventional Armaments (New York: United Nations, S/C.3/32/Rev.1, 1948).
2. See *Nature* **393**, 25 June 1998. Also J.D. Steinbrunner, "Biological weapons: a plague upon all houses", *Foreign Policy* **109**, Winter 1997, 88. And IHT, 7 February 1997, 26 June 1998 and 29 June 1998.
3. Protocol for the Prohibition of the Use in War of Asphyxiating, Poisonous or Other Gases, and of Bacteriological Methods of Warfare, 1925, preambular paras 1 and 3.
4. *Final document*, paras 2, 11, 15, 18.
5. Ibid., paras 1, 8, 28.
6. United Nations General Assembly resolution 1/I (1946).
7. *Final document*, para. 8.
8. United Nations General Assembly resolution 1378 (XIV), 20 November 1959 (UN Fact Sheet No. 4, DPI 656).
9. Examples include both multilateral and bilateral instruments:

    Proclaiming as their principal aim the speediest possible achievement of an agreement on general and complete disarmament under strict international control in accordance with the objectives of the United Nations which would put an end to the armaments race and eliminate the incentive to the production and testing of all kinds of weapons, including nuclear weapons (Treaty Banning Nuclear Weapon Tests in the Atmosphere, in Outer Space, and Under Water, 1963, 1st preambular para.);

    ... pursuant to a treaty on general and complete disarmament under strict and effective international control ... (Non-Proliferation Treaty, 1967, 11th preambular para.);

    Determined to act with a view to achieving progress towards general and complete disarmament, including the prohibition and elimination of all types of weapons of mass destruction ... (Convention on the Prohibition of the Development, Production and Stockpiling of Bacteriological (Biological) and Toxin Weapons and on their Destruction, 1972, 1st preambular para.);

    Declaring their intention to achieve at the earliest possible date the cessation of the nuclear arms race and to take effective measures towards reductions in strategic arms, nuclear disarmament and general and complete disarmament under strict and effective international control . . . (Threshold Test Ban Treaty, 1974, 1st preambular para.);

Reaffirming their desire to take measures for the further limitation and for the further reduction of strategic arms, having in mind the goal of achieving general and complete disarmament (SALT II, 1979, 8th preambular para.).

10. *Final document*, para. 1.
11. *Common security*, 96.
12. *Final document*, preamble and paras 43, 45.
13. The ten areas were: (i) nuclear weapons; (ii) chemical weapons; (iii) other weapons of mass destruction; (iv) conventional weapons; (v) military budget reductions; (vi) armed force reductions; (vii) disarmament and development; (viii) disarmament and international security; (ix) confidence-building measures; and (x) a comprehensive programme of disarmament leading to general and complete disarmament
14. Non-Proliferation Treaty, 1967, 11th preambular para.
15. Convention on the Prohibition of the Development, Production and Stockpiling of Bacteriological (Biological) and Toxin Weapons and on their Destruction, 1972 (Biological Weapons Convention), 1st preambular para.; Convention on the Prohibition of the Development, Production, Stockpiling and Use of Chemical Weapons and on their Destruction, 1993 (Chemical Weapons Convention), 1st preambular para.
16. Security Council Summit Meeting, 31 January 1992 (United Nations), 92.
17. NPT, Article 10; Biological Weapons Convention, Article 13; Chemical Weapons Convention, Article 16.
18. UNDH, 13 May and 1 June 1998.
19. UNDH, 14 May and 1 June 1998.
20. Because of the lack of firm Security Council action and because neither country has yet formally declared that it has deployed nuclear weapons, they will continue to be referred to in this book as the threshold states.
21. *Final document*, para. 44.
22. "The first submarine, equipped with the Trident II missile will become operational in late 1989, and this combination will gradually become the mainstay of the US submarine force as a reliable deterrent well into the twenty-first century", *US fiscal year 1988 arms control impact statements* (United States GPO, Washington, DC, June 1987, 39); *Annual report to Congress: Secretary of Defense Caspar Weinberger, F/Y 1985* (United States GPO, Washington, DC, 1 February 1984) which, *inter alia*, referred to the Advanced Technology Bomber as being able to penetrate Soviet air defences "well into the twenty-first century"; and: "Trident is intended to maintain a credible strategic nuclear deterrent from the mid 1990s when Polaris nears the end of its useful life until well into the next century", *United Kingdom parliamentary debates (Hansard)*, 29 June 1987, 38. And: " 'For the foreseeable future', said President Reagan, the world must rely on nuclear deterrence to preserve the peace'." *United States Daily Bulletin* (Geneva: 174, 29 September 1987), 5. See Chapter 4.1, n. 12, for further analysis.
23. See, for example, statement by India's BJP President Lal Krishna Advani: "BJP favours that India develop a nuclear deterrent of its own. We are for global disarmament, but we are against nuclear apartheid that is being imposed by the developed world" (IHT, 12 December 1997).
24. "In order to promote the establishment of international peace and security with the least diversion for armaments of the world's human and economic resources, the Security Council shall be responsible for formulating, with the assistance of the Military Staff Committee referred to in Article 47, plans to be submitted to the Members of the United Nations for the establishment of a system for the regulation of armaments" (UN Charter, Article 26).
25. "Recalling that, in accordance with the Charter of the United Nations, States must refrain in their international relations from the threat or use of force against the territorial integrity or political independence of any State, or in any other manner inconsistent with the Purposes of the United Nations, and that the establishment and maintenance of international peace and security are to be promoted with the least diversion for armaments of the world's human and economic resources" (NPT, 12th preambular para.).
26. Informally, suggestions have been made, such as, for example, a "threshold of planetary survival" defined as "the quantitative limit of combined destructive power of all weapons of mass destruction above which planetary survival would be threatened". See K. Graham, *National security concepts of states: New Zealand* (UNIDIR; New York: Taylor & Francis, 1989), 138.
27. "The aim must be to reduce arms holdings to levels commensurate with the genuine security needs of states", Boutros Boutros-Ghali, *The disarmament agenda of the international community and beyond: statements of the Secretary-General* (New York: United Nations, 1994), 4.
28. *Global governance*, 338.

CHAPTER FOUR

Nuclear disarmament

4.1 Introduction

Of all four weapons of mass destruction formally identified by the international community, nuclear weapons are the most widely deployed and potentially destructive.

THE GLOBAL PROBLEM

The threat to the planet and humankind posed by nuclear weapons was most clearly depicted by the international community in the 1978 *Final document* which referred to the

> ... unprecedented threat to the very survival of mankind posed by the existence of nuclear weapons ... [the] unprecedented threat of self-extinction arising from the massive and competitive accumulation of the most destructive weapons ever produced ... [The] accumulation of weapons, particularly nuclear weapons, constitutes much more a threat than a protection for the future of mankind ... Nuclear weapons pose the greatest danger to mankind and to the survival of civilisation.[1]

Ten years later, the UN identified in more rigorous terms the consequences of a nuclear conflict for humanity and the planet. In addition to the direct casualties in the combatant area, there would be a high risk of global environmental disruption, a severe threat to world food production and an almost complete breakdown in human health care. Long-term recovery would be uncertain.[2]

Two decades later, this perception of threat has not changed. The most recent estimation of the destructive potential of nuclear weapons was entered by the International Court of Justice (ICJ) in 1996: "[Its] characteristics render the nuclear weapon potentially catastrophic. The destructive power of nuclear weapons cannot be contained in either space or time. They have the potential to destroy all civilization and the entire ecosystem of the planet."[3] All nation-states take this global threat as a given, and as the basic premise for their judgements of the need for action.[4] At the fundamental level of threat perception, there is unanimity within the international community.

THE GLOBAL OBJECTIVE AND STRATEGY

Unlike the first disarmament conventions, the arms control treaties of the modern era refer to the interests of humankind as a single entity.[5] The United Nations is clear in its view of the vital planetary interest: "All the peoples of the world", stated the 1978 *Final document*, "have a vital interest in the success of disarmament negotiations."[6]

The Action Programme in the *Final document* envisaged a two-stage process concerning nuclear weapons. First, it was "essential" to halt and reverse the nuclear arms race in order to avert the danger of nuclear war. Secondly, the "ultimate goal" was the complete elimination of nuclear weapons.[7] The General Assembly did not, however, specify a timeframe for attaining the ultimate goal.

PRESCRIBED NATIONAL POLICIES

With a view to attaining the ultimate goal, the programme identified the following nuclear disarmament measures: (i) an end to the qualitative improvement and development of nuclear weapon systems; (ii) an end to the production of all nuclear weapons and delivery systems; (iii) an end to the production of weapons-grade fissionable material; (iv) a comprehensive nuclear weapons test ban; (v) the conclusion of START II negotiations; (vi) non-use assurances to non-nuclear weapon states; (vii) the establishment of nuclear weapon-free zones; (viii) development of a universal and non-discriminatory non-proliferation regime; (ix) a "comprehensive phased programme" with agreed time-frames "whenever feasible", for the reduction of nuclear weapon stockpiles and their delivery systems, leading to their ultimate and complete elimination "at the earliest time".[8]

These measures form the global strategy for nuclear disarmament as agreed, in non-binding manner, by the international community. As such they are the prescribed national policies for all nation-states. It does not follow, however, that they comprise the agreed strategy for global strategic security. A difference of outlook – a "strategic divide" – exists among nation-states, penetrating deep into the human psyche, thwarting any rapid progress towards the ultimate goal. In reality, humanity is not agreed that the goal of a nuclear weapon-free world is compatible with a lasting strategic stability. As a result, the international community is divided over the timeframe in which the "ultimate goal" might be realized. One school of thought believes it to be attainable within a relatively short timeframe, and thus within the immediate purview of formal negotiations. The other school sees it as unattainable within a specified timeframe, is not convinced that strategic stability can be ensured without nuclear weapons, and believes that the world must continue to rely on such weapons, possessed only by the major powers.

In trying to determine the global strategy for the vital planetary interest, the international community thus fails to speak with one voice. A bifurcation exists between the "global judgement" on the one hand and the strategic policies of the major powers on the other – manifest in a credibility gap between the UN's *Final document* and the bilateral arms control agreements of the two superpowers. While the General Assembly includes the major powers, these states perceive "strategic stability", as fashioned by them, to be the imperative, more important than the goal of a nuclear-free world.[9] For them, strategic stability is a necessary condition of the elimination of nuclear war but, paradoxically, this is to be attained through the deployment of nuclear weapons. When the global climatic effects of a nuclear conflict – the "nuclear winter" – were documented by the international community in the early 1980s, the US response was that the higher the stakes are for humanity and the planet, the more critical it is to ensure the avoidance of nuclear war – through nuclear deterrence.[10]

In terms of the global population, these divisions reflect majority and minority views. The minority are the five declared nuclear weapon states, representing one-third of humankind (1.9 billion) – even with the Western allied states included, the figure is some 40%. The majority are the 180 non-nuclear, non-allied states, representing two-thirds of humankind.

The majority: a time-bound strategy for a nuclear-free world

Non-nuclear powers and threshold states are committed to a nuclear-free world as part of the "short-term measures" enumerated in the 1978 Action Programme. The programme specified fulfilment "in the next few years", but the "majority strategy" currently envisages a longer period, with a nuclear weapon-free world attained by 2020.

The "majority strategy" rests on the political premise that the stakes involved in a nuclear-reliant policy – the devastation caused by a nuclear conflict – are so great that any level of risk is unacceptable. And it rests on the underlying juridical premise, contained in the Advisory Opinion of the International Court that ". . . the threat or use of nuclear weapons would generally be contrary to the rules of international law . . .".[11]

The minority: indefinite nuclear-reliant "stability"

A minority of nation-states opposes such a strategy.[12] While the nuclear powers acknowledge the desirability of a nuclear weapon-free world, the Western powers in particular see this as a philosophical, long-term prescription, not a political commitment today. In the 1990s, after the Cold War, they continue to foresee a reliance on nuclear weapons "into the indefinite future", or "well into the twenty-first century".[13] The global objective for the foreseeable future is not a nuclear-free world but rather strategic stability and the avoidance of nuclear war, relying upon nuclear weapons and nuclear deterrence with a first-use policy.[14] They concentrate on the elimination of the risk of nuclear war through strategic stability.[15] Allied Western states (NATO, Japan, Australia) accept this view.

In November 1997, the US adopted a new strategic doctrine for its nuclear forces, replacing the 1981 doctrine of maintaining a "protracted nuclear war-fighting" ability. The new doctrine reduces the number of nuclear targets to those focused on command centres and nuclear forces. It makes it the aim of US nuclear doctrine henceforth to promote deterrence through the threat of "devastating retaliation" – not unlike the original doctrine of the 1950s. It also permits US nuclear strikes after the use of chemical or biological weapons against the US.[16] The US and Russia now have a bilateral "detargeting agreement" not to aim nuclear missiles at each other, but China rejects such an arrangement until the US renounces its first-use policy. Russia's strategic doctrine of 1993, reflecting its reduced conventional force level, has placed greater reliance on the use of nuclear weapons, including first-use against a non-nuclear country allied to a nuclear adversary.[17]

This "strategic divide" stems from a lack of clear vision over how to replace nuclear deterrence with some alternative strategy for global stability. The United Nations has condemned the theory of nuclear deterrence as the proclaimed strategy for global stability,[18] advocating instead a return to the collective security provisions of the charter through the use of conventional weapons only.[19] The three Western nuclear powers, however, oppose this on the grounds that the elimination of nuclear weapons would "make the world safe for global conventional war".

Despite this fundamental cleavage, some progress has been made with nuclear disarmament measures over the past decade:

(i)   The qualitative improvement of nuclear weapons has been partially halted by the Comprehensive Test Ban. The treaty was, after four decades of intermittent negotiations, concluded in 1996. It will take effect, however, only when the three threshold states, India, Israel and Pakistan, ratify it in addition to the five declared nuclear powers. India currently opposes the treaty, for the same reasons it opposes the Non-Proliferation Treaty. The treaty, moreover, has tended to curtail the acquisition of weapons by non-nuclear states rather than the qualitative improvement of existing weapon types by the nuclear powers. The latter maintain plans for a continued reliance on nuclear weapons, such as the $40 million Science-Based Stockpile Stewardship programme of the United States which includes sub-critical testing and inertial confinement fusion – after the CTB has been concluded.

(ii)   A treaty banning the production of fissile material has become one of the main areas of focus recently. In 1995, the Conference on Disarmament agreed on a negotiating mandate, but no committee has been established to conduct the negotiations. The deadlock revolves around a different perception of the end goal – whether the ban covers only future fissile material or includes existing stockpiles as well. The nuclear powers and the threshold states favour the former; the "majority" favours the latter. One recent proposal suggests "voluntary transparency" measures for declaring current stockpiles.

(iii)   SALT II has been ratified by the American but not the Russian legislature. The two governments, however, are implementing its provisions, and in 1997 agreed to move towards a SALT III target of 2,000 to 2,500 strategic weapons on each side by 2007.

(iv)   The NPT, originally in force for 25 years and subject to review thereafter, was indefinitely extended at the 1995 review conference. The fundamental problem, however, remains, namely, the contention by certain threshold states, led by India, that the treaty institutionalizes a discriminatory regime, locking in a military superiority for the five nuclear powers.

(v)   Above all others, the goal of an elimination programme reveals the underlying strategic divide of the international community. The majority strategy has a clear enough policy: a 1996 draft programme, not yet endorsed by the international community. It foresees a three-phase process covering the late-1990s and the first two decades of the twenty-first century, at the end of which a nuclear weapon-free world would be attained. Details of the programme are set out in the annex to this chapter. Proponents of the majority strategy are pursuing this approach vigorously. At its 51st Session in 1996, the General Assembly called upon all states to commence multilateral negotiations in 1997 leading to the early conclusion of a Nuclear Weapons Convention prohibiting the "development, production, testing, deployment, stockpiling, transfer, threat or use of nuclear weapons and providing for their elimination". A draft convention exists but, because of the opposition of the nuclear powers, it is not yet under formal negotiation.

Progress thus continues, incrementally, but without a clear, firm vision on the part of the international community of what form of global security system can replace nuclear deterrence. The proclaimed planetary interest is a nuclear weapon-free world at the earliest possible date, yet a strategic divide reflects a lack of universal conviction over the goals proclaimed, and its achievement is accordingly deferred. The diminution in nuclear weapons reflects, not a fundamental change of mindset and policy by the nuclear powers with a view towards total elimination, but rather a rationalization of strategic forces – the elimination of numbers rendered superfluous by the end of the Cold War. Despite changed circumstances, the minority strategy has been retained and rationalized, rather than changed.

For the planetary interest to be attained, what is required is some melding of the majority and minority strategies into one vision of the future. The cardinal value of the majority is a nuclear-free "common security"; that of the minority is stability among the major powers. Can these two strategies be combined? Is it possible to attain a world of strategic stability among the major powers with a nuclear-free world – a "global strategic security" system?

LEGITIMATE NATIONAL INTERESTS

In such circumstances, what is the legitimate national interest of nation-states – both nuclear and non-nuclear?

The current trend of thought, on the part of both nation-states and citizens, is to move away from a reliance on nuclear weapons. In December 1996, a statement by 61 former generals and admirals in 17 countries stated that

> We, military professionals, who have devoted our lives to the national security of our countries and our peoples, are convinced that the continuing existence of nuclear weapons in the armories of nuclear powers, and the ever present threat of acquisition of these weapons by others, constitute a peril to global peace and security and to the safety and survival of the people we are dedicated to protect ... We know that nuclear weapons, though never used since Hiroshima and Nagasaki, represent a clear and present danger to the very existence of humanity. There was an immense risk of a superpower holocaust during the Cold War. At least once, civilization was on the very brink of catastrophic tragedy. That threat has now receded, but not forever – unless nuclear weapons are eliminated ... We have been presented with a challenge of the highest possible historic importance: the creation of a nuclear-weapons-free world ... The dangers of proliferation, terrorism, and new nuclear arms race render it necessary. We must not fail to seize our opportunity. There is no alternative.[20]

In many countries, citizens are acting on the basis of the ICJ Advisory Opinion, stopping convoys carrying nuclear weapons and upon arrest resting their legal defence on the grounds that such weapons are henceforth deemed to be illegal.[21]

The move away from such reliance is in fact a legal obligation. In its *Advisory opinion*, the court noted that "there exists an obligation to pursue in good faith and bring to a conclusion negotiations leading to nuclear disarmament in all its aspects". The court was simply reaffirming what had been clear from the time of the NPT in the 1960s. What is left unclear, however, is the pace at which that progress is to be attained. The "optimal pace" at which nuclear powers move towards complete nuclear disarmament would seem to be the clearest criterion of their legitimate national interest. This is, however, an essentially political judgement, not one for legal decision.

Recent opinion polls in two Western nuclear weapon-states indicate that a majority of citizens no longer believes that nuclear weapons provide them with national security. In an American poll of March 1997, 84% of respondents said they would feel safer in a world without nuclear weapons, 87% wanted their government to negotiate an agreement on their elimination, and 77% thought that excessive public funds were spent on nuclear forces.[22] A British poll of October 1997 showed that 59% judged Britain's national security to be enhanced without national ownership of nuclear weapons, 87% wanted their government to negotiate an agreement on their elimination (the same percentage as in the US), and 54% would unilaterally withdraw the Trident missiles from naval deployment.

Chapters 4.2 and 4.3 consider the national policies of two countries with vastly different experiences of national security, one a major power that led the former socialist military alliance, the other a former Western ally. Russia still possesses more nuclear weapons than any other nation-state. How it perceives its national security interests and what it might see as the planetary interest in global strategic security and its legitimate national interest within that context fundamentally affects other states. For its part, New Zealand has played a unique role in strategic thought in recent decades. It is the only country to have formally renounced nuclear deterrence as its national security policy. As part of that policy, New Zealand passed domestic legislation creating a nuclear-free zone over national territory that included a ban on any nuclear-armed warship. Its preference to remain an ally of the United States on terms of conventional defence alone proved unacceptable to the US and, apart from a conventional defence co-operation with Australia, it is now a non-allied state.

Is it possible to expect two such disparate nations to agree on what is to be done in the planetary interest, and what is the legitimate national interest of their own country, and the other? For if the planetary interest is to be attained, a common vision that can command a consensus among all nation-states is the first prerequisite.

NOTES

1. *Final document*, paras 11, 1, 47.

2. For all its apparent robustness, the planet on which we live exists in fragile balance ... The circumstances arising from nuclear war lie at the extreme end of the harmful actions that the human race can inflict upon itself. The Group's Report serves to confirm that a nuclear war cannot be won and must never be fought. It can also be seen as a strong argument for the pursuit of sharp reductions in, and ultimate elimination of, nuclear weapons ... The scientific evidence is now conclusive that a major nuclear war would entail the high risk of global environmental disruption ... The evidence assessed to date is persuasive that residual scientific uncertainties are unlikely to invalidate these general conclusions ... Global environmental disruption would result from temperature decreases occasioned by the elevation of smoke and dust particles into the upper atmosphere, as well as ozone depletion and radiation. A major nuclear war would constitute a severe threat to world food production, and the human impact would be exacerbated by an almost complete breakdown in health care in targeted countries and the likelihood of increases in ultra-violet radiation. The direct effects could kill hundreds of millions; the indirect effect could kill billions. Fatalities from starvation in one non-combatant country alone (India) could eventually exceed the number of fatalities in the United States and the USSR caused directly by nuclear explosions. Long-term recovery would be uncertain since a conflict would produce climatic and socio-economic consequences that are unprecedented. If recovery occurred, it would be slow and difficult, and it is most unlikely that any new social order would resemble, or be an improvement on, that which preceded it (*Study on the climatic and other global effects of nuclear war, Report of the UN secretary-general* (New York: United Nations, A/43/351, 5 May 1988), 5, 15, 16, 57).

3. International Court of Justice, *Advisory opinion on the illegality of the use or threat of use of nuclear weapons* (The Hague: International Court of Justice, 1996), 35 (hereafter ICJ *advisory opinion*).

4. Considering the devastation that would be visited upon all mankind by a nuclear war and the consequent need to make every effort to avert the danger of such a war and to take measures to safeguard the security of peoples, believing that the proliferation of nuclear weapons would seriously enhance the danger of nuclear war ... (NPT, 1st and 2nd preambular paras);
   Taking into account the devastating consequences that nuclear war would have for all mankind ... (Agreement on Measures to Reduce the Risk of Outbreak of Nuclear War between the USA and the USSR, 1971, 1st preambular para.);
   Proceeding from the premise that nuclear war would have devastating consequences for all mankind ... (Anti-Ballistic Missile Treaty, 1972, 1st preambular para.);
   Conscious that nuclear war would have devastating consequences for mankind ... (Agreement between the USA and the USSR on the Prevention of Nuclear War, 1973, 2nd preambular para.);
   Conscious that nuclear war would have devastating consequences for all mankind ... (SALT II, 1979, 1st preambular para. and INF, 1987, 1st preambular para.);
   Believing that and nuclear war cannot be won and must never be fought ... (Agreement between the USA and the USSR on the Establishment of Nuclear Risk Reduction Centers, 1987, 2nd preambular para.).

5. Recognising that it is in the interest of all mankind that Antarctica shall continue forever to be used exclusively for peaceful purposes and shall not become the scene or object of international discord ... Convinced that the establishment of a firm foundation for the continuation and development of such

co-operation ... accords with the interests of science and the progress of all mankind (Antarctic Treaty, 1957, 1st and 3rd preambular paras);

Recognizing the common interest of all mankind in the progress of the exploration and use of outer space for peaceful purposes ... (Treaty on Principles Governing the Activities of States in the Exploration and Use of Outer Space, including the Moon and Other Celestial Bodies, 1967, 2nd preambular para.);

Believing that agreement on measures for reducing the risk of outbreak of nuclear war serves the interests of strengthening international peace and security, and is in no way contrary to the interests of any other country (Accidents Measures Agreement, 1971, 3rd preambular para.);

Recognizing the common interest of mankind in the progress of the exploration and use of the seabed and the ocean floor for peaceful purposes; considering that the prevention of a nuclear arms race on the seabed and the ocean floor serves the interests of maintaining world peace ... (Treaty on the Prohibition of the Emplacement of Nuclear Weapons and Other Weapons of Mass Destruction on the Seabed and the Ocean Floor and in the Subsoil Thereof, 1972, 1st and 2nd preambular paras).

6. *Final document*, para. 28.
7. Ibid., 47.
8. Ibid., 50, 51, 52, 57, 59, 60, 66.
9. "Recognizing that the strengthening of strategic stability meets the interests of the Parties and the interests of the international community..." (SALT II, 1979, 7th preambular para.); "Guided by the objective of strengthening strategic stability" (INF, 1987, 2nd preambular para.).
10. "We are persuaded that a nuclear war would be a terrible thing, but we believe that what we are doing with respect to strategic modernization and arms control is sound, and we believe it is made no less sound by the nuclear winter phenomenon ... Rather than eliminating weapons, the most realistic method of preventing nuclear winter is to build enough weapons to make sure that the Soviets will be deterred from attacking" (US Assistant Secretary of Defense, Richard Perle, testifying to Congress, *Wellington Evening Post*, 16 March 1984).
11. ICJ *advisory opinion*, para. 105 (2.E).
12. "... immediate multilateral negotiations on the time-bound elimination of nuclear weapons. The United States has always opposed this idea in the past and will continue to do so because we remain convinced that the bilateral efforts which have already produced results in the area of nuclear disarmament remain, for the time being, the only realistic approach to arms control in this highly complex field" (US Explanation of Vote on draft resolution A/C.1/52/L.37, UN General Assembly, 12 November 1997). Also US statement in the Conference on Disarmament:

> The idea of discussing nuclear disarmament and a programme of reduction and elimination of nuclear weapons in a time-bound framework raises several questions. What does a "time-bound framework" mean? ... How could we be sure that the instituting of a "time-bound framework", dictated by those who bring nothing but pieties and rhetoric to the dialogue, would not be an artificial mechanism affecting adversely the current trend ... toward deep nuclear weapons reductions? ... the maximum capability of the United States to destroy the thousands of nuclear warheads resulting from the START treaties is already totally saturated, and will be well into the twenty-first century. How would a "time-bound framework" apply to this process? Another question is how negotiations leading to the elimination of nuclear arms in a "time-bound framework" would relate to the diverse situations of various States with varied nuclear holdings. There is also the question of whether and how nuclear reductions "in a time-bound framework" would affect certain nuclear-capable or "threshold" States ... (Geneva: Conference on Disarmament, 8 February 1996, CD/PV.724).

And:

> The United Kingdom is committed to the goal of the global elimination of nuclear weapons. We will press for mutual, balanced and verifiable reductions in nuclear weapons. When satisfied with verified progress towards our goal, we will ensure that British nuclear weapons are included in multilateral negotiations (UK Explanation of Vote on draft resolution A/C.1/52/L.37, UN General Assembly, 12 November 1997).

Also UK statement in the Conference of Disarmament:

> ... we simply do not see the value at this stage of trying to devise a complete blueprint for the final achievement of nuclear disarmament ... Oscar Wilde once said that "a map of the world that does not include Utopia is not even worth glancing at". He was right. We need to have high aspirations. But we also need realism about the best way of achieving those aspirations. I sometimes feel that in the

current debate about nuclear disarmament the more distant aspirational elements are in danger of drowning out the more immediately achievable elements (Geneva: Conference on Disarmament, 21 January 1997, cd/pv.751).

13. The Cold War reliance on nuclear weapons was reaffirmed in the 1997 presidential directive on strategic doctrine and targeting: "The United States will continue to rely on nuclear weapons as a cornerstone of its national security for the 'indefinite future'." (See *Washington Post*, in *Guardian Weekly*, 14 December 1997 and iht, 8 December 1997.)

14. "Recognizing that the strengthening of strategic stability meets the interests of the Parties and the interests of the international community..." (salt ii, 1979, 7th preambular para.); "Guided by the objective of strengthening strategic stability" (inf, 1987, 2nd preambular para.).

15. ... recognizing the need to exert every effort to avert the risk of outbreak of such a war, including measures to guard against accidental or unauthorized use of nuclear weapons (Accidents Measures Agreement, 1971, 1st preambular para.);

Proceeding from the desire to bring about conditions in which the danger of an outbreak of nuclear war anywhere in the world would be reduced and eventually eliminated ... (Prevention of Nuclear War Agreement, 1973, 3rd preambular para.);

Affirming their desire to reduce and ultimately eliminate the risk of outbreak of nuclear war, in particular, as a result of misinterpretation, miscalculation, or accident (Nuclear Risk Reduction Centers Agreement, 1987, 1st preambular para.).

16. *iht*, 8 December 1997.

17. See testimony to US Senate Intelligence Committee, *iht*, 8 December 1997.

18. "Enduring international peace and security cannot be built on the accumulation of weaponry by military alliances nor be sustained by a precarious balance of deterrence or doctrines of strategic superiority ... The most effective guarantee against the danger of nuclear war and the use of nuclear weapons is nuclear disarmament and the complete elimination of nuclear weapons" (*Final document*, paras 13, 56).

19. "Genuine and lasting peace can only be created through the effective implementation of the existing security system provided for in the Charter of the United Nations and the speedy and substantial reduction in armed forces, by international agreement and mutual example, leading ultimately to general and complete disarmament under effective international control" (*Final document*, para. 13).

20. Statement on Nuclear Weapons by International Generals and Admirals, Disarmament Clearinghouse, Washington, dc.

21. As examples: in Balloch, Scotland, citizens wearing judges' robes stopped a convoy carrying Trident nuclear warheads, claiming that the convoy was illegal. The thirteen arrested used the icj decision in their defence before the sheriff's court which acquitted them. In Germany, seven citizens who had broken into a nuclear base were acquitted. The judge agreed that since the end of the Cold War, no state could genuinely claim its existence to be endangered, thereby eliminating the only possible justification for nuclear weapon use allowed in the icj opinion. The decision is under appeal.

22. Lake Sosin Snell & Associates opinion poll, March 1997 (number of respondents = 1,006).

Annex

G-28 PROGRAMME OF ACTION FOR THE ELIMINATION OF NUCLEAR WEAPONS: 1996–2020

First phase: 1996–2000

A   Measures aimed at reducing the nuclear threat:

- immediate and concurrent commencement of negotiations and early conclusion of:
    - (i)   a legal instrument to assure non-nuclear weapon states against the use or threat of use of nuclear weapons;
    - (ii)   a convention prohibiting the use or threat of use of nuclear weapons;
    - (iii) a treaty to eliminate nuclear weapons;
    - (iv) a treaty banning the production of fissile material for nuclear weapons;
- an end to the qualitative improvement of nuclear weapons, by agreements on:
    - (i)   cessation of all nuclear weapon tests and closure of all nuclear weapon test sites;
    - (ii)   measures to prevent the upgrading of existing nuclear weapons systems;
- full implementation of the Treaties of Tlatelolco, Rarotonga, Pelindaba, and Bangkok,* and establishment of additional nuclear weapon free zones;
- declarations of the stocks of nuclear weapons and of nuclear weapons-grade material.

B   Measures of nuclear disarmament:

- stand down nuclear-weapon systems from a state of operational readiness;
- preservation of the ABM (Anti-Ballistic Missile) Treaty;
- moratorium and prohibition on testing of outer space weapons systems;
- ratification and implementation of the START II Treaty;
- conclusion of START III;
- IAEA safeguards for nuclear fissile material transferred from military to peaceful uses;
- an end to the production of nuclear warheads;
- recommendation to the General Assembly to declare 2000–2010 the "decade for nuclear disarmament".

Second phase: 2000–2010

Measures to reduce the nuclear arsenals and to promote confidence between states:

- entry into force of the treaty to eliminate nuclear weapons and establishment of a single integrated multilateral comprehensive verification system to ensure compliance, including measures such as:
    - (i)   separation of nuclear warheads from their delivery vehicles;
    - (ii)   placement of nuclear warheads in secure storage under international supervision leading to the removal of special nuclear materials from warheads;
    - (iii) transfer of nuclear materials including fissile materials and delivery vehicles to peaceful purposes;
- preparation under international auspices of an inventory of nuclear arsenals, including fissile materials, nuclear warheads and their delivery vehicles;

- reduction of number of missiles intended for carrying nuclear warheads;
- recommendation to the General Assembly to declare the decade 2010–2020 the "decade for the total elimination of nuclear weapons".

Third phase: 2010–2020

Consolidation of a nuclear weapon-free world:

- adoption of principles and mechanisms for a global co-operative security system;
- implementation of the treaty to eliminate all nuclear weapons through further measures as:
  - (i) conversion of all facilities devoted to the production of nuclear weapons to peaceful purposes;
  - (ii) application of safeguards on nuclear facilities on a universal basis; and
  - (iii) elimination of all nuclear weapons.

* The treaties establishing the Latin American, South Pacific, African and South East Asian zones, respectively.

4.2   New Zealand

David Lange

"Ideally, and other things being equal, I would like to see my country keep its word."

M. Michel Rocard, Prime Minister of France

There is a hint of understatement in the Security Council's judgement that the proliferation of weapons of mass destruction constitutes a threat to international peace and security. When the proliferation of nuclear weapons took the form of the arms race that characterized the Cold War, no less than the destruction of human life on the planet was threatened. While that era is over and the Security Council elects to define the threat posed by weapons of mass destruction in terms of the potential disruption of international order by their manufacture or deployment by states or rogue entities which do not yet possess them, or which do not acknowledge their possession, their graver potential has not diminished. Whatever the fate of the weaponry, the destructive capacity of thermo-nuclear fusion will always be with us.

Greater insight is to be found in the General Assembly's judgement a decade earlier, that nuclear weapons comprise more a threat than a protection for humanity. That judgement includes the nuclear weapons possessed by the major powers. It is a universal non-discriminatory judgement, and one that cannot be gainsaid. The global problem we confront is no more the acquisition of nuclear weapons by new states or other entities than it is their continued retention by the existing "responsible powers". That is the global problem which humanity must eternally face.

It is a commonplace that the international community, when speaking collectively, and whether or not it acknowledges the ultimate significance of the threat posed by nuclear weapons, is invariably less than wholehearted in its efforts to limit their manufacture and deployment. The threat of global conflict between opposing power blocs has receded, and the fear of the widespread use of the weapons of mass destruction with it. But the five permanent members of the Security Council manufacture and store the weapons and continue to refine their technology; the weapons are deployed, in lesser numbers than they were at the height of the Cold War, but deployed nonetheless; and the right to use the weapons in defence of the interests of their possessors is still asserted. Nuclear weapons remain at the heart of the defensive strategies of the five permanent members of the Security Council. Whatever broad agreement there may be about the destructive potential of nuclear weapons is immediately qualified by the insistence of their acknowledged possessors on maintaining their capacity to ensure such destruction.

In these circumstances, the definition of the planetary interest with regard to the control of nuclear weapons may amount to no more in the 1990s than the identification of a lowest common denominator. Strategies devised to secure that interest are similarly compromised. The five declared nuclear powers have agreed among themselves to limit the numbers of their weapons, and to restrict the forms of their testing. Yet they decline to commit themselves to the eventual elimination of the weapons or to the eventual abandonment of their right to threaten their use, or actually use them. Those states which possess nuclear weapons without acknowledging their possession or which attempt their manufacture or deployment have called for their elimination, while declining to take any uni-lateral action to achieve that goal. The allies of the major nuclear powers may be active in the pursuit of arms limitation agreements, and may acknowledge the desirability of the ultimate elimination of the weapons, yet must defer to the insistence of their more powerful protectors that the goal is not a practical possibility. The rest, having no interest which is served by the weapons, are free to assert unequivocally their interest in their elimination, but with small hope of enlisting the acknowledged and unacknowledged possessors of the weapons.

In such an environment, global security amounts to a negotiated reduction in the numbers of the weapons deployed by the five permanent members of the Security Council, roughly mirroring the lessening of the tensions between them since the end of the Cold War; and an attempt by the international community to prevent the spread of weapons technology and materials to terrorist organizations and states which harbour terrorists.

If these limited aspirations are placed in the context of the potential of the weapons of mass destruction to render the planet uninhabitable, they seem painfully inadequate. The number of weapons may be reduced as global tensions decrease; should global tensions re-emerge, there is nothing which suggests that the number of weapons will not again increase. If the doctrines of deterrence are reasserted, the planet's future capacity to sustain life in any recognizable form will once again be as much at risk as it was during the Cold War.

Deterrence is a theory that can never be proved successful and yet it is retained. It remains a paradox that, although one can be certain when it is too late that deterrence has failed, one can never have absolute proof of its success. The persistence of the nuclear powers in retaining the theory of deterrence, in strategic circumstances different from those on which the premises of the doctrine originally rested, indicates that no circumstances are envisaged, in the nation-state world, in which that retention will be relinquished.

While a re-emergence of the nuclear arms race between the great powers would be potentially disastrous, a more immediate risk is the proliferation of the weapons. A small number of states selectively maintain their right to manufacture and deploy nuclear weapons in the interest of their own security, and attempt to deny the weapons to other states. It is regrettable but unsurprising that some among the latter will choose to define their security in terms of the possession of nuclear weapons and will attempt to break the monopoly of the declared nuclear weapons states. Any such proliferation must threaten disorder, and carries with it the enhanced risk of escalation of nuclear armaments. To this potential danger must now be added the risk of the possible acquisition of nuclear weapons by terrorist or other rogue groups. The disturbing possibility of such acquisition has become an issue as a result of the erosion of civil and military order in the former Soviet Union. The dangers remain in prospect as long as the nuclear weapons culture is perpetuated in the world.

The lack of a global strategy for the elimination of nuclear weapons derives from a refusal by the major powers to distinguish between nuclear and conventional weaponry. For the world to make the necessary qualitative breakthrough, it will need to distinguish between nuclear weapons and all other forms of coercive or deterrent power. There is no case to be made against the policeman's truncheon. And in the present world, the state must arm itself with military force to protect its citizens against aggression. It does not follow that, for those reasons, the state must arm itself with nuclear weapons.

NATIONAL POLICY

In the absence of co-ordinated national policies over nuclear weaponry, New Zealand chose to develop a national strategy that was more demonstrably in the planetary interest than anything the world was able to offer, then or since. From 1984 when I took office as prime minister, New Zealand introduced a nuclear-free policy – the first and hitherto the only time an allied state has renounced nuclear weapons in its defence.

In short, the policy consisted of two main features: a regional initiative by New Zealand and neighbouring countries to create a nuclear-free zone in the South Pacific,[1] and a national initiative by New Zealand alone to create a stronger nuclear-free zone for its own land and sea territory.[2] The policy, enshrined in statutory law, excludes nuclear weapons from its territory and eschews any part in their manufacture or deployment. In its statutory expression it represents a commitment to the elimination of nuclear weapons.

This policy reflected a serious national expression of the belief by the international community, as recorded above, that nuclear weapons constitute more a threat than a protection to humanity. If we meant what we collectively said at the United Nations, if we intended to make policy reflect our stated judgements, then we needed to act accordingly. It so happened that I and my government believed it; we believed that nuclear weapons were more a threat than a protection to New Zealand, and I had already made this clear to the international community in a number of addresses overseas and at home.[3] Far from developing an irresponsible national policy on the subject, as most of our Western allies found it expedient to insinuate, New Zealand was in fact acting in a rational and calculated way, in the name of the traditional concept of strengthening national security. We were, simply, safer without nuclear weapons in our defence than with them.

This view contrasted with that of other allied countries, including our neighbour, Australia, which selflessly accepted nuclear targeting in the interest of global strategic stability – a diametrically opposed national strategy in pursuit of, presumably, the same planetary interest. Both countries, traditional allies, strategically close, brothers essentially, perceive things differently. Both see a nuclear-free world as a long-term objective – the planetary interest. But as a national strategy to that end, one renounces nuclear weapons as the central problem itself that needs to be resolved within a finite period of time, while the other accepts them indefinitely as the Faustian means to a flawed strategic stability.

So far as the limitation of nuclear weapons is concerned, New Zealand's policy had its greatest practical effect during the Cold War when its ally, the United States, actively deployed nuclear weapons in the South Pacific region on its military vessels and aircraft. The policy, both before and after its embodiment in statute, refused entry to New Zealand's ports and airspace to any vessel or aircraft which was carrying nuclear weapons, or was believed to be carrying nuclear weapons. The United States declined to bring any of its military vessels or aircraft to New Zealand on such terms, and while it did not formally withdraw from its alliance with New Zealand, declared itself to be relieved of any treaty obligation to defend its erstwhile ally. In effect, New Zealand detached itself from any defensive strategy based on the nuclear deterrent, and insisted that any conflict or lesser disturbance in its region would not escalate into nuclear-armed confrontation between the two great power blocs.

What has changed in the strategic environment since the Cold War? Certainly, there has been progress. Nuclear weapons have been withdrawn from non-nuclear weapon states in Asia, though not completely from Europe. Tactical nuclear weapons have been withdrawn from naval vessels around the world, though at least one strategic submarine still continuously patrols the oceans of Earth, a modern Cerberus guarding the gates of hell. The numbers of strategic nuclear weapons have been reduced, perhaps to half of what they were, so now the rubble will bounce three times instead of seven. A nuclear test ban has been concluded at last, though nuclear weapons can still be modernized through computer simulation and "sub-critical events". Missiles have been taken off high-alert, though they can be restored to their previous hair-trigger status within minutes. Targeting policies have been modified to reassure traditional adversaries of good intent, though they can be restored to their previous foci in the time it takes to reprogram the computer. And the International Court has opined that the use of nuclear weapons would generally be contrary to international law, though the nuclear powers are studiously ignoring the advice.

So there is progress, but it is qualified. Above all, the major powers retain the right of use of nuclear weapons. NATO has declared that nuclear weapons are now weapons of "truly last resort", but the only change from Cold War doctrine is the rather meaningless adverb tacked on to the front of the phrase. And the risk of missile launch through accident or misunderstanding still remains, as the Russian nuclear force alert in response to a NASA rocket launch over Norway in 1995 showed. So the significance of New Zealand's stand – a renunciation of nuclear weapons as a deterrent policy – remains confined to its own national policy, it not having been in any way emulated elsewhere.

Is the New Zealand nuclear-free policy still relevant to the world of the 1990s? Most certainly it is. With the size of nuclear arsenals reducing, and their deployment receding, the policy as expressed in law stands as a statement of the political will to eliminate nuclear weapons and a rejection of the doctrines of nuclear deterrence. While it seems unlikely that any military power would wish to bring nuclear weapons to New Zealand territory, their continuing legislative prohibition means that the possibility of their presence is wholly excluded. Strong public support for the exclusion of nuclear weapons from New Zealand means that any government is unable to repeal the statute which prohibits them, and it remains as an effective limitation on the deployment of nuclear weapons.

THE LEGITIMATE NATIONAL INTEREST

New Zealand's statutory nuclear-free policy stands as a legitimate expression of its national interest. It is consonant with the vital planetary interest, however that interest might ultimately be defined, because it is in accord with its expression at the highest level in which the potential of the weapons of mass destruction to render the planet uninhabitable is recognized. The aim of policy becomes the elimination of nuclear weapons and the renunciation of the doctrines of nuclear deterrence. The policy, which stands aside from any nuclear deterrent strategy, and limits, to a small but significant extent, the capacity of others to employ such a strategy, is both a statement of the political will to eliminate nuclear weapons and a practical expression of that will. It follows that New Zealand's policy must equally serve any lesser expression of the planetary interest. If the goal is not the elimination of nuclear weapons but a restraint on their proliferation, or denial of their components to rogue entities, New Zealand's policy is a complete practical expression of such restraint or denial. New Zealand must, in terms of its statutory policy, stand as a barrier against the further proliferation of the weapons; its domestic law requires it to stand aside from any future escalation in nuclear armaments; and it cannot by law offer any opportunity or encouragement to terrorism or other rogue elements.

The insistence of the United States on the removal of the statutory prohibition of nuclear weapons as a precondition of any resumption of the defence relationship with New Zealand is in itself adequate demonstration of the continuing effectiveness of New Zealand's policy. It is a policy which can readily be adopted by any other state that wishes to act in accordance with the Security Council's judgement that the proliferation of the weapons of mass destruction is a threat to international peace and security, since it is utterly consonant with any effort to prevent the wider distribution of the weapons. And it is a policy which might appropriately be adopted by any state that wishes to pursue the more ambitious goal of the elimination of nuclear weapons, since it expresses the political will to eschew the weapons on which their elimination must ultimately rest.

When the policy was adopted, New Zealand was taken to task by other members of the Western bloc for its willingness to open itself to Soviet influence (a demonstrable nonsense) and, more critically, for its failure to carry its share of the burden of responsibility of nuclear deterrence. Now that the Cold War is over, and the nuclear powers make great play of the reductions in their nuclear arsenals, the complaint most readily made by opponents of New Zealand's policy, at home and abroad, is that it has not reduced by one the number of the world's nuclear weapons. This is true, but it is irrelevant to a policy which has from the start been a means, not of enforcing a reduction in the numbers of a weapon which New Zealand never possessed, but rather of limiting their deployment. And it is wilfully dismissive of the possibility that the doctrines of nuclear deterrence might one day demand a re-escalation in the level of nuclear armaments.

The obvious answer to such critics was, and is, that New Zealand is pursuing a right to limit their deployment, and that the invitation in the NPT to the major powers to eliminate nuclear weapons from their national arsenals still stands. Those who are in a position to reduce the numbers are invited to do so and to refrain from criticizing those who are not. When it comes to the legitimate national interest, it must be palpably clear to all that the United States and Russia have a greater obligation than that which they are currently meeting. I remember the day in the early 1980s when the Soviet Union deployed a land-based missile that brought New Zealand, for the first time, within ICBM range. It still is. I do not see it as a legitimate national interest of Russia that it should have the capability to devastate my country with nuclear weapons and I invite Mr Kozyrev to agree with that judgement. I admired his work as foreign minister of his country, and I urge him to continue it as a member of the Russian *Duma*.

Nor do I believe that the United States is acting within the legitimate national interest when it retains some 7,000 strategic warheads to make the post-Cold War world safe. No nation should carry the moral burden of having the capacity to devastate the planet. This holds in the twentieth century, not simply the mid- or late twenty-first.

New Zealand's statutory policy amounts to a rejection of the insistence of the declared nuclear powers on the retention of their capacity to threaten the destruction of human life on the planet. The policy is readily dismissed by the nuclear powers, and by their adherents, at home and abroad, as idealistic and impracticable, since New Zealand's small size and physical isolation mean that its practical effect is necessarily limited. And it has cost New Zealand in terms of defence co-operation with its former ally, the United States. Such dismissal is a perfect reflection of the less than whole-hearted approach taken by the international community to the control and limitation of nuclear weapons. It suggests that the best which can be hoped for in the new century is more of the same: more reductions in the number of weapons as international tensions continue to decrease, accompanied by the continuing refinement of the weapons themselves and the strategies for their deployment, against the day when a renewal of tension will call for a re-escalation in the number of weapons.

As always with the weapons of mass destruction, there is something peculiarly self-serving in the self-restraint of their possessors, and little hope can be placed in multilateral fora at whose head stands a Security Council which cannot overrule the wishes of any one of the five declared nuclear powers which constitute its permanent membership.

Figure 4.2.1 "When we exclude nuclear weapons from New Zealand, we exclude the possibility of a nuclear defence of New Zealand. We do not ask to be defended by the nuclear weapons we exclude and we do not ask any nuclear power to deter any enemy of New Zealand by the threatened use of nuclear weapons against that enemy", Rt Hon. David Lange, Prime Minister of New Zealand, 1985. Citizens of Auckland, New Zealand, take to their private boats during Cold War days to block the entry of a US nuclear attack submarine into Waitemata Harbour. (Courtesy Auckland Peace Squadron/Doug Harris).

CONCLUSION

My country was subject to severe pressure from major Western powers when it introduced its nuclear-free policy in the mid-1980s. The United States terminated New Zealand's operational involvement in the trilateral alliance with Australia, with a consequent cessation of military and intelligence links. It refused to make high-level political visits to New Zealand and refused to accept ours to Washington.

The policy of France was equally stringent and more chauvinistic. Since the early 1960s it resented New Zealand's protests against its nuclear testing on the beautiful Mururoa and Fangataufa atolls in the South Pacific. It must be remembered that France, as a permanent member of the Security Council, has the primary responsibility to contribute to international peace and security and an obligation to that end to act on behalf of all UN member states and not purely in its own interests. In 1985 it violated the charter by sending secret service agents to blow up, in Auckland's Waitemata Harbour, a private protest vessel *en route* to the French testing site, causing loss of life. New Zealand police apprehended two of the agents who were tried in a civilian court on charges of murder and who pleaded guilty to manslaughter. Their sentence of ten years' imprisonment was followed by French trade sanctions against New Zealand, in itself an illegal act. New Zealand appealed to the UN secretary-general for an arbitration ruling to resolve the situation. The ruling, binding on the two parties, was for the agents to be transferred to a French military atoll in the South Pacific for the remainder of their term, which had some eight years to run. Within two years, France had returned both agents to Paris on medical and compassionate grounds, without consultation with New Zealand as was required under the ruling, feting them upon their return. This dereliction of global responsibility can scarcely be seen as in France's legitimate national interest.

Political pressure and illegal behaviour of this kind are simply part of the real world of human affairs. I had been around long enough in politics not to be surprised by them. Nor is any government, including New Zealand's, without reproach. But there are certain standards of civilized behaviour by governments below which we cannot descend if humanity is to stand tall in the face of the global problems we confront today. Violating the United Nations Charter and a ruling of the secretary-general is below that line. The notion of legitimate national interest, in pursuit of the vital planetary interest, will help us determine where the line is to be drawn in these areas.

New Zealand's statutory policy marks the limits of what a small state can do on its own part to reject nuclear weaponry and repudiate the doctrines of nuclear deterrence. This is probably as clear an example of the legitimate national interest as it is possible to have. It can do no more.

NOTES

1. The South Pacific Nuclear-Free Zone Treaty (Treaty of Rarotonga), 1985.
2. The New Zealand Nuclear-Free Zone, Arms Control and Disarmament Act, 1987.
3. "When we exclude nuclear weapons from New Zealand, we exclude the possibility of a nuclear defence of New Zealand. We do not ask to be defended by the nuclear weapons we exclude and we do not ask any nuclear power to deter any enemy of New Zealand by the threatened use of nuclear weapons against that enemy" (Rt Hon. David Lange, Prime Minister of New Zealand, address to the Conference on Disarmament (Geneva: Conference on Disarmament, CD/PV.296, 5 March 1985), 12).

4.3   The Russian Federation

Andrei Kozyrev

> "... for God sets us nothing but riddles. Here the boundaries meet and all contradictions exist side by side."
>
> Fëdor Mikhailovich Dostoevski, *The brothers Karamazov*, Bk III, Ch. 3

The global problem facing humanity is the capacity for self-immolation in the name of survival. Whether that is a riddle set by God or by man can be argued. But in our late twentieth-century security environment, the boundaries of irrationality meet, and all contradictions of human logic and reason exist side by side.

The dangers and dilemmas facing humanity through the development of weapons of mass destruction are identified in the introductory section and do not require repetition. They are awesome enough to be contemplated only once. The only thing to add, perhaps, is that we Russians perceived, and continue to perceive, those dangers as acutely as any other people – Americans, Chinese, Europeans, anyone. It is strange to have to say this, perhaps, but necessary if only to dispel any lingering "image of the enemy" that drove the arms race, and might still instinctively shade negative concerns over a resurgent Russia. We are, if I may belabour the point, equally concerned with our security as a people as any other.

Indeed more so. Security has always been more of a challenge for Russians than for others. Our vast land, once the Soviet Union and still now the Russian Federation, has a hugely disparate ethnic composition. It is underpopulated and underdeveloped. It is strategically located, inviting intrusion and foray – a troubled neighbour to Mackinder's "heartland" where the major trials and tribulations of our century have occurred and been felt. We border on most of the major powers in the world – the United States, China and Japan, and more than a few other countries as well – Mongolia, Kazakhstan, Iran, Ukraine, Belarus, Latvia, Estonia, Finland and Norway. Our land borders are long, some 20,000 km, and our coastline extends nearly twice that distance. Our history is replete with turmoil from outside, including invasion by France in the early nineteenth century and by Germany in the mid-twentieth. Everyone remembers Stalingrad, the world over. We know what it is to be invaded and to suffer. Our people lost more sons per mother in both world wars than any other country.

Circumstances are different now. The world is beginning to think as one. Are we all safer? It is difficult to say so. Certainly, the bombers are not flying towards the borders on "fail-safe" assumptions. But the world remains a dangerous place. In the Cold War, three factors drove those dangers. The existence of nation-states and the principle of national sovereignty meant that people saw others as threats and potential enemies. Political ideologies competed, heightening mistrust and inflaming tensions. And modern technology bequeathed to humanity a destructive capacity of genocidal proportion. Today in the post-Cold War world, two of those factors still remain. And in a world free of ideologically driven political tension, other tensions remain – cultural and religious. Huntington may not be completely right, but he is not completely wrong. In a world of continuing injustices and instability, the potential for the use of weapons of mass destruction remains.

What kind of future global security system can be developed that will guarantee to Russia, to all countries, a decent national security without weapons of mass destruction, as envisaged in the 1978

Final document? What is the best global strategy to achieve the planetary interest of a world free of such weapons of mass destruction? Does the "planetary interest" in fact require this?

The planetary interest of humankind is determined readily enough – it is security for all peoples at levels of weaponry which, in the event the latter are used, do not threaten devastation of the planet and the species they are employed to protect. What is missing from the present global security equation are two things: a clear appreciation of what weapons level is optimal for that balance of security of nations and safety of the planet; and, secondly, the global strategy for achieving it. The treaty that proclaims the goal of the elimination of nuclear weapons from national arsenals, the NPT, serves a profound and necessary purpose. But it does not include in its provisions, explicitly or implicitly, an agreed strategy for attaining that state. Nor does it contain any vision of the security system that would prevail when nuclear weapons are absent from all national arsenals.

The necessary parameters for thinking this through are future-oriented over the long term. To get a decent perspective, a proper historical grip, it is instructive to cast back in the past over an equally long term. In the pre-nuclear age, the goal was less to achieve disarmament than to outlaw war on moral grounds. The advent of nuclear weapons placed unrestrained conflict in a qualitatively new light, the nature of its avoidance transforming from a moral prescription into a rational imperative. But the avoidance of war and the levels of weaponry are intimately and somewhat perversely related. Deterrence strategy marries the two in an unholy modern alliance. In the pre-nuclear age, the strategy for peace rested on collective security, with the major powers using conventional force, to the maximum extent required, to deter aggression. In the nuclear age, global security rests not on the UN Charter but the nuclear weapon. In an unfortunate sense, collective security is the nuclear weapon. Yet because of its destructive nature, it cannot be used. The result is an inadequate security system in which minor aggression and conflict can illicitly occur under an impotent nuclear umbrella.

The major powers recognize the inadequacy of this readily enough. But how can they change it so long as they remain locked into the prism of national security? For the short-lens focus of official policy says that the nuclear weapon still ensures national security. But the longer-lens focus of human reason says that the same nation runs risks to its national security it cannot afford. What, asks the policy-maker, is the alternative? If, in the event of a supreme act of political will on all our parts, the major powers disarmed, multilaterally or unilaterally, and the world were nuclear-free, how would it be governed? Through the collective security provisions of the UN Charter using conventional weapons? Nation-state competition has the inflationary effect of weapons accumulation. How can it be stopped at the "firebreak"? How could the legitimate global authority structure – the UN Security Council – deter the acquisition of nuclear weapons by clandestine outlaw groups? We have all pondered these riddles, and each of us has a fallible view that provides no ultimate solution. The various concepts developed – "threshold of planetary survival", "existential deterrence", "pre-deployment", "zero-alert" – are useful enough. But they do not, critics contend, solve the riddle sent by God – that so long as aggression remains part of human nature, humanity's destructive capacity will henceforth threaten humanity itself.

NATIONAL POLICY

Despite a popular global perception that Russia, with a weakened "transitional" economy, should no longer be seen as having superpower status, the country still retains more nuclear weapons in its national arsenal than any other nation-state, including the United States. How Russia perceives its national security interests and maintains its national strategic policy is therefore crucial to the future of the planet and of humanity. In an era of rapid and rather bewildering change, this is a major conceptual challenge and political task.

Russia's national policy on nuclear weapons is inextricably linked to that of the United States. It cannot be otherwise. That is a strategic given, bequeathed by the geography of the planet. The variable is how the relationship is handled. It is in the planetary interest that it be handled with understanding and wisdom. The scorpions may be reconciled, but their tails can still sting. Russia's strategic policy, therefore, has tended to be reactive, in response to US policy.

Many observers, however, conclude that the US appears now to follow a policy that seeks to maintain strategic superiority over all other nation-states, including Russia. The policy of maintaining a capability to engage in two simultaneous major regional conflicts, a key objective of the 1993 "Bottom-Up Review", continues to underpin its global reach. If Russia responded to the reactive instinct, the old rivalries would continue.

Yet the policies of our two countries in the late 1990s must fairly be seen as responding broadly to the planetary interest of a world ultimately free of the nuclear threat. The bilateral strategic force reductions in the 1990s have been to date the single most far-reaching legacy of the end of the Cold War. The implementation of START I is proceeding. Under the US Co-operative Threat Reduction Program, US financial assistance has been devoted to supporting START implementation and demilitarization in Russia, and an additional amount for Belarus, Kazakhstan and Ukraine.[1] The last remaining Russian nuclear warhead was withdrawn from Ukraine in May 1996, leaving two of the three former Soviet republics party to the Lisbon Protocol, Kazakhstan and Ukraine, free of nuclear weapons. In the 1996 Memorandum of Understanding, Belarus declared that it still had 18 intercontinental ballistic missiles on its soil. Delay in withdrawing these was due to protracted negotiations over compensation from Russia for their value. Kazakhstan still had 24 ICBMs as did Ukraine, but without their nuclear warheads.[2]

START II has yet to be ratified by the Russian parliament, the *Duma*. The Russian president, however, has indicated that he supports a lower force level than the START II ceiling. There is therefore considerable thought currently being given to the likely levels for a START III. The US prefers an early accord since otherwise it would need to devote $5 billion over the next seven years to maintain weapons which could alternatively be eliminated with sufficient "national security" retained. For its part, Russia would prefer such an accord since otherwise it will need to devote an equal investment to deploy 500 new SS-27 ICBMs to replace some of the older missiles that START II requires to be eliminated.[3]

The strategic force reductions planned by the United States are understood to be as shown in Table 4.3.1. In determining Russia's strategic plans for the early twenty-first century, a number of issues must be addressed:

- the risk of illicit proliferation of Russia's current arsenal of nuclear weapons;
- its current nuclear force reliability;
- how it perceives US nuclear doctrine;
- how it perceives the proposed expansion of NATO and the prospects for European security; and
- how it perceives the status of the anti-ballistic missile defence understanding with the United States.

Table 4.3.1 Strategic forces reduction plans: United States

	Planned cuts in US strategic forces		
	1989	1997	Target force
ICBMS	1,000	580	500
SSBNS	32	17	14
SLBMS	576	408	336
Bombers	359	174	86

Source: *The military balance 1996/97* (IISS, Oxford: Brassey's, 1997), 15.

Proliferation of existing weapons

The US is giving high priority in its national strategic planning to "counter-proliferation" with a view to developing capabilities to detect and neutralize weapons of mass destruction before they can be used. Priority is being given to developing the means to locate underground storage sites, and to detect and track weapons shipments.[4]

For its part, Russia is pursuing the problem with equal seriousness. In February 1997, an *ad hoc* committee of the UN General Assembly commenced its work on elaborating conventions on the suppression of terrorist bombings and acts of nuclear terrorism. Two draft conventions are already before the committee. The first, submitted by Russia and the G-7 nations, covers the definition, detention and extradition of suspects, as well as efforts to prevent the actions to be proscribed by the Anti-Terrorist Bombing Convention. The second, submitted alone by Russia, concerns the suppression of acts of nuclear terrorism. This proposal seeks to have states parties co-operate in preventing and prosecuting such acts through national legislative and technical measures to protect nuclear material, installations and devices and prevent unauthorized access by third parties.[5]

Nuclear force reliability

The status and reliability of Russia's nuclear missile forces have recently been a source of dispute. In February 1997, the defence minister contended that they were "close to collapse". But shortly there-after, at the request of the president, the prime minister launched an enquiry and concluded that they were "under firm and effective control".[6]

Despite these problems, Russia intends in the future not only to maintain but also to modernize its strategic weapons. It has recently purchased a powerful IBM RS/6000 SP supercomputer for the purpose of simulating future nuclear tests. The minister of atomic affairs allegedly justified the purchase on the grounds that it would help secure Russia's future reliance on its nuclear arsenal to offset its current weakness in conventional weaponry. The United States has expressed its concern at the sale, including the possibility that the computer can be used not only for monitoring stockpile reliability but also for new weapons research.[7] Yet the US is doing precisely the same. Double-standards, I expect, are excluded from the legitimate national interest.

Nuclear doctrine

The United States has always retained a policy of first-use of nuclear weapons in response to aggression with conventional weapons. Recently it has linked use of its nuclear weapons to the growing threat posed by chemical and biological weapons. As part of its effort to achieve Senate ratification of the Chemical Weapons Convention, the US administration offered the Senate an undertaking to enter a formal commitment to carry out "overwhelming and devastating" retaliation against any adversary that attacked US forces with poison gas. The undertaking, which would be legally binding on the president, would constitute an unusual written pledge to military action that would imply, though not require, the use of nuclear weapons.[8]

For its part, Russia has recently adopted a policy of first-use as well, since it no longer possesses a conventional superiority. It has done this in the name of national security, as traditionally understood.

Expansion of NATO

NATO's eastward expansion has been a source of concern and controversy in Russia. The issue was blown out of proportion both in the West and in Russia, and neither side dealt with the issue reasonably or co-operatively. Certainly the matter has implications for Russia's own perception of its national security and thus for global strategic stability. The foreign minister declared that our country's aim was "to minimise the depth of those dividing lines which might appear in Europe" and to obtain "guarantees which would alleviate our concerns".[9] Russia's present leaders, concerned perhaps above all that new NATO member states in Eastern Europe could have Western nuclear weapons stationed on their territory, declared that they would consider taking "adequate measures" if NATO's plans were realized.[10] Former Soviet president and Nobel Peace Prize winner Mikhail Gorbachev expressed his profound concern over the issue, citing it as an emerging threat to Russia's national interests and constituting a "global problem".[11] In its consultations with NATO, Russia indicated it wanted a legally binding document addressing the issue of expansion, and demanded that no "sophisticated military equipment" be stationed on the new members' territories. For its part, however, NATO believed that a political document would be sufficient. And that is how it transpired.

Ballistic missile defence

The US policy on ballistic missile defence has been to focus on theatre defence for its forces abroad. In the longer term, the national policy is to provide for a capability for rapid development of such a defence if the US perceives a threat to emerge. Current US policy, however, is that it will not develop systems that contravene the 1972 bilateral ABM Treaty. For its part, Russia has always insisted on the continued integrity of the ABM Treaty. If nuclear deterrence is to continue "into the indefinite future", so must the doctrinal struts that underpin it.

THE LEGITIMATE NATIONAL INTEREST

What is the legitimate national interest of Russia in the world of global security underpinned by nuclear capability? What can it do to secure the safety of its own people yet avoid undermining the legitimate security interests of the rest of humankind?

The answer to Russia's future security, in my own view, turns less on exogenous issues such as the recent arrangement with NATO than it does on the future domestic political evolution of the country itself. If Russia attains a further strengthening of its democratic structure and market economy without undue hardship to its people, then it will feel secure within itself, and perceive the world, including the United States, in a more benign light. Failing that, the forces of nationalism might increase the perception of external threat from the West, and all hope of further accord over nuclear arms will wither on the vine.

During the Cold War, my country sought global strategic stability through a mutual force parity with the United States. More than the United States, we had a security problem with China to contend with, and also the nuclear forces of Britain and France to face. Our heavy land-based ICBMs counterbalanced the smaller and more accurate American land- and sea-based missiles. Our national policy was seen, at least by us, as a defensive one relying on nuclear weapons for a second-strike policy. Unlike the West, which relied on a first-strike policy and capability, my country renounced first-strike and also first-use in a conventional conflict. The West denigrated this as a propaganda stance and, given our first-strike capability, it was not possible to prove them wrong – another of God's riddles. The United Nations Charter sanctioned regional defensive arrangements such as the Warsaw Pact but proved insufficient to maintain a safe and assured international security order. Because the charter is silent on nuclear weaponry, we believed it should be supplemented with a treaty renouncing first-use, since this would render nuclear weapons ineffective. Precisely for this reason the West opposed the proposal. We favoured a comprehensive test ban treaty, the universal adherence to the NPT, strategic defence limited by the ABM Treaty, and a new treaty for the non-deployment of weaponry in outer space to supplement the charter and the Outer Space Treaty. Those were the days and the policies of the Cold War and I was heavily involved in framing my country's policies as a senior official in the foreign ministry. Then the USSR collapsed, the Cold War was over, and I was appointed foreign minister of the Russian Federation from 1991 to 1995. To what extent have things changed from then?

A recent private American study has described "loose" nuclear weapons and material as the "no. 1 threat to America's vital interests".[12] Nuclear weapons and weapons material, the study observes, are scattered in 200 sites across Russia, including storage depots and laboratories. Neither the Russian nor Khazak governments were aware, it says, of the existence of 1,000 lb of nuclear material in Kazakhstan. When it was discovered, Kazakhstan sold it to the United States and it is currently stored in Tennessee. At the time, however, Iran was also aware of it and endeavouring to acquire it. The study concludes that the combination of a number of factors – a weak Russian economy, dissatisfied nuclear workers, and interest backed by money from the Mafia and terrorists – makes nuclear leakage "inevitable". It is, believes the chief author of the study, simply a matter of time before a private nuclear weapon is detonated in the United States.

The report is somewhat sensational, but the overall concern is valid enough. And I agree with the view that such risks can only be lessened by strengthening democracy in Russia and increasing co-operation between Russia and the United States, and including other countries as well. This requires a better "political environment" between the Russian government and its nuclear ministry, and the

US executive and legislature. The recent pattern of behaviour within the two governments has permitted only slow and grudging progress to date.[13]

Much has been made of former Defence Minister Rodionov's lament that the authority structure for control of nuclear weapons was not adequate. Equal anxiety attends the failure of the parliament to ratify START II. As a member of the *Duma,* I am concerned by this. The treaty has become hostage to a conservative majority whose nationalistic misperceptions of the world negate the broader planetary interest. Russia, of course, is not alone in this respect. We follow certain senatorial distempers and fulminations in the US with a mixture of bemusement and concern as well.

In an important sense circumstances change but national interests do not. Russia retains its right to ensure national security for its people. It retains nuclear weapons – more than any other nation on Earth. Its conventional forces have been withdrawn from Eastern Europe and they are in a sorry state. The West no longer sees Russia, Russia no longer sees itself, as possessing a superior conventional force structure. That is why my country adopted the NATO first-strike policy for its nuclear force structure in 1997, to compensate for an inferior conventional force structure, just as NATO did in 1952. Those who are disposed to criticize Russia for this are denigrating themselves and their own policy. And Russia has plans for the modernization of its nuclear submarine force, with new strategic and attack submarines as quiet or quieter than those in the West – an asset which the West always prided itself in having and now a source of some concern to Western strategic planners. So long as the West retains nuclear weapons, so will Russia. Even in the post-Cold War world. That much is certain.

Yet there are positive developments. The Comprehensive Test Ban Treaty is completed along with the Chemical Weapons Convention. We have a non-targeting agreement with the United States for our nuclear missiles. Those who deride this on the grounds that the missiles can be retargeted within minutes are unmindful of the importance of delicate diplomatic and political signals of this kind. They do not save humanity in themselves; they are a critical small step along the way. Nothing is worse in the struggle for mutual survival than cynicism and nihilism. Even for professionals paid to think that way.

Nuclear weapons are the symbol of a security situation, not its driving force. If a state feels secure, it will not be disposed to accumulate vast amounts of expensive weapons, especially when its economy is weak and in transition. But if it feels insecure, it will do so, no matter what the cost and national sacrifice, for the sake of national security, as we saw in my country in the 1950s. The propensity of a state to reduce and eliminate its weapons of mass destruction depends upon this security environment – witness Argentina and Brazil as a positive example and India and Pakistan as a negative one. In the case of Russia, was it more secure in a Cold War environment when it was ringed with nuclear missiles at five minutes' delivery time but with a relatively stable global security environment? Or safer today in a post-Cold War environment when the missiles are less threatening but with a less stable global security environment? Some retain a nostalgia for the stability and predictability of the Cold War. I am not one of them. We are safer in today's world, all of us, despite the instabilities of a world in change and ferment, and we must continue to work towards a safer security system.

But the issue of NATO expansion, misperceived and abused by the nationalists among us, is what drives the debate over nuclear weapons in Russia, including the matter of ratification of START II in the *Duma.* NATO's expansion eastward through the inclusion of Poland, the Czech Republic and Hungary, and the likely further expansion to include other states has been interpreted as proof of a strategy for isolating Russia. To a large extent this is an internal problem – the immaturity of Russian democracy and its inability to date to pursue a stable and co-operative foreign policy as a great power, something which Russia deserves and will achieve once it completes its democratic transformation.

Yet the arrangement, the "Founding Act", between NATO and Russia of May 1997 is adequate in the circumstances. A permanent council will discuss all security matters from peacekeeping to arms control, terrorism and drug trafficking. This council is additional to NATO's main policy-making body and to the Atlantic Partnership Council that links it with East European countries. As President Yeltsin's spokesman, Sergei Yastrzhembsky, put it, Russia succeeded in incorporating in the document "numerous guarantees which to a significant extent reduce or minimise the negative consequences of NATO's expansion for Russia's national interests".[14] Certainly, President Yeltsin saw the outcome as achieving his stated need to "minimise the threat to Russia", and Foreign Minister Primakov saw it as a "big victory for reason, a big victory for the world community, and a big victory for Russia".[15] For the planetary interest, one might say. But does the outcome increase Russia's propensity further to reduce its nuclear forces? Does it feel more secure as a result of the Founding Act?

Does the legitimate national interest of Russia require that it unilaterally dismantle its nuclear weapons arsenal? No. Is it legitimate for Russia to retain nuclear weapons and illegitimate for India to announce its possession? Yes, if and only if Russia is demonstrably moving towards ultimate elimination of its own. If not, then any other nation-state has the right to possess them. Does the legitimate national interest require that the *Duma* ratify START II? Yes. Is there a planetary interest that could contemplate a reversal of the nuclear reductions process in the name of global security? No. The process must continue, even in the absence of an agreed end-state.

Figure 4.3.1   "Some retain a nostalgia for the stability and predictability of the Cold War; I am not one of them," says Andrei Kozyrev. "We are safer in today's world, all of us, despite the instabilities of a world in change and ferment, and we must continue to work towards a safer security system." Military officials and journalists view the remains of a former Soviet nuclear missile silo, Pervomaisk, Ukraine, January 1995. US, Russian and Ukrainian defence ministers jointly detonated the explosives. (Courtesy Popperfoto/Reuters)

CONCLUSION

None of us knows the answers to God's riddles. It is beyond our sober imaginings to envisage the kind of global security system that will prevail on Earth a few centuries from today. When Peter the Great travelled through Europe in 1698, he could scarcely imagine, let alone foresee, the politics and technology that would shape the security system three centuries from then. In all its affairs, humanity gropes forward blindly, and the torch of foresight shines but a few years ahead. We are continuously in need of conceptual creativity to lighten the way. If we but begin to conceive of the planetary interest, seek to agree upon and strive to attain it, we shall surely do better in our timeless search for survival.

NOTES

1. International Institute for Strategic Studies, *The military balance, 1996/97* (iiss, Oxford: Brassey's, 1997), 113.
2. Ibid., 107.
3. See iht, 24 January 1997. "I favour the next treaty, the start iii treaty, that would continue the reduction of nuclear weapons", Russian Minister of Defence, Igor Rodionov.
4. *The military balance 1996/97*, 18.
5. undh, 25 February 1997.
6. "Russian strategic missile forces are capable of carrying out all tasks entrusted to them . . . The nation's nuclear shield is in reliable hands", Prime Minister Victor Chernomyrdin, *iht*, 22 February 1997.
7. "The only protection throughout this period will be nuclear weapons", Minister of Atomic Affairs, Victor Mikhailov. A senior US official is quoted as saying: "We have made a policy decision not to assist the Russians in their stockpile stewardship program. Even though relations with the Russians are good, we are potentially a target for their nuclear forces if relations change." The US is concerned that the purchase of the US computer through a European middleman has circumvented US export controls. *iht*, 26 February 1997.
8. *iht*, 17 February 1997.
9. Ibid., 25 February 1997.
10. Ibid., 22 February 1997.

11.   [Leaving] aside the cynical motives of those who would use nato expansion for their own ends, the idea itself is a real danger – and not only for Russia. During the Cold War, arms manufacturers and merchants of hate decided the destiny of the world. Immense efforts were required to break a fatal logic that was dragging humanity toward suicide. Seven years have passed since the end of the Cold War, but its poisonous roots live on, infecting economies, international relations, nations' internal politics and the moral and psychological health of millions of people. And yet, the leaders of countries that are even more civilised, cultured and democratic than their predecessors of 50 years ago are creating a situation in which human survival could again be threatened . . . Certainly the world has many problems – ecological, demographic, economic, among others – but these are not solved by military blocs. They are global emergencies, affecting everyone, while military blocs exist to act against someone else . . . The issue of placing nuclear weapons in the bloc's new member states is being discussed at governmental levels . . . Nothing could be more effective in reviving the Russian complex of "being surrounded" . . . Such an atmosphere, despite all the reassurances that Russian leaders and anxieties will be taken into account, is not conducive to trust . . . It is perhaps strange that neither Russia nor the West has tried to put the matter on the agenda of the United Nations Security Council. We are talking, after all, about a global problem (*La Stampa* (Turin), quoted *iht*, 22 February 1997).

12. *Avoiding nuclear anarchy: containing the threat of loose Russian weapons and fissile material*, G. Allison, O.R. Coté, R.A. Falkenrath, S.E. Miller, Center for Science and International Affairs, Harvard University, csia study No. 12 (Cambridge, Mass.: MIT Press, 1995).
13. *iht*, 23 November 1996.
14. Ibid., 15 May 1997.
15. Ibid.

CHAPTER FIVE

Chemical and biological disarmament

5.1   Introduction

Chemical weapons preceded nuclear weapons by some fifty years, and remain today more readily available as weapons of mass destruction for countries that lack the technological capacity to produce nuclear weapons for deterrence purposes. Yet the proscription against their use is the oldest weapons ban of the modern age. In many respects, therefore, the conceptual task in relating the national interest of a country to the planetary interest of humankind is as pertinent and challenging as with nuclear weapons for the major powers.

THE GLOBAL PROBLEM

The problem confronting the international community rests formally on a moral basis rather than a rational concern over their destructive capacity. The Biological Weapons Convention expresses the conviction that "such use would be repugnant to the conscience of mankind and that no effort should be spared to minimize this risk".[1] But it has always been recognized that the threat of bacteriological devastation to humanity is real. In the fourteenth century, some 20 million people were killed by an infectious agent believed to have been the plague bacterium, including nearly one-quarter of the population of Western Europe. Another 20 million were killed by an influenza virus in 1918, over twice the number of combat fatalities during the previous four-year world conflict. Since 1981, the HIV virus has killed an estimated 29 million people. Although these were not the result of military weapons deployment, it is not impossible that such agents can be put to military use. Unlike nuclear and chemical weapons, biological weapons contain pathogens which are alive, reproduce themselves and can engage in adaptive behaviour. The scope and timing of use of a pathogen cannot be precisely controlled and the inability to cause them to act swiftly reduces their current potential for military purposes. But in the view of one expert, a lethal pathogen used for hostile purpose could efficiently spread from one victim to another, and "would be capable of initiating an intensifying cascade of disease that ultimately threatens the entire world population".[2] The devastation and horror of the use of chemical weapons in the First World War is well known.

Possession of both biological and chemical weapons is difficult to identify. Unofficial estimates are that at least 17 countries are understood to be conducting biological weapons research.[3] As at December 1997, eight countries had declared past or present possession of modern chemical weapons. Their identity, dependent on classified information given to the responsible agency, has not been disclosed to the public.[4] These states are, however, understood to include the United States, Russia, Iraq and India.[5] About 20 other countries are reported to have or be seeking the ability to make them, including North Korea, Pakistan, Libya, Iran, China and Israel.[6]

Beyond this traditional threat to national security of nation-states posed by each other lies the emerging threat of their clandestine use by terrorist or cult organizations, as has already occurred in Japan in 1995.

THE GLOBAL OBJECTIVE AND STRATEGY

The planetary interest is captured in the relevant treaties. The Biological Weapons Convention expresses the determination, "for the sake of all mankind", to exclude completely the possibility of bacteriological (biological) agents and toxins being used as weapons.[7] The Chemical Weapons Convention identifies the same objective regarding that class of weapons.[8]

The global strategy has been to develop two multilateral treaties that prohibit the possession of biological and chemical weapons. In each case, the judgement was made that the elimination of each category of weapon would facilitate the achievement of general and complete disarmament.[9]

PRESCRIBED NATIONAL POLICIES

The specific measures identified in the 1978 Action Programme included both biological and chemical weapons. The programme called for "consideration", by the non-parties, of adherence to the Biological Weapons Convention, and the urgent conclusion of the negotiations on a chemical weapons convention. The conclusion of the Chemical Weapons Convention and increased adherence to the Biological Weapons Convention since then has gone some considerable way to realization of these measures. The national policies deriving from the global strategy involve the mandatory elimination of any chemical or biological weapons and a permanent renunciation of intent to acquire them.

Thus, in the case of biological weapons, each state party to this convention undertakes never in any circumstances to develop, produce, stockpile or otherwise acquire or retain microbial or other biological agents or toxins, whatever their origin or method of production, of types and in quantities that have no justification for prophylactic, protective or other peaceful purposes. They also renounce the acquisition of weapons, equipment or other means of delivery designed to use such agents or toxins for hostile purposes in armed conflict.[10] In addition, each state party undertakes to destroy, or divert to peaceful purposes all agents, toxins, weapons, equipment or means of delivery which are in its possession or under its jurisdiction or control.[11] They also undertake not to transfer to any recipient, directly or indirectly, and not in any way to assist, encourage, or induce any state, group of states, or international organization to manufacture or otherwise acquire any of the agents, toxins, weapons, equipment or means of delivery.[12]

In the case of chemical weapons, each state party undertakes never to develop, produce, otherwise acquire, stockpile or retain chemical weapons, or transfer, directly or indirectly, chemical weapons to anyone; never to use chemical weapons; never to engage in any military preparations to use chemical weapons; and never to assist, encourage or induce, in any way, anyone to engage in any activity prohibited under the convention. Each state party undertakes to destroy chemical weapons it owns or possesses, or that are located in any place under its jurisdiction or control. It undertakes to destroy all chemical weapons which it may have abandoned on the territory of another state party as well as any chemical weapons production facilities it owns or possesses, or that are located in any place under its jurisdiction or control. And it undertakes not to use riot control agents as a method of warfare.[13]

As with the NPT, the two conventions allow withdrawal in the event that any state determines that its national interest must take precedence over the planetary interest. In exercising its national sovereignty each state party shall have the right to withdraw from the convention if it decides that extraordinary events, related to the subject matter of the convention, have jeopardized its supreme interests.[14] To date, however, there never has been an occasion when a state party has withdrawn from an arms control treaty on these grounds.[15]

The Chemical Weapons Convention requires elimination of all chemical weapons by 2007. It creates the most intrusive verification regime of any arms control treaty to date. A secretariat, the Organization for the Prohibition of Chemical Weapons (OPCW) conducts routine and unannounced inspections of companies using chemicals covered by the treaty. Intrusiveness varies with the risk that a facility or its produce could be used for prohibited purposes. It requires parties to report the location of chemical weapons storage sites, the location and characteristics of production and research facilities, details of all equipment transfers since 1946, plans for destroying chemical weapons, and the location and activities of any facility using or producing controlled chemicals. It allows any party to request a "challenge inspection" of any site in another country. The request may be denied if three-quarters of the 41 countries on the Executive Council object; otherwise the council must act within 12 hours. The country facing inspection may manage access to protect military secrets or proprietary information.

The Chemical Weapons Convention came into force in April 1997. By June 1998 there were 110 states parties, and an additional 58 states had signed. All five permanent Security Council members had become parties. In South Asia, the convention was ratified by both India and Pakistan. In the Middle East, North Africa and Gulf region, Jordan, Iran and Saudi Arabia had ratified; Israel had signed but not ratified; while Egypt, Iraq, Libya and Syria had not signed.[16]

The Biological Weapons Convention entered into force in 1975 and negotiations are underway to strengthen its verification regime with an additional protocol. The United States, Russia, UK, France and China have all ratified, as have India, Pakistan, Iran, North Korea, Libya and Iraq. As noted earlier, following Iraq's aggression in the Gulf War, the UN Security Council imposed binding resolutions on that country, effectively depriving it of the right to possess any weapons of mass destruction, and has maintained an intrusive inspection programme designed to detect any violations of that resolution and destroy any weapons of mass destruction thus detected. The UN has accused Iraq of continuing deception in seeking to conceal its weapons of mass destruction during this period. Although the international community deprived Germany of the right to manufacture poison gas following the First World War, this is the first time that the international community has deprived a sovereign state of the right to possess all weapons of mass destruction in the interests of international peace and security. It thus creates an important precedent in security thinking.

LEGITIMATE NATIONAL INTERESTS

Is it in the legitimate national interest of every nation-state to sign and ratify both the Chemical and Biological Weapons Conventions? Certainly, in the view of the opcw, this is so. The national security interest in ratifying the convention is explained by the secretariat as follows:

> The main impact of the Chemical Weapons Convention will be in the national security and economic fields. In the field of national security, it should first be noted that the small non-possessor States are the most vulnerable to the threat of chemical weapons. The Convention will increase the national security of States Parties because of the reduction of the cw threat. National security will also be enhanced for the States Parties by the access to the clarification mechanism of the Convention. This includes the right to request the Executive Council to assist in clarifying situations, as well as the right to request a challenge inspection to resolve questions concerning possible non-compliance. Another factor which will increase national security is the right to request assistance in case of use or threat of use of chemical weapons. States Parties might also possibly access the information on pledges of assistance in order to identify other States Parties that could be possible sources for bilateral assistance in case of chemical catastrophes.[17]

Is this judgement shared by all nation-states? The political commitment to eliminating weapons of mass destruction in the Middle East is shown in Table 5.1.1.

Table 5.1.1 Political commitment to eliminating weapons of mass destruction in the Middle East, by year of ratification

Country	NPT	CTB	BWC	CWC
Israel		Signed*		Signed
Jordan	1970	Signed	1975	1997
Egypt	1981	Signed	Signed	
Syria	1968		Signed	
Iraq	1969		1991	
Iran	1970	Signed	1973	1997
Libya	1975		1982	
Saudi Arabia	1988		1972	1996

* "Signed" denotes government signature of the treaty, but not ratification or accession; the government is not therefore a party to the treaty.
Source: United Nations, *Status of multilateral arms regulation and disarmament agreements*, 5th edn (New York: United Nations, 1996).

Two countries that face special difficulties in facing up to the issue of chemical and bacteriological weapons are Middle East neighbours – Israel and Jordan. Having fought three wars in the past half-century, the issue of national security is as stark for these two countries as for any. The political relationship, involving the Middle East peace process and the fate of the Palestinian Authority, lends added intensity to the bilateral relationship. Can these two states reconcile their national interests with the planetary interest as it pertains to global security?

Israel is not a party to either the Biological Weapons Convention or the Chemical Weapons Convention, although it has signed the latter. It is believed by most authoritative observers to possess nuclear weapons but not chemical or biological weapons. What is the formally stated reason why Israel does not accede to any one of the three treaties banning weapons of mass destruction? Does it envisage circumstances in which it could accede with guaranteed national security?

For its part, Jordan is a party to both the Biological Weapons Convention (1975) and Chemical Weapons Convention (1997) as well as the NPT (1970). It has thus decided to surrender the right to possess any weapons of mass destruction, irrespective of Israeli policy. The political significance of Jordan's accession to the CWC, in the view of the head of the new chemical weapons agency for implementing the convention, is that "the group of Arab countries that always linked this problem to Israel's refusal to sign has been broken. This opens the way for Egypt to reconsider its position".[18]

How, then, do these two countries – Israel and Jordan – see their legitimate national interests in this most volatile region of the world?

NOTES

1. Biological Weapons Convention, 10th preambular para. (BWC).
2. J.D. Steinbrunner, "Biological weapons: a plague upon all houses", *Foreign Policy* **109**, winter 1997, 88.
3. Ibid., 86.
4. Correspondence with Organization for the Prohibition of Chemical Weapons (OPCW), The Hague.
5. *IHT*, 26 April 1997.
6. Ibid.
7. BWC, 9th preambular para.
8. Chemical Weapons Convention, 6th preambular para. (CWC).

9. ... convinced that the prohibition of the development, production and stockpiling of chemical and bacteriological (biological) weapons and their elimination through effective measures, will facilitate the achievement of general and complete disarmament under strict and effective international control (BWC, 1st preambular para.)

And:

Convinced of the importance and urgency of eliminating from the arsenals of States, through effective measures, such dangerous weapons of mass destruction as those using chemical or bacteriological (biological) agents ... (BWC, 7th preambular para.).

And:

Convinced that the complete and effective prohibition of the development, production, acquisition, stockpiling, retention, transfer and use of chemical weapons, and their destruction, represent a necessary step towards the achievement of these common objectives (CWC, 10th preambular para.).

10. BWC, Article 1.
11. Ibid., Article 2.
12. Ibid., Article 3.
13. CWC, Article 1.
14. BWC, Article 13; CWC, Article 16.
15. North Korea did threaten to withdraw from the Non-Proliferation Treaty in the early 1990s, but did not proceed following an agreement with the United States over a replacement of its nuclear facilities with light water reactors.
16. http://www.opcw.nl:80/memsta/namelist.htm and ... ratifyer.htm (26 June 1998).
17. http://www.opcw.nl:80/advanta.htm (31 December 1997).
18. Statement by José Mauricio Bustani, Director-General of the OPCW, The Hague, *IHT*, 11 November 1997.

5.2 Jordan

Toujan Faisal

"A world free of weapons of mass destruction . . . will surely be to the benefit of the peoples of the South even before it benefits those of the North. Saving the planet requires saving us in the South first."

The two principal concepts explored in Part II of this book are the planetary interest and the legitimate national interest. They comprise the important pillars of legitimacy for global politics, and form the conceptual structure within which argument and counter-argument can be assessed.

I begin by accepting the definition of the planetary interest as set out in Chapter 1. I also accept the distinction developed between the vital and the normative planetary interest. That is an abstract categorization that intrinsically holds true. But my own analysis and reasoning from there may perhaps differ fundamentally from many other contributors to this book. For it is my contention that the substance of the twin concepts – what actually comprises the vital and the normative categories – is related to, and indeed draws from, the substance of the legitimate national interest.

I contend also that the perception by the United States of its own national interests in the 1990s is widely if not universally held, at least in the Western world, as the legitimate interest for the international community in general, operationalized through the United Nations. The UN Charter was, after all, largely the product of American thinking, and to a lesser extent British.[1] To this day the US remains the leading member of both the General Assembly and the Security Council. To this day, it continues to claim to be the caretaker of "international legitimacy". And, of course, to this day it claims, and has claimed even prior to the formation of the United Nations, to be the main, if not the sole, defender of freedom and democracy around the world.

Recognition of this reality is the logical and also ethical basis for my proposal not just to adopt one universal definition of the "legitimate national interest", but rather the one proposed by the US itself. This, and this alone, can prompt us to address the main sources of conflict around the planet which is causing so much damage to humankind.

This argument rests on an ethical basis, not realpolitik. Without a real moral conviction on the part of all individuals and nations, nothing can be achieved in serving humanity or the planet on which we dwell. For what we are aspiring to save is not the prevailing balance of power, but rather humanity itself. In essence, some form of new international order is needed that sheds the illogicalities, and indeed the ethical ugliness, that permeate much of past and present international relations. And a prerequisite to such fundamental change is an unprecedented popular conviction of the need for change, not a continuing compliance with the present order.

And so, writing from the Arab perspective in this book, I shall adopt the definition of the national interest used by the US itself as a common indicator of "legitimacy" and as a definition of the pursuit of the national interest of every other nation. Nothing less would, ironically, provide adequate conviction even for the Arab nation.

A recent Commission on American National Interests identified four levels of intensity for the US national interest: "vital", "extremely important", "just important" and "less important".[2] It is obvious that the first of these forms the core interest of a nation-state. In the view of the commission, the threats to the vital US national interests were five: nuclear, biological or chemical weapons attack on US territory; the emergence of a hostile hegemon in Europe or Asia; the emergence of a hostile power on US borders or controlling the high seas; catastrophic collapse of major global systems (trade, financial, energy, environmental); and threats to the survival of US allies.

It goes without saying that this definition should be re-articulated in terms responding to the same categories of interests and standards that can reflect the various geographical and strategic needs of each single nation-state. And, similarly, the spirit in which the nation-state is defined, acceptance of how far that nation-state can stretch its arm beyond its national borders to protect those interests, and what means it may employ to that end – all these should be maintained equally for every nation-state.

NATIONAL POLICY

For its part, Jordan is a party to all three treaties pertaining to the prohibition of weapons of mass destruction – the Non-Proliferation Treaty, the Chemical Weapons Convention and the Biological Weapons Convention. We have thus surrendered our sovereign right to acquire nuclear, chemical and biological weapons. Israel is a party to none. Jordan can, however, withdraw upon three months' notice – at least legally under the provisions of the treaties.

That is all I believe I need to record here about the official policy of my country. For my main contention is that the policy of all our countries, and especially those in the Arab world, are a distorted reflection of the state of the international order in the late twentieth century. And it is that which I thus wish to address in more depth. The legitimate national interest, in fact, not only of Jordan but of the Arab nation.

THE LEGITIMATE NATIONAL INTEREST

I do not assume that, in my individual capacity, I am mandated by the Arab nation to draft a definition of the "vital Arab interest". But I can definitely, based on the spirit and even the details of the US definition of national interest, explore on behalf of the Arab world some basic issues concerning the contemporary practices and policies, carried out and either condoned or overlooked by the international community. For these do not just imperil, but at times completely "confiscate" our national interests, including the most vital of all – the survival and viability of the Arab people in free and secure nation-states.

The issues are many and I shall address but a few. Our neighbour, Israel, was created not on the borders but in the midst of the Arab nation, on usurped Arab land, by the same nations that had colonized the Arab nation-states. Thereafter that state has engaged in expansionist wars in the West Bank of my country, in the Sinai, and in southern Lebanon. It has struck beyond the territories of neighbouring Arab countries to bomb Iraq's nuclear reactor, and to hunt PLO leaders on the shores of Tunisia. It issues a continual declaration, repeated by its national leaders of all parties, that the West Bank belongs to Israel. It operates a nuclear reactor in Daimuna and develops a weapons capability there. The reactor leaks radioactive waste, as confirmed by scientific reports appearing in the Israeli media.

Israel has recently begun speaking of its nuclear capability as a "counterforce" to other nations' advanced weapons. No longer does it conceive of nuclear weapons as a "last resort". It has adopted the phrase "nuclear capability", not yet an acknowledgement of deployment, as a deterrent to adversaries in the region. It has hinted that it might deploy its nuclear weapons in a "launch-on-warning" mode, releasing its own nuclear force immediately upon detecting an incoming missile attack, before the missiles are positively identified. The head of Israel's atomic energy commission has said that it could only "give up its nuclear capability when it reaches a 'utopia' with its neighbours, in the manner of Brazil and Argentina".[3] In November 1997 its minister of national infrastructure warned that Israel was "ready to respond with all our might" to Iran and Iraq, a phrase generally interpreted as implying nuclear retaliation. The defence minister has also indicated that Israel will strike pre-emptively rather than allow Iran to develop weapons which his prime minister has described as an "existential threat" to Israel. Israel has acquired 25 F-151 fighters, an advanced version of the main US strike aircraft used in the Gulf conflict. They have a range of 1,600 kilometres and were acquired with "Iran in mind", as an Israeli official is reported to have said.[4]

What future threats to the Arab world might be presented by a nation-state that engages in this conduct? A nation-state that, prior to fully developing its own nuclear weapons, ingratiates itself with the "exclusive club" of nuclear states and concomitantly leads the major powers to the self-humiliating pretence of ignorance of the universally known hazards which the Israeli nuclear programme poses?

Additional to this national threat is the more general challenge posed by the US military maritime dominance, and indeed land presence, in the Mediterranean and Gulf regions, thereby effectively laying siege to the Arab world. The purpose of such an arsenal, or one of its principal purposes, is control over Arab oil resources, whether through military action or economic pressure such as sanctions. And such pressure is focused on certain Arab leaders perceived and denigrated as dictators, while the US allies itself with other Arab leaders, equally undemocratic and more corrupt. That pressure, I contend, violates the legitimate national interest, and legitimate human rights and aspirations, of the Arab people.

Then there is the associated issue of the extreme poverty in which a majority of the people in the wealthy Arab nation live – this wealthy nation of energy-suppliers – as a result of such American and "international" policies. A quick glance at the suffering of the people in the Gaza Strip and the West Bank, in Lebanon and in Iraq testifies to the deprivation of what might legitimately be seen as the "vital Arab interests". Not "normative" national interests, but "vital".

Let me address the "vital planetary interest". Our land stands as one of the main examples of calculated US and UN action which has resulted in irretrievable damage to the planet and to humanity. Is this a biased judgement of one Arab politician? No. It reflects the judgement of many human rights organizations and conscientious leaders around the world. In November 1996, former US senator and presidential candidate Ramsay Clark presented a complaint against the US, UK and UN before a popular international tribunal in Madrid, justifiably charging them with "genocide, crimes against humanity, and the use of weapons of mass destruction".[5] Another US citizen, Randall Mollin, member of an American charity group, Voice of the Wilderness, which sent a fact-finding mission to Iraq, reported to the international media that what the US and UN were doing in Iraq was no less than "genocide".[6] Bert Sachs, president of the same group, told his own government that if it were interested in finding weapons of mass destruction in Iraq, it need look no further than the drinking water of Basra. A UNICEF survey in November 1997 found that nearly 1 million children were malnourished.[7]

Are these statements merely metaphorical in their relevance to the comparable effect of weaponry? No. I am aware of what the UN Conference on Disarmament has defined as weapons of mass destruction. But in the real world, weapons of mass destruction come in endlessly variant form. And their relative danger should be measured by the criteria laid down earlier in this book, namely, scale, time-period and severity. The scale on which economic sanctions operate as a weapon of mass destruction can be calculated as affecting a country's whole population. This is the case with Iraq, where 1.5 million citizens have been killed of whom half were children. Nor was the destruction confined to cities alone as occurred with Hiroshima and Nagasaki where 60,000 and 40,000 were killed directly in atomic attacks. Sanctions have now been in force for six years, similar to the timeframe during which one European country exterminated millions of Jews in mid-century. Some forty Iraqi children are now dying each day. If sanctions are maintained in the present manner, this rate will of course increase. The timespan, moreover, extends beyond the killing, for the wounded soul of a nation and indeed of humanity needs time to heal, as we have seen so often in this bloodied century with the two world wars, with Cambodia and Bosnia. It is, in fact, indefinite, because of the physical and psychological damage inflicted on the next generation through prolonged malnutrition and disease.

The presence and alleged use of weapons of mass destruction in the Gulf region have proved controversial. The United States initially claimed that Iraq had used chemical weapons during the Gulf conflict, causing the so-called "Gulf War syndrome" in US servicemen. Subsequently, reports have attributed the syndrome to leakage of chemicals from Iraqi chemical storage sites following US bombing or post-conflict detonations.[8] Other reported explanations have included the use of previously untested vaccines on its own soldiers, and even the possible side-effects of various medicines. But all these possibilities seem not to be sufficient explanation. In fact, a scientific study conducted by a German physician, Dr Siegwart-Horst Günther, on US missile remains in Iraq and on the Kuwaiti

Figure 5.2.1 A Palestinian confronts Israeli soldiers at the entrance to the Aidi refugee camp, November 1997. "There are two extreme defensive reactions on the part of Palestinians to Israeli occupation," says Toujan Faisal. "One is the collective choice of survival by outnumbering the statistics of death through procreation. The other is the individual choice of suicidal death. Between these, the general attitude of the vast majority of the Arabs is to support the idea of their acquiring any kind of weapon available that will meet their defensive and deterrent needs." The way forward, she suggests, "is to metamorphose, as an international community, into something qualitatively different". (Courtesy Associated Press)

border, offers a different possibility. It is that the warheads of such missiles contained depleted uranium, an illegal substance.[9] I understand that previous research on similar though accidental cases of depleted uranium release has shown that it triggered an identical syndrome in both humans and animals in the Iraqi and Kuwaiti deserts and in Basra city – essentially manifested as mutations in new-born babies. Such uranium pollution from the US warheads had, it seems, penetrated the surrounding land, permeating it through the effect of rain. Thus, on the criteria of severity and timespan, the damage perpetrated to the planet is not insignificant.

The Arab people, and indeed the international community as a whole, are told that weapons of mass destruction are safe only in the hands of a few nation-states, and must above all not fall into the hands of "rogue states". The Arab memory, however, stretches back to the only use in history of nuclear weapons, which was perpetrated, although in wartime still illegally, against the civilian population of two cities in Japan. We are told that weapons of mass destruction must never fall into the hands of terrorists. But as some of my more objective colleagues in the West often put it, one man's terrorist is another man's freedom fighter. A former prime minister of Israel is alleged to have been a member of the group which assassinated the United Nations mediator in the 1940s. And Arab memories do not need to go so far back, since two Israeli agents were arrested in my country in 1997 with false Canadian passports and nerve gas to carry out the assassination of a Palestinian leader. State-terrorism is just as odious as that perpetrated by private groups, perhaps more so. It is consistency and integrity in the application of global norms that is lacking today, and that is what bedevils our rate of progress towards a better planet.

People in my part of the world are known for their high fertility rate. But the reasons are in fact not those usually assumed. Beyond all economic, educational and social factors involved, there is a psychological and instinctive need on the part of all humans for survival – not only as individuals but as families. Even within the Arab world, the Palestinian people are known for a higher fertility rate. Why? Simple. They run the higher risk of losing their children and young adult offspring. Paying the price of one's child in "martyrdom" in the pursuit of freedom seems to be the destiny of Palestinian parents.

So there are two extreme defensive reactions on the part of Palestinians to Israeli occupation. One is the collective choice of survival by outnumbering the statistics of death through procreation. The other is the individual choice of suicidal death. Between these, the general attitude of the vast majority of the Arabs is to support the idea of their acquiring any kind of weapon available that will meet their defensive and deterrent needs. It is on this rationale that some Arab nation-states refuse to surrender the sovereign right to acquire chemical weapons, just as Israel does with both chemical and nuclear weapons, just as the five permanent members of the Security Council do with nuclear weapons. At present the world is governed by an exclusive superpower club which accords consent to those who "may be entrusted" with weapons of mass destruction. That includes Israel on a selective and clandestine basis. Such consent is totally denied to Arabs. But it is the same major powers that have declared their own national interests in the area, retain a policy of first-use of, and have indeed threatened to use, weapons of mass destruction. And if the definition is broadened as I have proposed above, it is the same powers that have already used certain kinds of such weaponry against the Arab peoples. So the Arabs are for their part left with the only choice available, namely, the "atomic bomb of the poor". But for "poor", I suggest, read "subjugated" as well.

Diplomatically, the Arab world sends mixed signals through its national governments over the issue of weapons of mass destruction. Some ratify the treaties, some do not. But my own experience demonstrates clearly to me that the general sentiment of the people is for the development of any available weapon that will enable them to face up to the challenges of self-defence and survival. This is likely to remain the case until a truly objective and equitable international order that genuinely serves the "vital" Arab interests as fully as those of some other peoples is in place.

CONCLUSION

There is a point of logic involved in the above strategic reasoning. It concerns moral logic. Those who do not truly care about the wellbeing and safety of their own country lack credibility when they claim to care about the national interests of others, let alone the interests of the planet and humanity. And, conversely, those who claim to care for the whole planet and humanity must be able to address the grievances of the marginalized and victimized nation-states as well.

A further point of logic concerns the weapons themselves. To truly care about the wellbeing of a living thing – be it one's child, or an animal, the human race or indeed perhaps the planet – means to be required courageously and honestly to define the sources of danger to the beloved object and accurately to assess the relative degree of threat. One might appear to fulfil one's protective charge by issuing warnings over slippery stairs or poor food. These can indeed cause temporary, if normally reversible, harm. But it is the loaded gun that will wipe the child from the face of Earth. The same logic applies to weapons of mass destruction. Biological weapons do serious damage to human bodies, individually; chemical weapons also. But it is the nuclear weapon that can wipe humanity, and perhaps other higher forms of life, off the planet.

Specialists maintain that elimination of the nuclear stockpile will require a quarter of a century. The hazards of such a process have not been fully appreciated, and the cost will be astronomical as we see from the process underway in the former Soviet Union. Yet it must be done.

Other global threats exist, as this book shows clearly. Which nation-states are principally responsible for ozone depletion and climate change – damage to the planet through behaviour practised openly and on a daily basis by the North? Ironically, this global damage is caused through the use of chemicals. And much of the disposal of hazardous waste is undertaken in – exported to – the South.

The price of such waste disposal in Africa is $40 per tonne. Some of this waste enters my own country, Jordan. Corruption can go a long way for the interests of the North, but it is not strictly in their legitimate national interest. For these kinds of practice to be rectified in the South will require the exercise of true democracy, transparency and accountability. I have watched my sister from Kenya, who writes in this book, take a stand for that, just as I have in my own country. Women will, I believe, make a difference in politics, both at the national level and also at the global level. It is happening already.

A world free of weapons of mass destruction, a world with lower rates of industrial gases and chemical waste, will surely be to the benefit of the peoples of the South, even before it benefits those of the North. Saving the planet requires saving us in the South first. But it will not be achieved through the current policies of the leading nation-states, nor by global theorists who reconcile themselves to such policies. The way forward, surely, is to metamorphose, as an international community, into something qualitatively different. A new charter, a new organization. The latter deriving its strength from a global charter and other basic laws that draw from the spirit of the constitutions of the national democracies around the world – yet another irony. And such a charter will deal with the planet as the one homeland of humanity, caring equally for each part of it. Where the small nation-states of the world will enjoy the status of minorities, or provinces, of the larger whole.

This is not a dream; it is a realistic set of reflections and a proposal for sober consideration. The nation-states have met before in this world, to address not only the wrongs that led to previous conflicts but also to learn from the flaws of earlier experiments in international organization. The UN Charter, it is universally recognized, contains flaws of its own. And since its inception, the practice has, in certain respects, exacerbated those shortcomings. The more noble and up-lifting sections of the charter have been ignored or even breached, not least by the "superpower virus" that infiltrated the international system. We have failed twice to protect the planet through experiments in international organizations. Trying a third time, benefiting from the experience of the twentieth century, learning from the lessons of wrongs already committed, seems a logical and realistic way to proceed. Not simply with respect to the hazards of weapons of mass destruction, but also the growing list of fundamental global issues and questions that confront humanity and the planet we live on.

> To each, God has given a goal
> Towards which he must turn
> And then everyone must strike together,
> To achieve all that is good.
> Qur'an, Sura II: 148, 20

NOTES

1. See:

> It was on this level of diplomats and bureaucrats in the ministries of Washington and London, under the leadership of the US Department of State and the British Foreign Office, that some rough outlines of the new organization gradually took shape. Within two and a half years, these governmental experts produced a series of working papers and memoranda, serving first to clarify their own positions and to examine the political aims of their respective governments and, secondly, as a means of securing domestic support for their diplomatic aims . . . A paper entitled Draft Constitution of an International Organization . . . completed in August 1943 under the dominating influence of Hull, it was re-named Charter of the United Nations . . . Soon after [Tehran . . . t]his working paper was submitted to the [US] President and approved by him . . . By familiarizing the President with the issues involved, the Department of State was able to yield to the British Government which was pushing for a diplomatic exchange. This became possible only after including Congress in the deliberations. B. Simma (ed.), *The charter of the United Nations: a commentary* (Oxford: Oxford University Press, 1995), 4–5.
>
> It is true that President Roosevelt played a special role in the creation of the United Nations, but his role was not that of a contributor of ideas. It was the role of a propagator and political promoter of a peace organization as such . . . As far as Churchill is concerned, we know he originally visualized a concept of the post-war world which differed from the American one. He sympathized, it is true, with Roosevelt's concept of the four Great Powers as a kind of directorate leading a world of nation-states and guaranteeing their peaceful behaviour. (ibid., 2–23).

2. *America's national interests* (Commission on America's National Interests, Kennedy School of Government, Nixon Center for Peace and Freedom, The Rand Corporation, 1996).
3. IHT, 19 December 1997.
4. Ibid.
5. C. Varea & A. Maestro (eds), *Guerra y sanciones a Irak: Naciones Unidas y el "nuevo orden mundial"* (Madrid: La Catarata, 1997), 93–7.
6. CNN report on Jordan Television News, November 1997; also reported by Reuters.
7. UNDH, 26 November 1997.
8. "Gulf War troops may have been exposed to chemical weapons", Associated Press, and CNN, 21 June 1996, Microsoft Internet Explorer. Also: "Several theories have surfaced as to the possible causes, including chemical or biological weapons exposure, experimental vaccines, parasites and environmental pollutants. The bottom line, however, is that we are not certain what happened over there in the Iraqi desert", in "The Gulf War Syndrome – does it really exist?", statement by Hon. Cliff Stearns, US Congress. Also: "Pentagon acknowledges circulation of chemical weapons report", especially: "High-level US government officials knew in November 1991 that chemical weapons had been stored in an Iraqi depot blown up by US troops earlier that year, the Pentagon acknowledged yesterday", CNN, 28 August 1996, Microsoft Internet Explorer.
9. Varea & Maestro (eds), *Guerra y sanciones a Irak*, 119–25.

5.3 Israel

Naomi Chazan

> "We seek to resolve the disputes of the past over frontiers and respond to the call of new horizons of our age . . . Israel suggests to all the countries of the region to construct a mutually verifiable zone, free of surface-to-surface missiles and of chemical, biological and nuclear weapons."
>
> Shimon Peres, Foreign Minister of Israel, 1993

The tension between national interests on the one hand and the "planetary interest" in eliminating chemical and biological warfare on the other may appear, on the surface, to be especially strange in the case of Israel. It is, however, my contention that the national, regional and planetary interests of both Israel and its neighbours ultimately lie in conforming to the global standards pertaining to chemical and biological weapons. On both the regional and international levels, agreement and compliance can be achieved only through clear and appropriate methods of co-operative and reciprocal involvement in international arms reduction and elimination agreements. Agreement on these levels must be consonant with the vital interests of participating states. Drawing on the US–Soviet nuclear arms reduction as a useful model, I submit that mutual disarmament is the best and, perhaps in effect, the only path to secure national interests and stabilize the Middle East, which has been so traumatized by mutual mistrust and a perpetual concern for security.

Discussions of weapons reduction in general and those pertaining to chemical and biological weapons in particular are especially germane to the concept of the planetary interest. The prototypical versions of this concept in the League of Nations, the United Nations Charter of the 1940s, the more recent arms treaties, and the global conferences of the 1990s reflect a clear consensus on the need for a global dialogue over non-conventional warfare. Motivation for such dialogue and agreement originates from a concern extending beyond political and geographic borders, a concern for humanity as a whole.

Yet such broad-minded concern, though rich in rhetorical and perhaps visionary power, has proved to be a great challenge in the real world of political tension and conflict. This certainly comes as no surprise, as the interplay of national and global interests remains one of vigorous competition, rather than a consciously delicate balancing act. The global community continues to suffer from a lack of conceptual clarity and hence a paucity of conventions that delineate its ostensible aims. As a result, policy instruments that have the interest of the planet, or the whole of humanity, in mind are meagre and often inadequate. In these circumstances, national and global interests will continue to exist in competition. Any effort to establish global agreement and co-operation must be viewed in this light.

Thus, when the planetary interest is overwhelming but conflicts with national security interests, concerned parties need to find appropriate methods for attaining the desired results. These include built-in assurances on the part of the parties in question, as well as by the international community, to enforce conformity to international arms control agreements.

For much of the twentieth century the global community has been striving to develop a united vision to guide its conduct. Progress has been painfully slow, particularly in the areas of peace and arms control. It took some forty years – from the 1930s to the 1970s – for the world to agree on a definition of aggression, and it took another forty – from the 1950s to the 1990s – for agreement to be reached on a nuclear test ban. It has taken a comparable period of time for the international community to ban chemical and biological weapons. Even with international agreements in place, compliance is always a problem. For example, poisonous gases were banned under declarations and accompanying annexes from The Hague Conferences of 1899 and 1907, yet their deployment during the First World War demonstrated the need for a renewed and more binding commitment to prevent their use. International agreements prohibiting the use of certain types of weapon often become moot when individual states, for whatever reasons, place their national interests not only ahead of broader international commitments but also in direct conflict with the planetary interest.

Efforts to reconcile these two levels of interest require considerable creativity. International agreements based on the planetary interest must take into account and be firmly rooted in bilateral agreements, enacted in good faith, that address the national interests of involved parties, particularly with reference to weapons and defence-related issues. Recourse to the withdrawal clause can thus be pre-empted by using arms control agreement as an additional means of conflict resolution. However compelling the planetary interest in a given situation might be, states will inevitably enter into agreements of this magnitude with their own "local" national interests in mind. This crucial consideration cannot be denied or ignored. The goal must be to create means for addressing such localized concerns within the framework of internationally binding agreements.

Within this context, an understanding of chemical and biological weaponry in the Middle East in general and Israel in particular must be grounded first in the context of international attitudes towards non-conventional weapons and, secondly, in the diplomatic, security and economic concerns particular to the region and to Israel itself.

The BWC and the CWC are based on globally oriented understandings of the planetary interest and the strategies such an interest implies. Both rely on the prototypical concept of the planetary interest implicit in the UN Charter to explain the need for complete exclusion of the possibility of biological and chemical warfare. In addition to bolstering the principles of the charter, these conventions aim to enhance the degree of confidence among peoples; from a global perspective, they are essentially political agreements enacted for the sake of humanity. On this premise, any use of weapons of mass destruction is repugnant to the conscience of humanity, and no effort should be spared to minimize that risk. The global strategy – working towards the common international objective – is therefore the complete and effective prohibition of the development, production, acquisition, stockpiling, retention, transfer and use of such weapons, and the destruction of any that exist.

But the planetary interest cannot be realized without the compliance of member states. And the compliance of member states depends on their perceived national interests in relation to their geostrategic position, their security requirements and capabilities, and their economic interests. Israeli debate over ratification of these conventions, particularly the chemical weapons ban, which Israel has signed but not ratified, provides a fascinating case study of these dilemmas.

NATIONAL POLICY

The CWC is widely considered to be the most comprehensive and intrusive treaty ever enacted. The underlying strategy, given the threat of chemical weapons and the objective of preventing their use, is to develop a coalition of states interested in protecting their own national security as well as global security by banning the production, sale and use of such weapons. The politics implied is extensive, touching on economic and international trade issues as well as those related to the military and security.

Given the wide-ranging impact of this treaty, Israel must carefully weigh its national interests and choose a path that will succeed in securing its desired place in the international arena as well as protecting its own vital interests. The primary considerations in the current debate over ratification can be broken down into security, diplomatic and economic issues.

Security concerns

Since the inception of the state in 1948, Israeli security policy has traditionally been defined by its existence within a hostile environment. In 1948, Israel confronted neighbours on all sides bent on its destruction. Even since signing peace accords, first with Egypt (in 1979) and then with Jordan (1994), and in times of relative quiet, some of Israel's neighbours have provided refuge to militant organizations committed to threatening Israel's survival, some of which enjoy moral and financial support from third countries. The Israeli war in Lebanon, which has continued since 1982, represents just one such example.

Existence within a potentially hostile regional atmosphere, together with the small size of the country, has denied Israel the luxury of relegating security concerns to a secondary status. In an era of long-range missiles, Israel must be prepared to face adversaries far from its borders as well as those at its borders. During the first 50 years of Israel's independence, in the post Second World War tradition of technological preparedness, Israel has devoted a good deal of its human, economic and intellectual resources to defending itself militarily.

Undoubtedly, Israel would face formidable challenges from its neighbours were war to break out tomorrow. Table 5.3.1 shows the air-to-surface missile capability of neighbouring states, together with Israel. Perhaps what concentrates the mind even more is the regional surface-to-surface missile capability, as Israel's experience during the Gulf War testifies. That capability is illustrated by Table 5.3.2.

Table 5.3.1   Air-to-surface missile launching capabilities in the Middle East

State	Air-to-surface missile launching capabilities
Israel	AGM-45 *Shrike*, AGM-62A *Walleye* AGM-65 *Maverick*, AGM-78D *Standard Gabriel* III (mod.), *Hellfire*, TOW, *Popeye*
Jordan	TOW
Iran	AGM-65 *Maverick*, AS-10, AS-11, AS-14, C-801
Iraq	AM-39, AS-4, AS-5, AS-9, AS-11, AS-12, AS-30L, C-601
Syria	AT-2 *Swatter*, AS-7 *Kerry*, AS-12, HOT
Libya	*Exocet AM-39*, HOT
Saudi Arabia	AGM-65 *Maverick*, A-15, AS-30, *Sea Eagle*, AGM-45 *Shrike*
Egypt	AGM-65 *Maverick*, *Exocet* A-39, AS-12, AS-30, A-30L HOT

Source: *The military balance 1997–98* (London: International Institute for Strategic Studies, 1997).

Table 5.3.2   Surface-to-surface missile launching capabilities in the Middle East

State	Surface-to-surface missile launching capabilities
Israel	*Lance, Jericho I, Jericho II*
Iraq	SCUD
Iran	SCUD-B, SCUD-C, CSS-8, *Fajr*
Syria	FROG-7, SS-21, SCUD-B, SCUD-C, SS-C-1B, *Sepal* SS-C-3 coastal
Libya	FROG-7, SCUD-B
Saudi Arabia	PRC, CCS-2
Egypt	FROG-7, *Saqr-80* (trials), SCUD-B

At present, surface-to-surface missiles are considered the greatest threat to Israel's security, and there has been considerable speculation that several states in the region are expanding their capabilities in this area. Syria, in particular, has diverted much of its defence budget away from ground, air and naval forces and is suspected of investing those resources in developing missile capabilities similar to those held by the Iraqis during the Gulf War. Israeli diplomatic efforts recently succeeded in blocking a Syrian–Chinese agreement to purchase Chinese M-9 surface-to-surface missiles. But Syria has probably explored other options. The current Syrian assumption is that until the Arrow missile, a joint US–Israeli project, is completed within the next few years, Israel has no effective response to long-range missiles, particularly those with chemical warheads. However, according to a senior adviser to the minister of defence, Iran, Egypt and Iraq are also developing or conserving their capabilities in this area.[1]

Israeli intelligence anticipates that within the next few years Iran too will possess a formidable store of long-range missiles and non-conventional weaponry, including chemical, biological and nuclear weapons. In fact, Iran's spiritual leader, Ali Khameini, has delineated two objectives for his country: the production of long-range missiles and the acquisition of non-conventional weapons. Iran is believed to be developing a missile with a 1,300 km range – capable of reaching targets in any part of Israel, and a missile with a 2,000 km range is expected to follow. Russian technology is thought to play a major role in these developments, and both Israel and the United States have sent messages to Moscow demanding the termination of this co-operation. Both Iran and Syria are also suspected of developing or improving their weapons of mass destruction. Syria is exploring the possibility of scud missiles with warheads containing nerve gas and possibly biological substances as well. Western intelligence sources suspect that Iran is ten years closer to possessing nuclear capabilities than was formerly predicted.

Without a doubt, issues of compliance with international treaties are pertinent to this discussion, as the activities described above are taking place in direct violation of the international commitments indicated in Table 5.1.1. To the detriment of national, regional and planetary interests, political commitment to curbing non-conventional weapons does not ensure compliance. Not surprisingly, the wide disparity between agreement to international arms reduction and compliance is a cause of significant hesitation in Israel's deliberations over ratifying the cwc. In this atmosphere, security remains an uppermost concern for Israel.

Diplomatic issues

In addition to the wide range of security concerns, Israel must also take into account the broad diplomatic issues involved in deciding whether to ratify the cwc.

First, many Israeli strategists believe that meeting the terms of the convention would eliminate a critical element of Israel's "deterrence equation" by opening its arsenals to investigations of chemical, and perhaps later nuclear, capabilities. Such a situation would be particularly ominous if surrounding Arab states refused to join and Israel were the only state in the region obligated to disclose its holdings.[2] In addition, Israel must factor in the possibility that certain token states would join primarily to gain access to Israeli facilities and disseminate that information to non-signatory states after, as one government expert put it, having "learned everything they've been dying to know about us".[3] Thirdly, some Arab states have made their agreement to the cwc contingent on Israel's signing the NPT, which, though desirable in the long-run, is not feasible at present because of consistent government opposition over a period of time.

Aside from these regional pressures, Israel must also consider the role of its international allies. In particular, the United States – whose president is a staunch supporter of the treaty – might place Israel in a position where continued US support becomes contingent on Israeli ratification. On the other hand, this alliance may provide an opportunity to enter the agreement with an assurance that certain non-chemical weapons facilities will be protected from unsolicited questioning while chemical facilities are opened for inspection by other signatories.

In short, Israel must take into account regional and international pressures as well as strategic moves to gain or shield access to weapons capabilities.

Figure 5.3.1   "You might ask me: are there any additional quantities? Quite frankly, we don't know. We have to verify that", UN expert on Iraq's chemical weapons programme, November 1997. A Patriot anti-missile missile streaks towards an incoming Iraqi Scud over Tel Aviv, February 1991. If Israel does agree to ratify the Chemical Weapons Convention, says Naomi Chazan, a balance must be struck between its national interests, its regional interests, and its stake in the planetary interest. (Courtesy Popperfoto)

Economic interests

Pharmaceutical and petrochemical production are rapidly growing areas of the Israeli economy. If failure to sign the CWC results in economic restrictions on the importation of raw materials for the production of these products, the impact on the Israeli economy could be severe. At this juncture, moreover, the economic aspects of the CWC non-compliance cannot yet be evaluated. The weight of this factor in an Israeli decision may ultimately be contingent upon the readiness of signatories to enact sanctions or trade restrictions.

Seeking a balance

If Israel does agree to ratify the CWC, a balance must be struck between its national interests, its regional interests within the context of the Middle East, and its stake in the planetary interest. Such a balance would require assurances that Israel's vital security interests will be protected while complying with the requirements of the treaty.

The planetary interest, as described at the beginning of this chapter, is of great significance to Israel. As a contemporary democratic state, the protection of human lives and the maintenance of political stability are powerful criteria in national and foreign policy decisions.

Israel also has a considerable stake in attaining regional stability and normalization. In the worst-case scenario, the Middle East will not be able to endure another war that includes the threat or potential use of chemical weapons. The sheer force of such a conflict would be technologically unprecedented, and the danger to civilians on all sides would be alarming. After the Gulf War, it is clear that long-range missiles are capable of hitting civilian targets with ease, and there now exists a precedent for such attacks on civilians. As a region, the Middle East must accept the challenge of finding practical, long-term strategies for reducing rather than strengthening its non-conventional weapons capabilities.

At the state level, Israel's interests in non-conventional arms reduction are equally forceful. In addition to safeguarding the lives of its citizens and enhancing the stability of the region, participation in this convention will protect its economic interests and potential for growth. By joining other progressive and forward-thinking states in signing this treaty, Israel will assuredly benefit politically, diplomatically and economically within the international community. Participating in global efforts to reduce the threat of non-conventional weaponry will put Israel in the front line of enlightened states and will open doors for greater involvement in the international community.

CONCLUSION

In the post-Cold War era, all key political concepts must be reviewed and revised. The concepts both of "interest" and "security" are especially relevant. The proliferation of chemical and biological weaponry in recent decades has yielded yet another revolution in the international political sphere. Chemical and biological weapons production has increased in recent decades. Possessor states have threatened to use these weapons and some, in fact, have been used, as in the case of Iraq's actions against both Iran and the Kurdish population. Long-range delivery systems are now capable of projecting chemical and biological weapons across previously unheard-of distances.[4] All these factors contribute to a stressful peacetime environment and unspeakably tense crisis situations in regions where such weapons exist.

The concept of the planetary interest will prove useful in surveying the needs and desires of the world's population, and it must serve as a lodestar in all bilateral and multilateral negotiations pertaining to arms control. But this concept in and of itself cannot propel mistrustful, antagonistic states to destroy their weapons and join hands in one swift motion. Practical, sustainable achievements in arms reduction must be rooted in a variety of even-handed, well-mediated confidence-building measures that ensure a stable entrance into the post-convention atmosphere.

Antagonistic parties jointly entering such an agreement must be assured of several points. First, signatories must be confident that they are entering a clearly articulated, well-explicated agreement that demonstrates, in detail, the kinds of protection available to them and their populations in the event that such agreement is violated. Additionally, while agreements such as the BWC and CWC focus on one particular category of weapons, negotiations must take into account the "strategic connectivity" between various types of weapons and address the vital interests of states in both reducing their non-conventional weapons stores and protecting their national security.[5] And, thirdly, the specific role of sanctions and other penalties in responding to non-compliance must be very clear; an international agreement of this order cannot be taken seriously unless it includes strong and evenly applied penalties for non-compliance.

Beyond these requirements, however, reduction of non-conventional weapons stores cannot wait until peaceful conditions exist, particularly in the tumultuous Middle East. Both the earlier American–Soviet arms reductions and the more recent, though unfulfilled, Oslo Accords demonstrate that mutual suspicion and low expectation need not eliminate the possibility of limited agreement on issues of mutual concern.

In his address at the signing of the CWC in 1993, then Foreign Minister Shimon Peres outlined Israel's ideal vision for a new Middle East. Principal goals included mutual confidence between states, a collective understanding of security and a "mutually verifiable zone" free of surface-to-surface missiles and non-conventional weapons. Such conditions can only be met if arms control negotiations are mutually agreed upon and inclusive of all states in the region.[6] The political environment in the Middle East has changed drastically since 1993, but these changes cannot allow the issue of chemical and biological weaponry to fall from the list of regional priorities. The national security of nation-states and regions is not yet a fact; it cannot be realized in absolute and immutable terms. It is a process, and an imperfect one, towards which all countries must continually aspire.

As such, it is in Israel's interest as an enlightened state, as a key player in the broader region and as a partner in the global community to work towards the goal of banning chemical and biological weapons. Ratifying the cwc, under the appropriate circumstances, is the first step. In the long run this goal is attainable, but only if other states within the region are willing to redefine their national interests and align them with these comprehensive planetary goals.

NOTES

1. R. Ben-Yishai, "Syrian missiles: the primary strategic threat to Israel", *Yediot Ahronot*, 22 June 1997, 8–9.
2. S. Rodan, "Bitter choices: Israel's chemical dilemma", *Jerusalem Post*, 15 August 1997, 10.
3. Ibid.
4. C. Flowerree & B. Roberts, "Chemical weapons arms control", in *Arms control and confidence-building measures in the Middle East*, A. Platt (ed.) (US Institute of Peace: Washington, DC, 1992), 103–4.
5. Ibid., 111.
6. Shimon Peres, "A farewell to chemical arms", address delivered at the signing ceremony of the Chemical Weapons Convention, Paris, 13 January 1993.

The author gratefully acknowledges the assistance of Ms. Sarah Willen, parliamentary assistant, the Knesset, Jerusalem, in the preparation of this chapter.

SECTION II

Global environmental integrity

The global environment is changing more rapidly than at any time in recent centuries. As a result, surprises must be expected and the twenty-first century could see significant environmental change. At the same time, the human consumption of energy, water and non-renewable resources is increasing on both a total and a per capita basis, and shortages may ensue in many parts of the world even if environmental conditions remain unchanged.[1]

THE GLOBAL PROBLEM

The Brundtland Commission spoke of the "environmental trends that threaten to radically alter the planet [and] threaten the lives of many species upon it, including the human species". The commission observed that

> The planet is passing through a period of dramatic growth and fundamental change. Our human world of 5 billion must make room in a finite environment for another human world. The population could stabilize at between 8 billion and 14 billion sometime next century . . . These related changes have locked the global economy and global ecology together in new ways. We have in the past been concerned about the impacts of economic growth upon the environment. We are now forced to concern ourselves with the impacts of ecological stress – degradation of soils, water regimes, atmosphere and forests – upon our economic prospects. We have in the more recent past been forced to face up to a sharp increase in economic interdependence among nations. We are now forced to accustom ourselves to an accelerating ecological interdependence among nations. Ecology and economy are becoming ever more interwoven – locally, regionally, and globally – into a seamless net of causes and effects.[2]

In 1988, one year after the Brundtland Report, the British prime minister noted that, because of population growth, potential agricultural technologies and the use of fossil fuels, "we have unwittingly begun a massive experiment with the system of this planet itself . . . Protecting the balance of nature is therefore one of the great challenges of the twenty-first century". The Soviet foreign minister likened environmental threats to a "second front" which was gaining an urgency equal to that of the "nuclear-and-space threat". Human activity was turning into a global aggression against the very foundation of life on Earth.[3] Concerned over the implications of climate change for their adult lives, youth leaders are expressing their views in similar manner.[4] And US Senator, now Vice-President, Gore has expressed the view that

> we must take bold and unequivocal action; we must make the rescue of the environment the central organizing principle for civilization. Whether we realize it or not, we are now engaged in an epic battle to right the balance of our earth, and the tide of this battle will turn only when the majority of people in the world become sufficiently aroused by a shared sense of urgent danger to join in an all-out effort . . . Adopting a central organizing principle – one agreed to voluntarily – means embarking on an all-out effort to use every policy and program, every law and institution, every treaty and alliance, every tactic and strategy, every plan and course of action – to use, in short, every means to halt the destruction of the environment and to preserve and nurture our ecological system.[5]

There is a close interrelationship between local, national, regional and global environmental issues: the Union Carbide disaster at Bhopal, the nuclear industry disaster at Chernobyl, the acid rain falling on forests in Europe and North America, ozone depletion and the hole over the Antarctic, the Rhine River chemical spill, the freighter carrying toxic ash which went from port to port for two years without being permitted to dock, the continuing deforestation in both temperate and tropical belts, species extinction, shore and riverine pollution, the *Exxon Valdez* oil spill, drought and desertification, excessively strong typhoons in South Asia and hurricanes in North America and the Caribbean and the forest-fire smoke and haze over South East Asia. Some of these are the result of an interrelated series of climatic and biospherical disturbances arising from human activity. Others are more localized accidents that do not impact on the planet as a whole.

Which environmental problems today threaten the vital planetary interest? In Chapter 1, the distinction was drawn between threats to the very existence or viability of the species and those which might affect the human condition but not its viability. The former involve the vital planetary interest; the latter do not. Applying this criterion to contemporary environmental problems is complex. It is contended here that the two most-recognized issues – ozone depletion and climate change – demonstrably meet the criterion of the vital planetary interest. Ozone depletion affects the whole planet in the sense of diminishing the stratospheric ozone layer of Earth, albeit in greater degree at present in the southern hemisphere. Climate change affects the whole planet in the sense of altered temperature and precipitation. Homo sapiens has survived radical changes in climate throughout its evolution, but those earlier experiences were natural phenomena to which our ancestors, few in number and innocent of the cause, responded nomadically in an instinctive and largely unwitting manner. In our modern time, such potential planetary change is anthropogenically produced, recognized for what it is by an international community of nation-states, and can only be responded to effectively through the provision of global political constructs. Such a construct is the vital planetary interest.

Might other environmental issues also be accepted as a threat to the vital planetary interest? Persistent environmentally mediated toxins, for example, such as PCBs and other "hormone-disrupter" chemicals which threaten reproductive potential and human development might indeed be so regarded. The dissipation of such synthetic chemicals, radiation from weapons testing and the leaching of heavy metals are of global proportion; it is possible, for example, to trace the planetary distribution of such phenomena in polar ice. Lead can be measured in the atmosphere in similar manner to chlorofluorocarbons or carbon dioxide. Few humans do not have traces of DDT and other pesticides in their body. Do these developments, if they risk a significant deleterious effect on human intelligence and fertility, not threaten the vital planetary interest? Another class of problem is the spread of infectious disease, as the global drama of AIDS vividly shows. Is the fight against AIDS not in the vital planetary interest?

The answers to such questions lie in the future. It is for humanity itself – the international community – to determine, with the passage of time, what meets the criteria for action in the vital planetary interest. It is sufficient now to note that ozone depletion and climate change have effectively been perceived as such. They are therefore explored in this section. The underlying point here, however, is that, as noted in Chapter 1, if any issue is accepted by the international community as threatening the vital planetary interest, then far-reaching political consequences will be set in train, involving judgements of the legitimate national interest and legitimate global power.

THE GLOBAL OBJECTIVE AND STRATEGY

The Brundtland Report introduced the concept of "sustainable development" which has become one of the principal goals of the international community in the 1990s. Sustainable development is defined as development that "meets the needs of the present without compromising the ability of future generations to meet their own needs".[6] There are, in the report's view, limits to economic growth, but not the "absolute limits" whose theoretical existence was proposed and vigorously debated in the 1970s.[7] Instead, the report notes the more elastic limitations "imposed by the present state of technology and social organization on environmental resources and by the ability of the biosphere to absorb the effects of human activities", not a "fixed state of harmony" but rather a "process of change".[8]

Those "elastic limitations" will depend henceforth on restoring a natural equilibrium to Earth, a harmonious balance between environmental integrity and the developmental aspirations of humanity. Environment and development, the twin foci of the two Earth Summits in 1992 and 1997, are two sides of the same coin – attaining humanity's objective over the next half-century of sustainable living on the home planet. The focus of Section II is on the environment – restoring a global environmental integrity that has already to a significant extent been lost through developmental activity. The focus of Section III is on the broader challenge of attaining an enduring equilibrium with Earth – a global sustainability in all human activities, with an optimal relationship between population size and economic activity.

The global objective for the environment, therefore, is the restoration of Earth's environment in the two areas that currently threaten the vital planetary interest: ozone depletion and climate change. The strategy to achieve that goal is through two legal instruments: the Vienna Framework Convention for the Protection of the Ozone Layer and its Montreal Protocol with revision; and the Framework Convention on Climate Change and its Kyoto Protocol.

PRESCRIBED NATIONAL POLICIES

With both issues, the framework conventions and associated protocols prescribe certain policies and measures for nation-states to carry out in order to attain the strategic goals of ozone protection and climate staibilization. In the former case, those measures are virtually universally accepted, are binding on the states, and specify a finite time-period for implementation. With the latter, such features are not yet in place. The Kyoto Protocol, as agreed in December 1997, frees the developing countries from any legal obligations – something that is the subject of continuing negotiation. Clearly, there is still some way to go before even the policy prescription on climate change is finalized. The specific policies and measures for both ozone protection and climate stabilization are explored in Chapters 6 and 7.

LEGITIMATE NATIONAL INTERESTS

Changes to the global environment and the global strategy to rectify their adverse effects and prevent further change bring into question the future of national sovereignty and the relationship of one nation's freedom to another's. In the view of one recognized expert:

> The nature of national sovereignty is changing. The global environmental trends – loss of species, ozone depletion, deforestation on a scale that affects world climate, and the greenhouse effect itself – all pose potentially serious losses to national economies, are immune to solution by one or a few countries, and render geographic borders irrelevant. By definition, then, they pose a major challenge to national sovereignty... National security depends on global security. Within that context, North–South relations will be profoundly different.[9]

It is generally believed that environmental concerns are confined mainly to the North, and that countries and citizens of the South are more concerned with economic development at the cost of the environment. An opinion survey of 24 countries, however, indicates otherwise. A "State of the Planet" international opinion poll was conducted in 1993 with significant findings. Nine questions were asked of citizens in 24 countries around the world. The results were as follows:

Health of the Planet 1993 (nine propositions):

1. Environmental problems are the most important problem facing my nation.
2. Environmental problems are a very serious issue in my country.
3. I am "greatly" or "fairly" concerned about the environment.
4. The quality of the environment in my country is very bad.
5. Environmental problems affect my health a great deal.
6. Protecting the environment is more important than economic growth.
7. I am willing to pay higher prices to protect the environment.
8. Citizens, rather than government or business and industry, should have primary responsibility for environmental protection.
9. Individuals and citizens groups can have a great effect in solving environmental problems.

Table II.1   Opinion survey on the environment: selected countries (% respondents in agreement with question)

Country	Q.1	Q.2	Q.3	Q.4	Q.5	Q.6	Q.7	Q.8	Q.9
North									
Canada	10	53	89	18	25	67	61	23	43
Denmark	13	26	53	12	11	77	78	24	22
Finland	28	21	63	13	10	72	53	13	19
Germany	9	67	63	22	61	73	59	25	13
Ireland	39	32	73	10	21	65	60	19	43
Japan	12	42	66	31	15	57	31	16	11
Netherlands	39	27	71	24	17	58	65	23	17
Norway	7	40	77	10	17	72	72	17	43
Portugal	25	51	90	30	39	53	61	32	35
Switzerland	20	63	42	21	20	62	70	35	36
UK	3	36	81	27	27	56	70	12	29
US	11	51	85	28	45	58	65	29	38
South									
Brazil	2	50	80	41	18	71	53	60	46
Chile	20	56	70	41	13	64	64	38	46
Hungary	1	52	79	48	24	53	49	25	9
India	21	51	77	44	40	43	56	34	39
Mexico	29	66	83	31	23	71	59	43	59
Nigeria	1	45	87	34	49	30	28	22	59
Philippines	2	37	94	28	50	59	30	43	57
Poland	1	66	25	71	59	58	49	9	17
Russia	9	62	78	69	65	56	39	9	17
South Korea	9	67	80	57	10	63	71	28	48
Turkey	18	61	40	44	31	43	44	24	52
Uruguay	3	44	82	28	26	64	54	43	41

Source: R.E. Dunlap & G.H. Gallup Jr, *Health of the planet* (Princeton, N.J.: George H. Gallup International Institute, 1993).[10]

Drawing conclusions from the survey, the analysts conducting the poll noted:

> the growing credibility of the core tenet of an environmental worldview; the inability of the Earth to cope with the increasing scale of human impact. Personal experience, combined with increased awareness of the global impact of human activities, has likely made people around the world begin to recognize that their welfare is inextricably related to that of the environment.[11]

The two issues comprising the vital planetary interest, ozone protection and climate stabilization, are the subject of Chapters 6 and 7.

NOTES

1. *Agenda 21 – The United Nations programme of action for sustainable development*, text negotiated by governments at the United Nations Conference on Environment and Development (UNCED), 3–14 June 1992, Rio de Janeiro, Brazil, para. 35.10 (hereafter *Agenda 21*).
2. World Commission on Environment and Development, *Our common future* (Oxford: Oxford University Press, 1987), 4, 5.
3. Prime Minister Thatcher (UK) and Foreign Minister Schevardnadze (USSR), quoted in J.T. Mathews (ed.), *Preserving the global environment: the challenge of shared leadership* (New York: W.W. Norton, 1991), 17.

4. See, for example, the statement of the International Youth and Student Movement for the United Nations (ISMUN), at Kyoto, December 1997:

> Young people and youth NGOs have taken the lead in many countries in the new search for the new production and consumption patterns which are required to avert the disastrous consequences of climate change. Yet little progress has been made because of the failure of the richest and most powerful countries to act in the interest of present and future generations ... The single greatest threat to the global climate and survival of mankind would be the use of nuclear weapons leading to a nuclear winter ... The threat of climate change represents a great challenge to generate the new and additional resources required for sustainable development (ISMUN; e-mail: jlonn@undp.org).

5. A. Gore, *Earth in the balance: ecology and the human spirit* (New York: Plume/Penguin, 1993), 269, 274.
6. *Our common future*, 8.
7. See, for example, D.L. Meadows et al., *The limits to growth* (New York: Universe Books, 1972).
8. *Our common future*, 8, 9.
9. Mathews, *Preserving the global environment*, 31, 33.
10. Also reported in "Of global concern: results of the health of the planet survey", *Environment* **35**(9), 7–39, 1993. See also, R.E. Dunlap, "International attitudes towards environment and development", *Greenglobe yearbook 1994* (Oxford: Oxford University Press, 1994), 115–26; and R.E. Dunlap & A.G. Mertig, "Global concern for the environment: is affluence a prerequisite?", *Journal of Social Issues* **51**(4), 121–37, 1995.
11. "Of global concern", *Environment* **35**(9), 7–39.

CHAPTER SIX

Ozone protection

6.1 Introduction

Ozone depletion is a clear example of, in the words of a former head of UNEP, "a global problem that requires global action".[1] The revolutionary implications of the global ozone issue for international politics and diplomacy are by now well recognized. As one of the policy-makers in the 1980s put it:

> Throughout most of the twentieth century, diplomats have concentrated on questions of political and economic relations among nation-states, the traditional subjects of diplomacy. In the period following World War II, other issues arose, spurred by the information revolution, the development needs of newly independent nations, and technical advances in nuclear energy and electronics. As the century closes, a third set of international problems – those relating to the health of the planet – is coming to the fore, presenting new challenges to diplomacy. These problems will test the ability of governments and their diplomats to organize themselves for new dimensions in foreign relations, and to negotiate agreements that require departures from the traditional nation-state orientations of diplomacy towards patterns of global management still to be developed. The threatened depletion of the Earth's ozone layer is a prime example of such challenges.[2]

THE GLOBAL PROBLEM

Ozone, which in natural conditions comprises less than one part per million (ppm) in the atmosphere, is 90% concentrated above 10 km in altitude. The ozone layer protects the Earth and its fauna and flora from harmful levels of ultra-violet solar radiation by filtering it down to acceptable levels for life.[3] Too great an exposure to ultra-violet rays causes skin cancer and eye cataracts in animals and humans, yield losses in crops and destroys the phytoplankton that underlies the marine food chain.

In 1985, scientific findings established that ozone levels over Antarctica between September and November had fallen by 50% since the 1960s. The "ozone hole", which has appeared over the Antarctic every southern spring, in September 1995 covered an area of 10 million sq. km, twice the area of the previous year, approximately 2% of the surface of the planet – the size of Europe. Subsequent findings suggest that ozone depletion has spread around the planet's stratosphere and has become a global phenomenon. In 1995, WMO reported "unusually low" levels over the northern hemisphere. Siberia was the worst affected, with 35% depletion. Between October 1994 and March 1995, the average loss over Europe was 11%, and over North America 7%. In March 1995, the Arctic recorded depletion for the first time, at 25%. The greatest ozone depletion recorded to date over a populated area was over a town in Argentina.[4] Recent UNEP scientific reports conclude that "reductions in stratospheric ozone are continuing, both in the Antarctic with the reappearance of the ozone 'hole' each spring, and at other locations and times in both hemispheres",[5] and that "new concerns have been raised by record low ozone, and associated higher UV-B radiation at the Earth's surface, over populated areas of the northern hemisphere during late winter and early spring".[6] One finding in 1997 reported a 20% reduction over the Arctic in March 1997 from the previous year.[7]

The threat was officially recognized by the international community in the context of the early negotiations for the 1985 Vienna Framework Convention for the Protection of the Ozone Layer which recorded an awareness of the "potentially harmful impact on human health and the environment through modification of the ozone layer".[8]

THE GLOBAL OBJECTIVE AND STRATEGY

The vital planetary interest lies in an early reduction and total phase-out of all ozone-depleting substances (ODS). The international community recognized the global objective, in response to that threat, as "protect[ion of] human health and the environment against adverse effects resulting from modification of the ozone layer".[9] Such adverse effects meant changes in the physical environment or biota, including changes in climate, which have significant deleterious effects on human health or on the composition, resilience and productivity of natural and managed ecosystems, or on materials useful to humankind.[10]

Over a period of four years, from March 1981 to March 1985, negotiations were completed on a framework convention on ozone depletion. Shortly thereafter and within a nine-month period, from December 1986 to September 1987, negotiations were completed on a protocol to the convention that restricted national production and consumption of ozone-depleting substances. In terms of traditional diplomatic action, this is rapid work by the international community.

The global strategy for attaining the above objective was identified in the 1987 Montreal Protocol, ratified by 163 countries by December 1997. Essentially, the strategy involves "precautionary measures to control equitably total global emissions of substances that deplete it [the ozone layer], with the ultimate objective of their elimination on the basis of developments in scientific knowledge, taking into account technical and economic considerations".[11] The negotiations revolved largely around agreeing on what was "equitable" in this context.

PRESCRIBED NATIONAL POLICIES

The 1987 Montreal Protocol imposed binding obligations on parties to implement national cuts from 1986 CFC production and consumption levels of 20% by 1994 and 50% by 1999. One major exception to the "national-global" formula was entered: in the name of global equity to atone for historical emissions by the North, a concession was entered for the South in which developing countries could defer the phase-out regime over a ten-year grace period, provided their annual calculated per capita consumption remained below 0.3 kg.[12] Thus, the "basic domestic needs" concept can be seen as relating directly to the legitimate national interest of developing countries.

No sooner had the Montreal Protocol been concluded than new scientific evidence showed its provisions to be inadequate in the face of increasing levels of global ozone depletion, requiring more urgent negotiations for further cuts in controlled and other substances. The ensuing 1990 London, 1992 Copenhagen and 1995 Vienna revisions were based on the same methodology. States agreed once more on national cuts, increasingly severe in each case. The current regime is laid out in Table 6.1.1.

Agenda 21 of the 1992 UNCED Earth Summit calls for a number of national policies with respect to ozone protection, viz.: ratify, accept and approve the Montreal Protocol and its 1990 amendments; pay contributions towards the Vienna/Montreal trust funds and the interim multilateral ozone fund promptly; make available substitutes for CFCs and other ozone-depleting substances and facilitate the transfer of alternative technologies to developing countries to help them comply with the protocol. *Agenda 21* also asked countries to support further expansion of the Global Ozone Observing System by funding additional systematic observation stations, especially in the southern hemisphere.[13]

Success of the phase-out regime depends on the transfer of ozone-friendly technologies to the South and financial assistance to facilitate it. In 1990 a financial mechanism was incorporated in the Montreal Protocol to address this need. Part of the mechanism is a Multilateral Fund, designed to meet the incremental costs faced by some countries and act as a clearing-house to facilitate such technology transfer. Some $668 million had been pledged by September 1997 (see Table 6.1.2), although only $526 million had been paid. A meeting in Costa Rica in November 1996 decided the replenishment level of the fund for 1997–9, and it is estimated that by 2000 contributions will exceed $1 billion. Yet, in the view of some countries this amount is not sufficient for the purpose, given the importance of the strategic objective.[14]

Observations show a slowing, and in some cases a reversal, of the increases in atmospheric concentrations of major ODS. Nevertheless, the risk of increased ozone depletion is likely to continue for the next three or four years, with depletion peaking around 2000. Recovery of the ozone layer is

Table 6.1.1 Phase-out regime of ozone-depleting substances (percentage cuts*)

Substance		1994	1995	1996	2001	2003	2005	2010	2015	2016	2020	2040
Halon	a	100										
	b						50	100				
CFC	a	75		100								
	b					20	50	100				
CT	a		85	100								
	b						85	100				
MCF	a	50		100								
	b					freeze	30	70	100			
Meth.br.	a				50	70	100					
	b								100			
HCFC	a							65	90		100	
	b									freeze		100

* Original base-line year is 1986; subsequent base-line years are, variously, 1989, 1991, 1995–97, 1989–2000, and 2015.
Key: CFC: chlorofluorocarbon; CT: carbon tetrachloride; MCF: methyl chloroform; HCFC: hydrochlorofluorocarbon; Meth. br.: methyl bromide.
Note: a = developed countries; b = developing countries (Article 5 parties).
Sources: Phase-out schedule agreed at 9th Meeting of the Parties, Montreal, September 1997 (supplied by Ozone Action Programme of UNEP IE, Paris). Also: UN press release HE/922, 8 December 1995.

Table 6.1.2 Contributions to the ozone multilateral fund (US $million)

Country	Accumulated contributions, 1991–6	1997 contributions (as at 30 September)
United States	174	39
Japan	99	28
Germany	72	17
Russia	55	8
France	49	12
United Kingdom	40	10
Italy	34	10
Canada	25	6
Spain	17	4
Other	103	23
Total	668	157

Source: UNEP/Oz/.Pro/ExCom/23/3 (UNEP IE Ozone Action Programme, Paris), 5.

projected to take about fifty years. Health and environmental impacts are projected to continue beyond that.[15]

There are, in UNEP's view, a number of approaches that would steepen the initial fall from peak haloncarbon levels in the early decades of the twenty-first century and speed up the eventual recovery of the ozone layer. They are: elimination of the emissions of methyl bromide from agricultural structural and industrial activity by 2001; elimination of the emission of HCFCs by 2004; and ensuring that halons and CFCs contained in existing equipment are never released to the atmosphere. Implementation of these measures could speed up the decline of industrial chlorine in the atmosphere by up to 30% over the next 50 years.[16]

LEGITIMATE NATIONAL INTERESTS

The Montreal Protocol with its amendments is widely viewed as a model of global co-operation against a global threat. The UN secretary-general has expressed the view that, in the case of ozone depletion, the international community has moved with "astonishing speed from concern to discussion, from discussion to agreement, and from agreement to action".[17] It is perhaps the clearest example to date of the "precautionary principle" in operation, with international action being taken after reasonable scientific evidence but in advance of any widespread impact on human health or ecosystems. Global production and consumption of the major ozone-depleting substances have decreased markedly – consumption has dropped by over 80% since the regime was introduced. But as the secretary-general noted, the ozone layer will heal only if the phase-out of all ozone depleting substances continues on an urgent basis. Some countries, for example, Belarus, Bulgaria, Poland, Russia and Ukraine, have indicated that they may miss their phase-out targets. There is, moreover, a disturbing new trend in the form of illegal trade in CFCs estimated at some 25,000 tonnes per year.[18]

There is also a degree of scepticism over the extent to which enlightened governmental leadership forged the way to success of the ozone regime, as compared with a dawning recognition of commercial advantage on the part of the manufacturers during the critical period of the late 1980s. Once the technical and financial viability of alternative technologies was discerned, opposition from the private sector diminished and governments found new space in which to negotiate. Thus, it is sometimes contended, it has yet to be demonstrated that humanity is capable of turning away from future global disaster when compelling corporate interests are in favour of "business-as-usual".[19]

In considering the legitimate national interests of all nation-states in the face of a global problem such as ozone depletion, responsibility and vulnerability are the relevant considerations. In the early stage of the ozone problem, the "responsible" states were few in number, with the US producing 46% of the global share in 1974, the EU 38%, and Japan and the USSR most of the remainder. The "victim" states were also few: non-producing countries close to Antarctica such as Australia and New Zealand, Chile and Argentina, have already been significantly harmed through the actions of northern hemisphere producer countries.

Of these, two countries are selected for consideration of the legitimate national interest: Argentina and Japan. Japan is the world's second largest producer and a minor "victim'; Argentina is perhaps the world's major "victim" and a minor producer. Japan contributes some 12% of the global ozone depleting substances and is thus seen as a major contributing country. Argentina produced a tiny fraction of global output. It has recorded the highest ozone depletion of any inhabited area in the world. Both countries can be seen as tied together inextricably, from vastly different historical national interests, in pursuit of the planetary interest. How do Argentina and Japan each see their country's legitimate national interest as relating to the planetary interest?

NOTES

1. M. Tolba, *Saving our planet* (London: Chapman & Hall, for UNEP, 1992), 19.
2. D. Newsom, "Foreword", in R. Benedick, *Ozone diplomacy: new directions in safeguarding the planet* (Cambridge, Mass.: Harvard University Press, 1991).
3. "Ozone layer" means the layer of atmospheric ozone above the planetary boundary layer: see Vienna Convention for the Protection of the Ozone Layer, March 1985, para. 1.1 (hereafter Vienna Convention).
4. World Meteorological Organization findings, in "Current state of the ozone layer", (http://www.greenpeace.org/~ozone/radiant/2rad.html).
5. "Environmental effects of ozone depletion: executive summary", United Nations Environment Programme, Nairobi, October 1996, 1.
6. Ibid., September 1997, 1.
7. Geophysical research letter, *IHT*, 17 November 1997.

8. Vienna Convention, 1st preambular para.

9. Ibid., 8th preambular para.

10. Ibid., para. 1.2.

11. Montreal Protocol on Substances that Deplete the Ozone Layer, September 1987, 6th preambular para. (hereafter Montreal Protocol).

12. Ibid., Article 5, Special Situation of Developing Countries. "Calculated" in this context means "tons multiplied by ozone-depleting potential (ODP)".

13. *Agenda 21*: 9.24 (a) and (b).

14. United Nations document HE/941, 8 November 1996.

15. Based on assumed compliance with the amended Montreal Protocol (Copenhagen 1992) by all nations, the stratospheric chlorine abundances will continue to grow from their current levels (3.6 ppB) to a peak (of about 3.8 ppB) around the turn of the century... After around the turn of the century, the level of stratospheric chlorine and bromine will begin a decrease that will continue into the 21st and 22nd centuries... Global ozone losses and the Antarctic ozone hole were first discernible in the late-1970s, and are predicted to recover in about the year 2045, other things being equal (UNEP, "Scientific assessment ozone depletion 1994: executive summary", 19 August 1994).

16. Ibid.

17. UNDH, 16 September 1997.

18. UN document E/CN.17/1996/22, 20 February, para. 14–16.

19. To cite one authoritative view:

It is increasingly clear that it will be companies, and not governments, that will trigger the political sea change necessary for real reductions in greenhouse gas emissions... These are the guys with the future in their hands. They could install millions of solar panels across North America for the money it will cost them to explore and develop the northeast Atlantic oilfield... Perhaps one day they will. And they will do it because they see a commercial advantage. Then, the American negotiating position will change. Cutting emissions of greenhouse gases will seem, even in the business heartlands of the US, as natural and self-evidently a good thing as banishing London's peasouper smogs did in the 1950s, or saving the ozone layer in the 1990s (Fred Pearce in *New Scientist*, 15 November 1997, 54).

6.2   Argentina

Dante Caputo

"We are facing a danger as big as humanity has ever faced."
Dr Mostafa Tolba, Executive Director UNEP, April 1992

Not many people have heard of Ushuaia. It is a small and undisturbed town of some 100,000 souls, lying at the southern tip of my country on Tierra del Fuego – far in the south, 55 degrees South, the most southern inhabited town on Earth if you exclude the settlements of Antarctica. It is not too far from Las Malvinas, the cause of so much sorrow and pain between Argentina and Great Britain. It nestles close to cabo dos Hornos, known to English-speakers as Cape Horn, the rough and bitterly cold tip of the Americas around which explorers were obliged to sail in centuries past and adventurers choose to sail today. The area itself is something of a Mecca for campers and trekkers. The tourist literature, with supreme and unwitting irony, calls it the "land of fire".

In 1996, Ushuaia recorded a 35% depletion in the stratospheric ozone layer above the town.[1] With that level of depletion, humans quickly develop skin cancer and cataracts, and crops experience genetic mutation. It is the highest recorded ozone depletion above any town on the planet. It is not natural and it is not pleasant. Without any ozone at all, higher life-forms on this planet would be destroyed.

Argentina did not request this national threat. We did nothing to invite it. Nor, for that matter, did other countries intend it. It is not the traditional national security problem that countries have been used to combating over the years, like the Malvinas dispute which took so many young men's lives in 1982. Ozone depletion is, to cite Dr Prins, of the new kind – one of our modern "threats without enemies". We Argentinians have no enemies over CFC production, even though our national security is threatened by its manufacture from other nations. Humanity simply produced it and brought the danger upon itself. Ozone depletion is a new kind of threat and humanity is unused to responding to it. Why? Because the threat comes from normal and non-belligerent behaviour, it is not directed aggressively at anyone, and a new kind of response is required – global co-operation rather than national defence for a new model of security. Perceiving the world as one, and acting together as one, not just in a philosophical manner but politically. We humans are on the edge of change. If we can respond to the threat of ozone depletion and resolve the problem, and others like it, we shall have turned a corner. A very important corner, and the world will finally have matured politically.

NATIONAL POLICY

Argentina is doing what it can to help resolve the problem of ozone depletion. It took us a while, back in the 1980s, to wake up to the call. We did not produce much in the way of chlorofluorocarbons in Argentina in those days. When the negotiations for the Montreal Protocol began in 1986, one country, located in the Americas, accounted for 30% of global output of the ozone-depleting substances. After the US, Japan was the second highest producer, with some 12% while the Soviet Union produced about 10%. So these three countries were responsible for over half of the planet's depletion of ozone. Other countries, of which mine was one, produced much smaller amounts – Canada, China, Australia, Brazil, Mexico, Venezuela, India and Argentina.

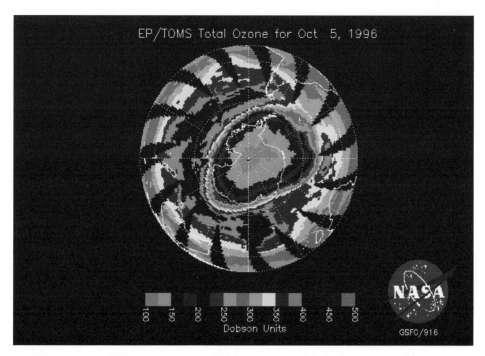

Figure 6.2.1 "Not many people have heard of Ushuaia", says Dante Caputo. But in 1996 the ozone layer above the small town at the bottom of Argentina recorded a 35% depletion. Here, NASA satellite imagery shows the ozone hole over Antarctica (the continent etched in white outline) in October of that year. Inhabited lands also identifiable are South America, southern Africa, Australia and New Zealand. "If we respond successfully to the threat of ozone depletion and resolve the problem", says Mr Caputo, "we shall have turned a corner. A very important corner, and the world will finally have matured politically." (Courtesy NASA).

As negotiations commenced, Argentina was largely uncommitted to the global objective of stratospheric ozone protection. The level of national awareness of the ozone threat was not yet sufficiently high. But, with the revelations from the scientific community in the months that followed concerning the ozone hole's appearance over the Antarctic each southern spring, that changed very fast. After it appears around September each year, the hole drifts north over the most southern countries on the planet – Australia and New Zealand, Chile and Argentina. But Chile and Argentina extend further south, so we suffer the most. And that began to drive national policy early in the negotiations over the protocol. We chose, along with Mexico and Venezuela, to support the proposal for a 50% cut in the substances then targeted.

When each of the negotiations has been concluded, Argentina has duly appended its signature. The Vienna Framework Convention we were an original signatory to in March 1985. Our parliament ratified it in January 1990 – ratification can take some time when there is a backlog of legislation following dictatorial rule.[2] The Montreal Protocol, completed in September 1987, we signed nine months later and ratified in May 1990.[3] The 1990 London revisions we ratified in September 1992 and the 1992 Copenhagen revisions in December 1994.[4]

In the late 1980s, we had already undertaken to initiate scientific investigation and evaluation, monitoring, development and legislation into the ozone layer and to seek out and adopt alternative technologies to ozone-depleting substances.[5] We then set to translating those international obligations into national law with implementing legislation. In 1991, we legislated for the control of CFCs 11, 12, 113, 114, 115, and halons 1211, 1301 and 2402.[6] In 1994 we established a Country Programme for supervising the phase-out of the substances, and in 1996 we established an Ozone Programme Office, inside the Department of Natural Resources and Sustainable Development, to implement the programme.[7] Under the programme, Argentina is completing the reduction and elimination of ozone-depleting substances by 2006, four years ahead of the 2010 deadline set out in the protocol. We have yet to legislate the requirement for companies to reconvert: for styrofoam products we are able to move ahead more firmly but with refrigeration, which is important both commercially and domestically, the process is proving slower. But the World Bank, UNIDO and other agencies are assisting us.

Under the protocol and its revisions, the countries of the South are accorded a grace period of ten years to develop their industries while the North was obliged to begin the phase-out immediately. Argentina has reduced and then increased its consumption, as Table 6.2.1 shows. Essentially, our consumption of substances with ozone-depleting potential was about 4,000 tonnes in 1992, meeting the criterion of less than 300 kg per person. We are one of the smallest producers and consumers in Latin America: of the 6,583 tonnes consumed in 1992, only 25% was home produced – that by our only producer firm, Frio Industrias Argentinas S:A, operating at 75% capacity – the rest being imported.

As with other countries, our substances relate to different uses: foam products account for 95% of our CFC 11; refrigeration accounts for 60% of our CFC 12 and 63% of HCFC 22; air-conditioners account for 26% of CFC 113/4, and 35% of HCFC 22; and solvents account for 100% of MCF.[8]

Table 6.2.1   Argentina: consumption of ozone-depleting substances, 1986–92 (tonnes)

Chemical	1986		1988		1990		1992	
	ODS*	ODP*	ODS	ODP	ODS	ODP	ODS	ODP
CFC 11	1,888	1,888	1,925	1,925	1,150	1,150	1,338	1,338
CFC 12	3,237	3,237	2,799	2,799	2,072	2,072	2,408	2,408
CFC 113	76	61	42	33	42	33	63	51
CFC 114	20	20	0	0	7	7	0	0
CFC 115	12	7	16	10	26	16	104	62
Sub-total	5,233	5,213	4,782	4,767	3,297	3,278	3,913	3,859
Halon 1211	38	114	51	153	23	69	76	228
Halon 1301	18	180	30	300	16	160	11	111
Sub-total	56	294	81	453	39	229	87	339
CFC 13	0	0	0	0	0	0	1	1
MCF	930	93	1,643	164	1,051	105	2,040	204
Sub-total	930	93	1,643	164	1,051	105	2,041	205
HCFC 22	N.A.	0	N.A.	0	N.A.	0	528	26
Meth. br.	198	138	N.A.	0	0	0	14	10
Sub-total	198	138	0	0	0	0	542	36
Total							6,583	4,439

Notes: * ODS: ozone-depleting substances; ODP: ozone-depleting potential.
N.A.: Data not available.
Totals not given for 1986–90
Source: Argentina Country Report: Executive Summary. World Bank, May 1994, 3.

In Buenos Aires, we have been measuring ozone since 1969 with financial help from Finland. Since 1990 the World Bank's Global Environment Facility has been financing the Dobson National Network with three stations operating across the country and one in Uruguay. An Ultra-Violet Network has been measuring depletion levels for the past four years with three stations, but its continuation depends upon financial assistance which is virtually non-existent. And there is an electrophotometre operating in Ushuaia. Yet our system of ozone measurement is basically inadequate because of the financial and technological deficiencies that are characteristic of the South. Satellite measurements are available but ground measurements are not – we simply lack the equipment. And the satellite information is not really detailed enough either. So it is not possible to obtain in Argentina a clear profile of ozone depletion. Yet we do know that in 1997 the depletion for the whole year averaged 2.5% above Buenos Aires. It was 4% above the cattle-rich northern Patagonia, 7% during July. And over 6% above Tierra del Fuego, 10% in October.

So there is a decision in the country to reconvert the ozone-depleting industries, given that it is one country recognized by the international community as a "victim" and justifying the contribution of facilitating multilateral financial assistance. But while it is seen as a victim, this is not adequately translated into a position of empowerment for the country through sufficient funding to rectify the impact of ozone depletion on activities such as agricultural health.

Under the regime of the protocol's revisions, our Country Programme envisages the phase-out regime illustrated in Table 6.2.2. So, as noted, we shall have completed the legal obligation four years ahead of the deadline. What is the financial cost? The government's Action Programme is costed at $0.4 million, while the financial assistance needed for all industrial reconversion projects is estimated at $90 million.[9] Clearly, we need help.

Table 6.2.2 Argentina: phase-out regime, 1996–2006 (tonnes)

Chemical	1996**		2000		2004**		2006	
	ODS*	ODP*	ODS	ODP	ODS	ODP	ODS	ODP
CFC 11	1,179	1,179	127	127	63	63	0	0
CFC 12	2,192	2,192	623	623	464	464	0	0
CFC 113–CFC 114	72	57	8	6	0	0	0	0
CFC 115	117	71	117	70	117	70	0	0
Sub-total	3,560	3,499	875	826	416	379	0	0
Halon 1211	8	23	0	0	0	0	0	0
Halon 1301	1	11	0	0	0	0	0	0
Sub-total	9	34	0	0	0	0	0	0
CFC 13	1	1	0	1	1	1	0	0
MCF	2,292	229	252	25	0	0	0	0
Total	5,862	3,712	1,127	852	426	380	0	0

* ODS: ozone-depleting substances; ODP: ozone-depleting potential.
Source: Argentina Country Report: Executive Summary. World Bank, May 1994, Table 6, 23.
** 1996 ODS and 2004 ODS and ODP totals not exact, but taken from original.

THE LEGITIMATE NATIONAL INTEREST

What is the legitimate national interest for all our countries over ozone depletion? Argentina, like other developing countries, wishes to avoid global, regional and national damage to the environment. Yet we also wish to develop. Countries of the North have accomplished their economic development effectively at the expense of the planet, whether through past colonial exploitation or depletion of their own forests, or more recent extraction of mineral and hydrocarbons far beyond their own borders. Or today, through ozone-depleting industrial and consumer activities. Still drawing down some four-fifths of the planet's resource base, they then require the other four-fifths of humanity to cease and desist from the activities which they have engaged in for centuries, lest the planet and humanity suffer. Those of us in the South have no wish for humanity and the planet to suffer, but we do not see the problem as our particular legacy, or our sole contemporary responsibility. Rather the reverse – it belongs to the North. So the requirement, the obligation, for redress is essentially upon the North. This of course has been the underlying debate for many decades now, but it is most recently pursued in environment and development fora on climate change and ozone depletion.

Thus, the notion of "common but differentiated responsibilities" surfaced in the ozone negotiations years before the Rio Conference enshrined it as a principle in 1992. Countries relatively more responsible for global environmental damage are obliged to acknowledge the fact and accept greater obligation for redressing it, while "victim countries" are assisted and developing countries are accorded less strict obligations. This is the key to much of the future in determining the legitimate national interest of otherwise disparate nation-states in an emerging global society.

CFC technology is not difficult to acquire, including by the South. Although their per capita consumption was low, their growing populations and rising consumer demand meant that, if the South acquired the old technology, the potential for future global emissions would have been huge, and with it the threat to the ozone layer. The negotiations over the Montreal Protocol had to accommodate the South for the common goal. They needed to enable these nations to meet, in the words of the chief US negotiator, their "legitimate needs" during a transition period while substitutes were being developed.[10] And to reduce incentives for them to become major new CFC producers and consumers. So the negotiations evolved into two groups of countries – the "Article 2 countries", those responsible for the ozone damage; and the "Article 5 countries" – those having contributed far less to the damage and yet still facing formidable developmental needs. Of course, it is never clear-cut: there are "victims" in the Article 2 group, and producers in the other. But the two groups negotiated together, in direct recognition of the common vital planetary interest.

In judging whether Argentina is meeting its legitimate national interest, we should look at what it is doing to phase out its own ODS and to develop alternative substances. Table 6.2.2 demonstrates that Argentina is meeting its legal obligations under the protocols and revisions even though its actual production increased slightly. Why, one might ask, have we allowed national production to increase when, as the major "victim" country, our ozone level is further depleted above the heads of our very own citizens? Can that be in our national interest? Does it not make a mockery of our claim for assistance from the international community and our demand for immediate cutbacks by the North?

The answer in politics is never straightforward. And it was given, essentially, in the course of the negotiations. The answer is no. Because of the developmental imperative which countries in the South face, Argentina is able to continue what it was doing for years in the name of development. It is obliged to phase out completely by 2010, and this it is on target to achieve. So our credentials in the legitimacy race are just fine.

Can we do more? Perhaps. Yet we have recorded a few breakthroughs. KOH-I-NOOR is a domestic refrigerator manufacturer. In the early 1990s, the company was dealing with the World Bank with a view to switching away from chlorofluorocarbons to hydrofluorocarbons (HFC 134a and HCFC 141b) in the manufacture of insulation foam in order to wreak less damage on the ozone layer. The conversion of the factory required assistance from the Multilateral Fund. In the course of the planning for this, it was established that the use of hydrocarbons might be viable. This was, however, opposed by some experts on safety grounds and there was also pressure for the early completion of project submissions to the fund. The issue generated considerable public interest and the final outcome was a decision by the company to choose the hydrocarbon option, using cyclopentane for foam blowing and isobutane for refrigerants. The project was approved for fund assistance in July 1995. There is, in fact, much scope for ozone-benign technology in refrigeration and many countries are now considering the change-over. Since 1993 when the first technology was manufactured, companies in Austria, Denmark, France, Germany, Italy, the Netherlands, Switzerland and the UK have been producing refrigerators using hydrocarbons, and China and India are also following suit.[11]

In judging the legitimate national interest of other countries, Argentina would look to two areas of action, at least on the part of the North: speed of their own emission reductions, and assistance to others to develop alternative technologies for their economic development.

The Multilateral Fund is of course the answer to the South's challenge of developing alternative technologies. But in assessing the legitimate national interest of both "victim" and "responsible" countries, the question must be addressed of how much is enough. The fund was opened in 1991. By late 1997, only $526 million had been paid in.

It is the countries of the North that pay into the fund. They comprise 15% of the global population, consume over 80% of the planet's resources, consume nearly 85% of the ozone-depleting substances, and have sold nearly $30 billion of such substances over the past decade. Is $500 million enough to remedy this? Does that reflect a legitimate national interest on their part, or does it fall short? And, fundamentally, is it enough to cover the needs of the South as they seek to develop their industries while avoiding ozone damage? Perhaps it is, but I believe it could be more. And the current three-year cycle of expenditure will leave some $80 million in the fund unspent.[12] Perhaps the management of the fund could do with some improvement. That is $80 million of missed opportunity to protect the ozone layer.

Is the United States, is Japan, meeting their legitimate national interest when, respectively, they pay $39 million and $28 million annually to the fund? Does Argentina, with an increased rate of melanoma since the 1970s, deserve more to assist it? Is there a moral obligation here? Yes. Does that translate into a political obligation? Yes. Does that translate into a legal obligation? The protocol called for state parties to take into account, in particular, the needs of developing countries.[13] Have they met this obligation? No, not entirely.

Japan is a wonderful country. I have visited there many times. Its people are, today, among the most hospitable and internationally minded in the world. They give the largest amount of aid of any country in the world today — some $9 billion in 1996. And they are the second largest producer of the substances that destroy the ozone layer over the heads of Argentinians. Is $29 million a year for the Multilateral Fund enough? Perhaps it is. But I believe it could be more.

CONCLUSION

When the Antarctic ozone hole was discovered I was foreign minister of the country which the statistics show to be the greatest victim of all. I served in that office from 1983 to 1989. That period covered the days of discovery of the hole, a belated awakening to the problem, formulation of national policy, completion of the Vienna Framework Convention and Montreal Protocol, recognition of the protocol's inadequacy and commencement of the London revisions. It was a time of environmental troubles, with the dawning awareness of possible climate change as well. A time when the age of innocence ended, and we began to realize, as a species, that we could affect our own fate, in an almost cosmic sense. I was, of course, deeply concerned.

But individuals in office cannot formulate policy alone in isolation from the opinions and interests of the populace. We were a democracy again after years of brutal military rule. Listening and responding to the people was the essence of our work. It took a while before the nation became cognizant of the severity of the threat. Some time again before the different nature of the problem was accurately understood and the different ways of responding to it developed. Some time, again, before Argentinian policy merged in a negotiating synthesis with that of other nations, first the other "victim states" and thereafter all states, producers and consumers, victims and those responsible.

Then it takes time for one or two hundred nation-states to reach agreement through negotiation, even if the nature of the threat is common, global and severe. After that it takes time for those states to ratify and implement the legal instrument, especially if the domestic politics are complex and fractious as so often happens in the larger federal polities such as the United States or, indeed, Argentina. And after that, it takes time for the implementation of the international agreement, assuming it is properly implemented, to take effect, and the problem to be mitigated and then overcome.

This is the way of the world in the twentieth century, and no doubt the early twenty-first century as well. Two hundred sovereign entities, with different national interests, some competitive, all ensuring that their own needs are properly accounted for, and obliged to go through the motions of their own national policy formulation and implementation procedures.

And then we must recognize the magnitude, the vastness, of the global problems. And the uncertainties, born of scientific imprecision, of these new threats which humanity is not used to dealing with, and which politicians must acknowledge even as they are balancing competing and often hostile partisan interests within their own countries. I know well the people in the environmental interest and lobby groups. They have a clear-sighted view of the global problems and solutions. They are good and attractive people, and I like their dedication and insight. But if they were running the country, they could do no better. They would have to confront, and deal with, the same problems as we do.

It is no wonder that the world works slowly. Let us hope, and pray, that no sudden global cataclysm engulfs our planet, until at least we have the political means of handling it.

NOTES

1. Reuters, 10 September 1996, reporting on WMO measurement findings. A newspaper report cited the depletion level at one time in 1995 at 50%, and a 40% depletion in 1997 is also believed to have occurred.
2. *Ley 23.724: Convenio de Viena para la Protección de la Capa de Ozono*, 13 September 1989.
3. *Ley 23.778: Protocolo de Montreal relativo a sustiancas agotadoras de la Capa de Ozono*, 10 May 1990.
4. *Ley 24.615: Conferencia de las Partes Londres*, 30 September 1992; *Ley 24.418: Conferencia de las Partes Copenhague*, 28 December 1994.
5. *Ley 23.724: Convenio de Viena*.
6. *Ley 24.040: Control de fabricación y comercialización de sustancias agotadores de la Capa de Ozono*, 27 November 1991.
7. *Decreto 265/96*, 20 March 1996.
8. Argentina Country Report: Executive Summary, World Bank, May 1994, 7.
9. Ibid., 29.
10. R. Benedick, *Ozone diplomacy: new directions in safeguarding the planet* (Cambridge, Mass.: Harvard University Press, 1991), 92–3.
11. See *La Desaparicion del ozono: un serio peligro. Greenfreeze: una oportunidad para evitarlo* (*Informe Greenpeace, Abril 1995*). Also, Domestic Refrigeration Case Study: KOH-I-NOOR, Argentina (http://www.greenpeace.org/~ozone/excuse/6excuse.html).
12. Greenpeace International: statement to 8th Meeting of the Parties to the Montreal Protocol (http://www.greenpeace.org/~ozone/costa/speech/index.html).
13. Montreal Protocol, Article 10.

6.3   Japan

Koji Kakizawa

"While the 1994 Assessment Panel Report confirms that we are heading in the right direction, we cannot afford to be complacent. The line that divides complacency from catastrophe is very thin."
        Elizabeth Dowdeswell, Executive Director UNEP, September 1994

Depletion of the ozone layer is one of the key global environmental issues requiring a long-term approach for solution. As one of the most populous nations of the world and one of its strongest economies, Japan carries a special responsibility to ensure environmental integrity in what it does. It is my duty, as a member of the Japanese Diet and a former foreign minister, to help ensure that we meet that responsibility.

Japan learned its environmental lesson relatively early. In the 1960s, during its high economic growth period, the country experienced serious pollution problems. The Minamata mercury pollution and the Yokkaichi asthma badly hurt our people. Smog and effluent from factories polluted the air and rivers. It seemed that every day brought news of further environmental pollution. For that matter, we know also about the lingering intergenerational effects of nuclear radiation.

Since 1970, however, with the enforcement of strong governmental policies in Japan, environmental conditions gradually improved. Visitors to Tokyo are surprised now to find the air unexpectedly clean despite the city's high population density. People can once again fish in the bay and a number of movements to restore fireflies along rivers have achieved good results. Most Japanese now understand the importance of taking responsibility for the protection of the environment in order to enjoy the beauty of our local nature.

Environmental consciousness on the part of the public does include a concern with the global environment. But the effects of measures to improve the global environment are not readily evident compared with the improvement of the local environment. Although the global situation is gradually worsening, it is not always easy to recognize the seriousness of global environmental issues. Because of this, continuous political effort for public co-operation is necessary.

NATIONAL POLICY

The Montreal Protocol on ozone protection was a unique event in the evolution of global politics. Montreal laid down concrete measures to protect the ozone layer in co-operation with all countries around the world. The adoption of the protocol was an epoch-making event for the protection of the global environment, the common asset of all human beings. Japanese people praised the adoption of this protocol, which regulated the production of specific chemical products. After the adoption of the Montreal Protocol, Japan enacted its own national legislation to protect the ozone layer in May 1988 – one of the first countries in the world to enact a new law for the protection of the ozone layer.

In the past, Japan faced several difficulties in carrying out its international responsibility for promoting measures for ozone layer protection. In particular, industries that were heavily dependent on the regulated chemicals, along with the Ministry of International Trade and Industries (MITI) as the bureaucratic representative of the related industries, argued that Japan should be more cautious in adopting strong measures.

There were also several reasons for Japan to be cautious of strong action. First, it was widely recognized that the reduction of chlorofluorocarbons (CFCs) used in the production of cleaning solvents for the electric appliance industry was not so easy in Japan, since it was one of the most important industries in the economy. This could be the reason why Japan was reluctant to reduce CFC 113 in the beginning – at the peak of CFC 113 production in Japan, it represented about 35% of world production. Among the five kinds of CFCs, production of CFC 113 used for the cleaning solvents was greater than of other CFCs for a long time.

Secondly, because Japan is located in a monsoon region, it experiences high temperatures and humidity in summer. So the CFCs used as coolants in air-conditioners were precious substances that brought comfort to the daily life of Japanese people. Since almost all cars were equipped with air-conditioners, the production of one type of CFC used for car air-conditioners had the biggest ratio among coolant CFCs.

Thirdly, it is difficult to find alternatives to the methyl bromide used to kill insects and micro-organisms that damage crops and Japan's many wooden artefacts. Farmers and agricultural officials were concerned that there might be a possibility of more adverse effects to the environment if we use, without caution, certain toxic chemicals as an alternative to methyl bromide. That is why it was important to have careful discussion on the "critical agricultural use" of methyl bromide at the Conference of the Parties to the Montreal Protocol.

Despite these problems, Japan, which had produced approximately 120,000 tons of CFCs as recently as 1986, abolished the production of CFCs at the end of 1995 without having any problems, thanks to the sincere efforts made by the government and related industries.

Japan's measures for the protection of the ozone layer can be analyzed in three areas: its role in international observational monitoring; its control measures under the Montreal-plus-revisions regime; and its financial support for the international community's efforts to strengthen protection measures and assist countries of the South. Let me explore each one.

Observation of the ozone layer

Using its high level science and technology, Japan has played an important role in understanding the problem of the ozone layer depletion. Although it is widely known that the British scientist Dr Joe Farman reported the ozone hole over Antarctica in December 1985, Mr Shigeru Chuhachi, a scientist at a Japanese meteorological institute, had reported 18 months earlier from Japan's 23rd Antarctic Winter Visit that the ozone layer over the Antarctic had decreased.

Observations at Japan's Showa Base in the Antarctic began in 1961. The Meteorological Agency has been observing the ozone layer since 1957 in Tsukuba, since 1958 in Sapporo and Kagoshima, and since 1974 in Naha, Okinawa. Since the observation points in the low latitude and from the ocean provide insufficient data, observation in Minami-Torishima began in January 1994.

The National Institute for Environmental Studies has been observing the vertical distribution of ozone in different altitudes using high technology, such as an ozone laser radar developed in 1988, and a millimetre wave sensor developed in 1995. An Improved Limb Atmospheric Spectrometer (ILAS) and a Retroreflector in Space (RIS), both developed to monitor and study the ozone layer, were deployed on the Earth observation satellite *Midori* in August 1996. The ILAS monitored the atmosphere at different altitudes and the RIS gauged vertical distribution of ozone layers over Japanese islands and the density of CFCs. Thanks to this monitoring equipment, the actual conditions and the mechanism of the changes of the ozone layer were expected to be further clarified. Unfortunately, *Midori* stopped its activities in June 1997 because of power failure.

Control measures on emissions of CFCs

Japan's ozone layer protection measures involve not only controls over the production of CFCs but also various measures to reduce the emission of CFCs into the atmosphere. In order to reduce emissions, equipment not using CFCs or equipment with a built-in mechanism for recovering them has been developed and widely used with the help of the government's financial assistance and tax measures.

Regarding car air-conditioners, there was a problem of leakage of coolant CFCs. However, car air-conditioners produced in Japan after 1990 have lower leakage, that is to say, leakage from a car filled with 700g of CFCs has been reduced from 50g in the past to 10g today. Because of these improvements, the demand for CFC coolants for replacement has been lowered. Furthermore, stocks of new CFCs remain even now. Accordingly, no cases of CFC trafficking have been reported in Japan, unlike in other developed countries, even after the production of CFCs was totally abolished.

The biggest issue in relation to protection of the ozone layer in Japan after the total abolition of CFC production is recognized as the recovery of CFCs. Since CFCs are no longer produced, it is difficult to identify those responsible for their emission into the atmosphere, and Japan did not enact a law that obligated any specific body to recover CFCs. However, the recovery of CFCs from domestic refrigerators through municipal activities has rapidly increased. According to the survey by the Environment Agency, CFC was recovered from 56% of refrigerators in 1996, and the ratio is rising sharply. With regard to their use in car air-conditioners, which accounts for the highest ratio of existing CFCs, the Japan Automobile Manufacturers Association will undertake initiatives to establish a recovery system with the co-operation of related companies, under the guidance of the Japanese government. Because of this development, the ratio of CFC recovery in this area is expected to rise considerably in the coming years.

Since the demand for coolants for replacement is small in Japan, only a small portion of the recovered CFCs are reused. Therefore, the technology for the destruction or breaking down of CFCs has been developed. UNEP has endorsed seven methods for destroying CFCs. Among them, the Environment Agency of Japan has developed technologies employing rotary kilns used as incinerators for industrial waste and cement kilns used at cement factories. MITI developed technologies to destroy CFCs using plasma methods, and is now developing technologies to increase the efficiency of the destruction of CFCs by improving the existing rotary kilns. Similar equipment is now being commercially produced by several companies.

There is a growing public consensus that all the parties involved in CFC production, sales and use should bear the costs of recovery, while there is a growing necessity for the government to provide financial support for their destruction. In my view, the government should provide a larger budget for that purpose.

International assistance

The most important issue in the protection of the ozone layer in the future will be for developed countries to assist developing countries through the provision of multilateral funding as well as of institutional advice and technical support in order to reduce the production of ODSs and to control their emission.

Japan is the second biggest contributor to the Multilateral Fund for the Protection of the Ozone Layer, next to the United States. It has given $99 million over the six-year period 1991 to 1996, and gave $28 million in 1997. Japan is also making the utmost effort to transfer technology for emission controls, recovery and destruction of CFCs and alternative substances.

THE LEGITIMATE NATIONAL INTEREST

Environmental problems are becoming trade issues, because if we fail to harmonize environmental regulations internationally, unnecessary distortions in trade may occur. It is not acceptable for a country to derive the benefits of trade by ignoring environmental issues and producing cheaply. That is against its legitimate national interest. On the other hand, selfish environmental regulations of a country may become non-tariff barriers to other countries. That, too, is against the legitimate national interest. If the environmental regulation of a country is aimed at punishing a specific country, there may be a violation of the latter's sovereignty and intervention in its domestic affairs. We need to discuss these issues in fora such as the World Trade Organization (WTO).

Citizen participation is critical in ensuring that governments pursue the legitimate national interest in the interests of the planet. Today, not only governments but also citizen groups are aware of the need to protect the ozone layer. Japan's Save the Ozone Network, a national-level NGO established to promote the recovery of CFCs, continues to urge governments and politicians to adopt stronger measures for recovery. In Japan, there were few active NGOs in the past, but today a number of NGOs including the Ozone Network are becoming more active. They have an increasing capacity to provide input into the decision-making processes.

Future measures for the protection of the ozone layer will still be needed. Observations of the ozone layer suggest that the amount of ozone is decreasing in the long term almost worldwide, except for tropical regions. The biggest ozone hole appeared in 1996 over the Antarctic, while one of the biggest decreases in ozone levels to date was observed over the Arctic in March 1997.

It is a relief to note the conclusion of the 1994 UNEP report, that the ozone layer will begin to recover in the early twenty-first century and the ozone holes should finally disappear around 2045. According to the National Oceanic and Atmospheric Administration (NOAA) of the US, the amount of CFCs in the troposphere peaked at the beginning of 1994, and since then there has been a gradual decline in the amount of CFCs. From this evidence, it is possible to say that the control of the production of ozone-depleting substances is working.

It is, however, too early to say that the scientific forecast of the UNEP panels will indeed be realized. Scientists admit that there is a lack of research into the interrelationship between ozone layer depletion and global warming. Since the depletion of the ozone layer is still progressing, we need to take measures as soon, and as extensively, as possible. Until the recovery of the ozone layer commences, we need to maintain the policy of strengthening controls of ODSS as much as possible.

The issues of ozone layer depletion and global warming are closely interrelated. CFCs and HCFCs have greater greenhouse potential than HFCs which are their alternative substances. Although the production of CFCs has ceased, the amount of CFCs emitted into the air when the existing appliances are discarded is very considerable. Further, CFCs and HCFCs are artificial chemical substances that are not recyclable in the natural ecosystem, in contrast to carbon dioxide. Therefore, in the coming years,

Figure 6.3.1   "The issue of ozone depletion," says Koji Kakizawa, "makes us aware of the importance of the planetary interest." A Japanese scientist prepares measuring equipment at the Showa Base in Antarctica during the 34th Japanese Antarctic Research Expedition. (Courtesy Environment Agency of Japan)

we should comprehensively evaluate these artificial chemical substances and take necessary measures from the perspective of the protection of the global atmosphere.

CONCLUSION

Since there are no national borders in the atmosphere, pollutants disperse over the entire Earth although taking a long time to create the damage. Thus the distantly intimate link today between Japan and Argentina. In this regard, the issue of ozone layer depletion makes us aware of the importance of the planetary interest. It is indispensable for us to have international frameworks in order to sustainably utilize the atmosphere, oceans and natural resources without polluting air or water, without exhausting resources and without destabilizing the ecological balance of the planet. In this regard, the Montreal Protocol is a valuable legal document since it lays down ways to reduce or abolish production of specific substances in a concrete manner, allows for the reduction schedule to differ between developed and developing countries and stipulates ways of channelling financial support.

I have always believed that the same type of protocol needed to be adopted for global warming. Kyoto is a big step forward. But although further reduction of carbon dioxide emissions is necessary, this will require us all to limit energy consumption, which is closely related to a country's economy, and could eventually limit the size of the economy. For this reason, global warming will be an even more difficult issue than the control of ozone depleting substances.

In order to address the environmental problem, which is becoming increasingly globalized, we must grasp internationally the reality of the problem, set up measures that take into account technical and economic capacities, provide legal frameworks and follow-up and review measures. To this end, I hope that international environmental organizations such as UNEP will be strengthened further.

We are now facing environmental problems which transcend national borders, while we still have an international system based on the sovereign nation-state. We need to address the difficult problems of evaluating and protecting the global commons, which are complicated and interrelated, while maintaining the free trade systems of the world. The planetary interest concept will be useful in helping us to realize this goal in the twenty-first century.

CHAPTER SEVEN

Climate stabilization

7.1 Introduction

Probably no other global issue has captured the concern and attention of the world in the 1990s as has climate change.

THE GLOBAL PROBLEM

Climate change poses a more difficult problem to the international community than ozone depletion, its causes being more integral to the functioning of modern society and the daily personal lifestyle. In addition, statistics are not readily available in some cases, and long time-periods are involved for assessing causal effects.

Climate change is caused by a complex interaction of physical and chemical phenomena, which results in an increased amount of gases emitted through human activity remaining in Earth's atmosphere, thereby trapping more of the sun's heat which would otherwise have been reflected back into space.[1] Four contributing greenhouse gases (GHGS) are involved, with various aspects of economic activity being responsible for each one. Carbon dioxide is emitted through fossil fuel burning, cement-making and deforestation. Methane is emitted through natural wetlands, rice cultivation, coal-mining, gas pipeline leaks and enteric fermentation from livestock. Nitrous oxide is emitted from adipic and acidic acid production, and chlorofluorocarbons are the same manufactured compounds that cause ozone depletion. Carbon dioxide is estimated to contribute 55% of the problem; CFCs 17%, methane 15%, nitrous oxide 6%, and other causes 7%.[2]

The annual emissions and atmospheric concentrations of the greenhouse gases are given in Table 7.1.1.

While each of these is a potent cause of global warming with a different "radiative forcing" factor, carbon dioxide has attracted most political attention because it is so central to the global energy system and the global economy. The "annual carbon budget" is depicted in Table 7.1.2. The volume of carbon in the atmosphere and its atmospheric concentration are shown in Table 7.1.3.

As Tables 7.1.1, 7.1.2 and 7.1.3 show, the current volume of carbon dioxide in the atmosphere is some 750 billion tonnes – already up 29% as a result of the Industrial Revolution from the 580 billion tonnes that had been constant over millennia until about 1800. Earth contains a massive reservoir of carbon – some 39,000 billion tonnes in the oceans, 1,500 billion tonnes in the biota on land, and 4,000 billion tonnes underground in the form of proven fossil fuel reserves (with additional unproven reserves of perhaps 10,000 billion tonnes). Some 190 billion tonnes of carbon are exchanged naturally between the planet's land and oceans and atmosphere each year. Anthropogenic emissions add a total of some 7.1 billion tonnes each year, about three-quarters through fossil fuel burning and cement production, and one-quarter through deforestation. About half of this (3.8 billion tonnes) is re-absorbed back through the planet's natural "sinks" – the result of the oceans and the trees "breathing".

With that amount re-absorbed, the net annual addition to the atmosphere from human activity is currently 3.3 billion tonnes – a 0.4% addition each year to the amount in the atmosphere today. The carbon concentration in the atmosphere in the mid-1990s was some 358 parts per million volume – up

Table 7.1.1 Greenhouse gases: anthropogenic emissions and concentrations (CFCs not included)

	Annual emissions (million tonnes)	Atmospheric concentrations		
		(ppmv)*		(% increase)
	1995	Pre-industrial	1994	
Carbon dioxide	7,100	280	358	28
– fossil fuels, cement	5,500			
– deforestation	1,600			
Methane	375	0.7	1.72	146
– fossil fuel related	100			
– total biospheric	275			
	(TgN)**			
Nitrous oxide	6	275	312	13

* ppmv = parts per million volume
** TgN = teragrams of nitrogen. Figure of 6TgN is for the 1980s.
Source: J.T. Houghton, L.G. Meira Filho, B.A. Callander, N. Harris, A. Kattenberg and K. Maskell (eds), *Climate change 1995 – the science of climate change: contribution of working group I to the second assessment report of the intergovernmental panel on climate change* (Cambridge: Cambridge University Press, 1996), Summary for policymakers, 3–7; Technical summary, 13–47. Also, M. Tolba, *Saving our planet* (London: Chapman & Hall for UNEP, 1992), 24–31; and J. Legget, "Anxieties and opportunities in climate change" in *Threats without enemies*, G. Prins (ed.). (London: Earthscan, 1993), 41–50.

Table 7.1.2 Carbon dioxide: annual average anthropogenic carbon budget, 1980–89

	Reservoirs (bill.tonnes)	Annual exchange (bill.tonnes)				
		Natural		Anthropogenic		Net addition to atmosphere
		Recycling (no net effect)	Net absorption from atmosphere	Source	Total annual emissions	
Oceans	39,000	90				
Land	1,500	100		Fossil fuels & cement	5.5	
				Deforestation	1.6	
Underground	4,000					
Total	44,500	190	3.8		7.1	3.3

Source: J.T. Houghton, L.G. Meira Filho, B.A. Callander, N. Harris, A. Kattenberg and K. Maskell (eds), *Climate change 1995 – the science of climate change: contribution of working group I to the second assessment report of the intergovernmental panel on climate change* (Cambridge: Cambridge University Press, 1996), Summary for policymakers, 3–7; Technical summary, 13–47. Also, M. Tolba, *Saving our planet* (London: Chapman & Hall for UNEP, 1992), 24–31; and J. Legget, "Anxieties and opportunities in climate change" in *Threats without enemies*, G. Prins (ed.). (London: Earthscan, 1993), 41–50.

28% from 1800. It is this increased concentration of carbon in the Earth's atmosphere that is causing the greenhouse effect and the global warming phenomenon. It is estimated that, at present rates of emission, the concentration of carbon in the atmosphere in 2100 will be 510 ppmv, an increase of 82% since 1800, and the volume would be some 1,070 billion tonnes.

Table 7.1.3 Atmospheric concentration of carbon dioxide

Year	Atmospheric volume (billion tonnes)	Atmospheric concentration (ppmv)
Pre-industrial	580	280
1995	750	358
2100	1,070*	510
(at current emission rates)		

* This figure is calculated from the projected atmospheric concentration given in the sources.
Source: J.T. Houghton, L.G. Meira Filho, B.A. Callander, N. Harris, A. Kattenberg and K. Maskell (eds),
*Climate change 1995 – the science of climate change: contribution of working group I to the second assessment
report of the intergovernmental panel on climate change* (Cambridge: Cambridge University Press, 1996),
Summary for policymakers, 3–7; Technical summary, 13–47. Also, M. Tolba, *Saving our planet* (London:
Chapman & Hall for UNEP, 1992), 24–31; and J. Legget, "Anxieties and opportunities in climate change" in
Threats without enemies, G. Prins (ed.). (London: Earthscan, 1993), 41–50.

The scepticism that surrounded the early scientific reporting and modelling on climate change largely diminished in the 1990s. Pockets of scientific scepticism remain over any anthropogenic cause of climate change or even over climate change itself. But the authoritative scientific opinion is that this is the reality. The most authoritative report on the subject, the 1995 Second Assessment Report of the Inter-Governmental Panel on Climate Change (IPCC), drew the following conclusions: carbon dioxide remains the most important contributor to anthropogenic forcing of climate change; projections of future global mean temperature change and sea-level rise confirm the potential for human activities to alter the Earth's climate to an extent unprecedented in human history; and the long time-scales governing both the accumulation of greenhouse gases in the atmosphere and the response of the climate system to those accumulations, means that many important aspects of climate change are effectively irreversible. "Our ability to quantify the human influence on global climate" said the report, "is currently limited because the expected signal is still emerging from the noise of natural variability and because there are uncertainties in key factors . . . Nevertheless, the balance of evidence suggests that there is a discernible human influence on global climate."[3] The World Meteorological Organization (WMO) has reported that 1996 was the eighth hottest year since records began in 1860, and the 18th consecutive year with positive global temperature anomalies.[4]

Climate change is likely to be manifest in temperature rise and changes in wind pattern, precipitation and ocean circulation. The temperature rise is the one most popularly understood, with its consequent sea-level rise, but the other effects could be equally detrimental to national interests. The 1995 IPCC models project an increase in global mean surface temperature from 1990 of about 1 °C. by 2025 and 2 °C. by 2100 in addition to what may have been induced by human emissions so far (range: 1 °C to 3.5 °C). The average rate of warming would probably be greater than any seen in the last 1000 years. Temperature levels would continue to increase beyond 2100 even if concentrations of GHGS are stabilized at that time. Sea-level rise is expected to be 0.2 meters by 2030, and 0.5 meters by 2100 (range: 0.15 m to 0.95 m). The sea level would continue to rise at a similar rate in future centuries beyond 2100 even if concentrations of greenhouse gases were stabilized at that time, and even beyond the time of stabilization of global mean temperature.[5]

More than half the world's population lives within 60 km of the shoreline, and this could increase to three-quarters by the year 2020.[6] The effect on humankind is expected to include flooded lowlands, loss of territory, severe storm damage, agricultural dislocation and the spread of infectious disease.

The international community has recognized the degree of threat which climate change poses for humanity and the planet itself. In the framework treaty negotiated in 1992, it acknowledged that "change in the Earth's climate and its adverse effects are a common concern of humankind". It then expressed the concern "that human activities have been substantially increasing concentrations of greenhouse gases, that these increases enhance the natural greenhouse effect, and that this will result in an additional warming of the Earth's surface and atmosphere and may adversely affect natural ecosystems and humankind".[7]

THE GLOBAL OBJECTIVE AND STRATEGY

The global objective has been identified clearly enough by the international community. It is, in short, to:

> protect the climate system for the benefit of present and future generations of humankind, on the basis of equity and in accordance with their [the parties'] common but differentiated responsibilities and respective capabilities.[8]

How, then, is the international community to protect the global climate system? The strategy is set out in the Framework Convention ratified, as at June 1998, by 174 nation-states. It is:

> stabilization of greenhouse gas concentrations in the atmosphere at a level that would prevent dangerous anthropogenic interference with the climate system. Such a level should be achieved within a time-frame sufficient to allow ecosystems to adapt naturally to climate change, to ensure that food production is not threatened and to enable economic development to proceed in a sustainable manner.[9]

The climate system, it is evident, has already been anthropogenically "interfered with". The question is whether such continued interference can be amended in a manner that falls short of the "danger level". Although the Convention defined the long-term aim to be stabilization of GHG concentrations, that level has not been formally determined.[10] While scientists have cited a "threshold of concern" above which the predicted climate changes could assume dangerous proportions, there is no clear consensus on what that threshold is. The debate over the desired "target" is pursued in the context of the associated economic costs to each nation and the world. To stabilize at the 1990 concentration level of 350 ppmv, for example, probably guarantees no adverse climate change but would require redistribution of global wealth or an absence of sustainable development in most of the world. A level of 450 ppmv is generally seen as acceptable in terms of the most adverse climatic impacts but also costly. A level of 750 ppmv can be readily accomplished in terms of costs of abatement but probably entails quite severe climatic impacts. Some experts have identified the maximum threshold as a doubling of CO_2 above the 1800 level of 280 ppmv, i.e. 560 ppmv.[11] Others have advocated a stabilization of CO_2 emissions at a concentration about 50% above the 1800 level (i.e. 420 ppmv), and thereafter a gradual reduction in the concentration. Although it is recognized that this would cause some climatic disruption, the "dangerous" level of damage would be averted. And others maintain that, with a current atmospheric concentration of 750 Gigatonnes of carbon, the maximum threshold permissible for future climatic stability will be another 300 Gt before the planet's climate becomes dangerously destabilized.[12] At the current rate of net annual emissions of 3.6 Gt, this would occur within about 80 years.

PRESCRIBED NATIONAL POLICIES

The attainment of such climate stabilization – at a level below the "dangerous interference" threshold that can meet the three goals of ecosystem adaptation, food security and sustainable development – is a major challenge to the international community. "The analysis of the social and economic dimensions of the climate change issue", says the IPCC chairman, "clearly shows that it will take time to introduce effective measures because of the inertia of the socio-economic system." The 1995 Assessment Report serves only "as an information basis for debates between conflicting interests within nations. The report is, however, not recommending one action or another. This is rather a matter for the political process".[13]

The prescribed national policies to implement the global strategy to date are comprised of two parts: the initial voluntary undertakings under the 1992 UN Framework Convention on Climate Change, and the commitments entered in the 1997 Kyoto Protocol which, when it comes into effect, will be legally binding.

The Framework Convention

The 1992 Framework Convention mandated effective obligations only for countries of the North – developed countries and those former socialist states with transitional economies – described as Annex I countries. Each undertakes to adopt national policies and take corresponding measures on the mitigation of climate change by limiting its anthropogenic emission of greenhouse gases and protecting and enhancing its greenhouse gas sinks and reservoirs ... To this end, each of these Parties shall communicate, within six months of the entry-into-force of the Convention for it and periodically thereafter ... detailed information on its policies and measures ... as well as on its resulting projected anthropogenic emissions by sources and sinks of green-house gases not controlled by the Montreal Protocol ... with the aim of returning individually and jointly to their 1990 levels these anthropogenic emissions of carbon dioxide and other greenhouse gases not controlled by the Montreal Protocol.[14]

The parties may implement such policies and measures jointly with other parties, and they may assist other parties in contributing to the achievement of the objective. Beyond that, all nation-states have a broad obligation to ensure that activities within their jurisdiction or control do not cause damage to the environment of other states or of areas beyond the limits of national jurisdiction. Subject to that responsibility, states have, in accordance with the UN Charter and the principles of international law, the sovereign right to exploit their own resources pursuant to their own environ-mental and developmental policies.[15]

How adequate are these binding national policies likely to be in collectively implementing the global strategy of climate stabilization below the anthropogenic interference threshold? The IPCC calculated "with confidence" that the long-lived greenhouse gases would require immediate reduc-tions in emissions of over 60% to stabilize their concentrations at today's levels, while methane would require a 15–20% reduction.

How successfully have nation-states met their obligations under the convention, even bearing in mind that these may not be adequate in any event? The convention came into force in March 1994. The Annex I states have to date reported once on their emission performance, with projected data for their emission levels for 2000. An interim report was submitted in September 1994 and a revised report in June 1996.[16] By the latter date, three Annex I countries had still not ratified the convention, and of the 34 that had, three failed to report in time. Of the 31 parties that did report in time, the results were as given in Table 7.1.4. Thus, 16 countries are projected to have cut their levels over this critical decade. Fifteen are projected to have increased their emissions level. The total change by all the reporting countries is projected at a 3% reduction in 2000 from 1990.

As noted, most attention has focused on carbon dioxide emissions. Global emissions from fossil fuel burning alone have increased nearly four-fold in the four decades since 1950. They continue to increase despite the 1992 Rio Conference, *Agenda 21* and the Climate Change Convention – increas-ing, in fact, by 5.5% since that year. The rate of increase is given in Table 7.1.5.

The 1997 Kyoto Protocol

It was well recognized at Rio that the Framework Convention would need to be augmented by a legally binding protocol with emission limits set for each country. The "Berlin mandate" agreed at the Second Conference of the Parties in 1995 set the goal of the Third Conference at Kyoto for the successful negotiation of such a protocol.

The Kyoto Protocol negotiated in December 1997 marks a watershed in humanity's battle with climate change. Under the protocol, negotiated by over 160 nation-states, 38 countries of the North are obligated to reduce their combined GHG emissions by an average of 5.2% from 1990 levels by the years 2008 to 2012. Because many such countries have increased their GHG emissions since the 1990 base year, the required reduction will be 10% on the projected emissions level for 2000.

After intensive negotiation, the protocol incorporated the "differentiation principle" under which nation-states have different national reductions. These are indicated in Table 7.1.6. Countries that do not meet their own emission targets can strike deals with nations that do better than required and purchase their excess "quota". A decision on obligations for the other 130 nation-states is delayed until the next conference, scheduled to take place in Buenos Aires in November 1998. A later meeting will decide on "appropriate and effective ways" to deal with non-compliance.

The protocol was opened for signature at UN Headquarters in New York in March 1998. It will enter into force upon ratification by 55 parties to the convention, including Annex I countries accounting for at least 55% of that group's 1990 emissions.

Table 7.1.4   GHG emission performance of the Climate Change Convention, 1990–2000

	Data from inventory	Data from projection		Variations from projection
		Net increases		
	Base level 1990	Base level 1990	2000 level	%
Portugal	51,045	38,689	54,274	40
Finland	67,114	67,734	84,158	24
Spain	310,070	222,908	276,523	24
Liechtenstein	265	208	245	18
Greece	94,888	94,888	107,288	~13
Canada	577,954	547,324	607,085	11
Ireland	63,757	63,757	70,968	11
Australia	465,305	465,275	512,811	10
Austria	75,286	~75,944	~81,844	~8
Italy	563,117	557,640	597,200	7
Sweden	75,573	75,625	79,310	5
Norway	52,235	52,322	54,627	4
Japan	1,206,523	1,221,850	~1,244,815	~2
New Zealand	80,266	76,480	77,755	2
United States	5,842,371	5,944,684	5,975,064	1
Sub-total	9,525,769	9,505,328	9,823,967	3
		Net decreases		
	Base level 1990	Base level 1990	2000 level	%
France	494,032	510,857	498,643	−2
Iceland	3,227	3,227	3,094	−4
Switzerland	58,196	52,401	50,552	−4
Netherlands	213,946	219,214	206,761	−6
United Kingdom	724,754	~746,520	~704,220	~−6
Hungary	88,674	83,506	77,536	−7
Denmark	65,517	71,660	66,106	−8
Bulgaria	123,755	112,213	101,011	−10
Germany	1,241,509	1,220,884	1,057,343	−13
Russia	3,078,892	2,330,000	1,978,000	−15
Slovakia	71,900	70,891	60,330	−15
Czech Republic	196,551	178,848	148,056	−17
Latvia	27,640	27,640	20,197	−27
Poland	572,257	629,830	459,886	−27
Luxembourg	12,123	12,081	8,417	−30
Estonia	46,479	37,800	20,250	−46
Sub-total	7,019,452	6,307,572	5,460,402	−13
Total	16,545,221	15,812,900	15,284,369	−3

Note: Relative data for 1991–94 and projections data for 2000 (CO_2 equivalent in gigagrams using IPCC 1994 GWPs, time horizon = 100 years). Monaco and Romania excluded because of insufficient data. Poland inventory base level is 1988 (~ signifies approximately).

Source: Second compilation of first national reporting: June 1996: GHG emissions (excluding land-use change and forestry), UN document FCCC/CP/1996/12, Add.1 and Add.2.

Table 7.1.5 Global carbon dioxide emissions from fossil fuel burning (billion tons)

1950	1960	1980	1990	1996
1.62	2.54	5.17	5.94	6.25

Source: Worldwatch Institute, *Vital signs 1997* (New York: W.W. Norton, 1997), 58–9 (1996 = preliminary).

Table 7.1.6 Kyoto Protocol: differentiated obligations for GHG reductions by 2012

−8%	−7%	−6%	0	+1%	+8%	+10%
European Union	United States	Canada	New Zealand	Norway	Australia	Iceland
Central Europe		Hungary	Russia			
Eastern Europe		Japan	Ukraine			
Switzerland		Poland				

Source: UNDH, 11 December 1997.

The negotiations leading up to Kyoto and the agreement itself have proved controversial. But in the view of UN Secretary-General Kofi Annan, "This will represent a major shift in the trend of emissions. It shows true political leadership by the largest industrialized countries. This is a sound foundation for a global co-operative strategy which will bring together, under the aegis of the United Nations, governments, civil society and the business community in a joint effort to protect a common environmental resource". And in the view of the chairman of the negotiating committee, the protocol will have a "real impact" on the problem of greenhouse gas emissions.[17]

LEGITIMATE NATIONAL INTERESTS

Few issues evoke as much concern among national leaders and citizens as the implications of reductions in greenhouse gas emissions. The question of the legitimate national interest becomes of direct relevance to the complex set of conflicting interests among countries. As with ozone depletion, the fundamental division is between countries relatively more "responsible" for climate change and those more likely to be "victims". As with ozone, there is considerable overlapping in this categorization – many states are responsible for climate change and are also a victim of its consequences at the same time. The major nation-states responsible for GHG emissions are given in Table 7.1.7, from which it is evident that the "top ten" countries collectively contribute some 63% of global warming.

Table 7.1.7 GHG anthropogenic emissions: major countries (percentage of global total)

		%			%
1	United States	18.4	6	Brazil	3.9
2	China	9.1	7	Germany	3.4
3	Former USSR	13.6	8	United Kingdom	2.2
4	Japan	4.7	9	Mexico	2.0
5	India	4.1	10	Indonesia	1.7

Source: K. Graham, *The planetary interest*. Occ. Paper no. 7 (Cambridge: Global Security Programme, University of Cambridge, 1995), 11. Based on Intergovernmental Panel on Climate Change, *Climate Change 92: the supplementary report to the IPCC Scientific Assessment* (Cambridge: Cambridge University Press, 1992).

The emission figures in Table 7.1.4 give total emission levels for greenhouse gases expressed in carbon dioxide equivalent terms. They do not depict how "clean" or "dirty" the national economies were in the base-year, 1990. Sweden, for example, with three times the population of New Zealand, emits 94% of the carbon dioxide that New Zealand does. Japan, with 49% of the population of the United States, emits 21% of the CO_2. The East European countries, whose economies were excessively "dirty" in 1990, are recording the greatest decreases in projected carbon dioxide for 2000 as they clean up their economies and close their dirtier factories.

Figure 7.1.1 illustrates the relativity between Annex I states as it pertains to two criteria: "economic cleanliness" (emissions per GDP); and "energy profligacy" (emissions per capita). As the graph shows, the "dirtiest" economies are six former socialist countries of Eastern Europe and Russia. The most energy-profligate lifestyles are led in Luxembourg, Estonia, the United States, Canada and Australia, while the most energy-sustainable lifestyles are led in Portugal, Spain, Switzerland, Sweden and France. So in terms of legitimate national interest, the total emissions must be discounted by the cleanliness of the country's economy. The situation is complex.

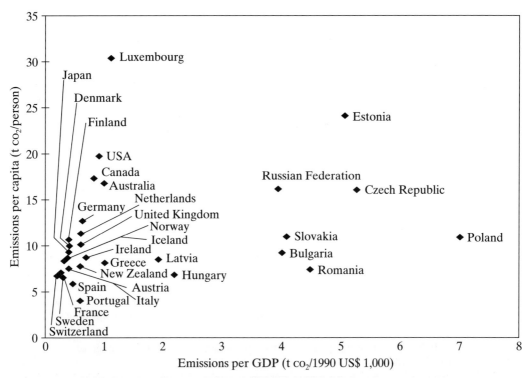

Figure 7.1.1   Economic cleanliness; energy profligacy: Annex I parties (CO_2 emissions per unit GDP and per capita).
Source: UN document FCCC/CP/1996/12, 11 June 1996, 6.

The principal "victim states" are of four kinds: small island states; those with low-lying coastal areas liable to floods; those with arid areas liable to drought and desertification; and those with fragile mountainous ecosystems.

* Low-lying states, in particular the Maldives, Marshall Islands and Kiribati, stand to lose a large proportion of their national territory.
* The major river delta states will be at risk: Bangladesh (from the Ganges); Brazil (Amazon); China (Yangzte); Egypt (Nile); India (Ganges); Italy (Po); Nigeria (Niger); Pakistan (Indus); Vietnam (Mekong); and the United States (Mississippi). In the case of Bangladesh, up to 15% of national territory is at risk.

The disasters faced by the Netherlands and the US in 1996, the states most advanced in coastal and river protection, portend the kind of global problem that must be expected to challenge the national interest of states in the twenty-first century.
- Arid and semi-arid states would experience changes in temperature, wind and rainfall, causing agricultural migration at a pace faster than the adaptability threshold of many plant and crop species. There may be severe decline in productivity of the states in some regions, most notably Brazil in Latin America, most Sahel states in Africa, some CIS states in Central-West Asia, and the ASEAN states of South East Asia.
- Fragile mountainous ecosystems in countries such as Nepal stand to experience more desiccated terrain and soil erosion on top of an already stressed national environment.

The Rio and Kyoto negotiations are essentially an attempt by humanity to alter the global energy system in one act of deliberate collective foresight, however long the process will ultimately take. They therefore evoke a clash of economic, political and cultural interests among the nation-states of the world more complex than the "responsible state/victim state" distinction portrays. The fault-lines reflect a cross-matrix of interests according to cause and effect. The "effect" divides those which are likely to be the most adversely affected from those that are not or that might even stand to gain a short-term illusory national benefit from global warming. The "cause" divides countries between living standards and export interests. The North maintains an affluent lifestyle through a reliance on fossil fuel burning. The South is determined to continue economic development, and the available means to that end remains the fossil fuel economy. Some countries (UK, Russia and East European countries) were fortunately placed in the negotiations and national reporting through having reduced their reliance on fossil fuels for reasons broader than purely environmental concerns. Others (oil exporters such as the Gulf States and coal exporters such as Australia) have a national interest in benefiting financially from the continued fossil fuel economy as long as deposits last. Still others (for example, the US) are caught between high per capita energy consumption and excessive reliance on the fossil fuel economy. The negotiating nexus between these States was evident in the fragile balance of interest that underpins Kyoto: the notion of trading emissions, for example, is critical, with the agreement perhaps hinging on the US having preferential access to Russia's expected surplus in emission credits. The situation thus reflects a complex skein of conflicting national interests, revealed in the negotiating positions put forward at Kyoto. (See Table 7.1.8.)

Table 7.1.8   Negotiating proposals at UNFCCC-COP3 (Kyoto): proposals for CO_2 reductions (%)

	2002	2005	2010	2012	2020
European Union	7.5		15		
G-77/China	7.5		15		35
AOSIS*		20			35
United States		0			
Japan				5	

* Alliance of Small Island States (see p. 117).
Source: Various media reports, December 1997.

Two countries most illustrative of the climate change problem are China and the Maldives. China is the second largest GHG emitter, contributing some 9% of the greenhouse gases. It has plans, moreover, for development of "dirty" coal reserves that could totally nullify all other collective efforts to contain global warming. It is the second largest contributor of carbon emissions (14%) after the United States (23%). Its rate of increase (27% between 1990 and 1995) is far higher than that of the US (8%). The Maldives is, perhaps, the biggest potential "victim" country facing climate change in the twenty-first century. It is, on average, 2 metres above sea level and stands to have significant parts disappear from the planet's surface if the sea level rises to what is currently forecast for the twenty-first century. How do these two countries view the planetary interest and their legitimate national interests with regard to climate stabilization?

NOTES

1. "Climate change" means a change of climate which is attributed directly or indirectly to human activity that alters the composition of the global atmosphere and which is in addition to natural climate variability observed over comparable time periods. UN Framework Convention on Climate Change, Article 1.2 (hereafter, UNFCCC).
2. L.R. Brown et al., *State of the world 1997*, (New York: W.W. Norton, 1997).
3. Climate change 1995 – the science of climate change: contribution of Working Group I to the Second Assessment Report of the Intergovernmental Panel on Climate Change, Eds J.T. Houghton, L.G. Meira Filho, B.A. Callander, N. Harris, A. Kattenberg and K. Maskell (Cambridge University Press, 1996) (hereafter 1995 IPCC Assessment), Preface. Other experts share the IPCC judgement: "There is a better scientific consensus on this than on any issue I know, except maybe Newton's second law of dynamics. Man has reached the point where his impact on climate can be as significant as nature's." James Baker, US National Oceanic and Atmospheric Administrator, IHT, 13 November 1997. And: "Under business-as-usual, we'll reach carbon dioxide concentrations that have not been seen on this planet in the last 50 million years. We will have achieved that in the geological blink of an eye, exposing as we do it, natural systems to a rate of temperature change faster than at any time in the last 10,000 years." Professor John Holderen, Harvard University and Nobel Laureate winner, IHT, 13 November 1997.
4. UNDH, 1 May 1997.
5. 1995 IPCC Assessment, 5–6.
6. *Agenda 21*, 17.3.
7. UNFCCC, first and second preambular paragraphs. "Adverse effects of climate change" means "changes in the physical environment or biota resulting from climate change which have significant deleterious effects on the composition, resilience or productivity of natural and managed ecosystems or on the operation of social-economic systems or on human health and welfare." (UNFCCC, 1.1.)
8. UNFCCC, 3.1. "Climate system" means "the totality of the atmosphere, hydrosphere, biosphere and geosphere and their interactions." (UNFCCC, 1.3.)
9. UNFCCC, 2.
10. Bolin, B. (Co-chairman, Inter-governmental Panel on Climate Change (IPCC), "The IPCC second assessment", paper presented at Second Générale des Eaux Cambridge Environment Lecture, Cambridge, England, 23 May 1996.
11. See, for example, *IHT*, 1 December 1997.
12. J. Leggett, "Anxieties and opportunities in climate change", in Prins, ed., *Threats without enemies*, 51.
13. Bolin, "The IPCC second assessment".
14. UNFCCC, 4.2 (a&b). "Greenhouse gases" means "those gaseous constituents of the atmosphere, both natural and anthropogenic, that absorb and remit infra-red radiation" (ibid.: 1.5). "Emissions" means "the release of greenhouse gases and/or their precursors into the atmosphere over a specified area and period of time" (ibid.: 1.4).
15. Ibid., 8th preambular para.
16. UN documents A/AC.237.81, and FCCC/1996/12 with Addenda 1 & 2.
17. Ambassador Raul Estrada Oyuela of Argentina, UNDH, 11 December 1997.

7.2   The Maldives

Ibrahim Hussain Zaki

"It is in the interest of all the world that climatic changes are understood and the risks of irreversible damage to natural systems, and the threats to the very survival of man, be evaluated and allayed with the greatest urgency . . . it is not too late to save the world. It is not too late to save the Maldives."

President Gayoom, 19 October 1987

The most pernicious aspect of ecological degradation, for me, is climate change. The changes in global climate patterns affect the thin film of matter that surrounds the Earth and sustains human habitation. As such, climate change poses dire threats to all countries.

Whether we live in a hilltop hamlet or reside near a reefside resort, climate change will cause enormous disruption and dislocation in our lives. Whether our countries are large with broad sweeping plains and rugged hilly terrain or small islands with coral beaches and little vegetation, climate change will impose a heavy burden on us. It will lead to loss of flora and fauna as localized ecosystems undergo thermal change. Agriculture will wilt under heat stress and loss of moisture. There will be some differences in exact impact across countries, but nothing as significant as the fatal price many small states, with little or no margin for adjustment, will have to pay, while some larger and wealthy states can hope for some adaptive options. But even that will only be buying time, and only a little time at that.

Few states, however, would have to pay as heavy a price as the Maldives. A rise in the mean temperature of Earth leads to thermal expansion of the seas. Not only would the fish upon which the islanders depend for their livelihood disappear, but sea levels could rise, swamping the entire island nation. That is why global warming, climate change and sea-level rise are of such urgent concern to the Maldives. That is why we have urged quick and effective international action to halt such change.

There are those among us, including some, not many, scientists, who query the scientific prognostications. Freedom of opinion and expression, and scientific integrity, must be respected. Majorities have been wrong in the past. But the majority is more usually right than wrong. Majority opinion and judgement got us to the moon and back, while a minority still claimed the Earth was flat and still claim the lunar landing to be a hoax. The precautionary principle laid down at the Earth Summit at Rio is no more than what each individual, each family, each nation accepts as a normal tenet in daily life. On the basis of normal precaution, humanity accepts the reality around us and prepares to act.

The Maldives, a sovereign state, is unlike others. It comprises 1190 tiny islands stretching 90,000 sq kilometres across the Indian Ocean. Only 200 are inhabited and the Maldives is, at 755 persons per square kilometre, one of the most densely populated nations on Earth. All told we number some 260,000 people. As many again visit the country each year. Male, the capital city, perches on an island 1,800 metres long and 1,200 metres wide. Above all, the archipelago is low-lying; indeed the Maldives is perhaps the lowest lying country in the world. My colleague Qian Yi observes that a 1 metre rise in sea level, combined with storms and spring tides, will flood areas in China below a 4 metre contour line. The average "altitude" of the Maldives is 1.6 metres.

The islands of the Maldives – Heyerdahl's "scattered emerald jewellery placed on blue velvet" – were discovered some four millennia ago. Settlers developed a peaceable and vibrant culture that has added, with the unfolding of time, to the rich tapestry of human life and drama around the planet.

Today, with the islands still relatively untouched by the ravages of modernity, Maldivians live off fishing and eco-tourism, and lay great stress on sustainable practices in development.

A 0.2 m rise in sea level by 2030 will mean that 80% of the area of the smaller islands will be lost, and 20% of the land area of the larger islands. The people will be forced "inland". Population density will increase intolerably. Housing, sewerage, food production, transport and other utilities will be disrupted. The psyche of the nation will be haunted by the very sea that sustains it. The low-lying islands will become so low-lying in the vastness of the ocean that human existence there will no longer be viable. At 3 metres above sea level there is no margin for error. Storm surges will sweep over the land, carrying all before them. In 1987 and in 1991 – two storms within five years of an intensity unknown in the past – unusually high waves inundated large areas of the capital and many other islands. The international airport was cut off. The first time, two islands were split in two. The second time, the damage equalled 22% of the country's GDP. In a sea-level rise scenario, living on these islands will not be viable. Essentially, what we are talking about is the death of a nation.

In the 1992 Climate Convention, the planetary interest and the global objective have been agreed. The global strategy is also set – the stabilization of greenhouse gas concentrations in the atmosphere at a level that will prevent dangerous interference with the climate system. Yet despite these developments and agreed intentions, progress has been slow. Let us therefore examine national policies and the extent to which they reflect the broader interest of all humanity.

NATIONAL POLICY

> "The North and the South must work out now an effective timetable for stabilizing and reducing atmospheric greenhouse gas concentrations and conserving global biodiversity – goals that are vital for the ultimate good of all human beings and life on Earth."
>
> President Gayoom, 12 June 1992

Two considerations are critical to the survival of a country like the Maldives:

- Are the national policies and obligations as negotiated among nation-states adequate to implement the global strategy?
- If so, are the nation-states meeting their national obligations?

What concentrates the mind, since enormous loss of human life could be involved, is the adequacy of the policies that are being pursued and the targets that are being achieved. What I wish to focus on now, therefore, is the national policies that flow from commitments identified above and the concept of the legitimate national interest that is so useful for making judgements about the continuing policies of various countries and the behaviour of their citizens.

The Maldives

When we recognized, in the mid-1980s, the likely phenomenon of global warming and its consequences for our country, we initiated a series of actions. President Gayoom was the first head of state to alert the United Nations to the threat to small island states posed by global warming and sea-level rise. In 1989 we convened a Small States Conference on Sea-Level Rise. The resulting Male Declaration on Global Warming and Sea-Level Rise called on all states to reduce emissions of greenhouse gases, enhance energy efficiency and undertake extensive afforestation.

In 1992, as the world community gathered at Rio for the Earth Summit, perhaps for the first time as a global society, the Maldives cried out. Our people signed a petition, addressed to the summit – 112,000 Maldivians, 74% of the population over ten years of age. It called for international action to save our country.

Domestically, we have legislated for environmental protection and biodiversity conservation, enforced sewerage and rubbish disposal standards, conducted our own afforestation programmes and strengthened our institutional capacity for environmental conservation. Specifically, we initiated a "million tree" programme in 1996, now increased to a 2 million target; we have 14 Marine Protected Areas; we are taking measures to protect our reefs, both for their intrinsic biodiversity value and as protective barriers to our islands. Facing coastal erosion already, we have transferred people from the four worst affected islands to safer ones elsewhere. In 1984 we set up a National Commission for the Protection of the Environment. In 1989 we developed a National Environmental Action Plan. In

1993 we enacted the Law on Environmental Protection and Preservation. Further, we are endeavouring to build coastal sea defences. But to do this for only 50 of the 200 inhabited islands, it will cost $1.5 billion, eleven times our annual GDP.

It reminds me of the statement by Sir Shridath Ramphal who is writing elsewhere in this book. "It is not", he once said, "a war of man against man, nation against nation, but rather a war of humanity against unsustainable living. It is the only war we can afford." As President Gayoom recently appealed to the world at the launching of the new Commonwealth Report, *A future for small states: overcoming vulnerability*, the quest for humanity's survival is a critical one, and the war against unsustainable living is one that must be made affordable, even for the small island states.

Without that assistance we are doing what we can. But it will be, to use a striking metaphor, a drop in the ocean. Nothing we do as a nation will have the slightest discernible effect on global warming. The 190 other nation-states, the 5.7 billion of our fellow humans – it is they who will determine our fate.

South Asian Association for Regional Co-operation (SAARC)

The South Asian Association for Regional Co-operation is also doing what it can, bearing in mind that two of its members are perhaps the most vulnerable countries in the world. We have undertaken regional studies of the causes and consequences of climate change so that we cannot be accused of not doing our homework or taking an alarmist approach. We set up a technical committee to co-ordinate action among our countries.

The New Delhi Declaration of 1997 established a common SAARC position towards the UNGA Special Session on the Implementation of *Agenda 21*. Five years after Rio, the declaration made some sombre points. It expressed concern that, despite the principle of common but differentiated responsibilities accepted by all at Rio, there was little evidence of a "major shift in attitudes and behaviour" on the part of the North. It found that the new and additional financial resources called for at Rio to assist the South had, to date, been "very disappointing". It noted that much of the environmental degradation resulted from unsustainable lifestyles in the North and stressed that protection of the environment required sustained effort to change consumption patterns there. It recognized that environmental degradation stemmed also from poverty and underdevelopment in the South, this being the result of a global macro-economic environment that was unsupportive of the South's "legitimate environment and development goals". SAARC urged the North to assist its low-lying countries most vulnerable to the negative impacts of climate change in meeting the costs of adaptation and capacity-building. For their own part, they agreed to co-operate in mitigating the adverse impact of sea-level rise on their own countries – referring essentially to Bangladesh and the Maldives.[1]

Shortly after the Delhi meeting, the South Asian heads of government met for their 9th summit in Male and called for the early implementation of the recommendations of the SAARC Regional Studies on Natural Disasters and the Greenhouse Effect. The Maldives convened a follow-up meeting of environment ministers in October which agreed to examine closer co-operation in coastal zone management, biodiversity conservation, monitoring of climate change and management of hazardous waste. They also formulated a common position for the Kyoto meeting of the Conference of Parties to the Climate Change Convention, seeking effective reductions in greenhouse gas emissions.

The Alliance of Small Island States (AOSIS)

Even small and vulnerable nations can act together. The Alliance of Small Island States was first convened in 1991 in face of the impending threat. Although they are small in land surface, collectively they are responsible for one-fifth of the planet's oceans and seas. These states are on the front line of the "war against unsustainable living".

AOSIS countries worked together in caucus at Rio in 1992. In 1994 they were the subject-matter itself of the UN Global Conference on Sustainable Development of Small Island States. The Barbados Declaration noted that such states "share with all other nations a critical interest in the protection of coastal zones and oceans against the effects of land-based sources of pollution". For its part, the international community was to "build new and equitable partnerships for the sustainable development of small island developing states through the implementation of the programme of action, and . . . send a powerful message to the world's people on the possibilities of joint action undertaken with a sense of common purpose and partnership".

In 1995 AOSIS presented a draft protocol to the parties to the convention under Article 17. The draft would have the North reduce carbon dioxide emissions by 20% below 1990 levels by 2005, and adopt timetables for other greenhouse gas reductions. For nearly two years it was the only effective proposal formally before the negotiations.

Small island states can work as one. They can speak with one voice and put forward proposals – send a "powerful message". But they cannot orchestrate decision-making at the global level. Not even for their own survival.

The international community

The survival of whole communities is at stake, in the Maldives, in South Asia and in AOSIS countries. What is the response of the international community? Are the national policies agreed upon to date adequate to achieve the global strategy?

Countries of the South, long colonized, economically exploited, and with their forests having been used for centuries for the benefit of the North, have been less than fully disposed to curb their economic development to atone for the activities of the North. For their part, countries of the North were more intent on seeing the preservation of the forests in the South as the necessary global carbon sink for the continued economic activities of the North. This was no basis for a global consensus. A house divided cannot stand.

The 1992 convention did incorporate some obligations upon the North. Annex I countries are to limit their greenhouse gas emissions with the "aim" of returning to their 1990 levels. Are these policies adequate? No. At the very first Conference of the Parties to the Climate Change Convention, it was acknowledged, with astonishing candour and lack of chagrin for only three years after the treaty's conclusion, that the 2000/1990 formula for the North "is not adequate to achieve the Convention's objectives". The "Berlin Mandate" that emerged from COP-1 established a process that would enable the parties to take appropriate action for the period beyond 2000, including stronger commitments by the North, through the adoption of a protocol or other legal instrument.

The Second Conference of the Parties, COP-2, was held in Geneva in July 1996. The conference president described the goal as being "to pave the way for a new era of trust, where all countries do their best to work for the common good of the global community". The planetary interest, more or less. But the preparatory negotiations leading up to the Third Conference of the Parties (COP-3) at Kyoto were long, arduous and fractious.

In December 1997, the Third Conference of the Parties met in Kyoto, Japan. In a political and diplomatic sense, the outcome is something of a breakthrough. But it is by no means clear that the agreement will be ratified by the United States or that, even if it is, the total future package will be enough to save my country. Is it a "common concern" of humankind that one nation-state perish through the actions of all others, in the name of material progress?

THE LEGITIMATE NATIONAL INTEREST

> "We did not contribute to the impending catastrophe to our nation; and alone, we cannot save ourselves."
> President Gayoom, 19 October 1987

How successfully have the most responsible nations met their current, "inadequate", obligations? The total emissions of Annex I Parties in 2000 are projected to be 97% of the 1990 level. It is, as I have said, basically business as usual. A 3% cut in emission falls hugely, and for my country and perhaps for the planet tragically, short of what is required – the 60% identified by the IPCC.

The legitimate national interest is a political, not a legal, concept. But those states whose survival is threatened attach political importance to it. The "common but differentiated responsibilities" of the Climate Convention has to be more than a ringing phrase. What is common is the collective interest of all nations and all peoples – the "planetary interest" – in meeting the challenge, and responsibility for doing so. What is differentiated is the degree of that responsibility.

The United States is the biggest contributor to global warming of all the nations of Earth. Its vibrant society makes it perhaps the most dynamic country of all, and the consequences of this are both good and bad for the planet and for the rest of humanity. Part of the good is the concern felt by many Americans over their own national lifestyle, and the commitment by some among them that has gone into allaying the worst features of the fossil fuel economy. I pay tribute to my colleague, Claudine Schneider, who did so much in the US Congress to that end. The debate is now on, fast and furious in the United States, as that country reflects on Kyoto and what the legislature will make of the outcome.

Two schools of thought compete in the US. Some believe that the remedial measures agreed are too far-reaching and that the economic shock will be severe, with mines and factories being forced to close, inflation rising and productivity falling. The other holds that energy conservation can pay for itself, and that new technologies can be found to offer new economic gains. A recent White House study has determined that energy policies aimed at cutting emissions might, over the next few decades, shave a fraction of a per cent off the US economic growth, but then be followed by a recovery. Stabilizing emissions at 1990 levels by 2010 would require steps equivalent to charging about $100 for every ton of carbon emitted when fossil fuel is burned. That would be the same as raising a tax on gasoline of about 26 cents per gallon, a tax on electricity of 2 cents per kilowatt/hour, a tax on coal of $52 per ton, and a tax on natural gas of $1.50 per 1,000 cubic feet.[2] As Lena Klevenås points out, Sweden already taxes gasoline by over $2 per gallon. It depends on how communally minded your people are.

What I find so intriguing in this profound and critical debate inside the United States is that the various argumentation is premised on continued economic shibboleths of growth, and not on the underlying and fundamental question of lifestyle. The US is undertaking some initiatives that are making a difference, and this is being translated into a certain constraint upon emission increases – the reporting shows near-parity for 2000 on 1990 levels. But that needs to be set against the realization that the US has one of the most energy-profligate lifestyles in the world. Ms Schneider's insights on sustainable consumption in the US are thus critical to the question of climate change and global warming. Her conclusions and recommendations are fundamental to the judgement of the legitimate national interest of the United States, and to the future of the planet – and especially my country.

China is the biggest unknown for the future of climate change, representing one-fifth of the global population, growing economically at about 10% per annum – development resting on a "dirty" fossil fuel economy. Its reserves of brown coal are absolutely vast and, if it extracts and consumes these reserves with older technology, the impact will be enormously bad for us all.

Japan has a more energy-efficient economy than the United States. It, too, has been undertaking measures to curtail carbon emissions: its projected increase by 2000 (102% on the 1990 level) is modest and it is committed under Kyoto to a sizeable reduction (94% on 1990). It has been helping us strengthen coastal defences and is by far the biggest and most generous donor of bilateral official development assistance to the Maldives.

Germany has done more than most unilaterally to curb emissions, and this national effort is manifested by a projected reduction in CO_2 to 87% of 1990 levels. Unification, it seems, has resulted in the closure of the most polluting factories in the East. In 1990 Germany adopted a National Carbon Dioxide Emission Reduction Programme. It has also helped us, by contributing towards the improvement of our water supply and sewerage system. And it is the country with the most tourists visiting the Maldives. Some 70,000 Germans come to our shores each year to enjoy the unique fauna and flora of our oceanic paradise.

The United Kingdom has supported us in the rehabilitation of our reefs. And the measures it is undertaking to cut emissions is having an effect – projected at 94% of the 1990 level.

Whatever their various policies might be, the fact remains that we have a vital national interest in survival, and they each must confine their national policy to their legitimate national interest. As my president appealed to the world at Rio, "Do not let our voice go unheard. For if you do, it might be forever".[3]

CONCLUSION

> "So let me say this to the world: Watch what happens to us, the small island states. The threats that we face today will not be limited to us alone ... Whatever our fate tomorrow, will be your fate the day after."
>
> President Gayoom, 27 March 1995

Most people around the world would agree that humanity has a moral obligation to prevent the disappearance of an entire nation. Morality, of course, has not been sufficient in the past for collective action at the global level. Rationality, however, is another thing. No individual, no nation, no collective group, consciously acts irrationally. The price of irrationality in a tough environment is often death. Darwin had it right in the natural world, and Hobbes in the political world. Only the threat to life truly concentrates the group mind. As early as 1989, my president offered a dramatic prescription for future global action: "... there is little in the way of action," he said, "and a great deal of reluctance to view environmental problems in a global perspective, perhaps because the issues of development and environment also tend to question the existing world economic order. It seems that nothing short of a sensational shock can bring some sense into those locked minds. That shock could very well be the annihilation of part of the human race."[4]

Sea-level rise will affect not only the Maldives. Elsewhere there will be increased frequency of inundation and flood damage. The rise will swamp fertile deltas, causing loss of productive agricultural and land vegetation, and increase saline encroachment into acquifers, rivers and estuaries. The increased costs of reconstruction, rehabilitation and strengthening of coastal defences may be beyond the resources of most countries.

A 1 to 2 metre rise would destroy up to 80% of coastal wetlands in the United States. Egypt could lose up to 20% of its arable land, disturbing 10 million people. Bangladesh would lose 15% of its land surface. In the Netherlands, a 1 metre rise will make it ten times more likely that its advanced coastal defences will be topped, with increased vulnerability to storm surge and flooding of the kind witnessed in Western Europe in 1995 and in Central Europe in 1997. A 1 to 2 metre rise, the figure estimated in the early 1990s, is higher than what is now expected by scientists. So divide the damage by half. Is this in the planetary interest?

And, of course, the 40 other countries that make up AOSIS, the Alliance of Small Island States – including Kiribati, the Marshalls, Tonga and Tuvalu in the South Pacific – face the same threat as the Maldives.

Figure 7.2.1   "So let me say this to the world. Watch what happens to the small island states. The threats that we face today will ... be your fate the day after", says the president of the Maldives. One of the atolls of the Maldives, 1 to 2 metres above sea level. "It is in the rational self-interest of us all to prevent sea-level rise", says Ibrahim Hussain Zaki. (Courtesy Maldives Tourist Bureau).

It is in the rational self-interest of us all to prevent unacceptable sea-level rise. What is unacceptable? The inundation of the Maldives is unacceptable. Unacceptable, not only to Maldivians, but to humanity. The vital planetary interest is the integrity of the Earth's atmosphere, the stabilization of climate change, the stability of the ocean level, the continued existence of the Maldives.

NOTES

1. 1997 New Delhi Declaration of Environment Ministers on a Common SAARC Position before the UNGA Special Session on the Implementation of *Agenda 21*, preamble and paras 7, 13, 14.
2. *IHT*, 18 July 1997.
3. President Gayoom, address to UN Conference on Environment and Development, Rio de Janeiro, 12 June 1992.
4. President Gayoom, inaugural address to Small States Conference on Sea-Level Rise, 16 November 1989.

7.3 China

Qian Yi

"China is aware of the impact its development will have on the planet and carries a feeling of responsibility for that … [It] is making efforts at saving energy through increased energy utilization rate, changing energy structure to reduce coal consumption and controlling population growth rate in order to reduce CO_2 emissions. That way, we shall stabilize Earth's climate and promote the sustainable development of the world."

The causes of climate change have been outlined in Chapter 7.1. The objective of the world community is to stabilize climate change in a manner that does not cause dangerous interference with the natural systems of Earth.

Ever since the reforms were introduced in the late 1970s, China has wished to open up to the world as a whole and play its part in contributing to the common endeavour of all of humanity. Our Chinese civilization, one of the oldest in the world, is unique in continuing through to modern times as one society with a direct lineage from the earliest times. Chinese people are very proud of that. Now, all the different civilizations around the world are slowly coming together into one common global civilization. Once, Chinese people, like many early people, saw themselves as the centre of everything. Now we realize there is no centre of humanity – all humanity is equally important and all humanity is now coming together. It will still take a long time to learn how best to live together with our different cultural values and political beliefs. That will take dialogue among nations. Meanwhile, we can identify together what needs to be done for our common survival, and work together for that. Climate stabilization is one of those areas. It is in the planetary interest.

We realize also that climate stabilization is in the national interest of Chinese people too. China itself will suffer through any dangerous change to the global climate. Using a leading climate change model, the changes for China from a doubling of atmospheric CO_2 have been simulated and are shown in Table 7.3.1.

Table 7.3.1 Simulated changes in China's climate with a doubling of CO_2

	Winter	Summer
Surface air temperature (°C)	4.8	3.9
Precipitation(%)	12.7	9.3
Soil moisture(%)	−2.4	−2.9
Total cloud cover(%)	−5.1	−2.9

Source: *China: issues and options in greenhouse gas emissions control*, Eds. T.M. Johnson, Junfeng Li and R. Taylor, World Bank Discussion Paper No. 330 (Washington, DC: World Bank, 1996), 10.

In summary, the warming would be greater in winter than in summer. Rainfall would increase in areas of the north and west as well as in coastal areas. Summer flooding would become more frequent in the areas of the Yangtze, Liaohe and Huaihe Rivers, as would typhoons and storms, which affect

China's southeast coast. Many parts of China could experience an increase in drought, hot dry winds and soil evaporation, especially in the spring and early summer.

Based on these results and historical climate change data for different parts of China, four principal impacts for China from climate change have been predicted by Chinese researchers: a general warming trend which would extend China's tropical and northern growing regions; lower crop yields due to reduced water availability caused by increased evaporation; a greater threat of soil erosion caused by higher precipitation levels and a decline in soil moisture; and increased flooding of coastal and low-lying plains caused by sea-level rise and more frequent and severe storms.

It is not just China, of course. Less developed countries in general are likely to be most affected by climate change because their economies are more dependent on climate-sensitive sectors, such as agriculture, and because they are least able to afford mitigating or adaptive measures, such as the building of dikes. Chinese researchers have predicted that a doubling of CO_2 will have a negative impact on rice, wheat and cotton production because of the combined effects of higher temperatures, increased soil evaporation and more frequent and severe storms. The modelling results by IPCC showed that agricultural production would fall by 6% to 8% worldwide, and 10% to 12% in developing countries, with doubling of atmospheric CO_2 concentrations.

Rising sea level is another concern for China and other countries with large populations living in low-lying coastal plains. According to studies by Chinese researchers, a 1 metre increase in sea level, when combined with storm surge and the astronomical tide, will flood areas below a 4 metre contour line in China's coastal plains. The inundated land would cover an area the size of Portugal, including the cities of Shanghai and Guangzhou, and would displace 67 million people at current population levels.

In the last few years, considerable progress has been made using models for climate simulation. These are able to provide more satisfactory and realistic descriptions of the interactions between the atmosphere and the oceans as well as of the water cycle. There are, however, a number of areas where we still need more information. One area is the role of clouds, which have both radiative and dissipative properties and influence the way in which the atmosphere reacts to greenhouse forcing. Another is the role of oceans, whose thermal exchanges with the atmosphere and circulation influence the rate of global climate change and its regional distribution. And finally the role of the polar ice caps, which affect forecasts of sea-level rise. There is much that we still do not understand about the climate system and humanity's impact on it. But the level of uncertainty in climate models should not be exaggerated. It is no greater than the uncertainty in the economic data and models on which equally far-reaching policy decisions are based. Although uncertainties remain, we know enough to say with confidence that the risk of climate change is genuine and serious.

NATIONAL POLICY

China has a developing economy on an unprecedented scale, and such a trend of economic development inevitably raises pressing environmental issues. Many problems remain to be solved, step by step, for China to achieve national sustainable development. The problems lying ahead for China, especially those related to climate change, are also ahead for the world at large. Thus there is wide interest in the formulation of China's policy on climate change, not only in domestic circles but also among the international community.

China has been undergoing dramatic change since its economic reforms began in the late 1970s. The economy is now increasing at a rate of 8% annually based on the 9th Five-Year Plan. In the first half of the 1990s, our national economy grew annually by 8%, 14%, 14%, 12% and 10%. As World Bank president James Wolfensohn has observed, "China's success has been truly remarkable. Less than a generation ago, eight in ten Chinese eked out an existence by tilling the soil for less than a dollar a day. One adult in three could not read or write. Since then, 200 million people have been lifted out of absolute poverty and illiteracy has fallen to less than one in ten".[1] In decade terms, the economic growth rate is projected to be 9% from 1990 to 2000, 7.5% from 2000 to 2010, and 6% from 2010 to 2020. Energy demand will increase with the development of the economy and the improvement in people's living standards.

These forecasts indicate that the total primary energy consumption will increase significantly. Commercial energy consumption will more than double by 2020 from current consumption. The share of coal in end use will decrease significantly, but still dominate the primary energy supply. Use of natural gas will increase but will remain limited by national supply.

It is estimated that energy consumption will reach 1.9 billion tonnes of coal if the utilization efficiency level remains unchanged. With the increase in energy consumption, particularly increased coal utilization, CO_2 emissions will further increase in the future. It is forecast that CO_2 emissions, some 570 Mt-c in 1990, will be 840 Mt-c in 2000, 1.1 Gt-c in 2010, and 1.33 Gt-c in 2020.

Energy consumption is by far the largest contributor of GHG emissions in China, accounting for 82% of total emissions in 1990. Coal accounted for 76% of primary energy use in 1990, followed by oil (17%), hydropower (5%) and natural gas (2%). Industry and electric power generation accounted for 75% of China's CO_2 emissions from commercial energy consumption, while the residential sector accounted for 14% and transportation 4%. Industrial boilers used outside the power sector consumed more than 350 million tonnes of coal in 1990, accounting for about 35% of the country's coal use.

Methane accounted for approximately 13% of China's GHG emissions in 1990 (CO_2 equivalent) with coal mining, rice fields, ruminant animals and animal waste contributing 88% of methane emissions. All other sources of emissions, including CO_2 from cement manufacturing, methane from landfills, N_2O from fertilizer, and non-CO_2 emissions from forests and land use changes, accounted for about 6% of China's total GHG emissions in 1990.

China is aware of the impact its development will have on the planet and carries a feeling of responsibility for that. It participates actively in international activities and decision-making concerned with global environmental issues. It is a signatory to the Framework Convention on Climate Change, and played an important role in its formulation and the development of international support for it, as it does in its implementation. The global nature of climate change calls for international co-operation of all countries in accordance with their common but differentiated responsibilities and their various socio-economic conditions.

To co-ordinate its national policy on climate change, China's National Co-ordination Panel on Climate Change (NCPCC) was established in 1990 under the jurisdiction of the State Environmental Protection Commission of the State Council. It organizes the government departments and experts participating on China's behalf in the work of three working groups and also the conferences of the Inter-Governmental Negotiating Committee. Four sub-groups have been established under China's NCPCC: on scientific assessment, environmental impact assessment and counter-measures, socio-economic impact assessment, and treaty negotiations. These groups conduct research, prepare relevant reports and manage international negotiations. Through this state mechanism, China has exchanged ideas and co-ordinated positions with the rest of the international community since Rio.

In 1990, the Chinese government compiled the National Environment and Development Report. The report reflects the basic policies of China on the issue of climate change, and contains five main principles. First, the development of the economy and the progress of society must be based on sound ecological and environmental principles, and on sustainable use of natural resources. Secondly, in international co-operation for environmental protection, it must be recognized that developing countries are faced with special tasks such as eliminating poverty. Thirdly, while environmental protection is a common task of all human beings, developed countries should take the greater part of the responsibilities that flow from it. They should supply new extra funds and transfer environmentally sound technologies on favourable terms to the developing countries. Fourthly, every country's sovereignty must be respected and there must be no interference in one another's internal affairs in the course of international co-operation to protect the environment. Finally, it must be accepted that China is a large developing country; to solve its environmental issues properly is not only a responsibility owed to the Chinese people and their descendants, but is also a great contribution to the common cause of humanity. It is our duty to international society.

After the Rio Earth Summit, China carried out a series of follow-up activities to implement the Framework Convention. In accordance with the principles of Rio and with the national conditions of China, the Chinese government proposed in September 1992 ten major strategies for environment and development. These were to:

1 implement the strategy of sustainable development;
2 carry out effective measures to prevent and control industrial pollution;
3 strengthen administration of the urban environment;
4 improve energy efficiency and the energy consumption structure;
5 popularize ecological agriculture, develop afforestation continuously and strengthen biodiversity;
6 promote the progress of science and technology energetically, strengthen scientific research on environmental protection and actively develop environmental industry;
7 use economic measures for environmental protection;
8 strengthen environmental education to improve public awareness on environmental protection;
9 complete environmental laws and regulations and strengthen environmental management; and
10 formulate China's action plan on the basis of the principles of the Earth Summit.

In March 1994, the 16th Executive Meeting of the State Council adopted China's *Agenda 21*, a White Paper on China's population, environment and development in the twenty-first century. China's *Agenda 21* covers the strategies and action framework for sustainable development in the fields of population, the economy, society, resources and the environment. The *Agenda* identifies four broad goals: an overall strategy for sustainable development; social sustainable development; sustainable development of the economy; and rational utilization and protection of resources and the environment.

As a guideline document, China's *Agenda 21* will be integrated into the mid- and long-term plans of national economic and social development. These include two areas directly relevant to climate stabilization. The first is the strengthening of measures for conservation of forest resources. To strengthen the management of forest resource consumption, the "permit" system is employed for deforestation and timber trade. Meanwhile, the strategic guideline for saving timber and using alternatives should be upheld in order to achieve a little higher carbon accumulation than that released by forests.

The second is continued and effective population control. Given the fact that China amounts to one-fifth of the total population in the world, the resulting relative shortage of natural resources per capita becomes the basic constraint on the improvement of the eco-environment. Since the 1970s, due to continued family planning over a long period, China has avoided a population growth by a magnitude of 300 million. For the purpose of achieving the set objective of population control, the Chinese government will continue to carry out the policy of family planning. This will incorporate comprehensive considerations of human capital improvement and age-mixture optimization.

Taking the above preparatory actions into account, China will pursue a two-pronged strategy for reducing greenhouse gas emissions:

- it will further promote economic reform, whereby market incentives and regulatory controls are adjusted or introduced to improve resource allocation and encourage energy efficiency; and it will
- implement a set of priority investment and technical assistance programmes to accelerate the adoption of more efficient and low-carbon technologies, improving the institutional and human resource capacity necessary to implement and sustain these programmes.

This strategy for global climate change mitigation is largely consistent with China's domestic environmental and economic modernization objectives, and thus does not pose a major new or different set of conditions or constraints on the public sector or enterprises.

In order to encourage energy saving in China, an Energy Saving Law was issued by the National People's Congress in November 1997, effective from 1 January 1998. The main purpose of the law is clearly stated: "This is for promoting energy saving, increasing energy utilization efficiency in order to protect the environment, to ensure the sustainable development and to meet the requirement of the people in China." It is also clearly pointed out that all the institutions and people in China have the responsibility to save energy. The national policies and plans for energy saving will be defined by the government and should be co-ordinated with the plan for economic development.

The State Council and the official authorities at different levels take responsibility for the planning, supervision, inspection and implementation of the Energy Saving Law. The policies for saving energy include: prioritizing those projects which may save energy; allocating more funds for energy saving projects; encouraging the utilization of renewable energy; setting the standard for rational energy use and requiring all enterprises and institutions to meet the standard; eliminating the technologies which waste energy through selection and competition; eliminating the products and equipment which consume large amounts of energy; and enhancing the management of the main energy consumers.

The importance of enhancing management of energy saving is emphasized and the main measures for doing so are identified. They include the management of statistics and analysis of energy use. The personnel who work in posts of energy utilization should be well trained. Energy utilization quotas should be set for the main products and institutions. All the large energy consumers should report on their energy utilization to the authorities, including energy consumption, the energy utilization rate, counter measures for saving energy and the economic benefit of saving energy. And also, all residents should pay energy fees.

The new law also encourages and supports research and development into energy saving technologies. The state will support priority projects and demonstration sites of energy saving technologies and the popularization of those technologies. Imports of advanced technologies from abroad for energy saving are to be encouraged. Attention will be paid to developing energy saving materials and improving the design of buildings. Development of solar energy, methane gas, wind energy and other renewable energy sources will be speeded up. All enterprises and institutions are urged to develop and use new technologies for saving energy and to eliminate backward technologies.

The legislative obligations of the law are defined firmly. Enterprises or institutions which act against the Energy Saving Law will be penalized in different ways. Fines may be imposed; time-periods for rectifying a violation may be granted; and if necessary a production line of enterprises may be closed down. Officers who are responsible for energy saving but who act against the law will be penalized in accordance with the particular circumstances; all are expected to assume proper responsibility.

The only way for China to meet its huge energy requirements is to improve energy efficiency while developing new energy sources and energy savings as the first priority. In addition to the Energy Saving Law, a Technical Policy Outline for Energy Saving in China was issued jointly in May 1996 by the State Planning Commission, the State Economy and Trade Commission and the State Science and Technology Commission. The Policy Outline has identified the target of energy saving for the year 2000 and the main measures for achieving it. The policy incorporates a range of areas for action. First, ensure an optimal disposition and the rational utilization of energy sources and natural resources. Then, speed up the technical reform and renewal of industrial furnaces, boilers and other energy consuming equipment. Increase the efficiency of heating systems. Use the residual heat and residual energy of industrial furnaces. Recover flammable gas emitted from industries. Develop new energy sources and substitute energy sources. Develop and promote energy saving materials. Enhance the measurement, control, supervision and scientific management of energy sources. Establish an energy saving transportation system, including better railway, highway and waterway systems. Pay more attention to energy saving in building construction. And enhance the management of energy development and energy saving in urban and rural areas. The Policy Outline places a priority on energy saving processes for the main industries, including power, iron and steel, non-ferrous metal manufacturing, construction and materials, chemicals, coal, petroleum and natural gas, petrochemicals, mechanical manufacturing, light industry, textiles, and energy use for local production in the rural areas.

China is trying to improve its coal utilization. It has the third largest coal reserves in the world, with 11% of the global total. Since 1989 it has ranked first in the world for national coal production. Production has increased 16-fold since 1952, and 94% since 1979. The quality of the coal is fairly good – 70% bituminous, 16% anthracite and only 14% lignite. The sulphur content is low. The problem is that only 16% of the coal is washed, and so impurities remain. The target is to have 40% of our coal washed by 2000. But this compares with 90% in the US, Canada and Western Europe. If more of the coal is washed, not only would output increase but air pollution would be lessened.

China is also trying hard to develop alternative energy sources to fossil fuels. It is proud of its new hydro-electric project in the Yangtze River. The Three Gorges Dam will be the world's largest, 185 m high and 1.6 km long, creating a lake 560 km in length. Its planned output is 18,200 megawatts of electricity, which will save the equivalent of 50 million tonnes of coal each year. The diversion was started in November 1997 and attended by President Jiang Zemin who said, "blocking the Yangtze is a great moment in the modernization of our country". Over 1 million people had to be relocated, but this was a necessary part of modernizing China while developing non-fossil fuel energy sources to help stabilize the planet's climate.

International co-operation will play an important role in reducing GHG emissions in China. It will take two forms. First, conventional international and bilateral assistance to China will continue to be important for improving resource allocation in general and energy efficiency in particular. Both are essential for GHG reduction. The technical assistance and lending programmes of international agencies have helped to advance energy price reform, capital market development, enterprise management and ownership reforms in China. Continued and expanded support from international agencies is also needed for China to implement many of the priority investments in GHG reduction, such as energy conservation, efficient power development, high-yield timber plantations, improved animal feed and alternative energy technologies.

Secondly, there is the Global Environment Facility. To support China's priority policies, investment and technical assistance projects for GHG reduction, GEF resources should be used primarily to overcome market and non-market barriers to implementing "no-regrets" projects and for accelerating the development of promising alternative energy technologies for the longer term.

China has a large number of projects underway with international agencies on climate stabilization. The biggest are those financed by the GEF in co-operation with the World Bank or UNDP. The largest focus on energy conservation (at $190 million), Sichuan gas transmission and distribution rehabilitation ($123 million), and efficient industrial boiler promotion ($101 million). Others include renewable energy commercialization ($27 million), coal-bed methane development ($20 million), methane recovery ($19 million), GHG abatement strategy ($10 million), GHG monitoring ($6 million) and rice methane emission research ($5 million).[2]

Figure 7.3.1 Chinese lorries dump the last truckload of rock into the Yangtze River during construction of the huge Three Gorges Dam. Over 1 million people had to be relocated, says Qian Yi, "but this was a necessary part of modernizing China while developing non-fossil fuel energy sources to help stabilize the planet's climate". China emits 10% of the global carbon emissions, but its emissions per capita are only 0.7 tons compared with 5.3 tons in the US. (Courtesy Popperfoto/Reuters)

THE LEGITIMATE NATIONAL INTEREST

The negotiations over the Kyoto Protocol showed that every country has a special national interest in the issue, but they are often very different. To reconcile these is not easy. Many people around the world are concerned over the possibility that China's development of a national fossil fuel economy could harm Earth's atmosphere, even while the international community is trying to avoid that. The Chinese government asks itself: what is legitimate for China and Chinese people?

In 1990, global anthropogenic CO_2 emissions were nearly 5.7 billion tons, of which China accounted for about one-tenth. But per capita CO_2 emissions from China were only 0.7 tons of carbon (tC), compared with the United States (5.3 tC), Russia (2.9 tC) and Japan (2.4 tC). As Table 7.3.2 shows, China is one of the lowest carbon emitters per capita in the world. That, above all else, is the clearest indicator of the legitimate national interest of a country.

Table 7.3.2   Carbon emissions from fossil fuel burning (1995): selected countries (ranked by volume per capita).

	Total		Per capita (tons)	Annual growth rate (%)
	Volume (mtons)	Global share (%)		
United States	1,394	23	5.3	6
Russia	437	7	2.9	−28
Germany	234	4	2.9	−10
Japan	302	5	2.4	9
China	807	13	0.7	28
Brazil	62	1	0.4	20
India	229	4	0.3	28
Indonesia	56	1	0.3	39

Source: Worldwatch Institute, *State of the world 1997* (New York: W.W. Norton, 1997), 11.

CONCLUSION

Climate change is a global concern and China's as well. The large population, energy source structure and low energy utilization rate make China a country with a large CO_2 emission level. China is making efforts at saving energy through increased energy utilization rate, changing energy structure to reduce coal consumption and controlling population growth rate in order to reduce CO_2 emissions. That way, we shall stabilize Earth's climate and promote the sustainable development of the world.

NOTES

1. J.D. Wolfensohn, "The challenge of inclusion", address to the annual meeting of the World Bank Group and the IMF, Hong Kong SAR, China, 23 September 1997.
2. For details, see UNFCC website: China section of CC:Info Country Profile. (http://www.unfccc.de/fccc/ccinfo/chn.htm).

The author gratefully acknowledges the assistance of Professor Hao Jimin in the preparation of this chapter.

SECTION III

Global sustainability

The third "vital planetary interest" is global sustainability. It is axiomatic that a living entity, to survive over the long term, must be sustainable – a living organism that is not sustainable will die. This holds for micro-organisms, plants, animals and humans. Societally, it holds for individuals, tribes, cities and nations. Ultimately, it holds for humanity as a species.

In the past, human groups have been organized on a sub-global basis – in early times as tribes, in classical times as empires, in modern times as nation-states. The boundaries of their values and judgements have been sub-global. For them, the world was an open system, which they drew upon in their own interests without responsibility for the larger entity. In recent centuries some nation-states, having developed a global reach, drew upon the planet at large through colonial relationships, effectively subsidizing their standards of living from elsewhere. But in the twentieth century the world has become a closed political system. Humanity is beginning to perceive the planet as a closed ecological and economic system for the first time. The sustainability of humanity, as opposed to a national society, is emerging as a major challenge. The relationship between global and national sustainability must now be addressed.

THE GLOBAL PROBLEM

What population can Earth support? What is its carrying capacity?[1] How is the international community to explore the issue of global and national carrying capacity and quantify its vital planetary interest in this respect? These questions evoke philosophical and moral as well as material considerations. The issue is complex, involving both technical and cultural factors.

Earth contains finite resources (land, water, atmosphere, minerals, hydrocarbons) which act as a constraint upon human productive capacity. Humanity, however, possesses a creative capacity to develop technology that can utilize such resources in an elastic way. Examples are the discoveries of increasingly potent techniques for harnessing energy; and the Green Revolution of the 1960s that exacted higher yields per unit of land, albeit at a certain economic and social cost. Can future technological breakthroughs, applied to a finite resource base, produce a continuously expanding carrying capacity for the planet? Does any one of the finite resources (land or water) act as a fixed constraint?

In determining the carrying capacity, it is necessary to consider the cultural dimension of the quality of human life. Human existence may be maintained at greater numbers at a lower standard of living or fewer numbers at a higher standard of living. When dealing with human beings there is no unique figure for carrying capacity. The assertion by some that the world can support 50 billion people cannot be directly contradicted. As one authority put it: "The naive question, 'What is the human carrying capacity of the Earth?' evokes a reply that is of no human use. No thoughtful person is willing to assume that mere animal survival is acceptable when the animal is *homo sapiens.*"[2] Thus, it is necessary to ask, more precisely: what is the carrying capacity of the planet for basic human needs at the level of technology prevailing today?

The concept of "basic human needs" is generally taken to include four elements: minimum requirements of private consumption: food, shelter and clothing; essential services provided for and by the community: safe drinking water, sanitation, public transport, health and recreational facilities; employment that yields an output, provides an income, and secures self-recognition; and participation in community decisions.[3] Humans living without these basic human needs – essentially nutrition, shelter, health and education in material terms, and employment and social participation in societal terms – remain in "absolute poverty". This is defined by UNDP as "some absolute standard of minimum requirements" below which the human potential for human dignity and self-realization is denied.[4]

Over the past half century, material economic growth has grown enormously, having tripled in pure monetary terms from \$3.8 trillion (i.e. 3.8×10^{12}) in 1950 to \$19.3 trillion in 1993.[5] But the draw-down on the planet's natural resource base has been considerable, and that capital depletion is not recorded in traditional economic accounting. As the global population grows, and per capita consumption rises concomitantly, the global ecological draw-down is increasing fast.

How has the international community responded to this global problem? The 1992 Rio Earth Summit expressed concern that

> The growth of world population and production combined with unsustainable consumption patterns places increasingly severe stress on the life-supporting capacities of our planet. These interactive processes affect the use of land, water, air, energy, and other resources . . . Present land use often disregards the actual potentials, carrying capacities and limitations of land resources, as well as their diversity in space . . . The need to increase food production to meet the expanding needs of the population will put enormous pressure on all natural resources, including land. [6]

There is, however, a lack of knowledge today over what the carrying capacity of the planet actually is. This was acknowledged at Rio:

> In order to promote sustainable development, more extensive knowledge is required of the Earth's carrying capacity, including the processes that could either impair or enhance its ability to support life.[7]

Behind this is a lack of scientific understanding of the ecological base for the global carrying capacity:

> A first step towards improving the scientific basis for these strategies is a better understanding of land, oceans, atmosphere and their interlocking water, nutrient and biogeochemical cycles and energy flows which all form part of the Earth system. This is essential if a more accurate estimate is to be provided of the carrying capacity of the planet Earth and of its resilience under the many stresses placed upon it by human activities.[8]

Thus, the fundamental problem threatening the "vital planetary interest" in sustainability of the human species is the current stress on the life-supporting capacities of the planet, and a lack of knowledge and understanding of its precise nature and severity.

THE GLOBAL OBJECTIVE AND STRATEGY

The global objective was explicitly identified at the 1992 Earth Summit – sustainable development. The Rio Declaration identifies the fundamental aim as follows:

> Human beings are the centre of concern for sustainable development. They are entitled to a healthy and productive life in harmony with nature . . . The right to development must be fulfilled so as to equitably meet developmental and environmental needs of present and future generations.[9]

Sustainable development is defined in the Brundtland Report, which was produced as the preparatory document for Rio, as development "which meets the needs of the present generation without compromising the ability of future generations to meet their own needs".[10] This is accepted today as the overarching objective of the international community in global sustainability.

Agenda 21 sought to redress the lack of knowledge of the global carrying capacity through three strategies: research programmes, new analytical tools and five-year audits of the planet's life supporting systems. Specifically, this would be done by:

> carrying out research programmes in order better to understand the carrying capacity of the Earth as conditioned by its natural systems, such as biogeochemical cycles, the atmosphere/hydrosphere/lithosphere/ cryosphere system, the biosphere and biodiversity, the agro-ecosystem and other terrestrial and aquatic ecosystems;

developing and applying new analytical and predictive tools in order to assess more accurately the ways in which the Earth's natural systems are being increasingly influenced by human actions, both deliberate and inadvertent, and demographic trends, and the impact and consequences of those trends; . . .

developing a methodology to carry out national and regional audits and a five-year global audit on an integrated basis. The standardised audits should help refine the pattern and character of development, examining in particular the capacities of global and regional life supporting systems to meet the needs of human and non-human life forms and identifying areas and resources vulnerable to further degradation. This task would be to involve the integration of all relevant sciences at the national, regional and global levels, and would be organized by government agencies, non-governmental organizations and United Nations bodies, when necessary and as appropriate. These audits should then be made available to the general public.[11]

What is the international community doing to identify "new analytical and predictive tools", and develop a methodology for global, regional and national ecological audits? Research in this area goes back some way,[12] but recent work holds new promise. Three concepts in particular – "earth-share", "ecological footprint" and "sustainability deficit" – can be used to help humanity understand the nature and severity of the problem and how to measure the damage being wrought by each nation-state.

Earthshare

On a finite planet, an increased global population will have less productive land area per capita. The natural asset base of Earth is set out in Table III.1. It can be seen that, under current technology, of the planet's total surface of 51 billion hectares, only 7.4 billion hectares, some 15%, is ecologically available land. With the increase in the global population, the individual human "earthshare" will have dwindled, from 5.5 hectares per person in 1900 to about one-third of that by 2000. The "earth-share" is the amount of land every human has if the ecologically productive land on Earth is divided evenly. If an individual's present earthshare were a circular island, it would have a diameter of 138 metres. One-sixth of the island would be arable land, the rest pasture, forest and wilderness, and built-up area.[13]

Table III.1 Earth's land surface (billion hectares)

	Marginally or non-productive land	Ecologically productive land	Total land surface	Ocean	Total surface
Degraded (built-up)	0.2				
Grasslands	1.3				
Semi-arid	1.2				
Desert	1.5				
Ice	1.4				
Wilderness		1.5			
Actively available		7.4			
Total	5.6	8.9	14.5	36.5	51.0

Source: M. Wackernagel & W. Rees, *Our ecological footprint* (Gabriola Island, BC: New Society Publishers, 1996), 89.

Ecological footprint

The "ecological footprint" of humanity, the "load" imposed by a given population on nature, is becoming larger. The ecological footprint of a specified population is the area of ecologically productive land and water required, on a continuous basis with prevailing technology, to provide all the energy and material resources consumed and absorb all the wastes discharged by that population.

The size of the ecological footprint is not fixed, but is dependent on money income, prevailing values, other socio-cultural factors and the state of technology.[14]

A rough assessment of the four major human requirements shows that the current appropriation of natural resources and services already exceeds Earth's long-term carrying capacity. Agriculture already occupies 4.8 billion hectares (3.3 billion hectares of pasture and 1.5 billion hectares of cropland). Sustainable production of current roundwood harvest, including firewood, would require a productive forest area of 1.7 billion hectares. To sequester the excess CO_2 released by fossil fuel combustion, a further 3.1 billion hectares of carbon-sink land would need to be set aside. This totals 9.6 billion hectares, some 30% above what is available today, and 10% above all potential land.[15]

Thus there is evidence that humanity's ecological footprint already exceeds global carrying capacity. The "global footprint" has been estimated today at 2.8 hectares per capita – one third above the average earthshare of 2.1 hectares. That is to say, the draw-down on the planet's natural resources exceeds the sustainability level by one-third.[16]

Sustainability deficit

The "sustainability deficit" or "ecological deficit" is a measure of overshoot. It estimates the difference between an area's ecological capacity and its actual "footprint". It therefore reveals the extent to which that area is dependent on extraterritorial productive capacity through trade or appropriated natural capital. The "global ecological deficit", unlike "national ecological deficits", cannot be subsidized through trade and draw-down from other surplus countries. It depends instead on the liquidation of natural capital stock. It cannot be spatial, imposing the burden on other areas at a single point in time. It can only be temporal, imposing the burden on future generations.

The current generation, then, is drawing down on Earth's natural resource base at an unprecedented rate. If this continues, today's inhabitants of Earth will leave a degraded planet for future generations – possibly to an irretrievable degree. Without a concerted effort today to reduce material throughput, the generations of the twenty-first century will be left to satisfy their needs from a much-diminished stock of natural capital.[17] As the authors of the concept put it, there is now "solid evidence that the human enterprise already far exceeds the long-term biophysical carrying capacity of the planet. People today are living on the biophysical heritage of their children".[18]

The Brundtland Report argued for "more rapid economic growth in both industrial and developing countries", and suggested that a "five-to-ten-fold increase in world industrial output can be anticipated by the time world population stabilises some time in the next century". It has been contended, however, that to accommodate this sustainably, on present technology, would require 6 to 12 additional planets. To accommodate it on Earth alone would require a heightened level of technology that can do the same with 6 to 12 times less energy and material.[19]

PRESCRIBED NATIONAL POLICIES

Four national policies are identified in *Agenda 21* to achieve the above global strategies, namely: new systems of national accounts, improved assessments of the national population impacts, and national and regional carrying capacity assessments:

> Consideration should be given to the present concepts of economic growth and the need for new concepts of wealth and prosperity which allow higher standards of living through changed lifestyles and are less dependent on the Earth's finite resources and more in harmony with the Earth's carrying capacity. This should be reflected in the evolution of new systems of national accounts and other indicators of sustainable development.
>
> Existing plans for sustainable development have generally recognized demographic trends and factors as elements that have a critical influence on consumption patterns, production, lifestyles and long-term sustainability. But in future, more attention will have to be given to these issues in general policy formulation and the design of development plans. To do this, all countries will have to improve their own capacities to assess the environment and development implications of their demographic trends and factors.
>
> An assessment should be made of national population carrying capacity in the context of satisfaction of human needs and sustainable development, and special attention should be given to critical resources, such as water and land, and environmental factors such as ecosystem health and biodiversity.

Although many of the long-term environmental changes that are likely to affect people and the biosphere are global in scale, key changes can often be made at the national and local levels. At the same time, human activities at the local and regional levels often contribute to global threats – e.g. stratospheric ozone depletion. Thus scientific assessments are required at the global, regional and local levels. Many countries and organizations already prepare reports on the environment and development which review current conditions and indicate future trends. Regional and global assessments could make full use of such reports but should be broader in scope and include the results of detailed studies of future conditions for a range of assumptions about possible future human responses, using the best available models. Such assessments should be designed to map out manageable development pathways within the environmental and socio-economic carrying capacity of each region.[20]

LEGITIMATE NATIONAL INTERESTS

What analytical tools are available for countries to determine the legitimate national interest of countries in this complex area? Just as it is applied at the global level, the ecological footprint analysis can be used as a key indicator at the national level. Using this concept, a national sustainability deficit can be arrived at, country-by-country.

Table III.2 portrays the ecological footprint of 51 nation-states (plus Hong Kong, treated separately), estimated in a study commissioned by the Earth Council for the Rio+5 Conference in June 1997 (and subsequently updated). These countries comprise 80% of the global population and generate 95% of World Domestic Product. The countries are ranked according to their ecological footprint per capita. Their ecological deficit or surplus is the amount of land they draw down from, or contribute to, the global availability. The world average is included, at 2.8 hectares per capita, for Earth.

Table III.2   Ecological footprint analysis: selected nations (ranked by footprint size)

Country	Population (1997) (million)	Ecological Footprint (ha/person)	Available Ecol. Capacity (ha/person)	Ecol. Deficit or Surplus (ha/person)
United States	268.2	10.3	6.7	−3.6
Australia	18.6	9.0	14.0	5.0
Canada	30.1	7.7	9.6	1.9
New Zealand	3.7	7.6	20.4	12.8
Iceland	0.3	7.4	21.7	14.3
Singapore	2.9	7.2	0.1	−7.1
Norway	4.4	6.2	6.3	0.1
Hong Kong	5.9	6.1	0.0	−6.1
Finland	5.1	6.0	8.6	2.6
Russia	146.4	6.0	3.7	−2.3
Denmark	5.2	5.9	5.2	−0.7
Ireland	3.6	5.9	6.5	0.6
Sweden	8.9	5.9	7.0	1.1
Germany	81.8	5.3	1.9	−3.4
Netherlands	15.7	5.3	1.7	−3.6
United Kingdom	58.6	5.2	1.7	−3.5
Belgium	10.2	5.0	1.2	−3.8
Switzerland	7.3	5.0	1.8	−3.2
Czech Republic	10.3	4.5	4.0	−0.5
Japan	125.7	4.3	0.9	−3.4
Italy	57.2	4.2	1.3	−2.9
Austria	8.1	4.1	3.1	−1.0
France	58.4	4.1	4.2	0.1
Greece	10.5	4.1	1.5	−2.6

Table III.2   (cont'd)

Country	Population (1997) (million)	Ecological Footprint (ha/person)	Available Ecol. Capacity (ha/person)	Ecol. Deficit or Surplus (ha/person)
Poland	38.5	4.1	2.0	−2.1
Argentina	35.4	3.9	4.6	0.7
Portugal	9.8	3.8	2.9	−0.9
Spain	39.7	3.8	2.2	−1.6
Venezuela	22.8	3.8	2.7	−1.1
Korea, Republic	45.9	3.4	0.5	−2.9
Israel	5.9	3.4	0.3	−3.1
Malaysia	21.0	3.3	3.7	0.4
South Africa	43.3	3.2	1.3	−1.9
Brazil	167.0	3.1	6.7	3.6
Hungary	10.0	3.1	2.1	−1.0
Thailand	60.0	2.8	1.2	−1.6
EARTH	5,892.5	2.8	2.1	−0.7
Mexico	97.2	2.6	1.4	−1.2
Costa Rica	3.6	2.5	2.5	0.0
Chile	14.7	2.5	3.2	0.7
Turkey	64.3	2.1	1.3	−0.8
Colombia	36.2	2.0	4.1	2.1
Jordan	5.8	1.9	0.1	−1.8
Peru	24.7	1.6	7.7	6.1
Nigeria	118.4	1.5	0.6	−0.9
Philippines	70.4	1.5	0.9	−0.6
Indonesia	203.6	1.4	2.6	1.2
China	1,247.3	1.2	0.8	−0.4
Egypt	65.4	1.2	0.2	−1.0
Ethiopia	58.4	0.8	0.5	−0.3
India	970.2	0.8	0.5	−0.3
Pakistan	148.7	0.8	0.5	−0.3
Bangladesh	125.9	0.5	0.3	−0.2

Source: Updated Ranking List (1993 data) after introducing equivalency factors, new forest productivity and CO_2 absorption (after IPCC data), November 1997 (supplied by e-mail by M. Wackernagel, May 1998); updating M. Wackernagel, L. Onisto, A. Callejas Linares, I.S. Lopez Falfán, J. Mendez Garcia, A.I. Suárez Guerrero, G. Suárez Guerrero, *Ecological footprints of nations*. Study commissioned for the Rio+5 Earth Summit, 1997, by the Earth Council, San José, Costa Rica, March 1997, 10.

The statistics themselves must be treated with caution at this early stage of development of the concept.[21] They are, as the originators put it, "just the beginning of our efforts to monitor national footprints".[22] It would seem to be too early to advance binding prescriptions concerning the legitimate national interest of each country based on the state of development of the methodology. Yet such work is an important harbinger of future statistical analysis and political judgement of this kind; and it has already appeared as a prescriptive concept in a UN action programme.[23]

From this work it is clear that the ecological footprint of the North exceeds its fair "earthshare" by a factor of two to three. If all humanity maintained the same consumption pattern, three planets would be required to satisfy aggregate demand, on current technology. In the words of the authors, "Not even the present population of 5.8 billion people let alone the 10 billion projected by 2040 can hope to achieve North America's material standards without destroying the ecosphere and precipitating their own collapse".[24] Moreover, as they put it, "Governments everywhere are obsessed with reducing their fiscal deficits but ignore their cumulative debt to nature. Material consumption in high-income countries today increasingly exceeds their sustainable natural income. Unless the wealthy nations act to reduce their growing ecological deficits, global sustainability will remain a receding dream".[25]

This section considers the three main elements of global sustainability – population, development and consumption.

Sustainability turns equally on each of these factors. But the international community has not yet demonstrated an equal commitment to each. The term "sustainable development" tends to prioritize development over consumption. While the UN conference at Rio addressed development (along with the environment) and Cairo stressed population (along with development), no global conference has to date focused on consumption. The result is a lack of clarity over the global limits to Earth's carrying capacity, and an implicit political premise that there is no limit or that the constraints are considerably elastic.

Six countries are chosen for the primary focus on these issues – India and Australia for population stabilization, Bangladesh and Kenya for development, and Sweden and the United States for consumption. In addition, a case study is chosen, forest management, as an example of a specific challenge for sustainability, and two key countries, Indonesia and Brazil, are chosen for analysis and comment on this. The basic indicators of these eight countries are set out in Table III.3.

Table III.3 Selected countries: basic lifestyle indicators

Country	HDI Ranking	HDI	Life expect.	Adult literacy (%)	GDP/p.c. ($000)	Ecological footprint (ha. p.c.)	Ecological surplus/deficit (ha. p.c.)
USA	4	0.942	76	99	26,400	10.3	−3.6
Sweden	10	0.936	78	99	18,500	5.9	+1.1
Australia	14	0.931	78	99	19,300	9.0	+5.0
Brazil	68	0.783	66	83	5,400	3.1	+3.6
Indonesia	99	0.668	64	83	3,700	1.4	+1.2
Kenya	134	0.463	53	77	1,400	n.a.	n.a.
India	138	0.446	61	51	1,300	0.8	−0.3
Bangladesh	144	0.368	56	37	1,300	0.5	−0.2

Sources: UNDP Human Development Report 1997, Human Development Index, 146–8; M. Wackernagel et al., *Ecological footprint of nations* (San José, Costa Rica: Earth Council, March 1997).

Thus, it can be seen that, according to the basic indicators used by UNDP of life expectancy, adult literacy and economic activity, the United States ranks fourth in the world. But the ecological footprint of each American is estimated to be 10.3 hectares, nearly four times larger than the average earthshare for each human on the planet. Despite its huge size and enormous natural wealth, the US runs an ecological deficit per capita of 3.6 hectares. Sweden ranks tenth in the world, but the Swedes' footprint is still unacceptably large at 5.9 hectares per capita. Because of its light population density, however, it runs an ecological surplus as a country. Similarly, Australia ranks 14th, although the footprint of the average Australian is huge, at 9.0 hectares. Yet its vast size and small population result in a large ecological surplus of 5.0 hectares per capita. Essentially, Sweden and Australia are subsidizing the rest of the world, although they should be subsidizing it by considerably more than they are.

In contrast, India and Bangladesh rank 138th and 144th respectively. Their citizens are denied the lifestyle benefits of Australia, Sweden and the US. Their footprints are exceedingly small, less than 1 hectare per capita. Despite being the second most populous nation in the world, India runs only a small deficit – scarcely drawing down on the world's ecological asset balance (0.3 hectares per capita).

For its part Bangladesh, with its 126 million crowded into a tiny slice of Earth's land space, also runs a deficit on the global asset balance by a small fraction (0.2 hectare per capita). Both Indonesia and Brazil are in the world's spotlight through their rainforest resources. Even the Brazilians, not regarded as an unduly rich people, nonetheless draw down 3.1 hectares per capita, 48% above the average earthshare. Yet because of its vast size and resources, Brazil runs a large ecological surplus. For their part, Indonesians live at two thirds the earthshare level, and despite their large population density, run an ecological surplus of 1.2 hectares per capita. Figures for Kenya are not yet available.

The conclusions of this analysis are stark. Wealthy and underpopulated countries such as Australia and Sweden are subsidizing the world through their small populations. Impoverished and populous countries such as Bangladesh and India are just about "breaking even" in the national contribution to global sustainability, while Brazil and Indonesia are subsidizing the world. A "wealthy" and populous country such as the United States is ecologically overshooting by a huge factor, and borrowing off the rest of the world – being subsidized by other countries for the lifestyle it leads.

In Chapters 8 through 11, the contributors from these eight countries are asked to consider their country's national policies in light of the vital planetary interest in global sustainability and its legitimate national interest in this respect.

NOTES

1. The basic definition of sustainable carrying capacity is: "the maximum number of persons that can be supported in perpetuity on an area, with a given technology and a set of consumption habits, without causing environmental degradation". See P.M. Fearnside, *Human carrying capacity of the Brazilian rainforest* (New York: Columbia University Press, 1986), 73; and J.W. Kirchner, G. Ledec, R.J.A. Goodland & J. Drake, "Carrying capacity, population growth and sustainable development", in *Rapid population growth and human carrying capacity: two perspectives*, D.J. Mahar (ed.), World Bank Staff Working Papers No. 690, Population and Development Series No. 15 (Washington, DC: World Bank, 1985), 40–89. Quoted in J.E. Cohen (ed.), *How many people can the Earth support?* (New York: W.W. Norton, 1995), 419–25.
2. G. Hardin, "Cultural carrying capacity: a biological approach to human problems", *Bio Science* **36** (9), 599–606, in Cohen, *How many people?*, 421. See also, G. Hardin, *Living within limits: ecology, economics and population taboos* (Oxford: Oxford University Press, 1995).
3. See A.H. Maslow, *American Psychological Review* 1942; and *Employment, growth and basic needs* (Geneva: International Labour Office, 1976).
4. See UNDP Human Development Report 1997, ". . . a person is absolutely poor if her income is less than the defined income poverty line". This compares with the concept of "relative poverty": ". . . she is relatively poor if she belongs to the bottom income group (such as the bottom 10%)".
5. *Vital signs 1994* (New York: Worldwatch Institute, 1994). Figures in 1987 US dollars.
6. *Agenda 21*: 5.3, 14.34
7. Ibid., 5.10
8. Ibid., 35.2
9. Rio Declaration: Principles 1 and 3.
10. *Our common future*, 8.
11. *Agenda 21*: 35.11(a&b); 35.17(b).
12. See for example:

> Studies about nature's capacity to support human life go back many centuries. Some focus more on energy requirements, others on non-renewable resources, and others again on photosynthetic potentials. But all are based on the same principle: tracing resource and energy flows through the human economy. Much intellectual ground-work was laid in the 1960s and 1970s. Examples are Eugene and Howard Odum's eMergy analysis examining systems through energy flows, Jay Forrester's advancements on modelling world resource dynamics, John Holdren's and Paul Ehrlich's IPAT formula, or, in the spirit of the International Biological Programme, Robert Whittaker's calculation of net primary productivity of the world's ecosystems. The last ten years have witnessed exciting new developments: life cycle analyses (e.g. Muller-Wenk), environmental space calculations (Johann Opshoor and the Friends of the Earth), human appropriation of net primary productivity (Peter Vitousek at al.), mass intensity measures such as MIPS (Friedrich Schmidt-Bleek and the Wuppertal Institute), the Sustainable Process Index SPI (Christian Krotscheck, Michael Narodoslawsky), the "Polstar" scenario model (Stockholm Environment Institute), or the ecological footprint concept (Mathis Wackernagel and William Rees, and similar studies by Carl Folke); to name just a few. Their applications may vary, but their message

is the same: Quantifying human use of nature in order to reduce it. As most of them are compatible, results from one approach strengthen the other. M. Wackernagel et al., *Ecological footprints of nations* (San Jose, Costa Rica: Earth Council, 1997).

See also E. Elgar, *Measuring sustainable development* (London: UCL Press/World Bank, 1997) which reviews the various ecological indicators and economic measures of sustainable development, ranging from indicators of biological diversity through to "adjusted GNP".

13. M. Wackernagel & W. Rees, *Our ecological footprint: reducing human impact on the Earth* (Gabriola Island, BC: New Society Publishers, 1996), 88, 53.
14. Ibid., 5, 51–2.
15. Ibid., 89–90.
16. Wackernagel et al., *Ecological footprints of nations*, 5, 10, 13. See also Wackernagel & Rees, *Our ecological footprint*, 85, 90, and A.J. McMichael, *Planetary overload*. (Cambridge: Cambridge University Press, 1993). The figures used here were updated by M. Wackernagel, May 1998.
17. Wackernagel & Rees, *Our ecological footprint*, 55.
18. Rees, in Wackernagel et al., *Ecological footprints of nations*, 17.
19. Wackernagel & Rees, *Our ecological footprint*, 91.
20. *Agenda 21*, 4.11, 5.16, 5.23, 35.15
21. An earlier version of the same analysis for a smaller number of countries, for example, had significant statistical differences. See Wackernagel & Rees, *Our ecological footprint*, 97.
22. Wackernagel et al., *Ecological footprints of nations*, 26.
23. "We [the participating States] commit ourselves to: ... Promoting changes in unsustainable production and consumption patterns ... thereby ... reducing the ecological footprint of human settlements". United Nations Conference on Human Settlements, Habitat II Agenda, 43 (j).
24. Wackernagel & Rees, *Our ecological footprint*, 90.
25. Rees, in Wackernagel et al., *Ecological footprints of nations*, 17.

CHAPTER EIGHT

Population stabilization

8.1   Introduction

The most critical determinant of all in considering the planet's carrying capacity is the growing human population. Everything else is secondary to the phenomenon of the "demographic transition" which the world is currently experiencing.

THE GLOBAL PROBLEM

It took some 100,000 years for humanity, upon evolving into modern homo sapiens, to reach 1 billion in number. It reached this figure around AD 1804. Thereafter, the global population has grown almost exponentially, with succeeding increments of 1 billion respectively taking 123 years, 33 years, 14 years, 13 years and 11 years.[1]

The average annual global population growth was 87 million from 1985 to 1990, declining to 81 million from 1990 to 1995. The period 1985 to 1990 appears to have been the peak period of global population growth. The annual rate of growth was 1.72% from 1975 to 1990, reducing to 1.48% from 1990 to 1995.[2] The annual increase in the global population will remain at around these levels for the next two decades – about a quarter of a million each day, for the next twenty years.[3]

This unprecedented increase is due to the demographic transition, defined as the "historical shift of birth and death rates from high to low levels in a population". The decline of mortality usually precedes the decline in fertility, thus resulting in rapid population growth during the transition period.[4]

The magnitude of the problem confronting humanity over the next century is displayed in the global population projections compiled by the United Nations as illustrated in Table 8.1.1.

Table 8.1.1   Global population projection: 2000–2150 (billion)

Year	Low	Medium	High	% Increase Medium/1996
1995		5.70		
2000	6.06	6.09	6.12	7
2010	6.73	6.89	7.06	21
2025	7.47	8.39	8.58	47
2050	7.66	9.37	11.16	64
2100	5.58	10.41	17.50	83
2150	3.55	10.81	26.98	90

Sources: World Population Prospects: the 1996 revision, Annex I (New York; United Nations, 1996); and Long-Range World Population Projections, 1950–2150 (New York; United Nations, 1998).
See also earlier projections in *Agenda 21* and the Cairo ICPD Programme for Action. The latest figures project significantly lower growth than the projections of the early 1990s (4% lower for the medium projection of 2050 and 7% lower for 2100).

Whatever the degree of stress there is on the planet's environment and carrying capacity today, it will double by the middle of the twenty-first century if the level of technology and current development and consumption patterns continue unchanged. The medium-fertility scenario indicates that the global population will reach 9.4 billion in 2050, 10.4 billion in 2100 and 10.8 billion in 2150. It will, in this scenario, ultimately stabilize at just under 11 billion around 2200. A doubling of environmental stress is clearly untenable for human sustenance. Every effort must therefore be made to curtail the human population growth over the next critical decade of the "transition".

THE GLOBAL OBJECTIVE AND STRATEGY

The global objective, as proclaimed at the 1994 UN International Conference on Population and Development, is the improvement in the quality of life of present and future generations through the stabilization of the world population with sustainable development and economic growth:

> Recognizing that the ultimate goal is the improvement in quality of life of present and future generations, the objective is to facilitate the demographic transition as soon as possible in countries where there is an imbalance between demographic rates and social, economic and environmental goals, while fully respecting human rights. This process will contribute to the stabilization of world population, and, together with changes in unsustainable patterns of production and consumption, to sustainable development and economic growth.[5]

By "stabilization" is meant a level of recurring population growth below the medium-term projection of the UN population projections:

> During the remaining six years of this critical decade, the world's nations by their actions or inactions will choose from among a range of alternative demographic futures . . . Implementation of the goals and objectives contained in the present 20-year Programme of Action . . . would result in world population growth during this period and beyond at levels below the United Nations medium projection.[6]

Thus the objective is to have a global population at or below 9.8 billion in 2050 and 11.2 billion in 2100 (the medium projection figures used at the Cairo conference).

The strategy for the earliest possible completion of the demographic transition is essentially the Cairo Programme of Action. The programme makes it clear:

> World population grew at the rate of 1.7% per annum during the period 1985–90, but is expected to decrease during the following decades and reach 1.0% per annum by the period 2020–2025. Nevertheless, the attainment of population stabilisation during the twenty-first century will require the implementation of all the policies and recommendations in the present Programme of Action . . .
>
> The Programme of Action will require the establishment of common ground, with full respect for the religious and ethical values and cultural backgrounds. The impact of this Conference will be measured by the strength of the specific commitments made here and the consequent actions to fulfil them among all the world's countries and peoples, based on a sense of shared but differentiated responsibility for each other and for our planetary home.[7]

The Global Population Programme is an interrelated series of policies for reducing the rate of population growth, primarily through five measures: family planning including contraceptive techniques; improved reproductive health services; the suppression of sexually transmitted diseases; improved education, especially for girls; and heightened male responsibility. The annual cost of the programme is estimated as set out in Table 8.1.2. It is "tentatively estimated" that up to two-thirds of the above costs will continue to be met by the countries themselves and in the order of one-third from "external sources", i.e. financial assistance from North to South.[8]

In the Cairo Statement of Principles, the developed countries "acknowledge the responsibility they bear in the international pursuit of sustainable development". They accept the obligation to "continue to improve their efforts to promote sustained economic growth and to narrow imbalances in a manner that can benefit all countries, particularly the developing countries".[9] The programme stipulates that governments, NGOs, the private sector and local communities, "assisted upon request by the international community", should "strive to mobilize and effectively utilize the resources for population and development programmes". They should "strive to further mobilize the resources needed to meet the goals in the present Programme of Action. In this regard, governments are urged

Table 8.1.2 Global population programme: estimated annual cost of implementation ($ billion)

Programme	2000	2005	2010	2015
Family planning	10.2	11.5	12.6	13.8
Reproductive health	5.0	5.4	5.7	6.1
Disease control*	1.3	1.4	1.5	1.5
Research	0.5	0.2	0.7	0.3
Total	17.0	18.5	20.5	21.7
External sources	5.7	6.2	6.8	7.2

Source: ICPD, 13.15; 14.11.
* Sexually transmitted diseases.

to devote an increased proportion of public-sector expenditures to the social sectors, as well as an increased proportion of official development assistance . . .".[10]

More specifically, the Cairo programme recalled the 1989 Amsterdam Declaration on a Better Life for Future Generations, which urged governments to double global expenditure on population programmes, and donors to "increase substantially their contribution".[11] Cairo then asserted that "additional resources are urgently required to better identify and satisfy unmet needs in issues related to population and development".[12]

Much of the content of the programme addresses sensitive social and moral issues such as contraception and abortion, and the individual right of parental choice compared with individual responsibility. The strategy of coercion was adamantly rejected in favour of the "reproductive right of free and responsible choice" and the "principle of informed choice". As the programme stated it:

> Reproductive health is a state of complete physical, mental and social well-being . . . Reproductive health implies that people are able to have a satisfying sex life and that they have the capability to reproduce and the freedom to decide if, and when and how often to do so. Implicit in this last condition are the rights of men and women to be informed and to have access to safe, effective, affordable and acceptable methods of family planning of their choice, as well as other methods of their choice for regulation of fertility which are not against the law, and the right of access to appropriate health-care services that will enable women to go safely through pregnancy and childbirth and provide couples the best chance of having a healthy infant.[13]

These rights, stated the programme, rest on the recognition of the basic right of all couples and individuals "to decide freely and responsibly the number, spacing and timing of their children" and to have the information and means to make those decisions. Couples and individuals have the right to make decisions concerning reproduction free of discrimination, coercion and violence. The "principle of informed choice" is essential to the success of family-planning programmes.

A key concept in this respect concerns the "unmet needs" of couples requiring family planning services. It is estimated that some 350 million couples lack access to modern family-planning methods and another 120 million women would use such methods if more accurate information and affordable services were easily available.[14] Millions of deaths each year are due to the denial of "reproductive rights" – including "free choice" with regard to pregnancy and childbearing.[15] The UNFPA has warned that shortfalls in population assistance may result, between 1995 and 2000, in 120 million additional unwanted pregnancies, 49 million abortions, 5 million infant and young children deaths and 65,000 maternal deaths.[16]

PRESCRIBED NATIONAL POLICIES

All countries, stated the Cairo programme, should recognize their "common but differentiated responsibilities" in sustainable development and social progress.[17] Two years earlier, Agenda 21 had called upon nation-states to intensify their national policies for the attainment of a global strategy:

National population policy goals and programmes that are consistent with national environment and development plans for sustainability and in keeping with the freedom, dignity and personally-held values of individuals should be established and implemented. National reviews should be conducted and the integration of population policies in national development and environment strategies should be monitored nationally.[18]

Specifically, the Cairo programme urges governments to undertake a wide range of measures. They should strive to make accessible, through the primary health care system, reproductive health to all individuals of appropriate ages as soon as possible and no later than 2015. Governmental goals for family planning should be defined in terms of unmet needs for information and services. Demographic goals should not be imposed on family-planning providers in the form of targets or quotas for the recruitment of clients. All countries should assess the extent of additional unmet need for good-quality family-planning services.

All countries should, the programme said, take steps to meet the family-planning needs of their populations as soon as possible and should, in all cases by 2015, seek to provide universal access to a full range of safe and reliable family-planning methods and to related reproductive health services which are not against the law.

For their part, "leaders and legislators at all levels" are enjoined to translate their public support for reproductive health, including family planning, into adequate allocations of budgetary, human and administrative resources to help meet the needs of all those who cannot pay the full cost of services.

Finally, the vexed question of abortion. Governments should take appropriate steps to help women avoid abortion, which "in no case" should be promoted as a method of family planning, and "in all cases" provide for the humane treatment and counselling of women who have had recourse to abortion.[19]

The programme lays out a model "national action plan" for countries to incorporate population concerns into their national development strategies. They should foster the active involvement of elected representatives of people, particularly parliamentarians, in formulating rational strategies for population and development. Governments, with the active involvement of parliamentarians, should work to increase awareness of population and development issues. Governments and parliamentarians, in collaboration with the international community and non-governmental organizations, are expected to make the necessary plans in accordance with national concerns and priorities. They should also monitor and evaluate progress towards meeting the goals of the present Programme of Action.[20]

LEGITIMATE NATIONAL INTERESTS

Two countries that symbolize the extremes in the global population drama are India and Australia. India has 914 million people; Australia has 19 million. With 2% of the planet's land surface, India has 16% of the global population; with 5% of the land, Australia has 0.3%. The average human population density on the planet is 38 persons per square kilometre. In India it is 278; in Australia, 2. Australia, which is two and a third times larger than India, has one-fiftieth the population. Although much of the Australian continent is desert, its habitable area is still a huge area. Yet the population growth rate in India (1.8%) is higher than that of both Australia (1.5%) and the world average (1.48%). By 2000, the population of India is projected to exceed 1 billion. In a few decades, India is expected to pass China's population, and become the most populous country on the planet.

What happens in India is therefore critical to the future of Earth's population. With a GNP per capita of $320, it is a country in need, and it is in the vital planetary interest that the rest of the world help. For its part and with a GNP per capita of $18,000, Australia is a country that can help. What Australia does in this respect is, in turn, critical to that task.

NOTES

1. Programme of Action of the International Conference on Population and Development, Cairo, 1994: 6.1 (hereafter ICPD).
2. 1996 Revision of UN Population Estimates and Projections, Population Division, United Nations (UNDH, 15 November 1996).

3. ICPD, 1.3.
4. Population Handbook, Population Reference Bureau.
5. ICPD, 6.3.
6. Ibid., 1.4.
7. Ibid., 6.1, 1.15.
8. Ibid., 13.16.
9. Ibid., Principle 15.
10. Ibid., 13.22, 13.23.
11. Amsterdam Declaration on a Better Life for Future Generations, adopted at the International Forum on Population in the Twenty-First Century, Amsterdam, 1989.
12. ICPD, 14.8.
13. Ibid., 7.2, 7.3, 7.12.
14. Ibid., 7.13.
15. United Nations Fund for Population Activities, 1997 State of the World Population Report: *The right to choose: reproductive rights and reproductive health* (UNDH, 29 May 1997).
16. UNDH, 14 May 1997.
17. ICPD, Chapter 2, Principle 15.
18. *Agenda 21*, 5.31, 5.35.
19. ICPD, 7.6, 7.12, 7.16, 7.17, 7.19, 7.20, 7.21, 7.22, 7.23(b), 7.24.
20. Ibid., 13.4–6.

8.2 India

Margaret Alva

> ... reducing the birth rate to the extent necessary to stabilize the population at a level consistent with the requirement of the national economy.
>
> Family-Planning Programme, Government of India, 1951

From the warnings of Malthus in 1798 to the Cairo Declaration of 1994, population pressure, sustainable development and human survival have been irrevocably linked. They are, taken together, the key issue for global policy-makers. While the primacy of national laws and local religio-cultural traditions in determining national policies were accepted, the nations assembled at Cairo and earlier at Rio acknowledged that our planet cannot sustain life for long if the present trend of population growth, poverty, pollution and indiscriminate exploitation of natural resources continues. Recent disasters, natural or man-made, have proven beyond doubt that national boundaries and regional might are of no consequence when such calamities occur. Humanity must survive or be destroyed together – the big and the small, the strong and the weak, the developed and the developing – as the people of the world.

The demographic projections of the world are clear. Today's population of 5.8 billion will reach around 9 billion by 2050. Most of this growth will occur in the South. India and China will account for 50% of that. Simultaneously, the North will have an aging population, increasingly dependent on a diminishing productive workforce, making it difficult for them to sustain their economic momentum. Imbalances and scarcities will force mass migrations, peaceful or otherwise, leading to tension and conflict between and within nations. All in all, a rather dreadful scenario to look forward to.

And what of my country? Celebrating the Golden Jubilee of her independence, India is proud of the progress made these past 50 years. We are self-sufficient in food. We have a strong industrial base. Our economy is now of global reach while our achievements in space technology are acknowledged. We have preserved, in fact strengthened, our democratic institutions.

Yet none of this seems to have in any way mitigated the social and economic condition of millions of our people, steeped in poverty, illiteracy and hunger. While one could cite excuses for this, the single most important reason is an inability to keep our population under control. The benefits of our achievements have been eroded by the ever-growing requirements of the multiplying millions.

The statistics of India are staggering. We are 3.3 million sq. km. That is larger than Europe – 13 times the size of Britain. In 1947 our population was 342 million. Half a century later, it stands at 974 million – almost three times larger – one-sixth of humanity. Yet our population density, at 296 per square kilometre, is not as great as some; Britain, at 246, is almost as densely populated. The difference, however, is that Britain and other countries of the North have completed their "demographic transition" while India has not. Our population is still growing fast.

NATIONAL POLICY

The Cairo Conference called upon countries to introduce or intensify their national population goals and programmes consistent with national sustainability. Governments and parliamentarians, "in collaboration with the international community", are to make the necessary plans to meet the goals of the global Programme of Action.

India, of course, has been striving to do essentially this for decades. It was the world's first country to launch an official Family-Planning Programme, back in 1951. The stated aim even then was "reducing the birth rate to the extent necessary to stabilize the population at a level consistent with the requirement of the national economy". That is close to saying keep the population within the national carrying capacity. If our population growth had been effectively contained, the number today would have been around 700 million, with dramatic positive effects on the economic and social life of the people.

Over the years, various initiatives have been taken by successive governments. In 1976, the National Population Policy emphasized the "crucial role of fertility control in India's movement towards economic development and social transformation". All the states of India sought to implement it in earnest, with a certain degree of coercion and compulsion. Results were initially achieved with 8.4 million sterilized in 1976–7. But a strongly negative public reaction followed and in turn, a rapid decline in the number of those sterilized to 0.95 million in 1977–8. The message was clear: population control is too sensitive and personal a matter to be forced on citizens without repercussions, be they social or political. In the parliamentary elections of 1977, the Congress Party lost the government benches for the first time since independence in 1947.

The new government, realizing the price its predecessor had paid for such coercive family-planning measures, advanced a new policy statement upon election. Family planning was included as an integral part of the total welfare programme. The problem was to be tackled henceforth through education, information and motivation. Significantly, the name of the department handling the subject was changed from Family Planning to Family Welfare. This was almost 20 years before Cairo.

Returning to power in 1980, Indira Gandhi announced a new National Health Policy. It emphasized the need for "securing a small family through voluntary efforts to move towards the goal of population stabilization". The wishes of the people had been taken into account. India was a vibrant democracy. Government could not thrust anything, certainly not sterilization, on the people. Acknowledging the past lack of political will and poor programme implementation, parliament passed a unanimous resolution making population issues a "national priority", with political parties committing themselves not to politicize the issue. The freezing of seats in parliament up to AD 2001 through a constitutional amendment was a special measure intended to remove the disadvantages that would accrue to states within the Union which achieved positive results in population control.

After Indira Gandhi's assassination and Rajiv Gandhi's assumption of the leadership, the young prime minister gave a new dimension to the population issue in 1985. He asserted that India's population, two-thirds of which were under the age of 45 years, could in fact be its greatest asset, so long as our human resource was turned into a disciplined, trained and productive workforce for national development. The Ministry of Human Resource Development was created to deal with education and training, childcare, women's health and development, youth affairs, sports and culture. "Our numbers must become a positive factor for development," he said.

Then came the 1994 Cairo Conference. How has India responded?

Containing population growth has been one of the six most important objectives of India's 8th National Plan (1992–7). The aim is three-fold: to reduce the birth rate from 30 per thousand in 1990 to 26 in 1997, with a decrease in the Infant Mortality Rate (IMR) from 80 per thousand in 1990 to 70 in 1997, and increase the couple protection rate to 56%. But the programme is linked to various factors such as improving the literacy rate, female education, socio-economic status of individuals and families and other human resource indicators, emphasizing a broad-based and integrated approach to population stabilization. Suggestions are now made for incentives and disincentives such as debarring those who did not follow the two-child norm from contesting elections; debarring from the civil service those who had married below the legal age; recruitment and promotion within the services and several benefits provided to be linked to adoption of the two-child norm; and amendments of existing laws to ensure that the official norm is followed. But will they be implemented? I doubt our capacity to do so.

Cairo recommended that family-planning programmes in developing countries should not be viewed as policy intervention measures for manipulating the fertility rates of the population at the macro level. Rather, they were to be an integral part of the health programmes for the empowerment of women, respecting their rights with regard to their family size and the spacing of children. Such programmes were not to be guided by contraceptive targets.

India, as a signatory to the Cairo Programme of Action, abolished targets in its national family-planning programme in April 1996. The important elements of the new policy are: target-free programmes, greater emphasis on quality of services, decentralized participatory planning, integrated reductive health packages, integrated child health services, state-specific interventions, increased male participation, gender sensitivity and an increased involvement of NGOs and private practitioners.

THE LEGITIMATE NATIONAL INTEREST

The short experience to date since the introduction of the "target-free approach" in the states of Uttar Pradesh, Bihar, Rajasthan and Madhya Pradesh has been disappointing. Acceptance levels were less than 50% of the corresponding period in the previous year when targets were in vogue. On the other hand, such a drastic change in acceptance has not occurred in the progressive southern states. Thus, while the need for rapid increase in contraceptive use and reduction in the fertility levels is the highest in the four states identified, policy changes are slowing efforts in this direction. The abolition of targets may have a rebound effect in reducing family-planning acceptance and increasing fertility. Besides, policy changes involve retraining 250,000 grass-roots workers who have been implementing the programme in a particular way. This will adversely affect the delivery system as well as diverting scarce funds. And the emphasis on the total health package as a precondition of fertility management will involve providing many services without extra allocations, automatically reducing the outreach of the programme at a very crucial time.

There is near unanimity in the country that the population situation is critical and calls for urgent corrective action. With such intense political focus, why has India's population planning largely failed?

The reasons are many. Some 80% of India's population is rural based where poverty, illiteracy, unemployment and lack of basic facilities still persist. As numbers multiply the limited resources of human survival – water, fuel, fodder – are diminishing, and the pressure on forest wealth is mounting, resulting in growing conflict between man and animal. Urban migration and the resulting slums surround industrial and city centres, creating problems of housing, sanitation and drinking water and leading to heavy pressure on an infrastructure that is stretched beyond manageable limits. But in a multi-religious, tradition-bound society, population issues can become explosive. Sensitivities of minority groups can be exploited for narrow political gain, negating governmental initiatives and inhibiting bold action. This is one of the main reasons for the slow results seen in India to date.

The family-planning programme, now secured on a voluntary basis as a people's movement, seeks to promote responsible parenthood with a two-child norm, irrespective of gender, through independent choice of the method best suited to the couple. But progress is slow because the task is gigantic, involving 500 million people in the productive age group spread over 3.3 million sq. km of territory. The government has been playing the role of facilitator by providing free family-planning services through a vast infrastructure comprising the Primary Health Centres (PHC) and Child Health Centres (CHC), besides pressing into service health workers, traditional midwives and "bare-foot" nurses to reach the people in distant and remote areas. The central government alone spends around 2,000 crores ($500 million) annually on this.

In spite of the marginal decrease from 2.2% in 1971–81, the annual population growth rate of 1.8% is still high. Yet India's experience is not to be viewed as historically unique. The North has gone through this phase of population explosion before achieving manageable rates of growth. But, the demographic transition in India seems to be taking longer compared with many other developing countries. Nor do we seem to be using to our advantage the experience of others, or even of two or three states in our own country, to hasten the transition.

Poverty and population have a close link. Most poor parents view children as a means of income, and especially their sons as a means of security in old age. The choice therefore is for more children, preferably sons. As the Chinese say, "a girl is her mother's cotton padded winter-coat while her son is her down-jacket". The need for sons is embedded in the psyche of most Asian cultures. It is the son who ensures that the family name continues. It is he who will light the funeral pyre of his Hindu parents, after caring for them in old age. Parents see nothing wrong in preferring sons and if modern science can be exploited to ensure the birth of male children, then why not? Today medical inventions and traditional practices combine to perpetuate female foeticide despite a law banning sex determination tests and forbidding doctors from telling parents the sex of their unborn child. For those who are willing to pay, the facility exists. Female infanticide is a criminal offence but the investment that a family has to make in the form of dowry at the time of her marriage prompts them to do away with her at birth. And the girl-child is neglected, ill fed and burdened with household chores at every stage of her development, resulting in much higher IMRs for the female child than for that of the male.

This discrimination can clearly be seen in the 1991 census with a female/male ratio of 927 per thousand as compared to 934 in 1981. Population experts warn against what they term the "deliberate tampering" with India's demographic profile, the repercussions of which will be felt in the decades to come. Currently, only one state in India, Kerala, has a sex ratio exceeding unity, coupled with a declining population. Alarmed at these trends, the government launched in October 1997 the *Balika Samriddhi Yojana* which gives every mother of a female child born after 15 August 1997 who is below the poverty line Rs500 ($13) as a gift.

India is trying. But ultimately the only effective way to deal with all these social ills is the education and empowerment of women. Literacy plays an important role in controlling the birth rate by influencing the two most important determinants of fertility – age of marriage and contraceptive use. Comparative analysis of two Indian states, Kerala and Rajasthan, demonstrates this. Kerala, with the highest literacy levels in the country (approaching 100% in several districts) and with the average female age of marriage at 22 years (nearly four years above the minimum), has a CBR (crude birth rate) of 19 and IMR of 17. In stark contrast, Rajasthan, with a female literacy rate of 21%, an average age of marriage for females of 16 years (two years below the legal minimum) has a CBR of 33 and IMR of 83. Kerala has often been presented by demographers as a success story – the perfect case study where universal education, the high status of women and social awareness have combined to record a population decline. But Kerala also has the largest incidence of migration out of the state and out of the country, a factor which in terms of actual numbers and in prevented conceptions due to divided couples, cannot be ignored. And while the breakthrough achieved in Tamil Nadu can no doubt be attributed to the midday meal scheme in schools which has released mothers for full-time employment, with its natural consequences, the practice of female infanticide is also widespread there.

Illiterate women are just as receptive as literate women to family planning, provided they are organized into groups at the local level. A classic example of this is the small Muslim-dominated village of Mammalapuram in Kerala, where the women organized themselves into groups, fought religious orthodoxy and bigotry that bans family planning, and had themselves sterilized, despite the hostility of the clergy and their menfolk.

I believe that ultimately it is the young women who have to be targeted, even though this does not find favour with the intellectuals and activists. In a society that is paternalistic, prescriptive and coercive, tubectomy rates are naturally 50 to 100 times higher than vasectomy rates, though the latter is a simpler and safer procedure. The men are willing to let their wives be subjected to family limiting methods while the women are willing to consider alternatives to repeated childbirth. They are receptive to family planning once convinced of its efficacy. It is true that the number of children per woman has decreased but the number of women bearing children has increased. It is this higher number of child-bearing women who have to be convinced to adopt family-planning methods if population growth is to be contained.

The National Family Health Survey has shown that there exists a substantial unmet need among 20% of currently married women of which 11% desire spacing and 9% limitation methods. As more people enter the reproductive age group the number is set to multiply. And therefore a focused programme for young couples who are already motivated can achieve a rapid decline in fertility. But contraceptive supply rarely matches the demand.

Recent constitutional amendments for local self government reserved 33% of seats in elected bodies for women. As a result 1 million women have been elected to positions of power and authority at the local and district levels. This is seen as another means by which population planning and control will filter down to the grass roots through women.

Cairo, of course, called upon all governments to mobilize financial resources for the global Programme of Action, noting the Amsterdam call for a doubling of ODA population programmes. What has happened since 1994 in this respect? Is India receiving adequate international assistance for its

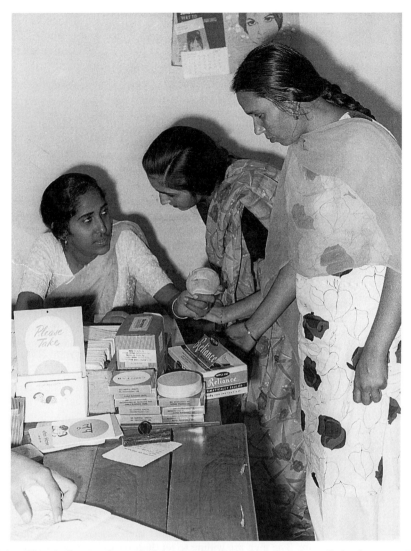

Figure 8.2.1   "The challenge of population planning in India is immense. It is also one of the biggest challenges for the world to solve in the vital planetary interest", says Margaret Alva. A woman doctor distributes free contraceptives to women, New Delhi. (Courtesy Popperfoto)

population planning? As Table 8.2.1 shows, our aid inflows for population programmes fluctuated greatly over the ten years before Cairo.

Over the decade before Cairo, India received some $130 million annually from the international community for population planning. Over three-quarters of this came from the International Development Agency which, in my view, is the best means of delivering assistance of this kind – in the name of the international community as a whole, on grant terms and with no bilateral strings attached that might answer to any special national interest. The United States gave 10%, and Norway, Sweden and the UK nearly 5% each. Australia gave nothing. Nor did Germany or Japan.

Since Cairo, the international community should theoretically have increased its ODA to India for population planning. The figures are as yet incomplete. Table 8.2.2 shows what has been recorded to date.

Table 8.2.1 Population assistance (ODA) to India: 1985–94 ($ million)

Country	1985	1986	1987	1988	1989	1990	1991	1992	1993	1994	Total
I.D.A.	51.0			57.0	113.3	182.7		298.5	194.0	88.6	985.1
United States	2.9	22.0	14.1	11.8	6.7	2.2	4.9	26.3	11.2	20.0	122.1
Norway		0.9	39.3		7.5		8.3		0.1	1.3	57.4
Sweden								51.5			51.5
U. Kingdom						32.0		13.2		2.5	47.7
Netherlands						5.5	0.1				5.6
Canada		0.6	0.3		0.1			0.1	2.3		3.4
Denmark				0.6		1.2					1.8
Switzerland			0.1				0.1				0.2
Germany											
Australia											
Total	53.9	23.5	53.8	69.4	127.6	223.6	13.4	389.6	207.6	112.4	1,274.8

Source: OECD Reporting Systems Division: e-mail information, 13 October 1997.

Table 8.2.2 Population assistance (ODA) to India: 1995–6 ($ million)

Country	1995	1996
I.D.A.		
United States	20.7	
Norway	0.1	
Sweden		
United Kingdom	0.6	8.0
Netherlands	10.9	0.1
Canada		
Denmark		
Switzerland		
Germany		10.0
Australia	1.6	
Total	33.9	18.1

Source: OECD Reporting Systems Division: e-mail information, 13 October 1997.

It is too early to draw conclusions over the international response to the call of Cairo. But it is good to see a response from Australia. That will help us develop our policies in light of the input from the Cairo conference. And it is not only in the planetary interest that we receive funds of this kind, but it is in Australia's best interest as well.

CONCLUSION

The challenge of population planning in India is immense. It is also one of the biggest tasks for the world community to solve in the vital planetary interest. Besides the challenge of an acceptable policy statement, the practical problems of implementing such policies are limitless due to the Federal Constitution and the powers of the states. As a practical politician with a vision of India's future, I had painful personal experience in encountering the obstacles that can arise. As India's minister for personnel, I sought to implement some of these policies by amending the service rules whereby maternity benefits to government servants would be limited to two children in keeping with the two-child norm. Yet I was criticized by women activists, unions and NGOs. They argued that such a policy was discriminatory since it only applied to women workers who availed themselves of maternity benefits. They insisted they were being penalized for a decision that was not theirs to make.

Here was I, a leader of the women's movement in India, trying to implement a policy for modern, urban, educated Indians who were part of government and whose duty it was to implement government policy; and I was being told that it was an infringement of human rights and that they had the right to decide how many children they wanted to have! Strangely enough, none of them saw it as a way of taking charge of their own fertility, as a policy that would free women from the constant cycle of childbirth and rearing that leaves them weak and worn out. When urban educated women claim that they have no control over their fertility, then one can imagine the fate of the women who are our rural poor, with low literacy and age-old perceptions of their low status.

Today I head an NGO that is pioneering training programmes for women elected to local bodies, often illiterate and generally inexperienced, to equip them with the basic knowledge of issues and systems to be able to undertake their responsibilities effectively. I believe that these women will usher in a quiet revolution in our villages. Almost all of them say the same thing, though in different ways: "Looking after the needs of a village is like looking after a family; education, health, drinking water and sanitation before tarred roads and office buildings. The fewer we are the better our conditions and the chance for a better life."

This, then, is India, a land of striking contrast where the gap between the literate and the illiterate, between the urban and the rural, between the administrator and the administered is so great that they often end up working against each other, rather than together for mutual growth and development. The challenge is immense; the problems are limitless. Yet the nation at 50, slowly but surely, is set on the democratic path to success. India realizes that population and development are interlinked and acknowledges its duty to ensure the survival of the human race.

8.3 Australia

Margaret Reynolds

"While the Coalition is committed to an immigration intake that serves the national interest in terms of our social, economic and humanitarian objectives, I see no need for a significant expansion of the intake."

Philip Ruddock, Minister of Immigration

The term "planetary interest" is, I believe, emerging as the most significant challenge for policy-makers in tackling the complex demands of today. Population policies are indicative of the need for defining a planetary interest as distinct from relying on the national interest. The Cairo conference of 1994 generated a fresh initiative for shaping international policy development in this respect. As US Under-Secretary of State Timothy Wirth put it at the time, "I think the world is never going to be the same after Cairo".

The global strategy for the world laid down at Cairo was essentially the stabilization of the world population at a level compatible with sustainable development in the twenty-first century – taken to be at, or below, 10 billion. Nation-states are called upon to establish and implement national population policy goals and plans to that effect. Their governments, and their parliamentarians, in collaboration with the international community, are urged to make these plans "in accordance with national concerns" and to take the action required for progress towards the global objective in the Programme of Action.

To what extent does Australia have an obligation, in the planetary interest, to contribute to curbing the global "population explosion" in the twenty-first century through financial assistance to the rest of the world in the 1990s? To what extent is it obliged to alleviate the current problem of global numbers by absorbing a significant fraction of the global population today? Is it part of its legitimate national interest to do so? What is Australia's overall population policy in response to the call of Cairo?

Australia is a huge country, 7.7 million sq. km, the only island continent floating on the crust of the Earth. That is four-fifths of the size of the United States, yet it has 8% of its population. It is 32 times larger than the United Kingdom, the original "mother country", but with one-third the population. And it is twice as large as India, with 2% of its population. At two persons per square kilometre, it is the most sparsely populated wealthy country in the world.[1]

Pure statistics, of course, can be misleading. Australia is, for the most part, rolling dry land and desert. A strip of habitable land etches its way around the shores. The Aborigines, one of the world's oldest people, found it some 60,000 years ago, migrated here and spread across the continent. Europeans found it only a few centuries ago, and settled mainly around the edges. Only 6% of the land is arable. That compares with 21% for the United States, 29% for the United Kingdom, 52% for India. But it still means that the 0.5 million sq. km of arable land supports about 36 persons per square kilometre. And that compares with 129 in the US, 741 in the UK and 503 in India. Australia is blessed, by even the strictest standard.

Half a century ago, Australia's population was 7 million. Today, it is 19 million. The government believes it can predict with some accuracy that, half a century from now, around 2040, it will be almost stationary at 23 million. But this is based on two assumptions: that fertility will remain at 10% below replacement levels; and that immigration will be set at approximately 50,000 annually. If social change were to see fertility levels restored to replacement levels at the same time as immigration were to increase to 1% (the post-1945 rate) then Australia's population by 2040 would be 30 million with the potential to reach 53 million by 2067.

NATIONAL POLICY

Australia's colonial history and its geography as an island state have contributed to a "fortress" mentality that has influenced successive governments throughout its political history. Such a psychosis peaks when high unemployment prompts some in the community to blame the latest group of immigrants for their own insecurities.

The psychosis is at a peak today. In recent policy statements, government leaders have emphasized the "national interest" ahead of Australia's global responsibility – indeed, the most current foreign policy White Paper is titled "In the National Interest".[2] Yet that document fails to define or describe precisely what that national interest might actually be beyond a generalized rhetoric about security and living standards. While recognizing the scope of global environmental degradation the statement concludes:

> In its pursuit of international action which contributes to sustainable development Australia must be active in protecting its fundamental national interests. The difficulties this will entail should not be underestimated.[3]

The nexus between environment and trade policy development is acknowledged by the government today but, as a recent comment by the foreign minister indicates, the policy specifically contradicts any acceptance of global responsibility:

> On the relationship between trade liberalization and environmental protection the Government will work for an outcome which ... prevents environmental objectives being used to support protectionism and which allows Australia to resist the imposition of solutions to environmental problems which are contrary to Australia's national interests ... the Government will apply a basic test of national interest: does it advance the security of the Australian nation and the jobs and standard of living of the Australian people?[4]

When it comes to population issues, Australian policy-makers wrestle with two contradictory arguments. We must limit our population growth from immigration. Yet we must accept a global responsibility to help curb population pressures through aid programmes, the sharing of our abundant resources and a reduction in consumption levels and a polluting lifestyle.

Australia was a signatory to a declaration by the world's scientists, meeting in New Delhi in 1993, that the world population goal should be "zero population growth" within our children's lifetime. And the government itself signed on to the Cairo Declaration and Programme of Action. In terms of a national policy to meet the planetary interest, however, Australia's policy is not wholly co-ordinated, nor even consciously aspiring to the stated global goal. The government's uncertainty over meeting these competing national and global objectives in population planning is reflected in official comment to the Cairo conference:

> Australia does not have an explicit or formal population policy ... After considerable public debate, the Government decided that a formal population policy, particularly one which would specify population targets, would not be appropriate. The Government's views on this issue are not shared by all in the community. Strong opinion persists that the development of a formal population policy is desirable and that there is a need to stabilize population numbers and resource use in Australia.[5]

In reality, of course, a country has a policy on any issue, either explicitly through policy development and public pronouncement, or implicitly by default. Australia does, thus, have a policy on all three major areas affecting the global population issue – domestic population growth, immigration and international development assistance in family planning to other countries.

Domestic population policy

Australia has always suffered a paranoia that its population numbers are insufficient to develop its vast island continent. The strength of parochialism in this regard has been played out in policies which can be traced to its convict heritage. To counter-balance the rogues and thieves of a penal colony, free settlers with strong wives who would produce large numbers of healthy children for the new country were in demand. By the early twentieth century, the emergence of contraception was seen to threaten Australia's population growth. One editor of a medical gazette was in no doubt, in 1903, that women themselves were to blame. "For some reason or reasons", he lamented, "women of today decline the responsibility of maternity, and resort largely to artificial preventives against conception."[6] Pro-natalism – the theory that an increase in population is necessary for the health of a nation – flourished as successive governments advocated the need for more people to fill the emptiness of the Australian interior. As one politician claimed in 1905, "the best of all immigration is the Australian baby" – a statement still supported by two-thirds of Australians six decades later.[7]

Australia's population, although small, is today one of the fastest growing in the North. Pressure is building for a formal policy that limits the rate of growth and is environmentally sustainable. Current arguments include: concern over increasing environmental degradation, the need to plan for the future; recognition that Australia's population consumes a disproportionate amount of the world's resources; and the need to show solidarity with the South over population issues. Yet it is significant that, in preparing for Cairo, the government chose the Immigration Department to co-ordinate national policy. Health, environment, international obligations and women's rights were issues to be considered from an immigration perspective. Nor, in the event, was there any official enthusiasm for developing a population policy.

Australia's national report to Cairo reflects this ambivalence and uncertainty in policy direction. In describing popular perceptions of population issues the report comments:

> The desirability and character that a formal population policy might take is not clear-cut in a country such as Australia, where low levels of domestic fertility are generally not considered a problem, and where diverse and often conflicting views on the objectives of a population policy exist. In highlighting the range of opinions about an optimum population for Australia, the report avoids coming to terms with its international role and responsibility.[8]

Australian governments have in fact rejected recommendations in the past to develop a formal population policy, on the grounds of Australia's relatively small population and low fertility rate; a lack of evidence that Australia is approaching the limits of its carrying capacity; the unlikelihood of achieving community consensus given the broad range of views that exist; and the potential divisiveness of an "environment versus development" debate.

A parliamentary committee, however, did prepare a report in 1994 on population and national carrying capacity, just as Rio had urged. The Jones Report concluded that carrying capacity was a complex issue.[9] It involved not only population numbers, but factors such as population and distribution patterns, levels of consumption, technological change, environmental management and the level of tourism. The report recommended that government adopt a population policy, and that political and administrative responsibility for population and immigration policy be separated. It did not, however, propose an optimal population figure.

So much for the preparation for Cairo. How did Australia respond to the 1994 Programme of Action? In 1995 the government detailed its national policy, highlighting the overriding goals of integrating population and development strategies.[10] Immigration, it said, should meet economic, social, cultural and humanitarian objectives, "recognizing Australia's right to control the flow of people across its borders". Development should be ecologically sustainable, so that Australia's unique biodiversity is protected.

In 1997 my own party, now in opposition, committed itself to a national population policy, and called on the government to implement the recommendations of the Jones Report.[11]

Some policy-makers argue that population growth via immigration is essentially "population transfer" as migrant women tend to have fewer children in their adopted country. While there is limited research validating this claim, anecdotal material suggests there is a greater chance of migrant women following the national trend, especially when education and employment options are enhanced.

Despite Australia's small numbers, the population is still taking a toll on the land. National policy identifies "the increasing tendency of Australians to migrate from the south-east metropolitan areas to smaller urban centres on the coast, particularly the east coast".[12] This is putting stress on the environment of cities and towns along Australia's east coast. Rapid urbanization along Australia's coastal seaboard has escalated over the past 20 years. A 95% population increase, from 2.1 million to

4.1 million, has occurred in non-metropolitan areas of the south east and far north of Queensland, the central and north coast of New South Wales and the south west of Western Australia. It is estimated that Australia's coastal zone supports 86% of the total population and projections show this trend continuing. Urbanization and fringe development are impacting severely on coastal ecosystems, with loss of native species and declining coastal and marine biological diversity. In response, a national coastal policy, *Living on the Coast,* has allocated $38 million for sustainable development there. It includes initiatives to build co-operation between users and managers through the development of strategic plans for those areas under pressure from competing land use.

Thus it can be concluded that, in its national population policy, Australia was reluctant and ambivalent before Cairo, and is cautious and rather defiant since, with an expectation of, rather than plans for, a slow and steady growth from 19 million to 23 million over the next half century.

Immigration policy

If we do not have a clear domestic population policy, and if we are sparsely populated, what is Australia's immigration policy?

Immigration policy has contributed significantly to the national debate on population size and composition. Before federation in 1901, the Australian colonies had imposed restrictions on non-European immigration, influenced by concern over the rapid expansion of the Chinese population during the gold rushes of the 1850s and 1870s. After federation one of the first actions of the new commonwealth government was to pass the Immigration Restriction Act. The "White Australia Policy" as it has become universally known, remained in force for the first 70 years of the twentieth century. The population remained not only white but also overwhelmingly British–Irish until the 1940s when the fright of an invasion from Asia altered post-war attitudes.

By mid-century, however, nobody doubted that the population needed to be increased and the idea of doing so through large-scale immigration caught the public imagination. When insufficient migrants were forthcoming from northwest Europe, the "acceptable" source areas were progressively widened to include eastern and southern Europe, and then Turkey, Lebanon and Egypt, whose proximity to Europe apparently made them more acceptable than Asian countries. In 1966 the first substantial modifications were finally made to the White Australia Policy, and it was subsequently omitted from the platforms of the two main political parties, being totally abandoned in 1972.

Since immigration has largely determined the rate of population growth, debate about population has focused on immigration. The immigration debate now has an environmental focus, rather than a "social cohesion" focus of the mid-1980s. Defenders of immigration argue that equating population numbers, and particularly immigration, with environmental degradation is simplistic. To date, however, the government has not indicated any support for population policy. "The Coalition", says Immigration Minister Philip Ruddock, "has no intention of trying to influence fertility levels . . . While the Coalition is committed to an immigration intake that serves the national interest in terms of our social, economic and humanitarian objectives, I see no need for a significant expansion of the intake."[13]

It appears to be the general consensus of those advocating a population policy on environmental grounds that an immigration programme advocating an in-take of 30,000 to 50,000 per year is appropriate. This would allow for an ongoing non-discriminatory immigration programme that encompasses genuine refugees, close-family reunions and some skilled migration. It might, however, be difficult to achieve a reduction to these levels: in 1995–6, 59% of immigrants were preferential family migrants (essentially spouses, non-working-age parents and dependent children). Another 20% were humanitarian entrants or refugees.

In fact, Australia maintained an annual immigration intake of 83,000 in the 1980s and early 1990s. This has been reduced in recent years to 74,000 under the current government, which announced a further reduction to 68,000 for 1997–8. With annual departures at about 30,000, this means a net addition of about 53,000 in the early 1990s, down to 38,000 in the mid-1990s.[14]

Rational debate, however, is a rare political luxury. Expert opinion and reasoned discussion have recently ceded to a negative populism, and the whole political and social atmosphere has changed in the country. One new and independent member of parliament in particular has attracted renewed attention to Australia's immigration policy. Her trenchant and unfortunate criticism of immigration, particularly from non-English speaking countries, has ignited a polarized national race debate. Racist violence and vilification are on the increase, following Ms Hanson's recently launched One Nation Party, fuelling divisions in the community. Australia, however, is not alone in this: it is a sign, it seems, of the distemper of our time, all around the world.

Current government policy and rhetoric have failed to protect Australia's previously admired multicultural policies. A national anti-racism campaign announced in the 1996 budget has yet to be developed since there is a reluctance within government directly to challenge the racism which has so polarized the Australian community. The consequence of this aspect of current policy is to blunt specific repudiation of racist themes. The failure to do so is damaging Australia's reputation as a tolerant society. Given the recent history of the White Australia Policy, combined with earlier genocidal policies toward Aborigines, it is scarcely surprising that the international community is questioning the apparent shift in Australian multicultural policy.

Aid policy for global population planning

Australia is perhaps making a more constructive contribution to global population planning through its official development assistance (ODA). The stated rationale for Australian aid rests on a mix of both the planetary and the national interest. In the words of AUSAID, Australia's aid agency:

> In a world where there is poverty, hunger, war and disease, it is appropriate that our humanitarian concern extends beyond our shores . . . Whether we realize it or not, we've all got a big stake in the future of developing countries – more particularly those in our region. As Australia and countries in the rest of the world become more interdependent, we increase our economic prospects, but also our exposure to the effects of international economic inequality, such as environmental degradation, war and the illegal movement of people and products . . . It is in our own interests then, as well as our neighbours', for us to help them address their development problems, before they cause crises, instability and conflict. And of course, when we provide Australian aid, it can also help provide Australian jobs.[15]

Australia's annual ODA stands at $1.1 billion, some 0.3% of GNP. This compares with the OCED average of 0.25%, the lowest ratio on record for the 30 years of the OCED's existence. Aid is no longer fashionable.

Australia's population and family-planning programmes rest on principles that reflect the priorities of Cairo. Individuals should decide freely the number and spacing of their children and have the information and means to exercise this choice. Access to safe and effective family-planning services is a fundamental right. Women should have access to a wide range of reproductive health services and should participate fully in defining the services they need. Family-planning programmes should include men and cater for all people who may be sexually active. And in general, the assistance should involve the local communities in planning programmes appropriate to their needs; increase the choice of family-planning methods available; improve the skills and competence of family-planning service providers; give information and counselling to clients; and provide follow-up advice to clients to ensure continued contraceptive use, if desired.

The annual level of Australia's population and family-planning assistance has increased to $27 million, some 2.5% of the total amount. This constitutes, in fact, a trebling of such assistance. In 1993 a four-year programme, the "Population Initiative" totalling $93 million, was introduced, and now funds the UN Population Fund, the International Planned Parenthood Federation and WHO's Human Reproductive Programme.[16]

Most assistance, however, focuses on Australia's immediately proximate region – the South Pacific and East and South East Asia. The major recipients of Australia's population aid are Indonesia, China, the Philippines, Vietnam and Papua New Guinea.[17] AUSAID collaborates with these governments to provide partnerships in developing policy, training and the marketing of contraceptives. In Indonesia, AUSAID has introduced the Healthy Start for Child Survival project which is a preventative health service aimed at a reduction in infant mortality. Similar programmes have been developed in the Philippines and China. In the South Pacific, Project Excel is a regional family health programme aimed at improving access to contraceptives and educating against the spread of sexually transmitted diseases. In Vietnam and Thailand, AUSAID funding is being utilized to train local health workers in women's health policy development and support the Planned Parenthood Association of Thailand.

India falls outside this priority area. Australia's total aid to India is some $15 million. It goes mainly to telecommunications, industrial waste management, rail transportation and smelting operations. Some additional funds go for training scholarships and to NGOs in health, environmental management and community development. And some $1.4 million goes in food aid through the World Food Program. Thus a total of some $19.3 million is expended in aid to India each year – at 1.8% a tiny fraction of the total Australian aid programme.[18]

Australian population assistance to India is negligible. Australia gave a grant in one year following the Cairo conference, but no direct bilateral aid on population is currently given. For 1997 Australia was considering a grant of $1.8 million in multilateral form, to UNICEF's Child Survival and Safe Motherhood Programme.

THE LEGITIMATE NATIONAL INTEREST

Are we doing enough? Is Australia, with 0.27% of the global population consuming 1.0% of the global energy resources, acting in the legitimate national interest with its population, immigration and development assistance policies? Is it playing its part in striving for the planetary interest? Should it specifically be helping India? Should India's nuclear weapon testing affect this?

In the late 1990s, nations have seen a shift of focus from global concerns to a preoccupation with increased nationalism. Some of this is based on destructive ethnic chauvinism. As the threat of nuclear conflict has receded many states have turned inwards, relying heavily on the rhetoric of "national interest".

Figure 8.3.1   Immigrants commence a new life in Australia in the 1960s. Australia has one of the least-dense populations in the world. To what extent should it accept greater numbers of immigrants to ease the global population pressure? "The agenda of the new millennium," says Margaret Reynolds, "must set down the principles of global citizenship and the social obligations we have for each other". (Courtesy National Library of Australia)

Australia is experiencing the same upheaval in determining its identity and future directions. In recent years there have been serious challenges to the nation's multicultural policy. Its immigration programme has been replaced. Its aid programme has declined to a record low, including a near-total absence of bilateral population aid to India, projected to be the most populous nation on the planet in the twenty-first century. On all counts, we are, I believe, falling short of our legitimate national interest.

In recent years, the main immigration-receiving countries of the world registered a net migration intake of some 1.4 million persons annually.[19] Australia's net intake of some 40,000 comprises 2.9% of this. I believe we could do more – much more.

Australians spend, for every $100 from the public purse, $36 on social welfare, $14 on health, $8 each on education and defence, and $1.20 on foreign aid. The legitimate national interest requires that Australians put themselves first – that has never been in question. But should they have a priority on their own welfare above that of their fellow humans by a factor of 30? Should they prepare to defend themselves against their fellow humans by six times the expenditure through which they help them survive and live decently? It is a question of priorities, of human values. The ratio of public spending in my country is violating the legitimate national interest. We are not doing enough for the species of which we are part.

In November 1997, one of Australia's regional neighbours, President Fidel Ramos of the Philippines, gave the UNFPA's Raphael Salas Memorial Lecture. First, he urged all countries to accede to the International Covenant on the Rights of All Migrant Workers and Members of their Families. Secondly, he repeated his country's offer to host an international conference on migration and development. Thirdly, he urged his friends in the developed world to meet the UN target of 0.7% of their GNP for ODA. Recalling Cairo's target of $17 billion for reproductive health and related programmes, President Ramos thought that "considering the great human good that it will do, this is a low-cost budget". Humanity, he noted, spends more on military expenditure in one week. "Surely, if we pull together in a world economy of $25 trillion in size, we can pay this bill", he said.[20] I agree with our neighbour, and I invite all my fellow Australians to do so as well.

CONCLUSION

How should the international community respond to this preoccupation of a country that is currently determined to put its perceived national interest ahead of both its immediate international obligations and a longer-term global interest? Sadly, most governments have only a short-term attention span in formulating public policy. They respond to the immediate demands of the most powerful voices in the community and have one eye on the more popular policy direction. There is little doubt that in Australia it is difficult for government to advocate policy from an international perspective. The slogan "think globally, act locally" may well be adopted by those who are well informed and committed to their role as global citizens, but the majority of Australians are more restricted in their focus. Recent opinion polls cite immigration and unemployment as the major causes of national insecurity.

In this climate it would seem that far-sighted leadership is required to educate citizens that their children's future will best be secured through an acceptance of global responsibility. The agenda of the new millennium must set down the principles of global citizenship and the social obligations we have for each other. This will not be an easy task in affluent nations such as mine where we so readily rely on our current level of resource consumption and privileged lifestyle. Nor will it be easy to communicate to the people in the South where basic human survival preoccupies the lives of so many.

But a strategy must be formulated in the planetary interest. If a country such as Australia cannot grasp the urgency of this imperative then it may be necessary to develop both moral and actual international sanctions to persuade and directly enforce governmental implementation of its obligations to all of humanity.

NOTES

1. Four other countries, Botswana, Namibia, Mauritania and Mongolia also have 2 persons per square kilometre. Canada has 3 per square kilometre. *Atlaseco World Economic Atlas* (Paris: EOC, 1994).
2. Department of Foreign Affairs and Trade, *In the national interest: foreign and trade policy white paper*, Canberra, August 1997.

3. Ibid., 49.
4. Minister of Foreign Affairs, the Hon. Alexander Downer; press statement, August 1997.
5. Australia: National Report on Population for the United Nations International Conference on Population and Development, Cairo, 1994, 29.
6. S. Siedlecky & D. Wyndham, *Populate or perish: Australian women's fight for birth control* (Sydney: Allen & Unwin, 1990), 5.
7. Ibid., 17.
8. Australian national report to the Cairo conference, 29.
9. Report of the House of Representatives Standing Committee on Long-term Strategies, *Australia's population carrying capacity* (Canberra, December 1994).
10. Australia and the ICPD: Australia's Position against the Programme of Action of the United Nations International Conference on Population and Development, Cairo, 1994 (Canberra, Dept. of Immigration and Ethnic Affairs, September 1995), 19.
11. D. Kerr, "Labor takes lead on population policy and calls on government for action", *Shared Future*, a newsletter for Multicultural Australia, April 1997.
12. Australian national report to the Cairo conference, 93.
13. Philip Ruddock address, "Population policy: issues for consideration", 4 March 1997.
14. *Far Eastern Economic Review*, 19 June 1997.
15. Australian Agency for International Development, *About Australia's aid program* (Canberra: AUSAID Public Affairs Division), 1.
16. Australia and the ICPD, 189.
17. AUSAID, correspondence with Social Sector and Gender Section, 6 March 1997.
18. AUSAID, *India – country in brief* (Canberra: AUSAID, 1997), 1–2.
19. ICPD, 10.1.
20. UNDH, 26 November 1997.

CHAPTER NINE

Development

9.1   Introduction

The relationship between environmental and developmental goals is well recognized. *Agenda 21*, itself opens:

> Humanity stands at a defining moment in history . . . integration of environment and development concerns and greater awareness to them will lead to the fulfillment of basic needs, improved living standards for all, better protected and managed ecosystems and a safer and more prosperous future. No nation can achieve this on its own; but together we can – in a global partnership for sustainable development . . . Agenda 21 . . . reflects a global consensus and political commitment at the highest level on development and environmental co-operation . . . This process marks the beginning of a new global partnership for sustainable development. In order to meet the challenge of environment and development, States have decided to establish a new global partnership . . . Governments recognize that there is new global effort to relate the elements of the international economic system and mankind's need for a safe and stable natural environment.[1]

The Rio Declaration proclaimed 27 non-binding principles for nation-state behaviour to translate this "global partnership" into action, including:

> States shall co-operate in a spirit of global partnership to conserve, protect and restore the integrity of the Earth's ecosystem. In view of the different contributions to global environmental degradation, States have common but differentiated responsibilities . . . To achieve sustainable development and a higher quality of life for all people, States should reduce and eliminate unsustainable patterns of production and consumption and promote appropriate demographic policies.[2]

The principle of "common but differentiated responsibilities" reflects an appreciation of the diverse national interests of nation-states in face of the global environmental threat: those that have caused relatively greater damage in pursuit of economic development at an unsustainable level, and those that have suffered relatively more as a result. Using the planetary interest, nation-states can more clearly perceive their legitimate national interest in this respect. In the case of the former, that is essentially a curtailment of activities that breach the sustainability threshold or cause third-party damage; with the latter, it comprises reparation for or protection against the damage inflicted.

The 1997 Second Earth Summit in New York ("Rio+5") made an assessment of progress since 1992. The General Assembly adopted the Programme for Further Implementation of *Agenda 21*, which reaffirmed the 1992 programme as the fundamental basis for sustainable development. "We emphasize", said the assembly in a statement of commitment, "that the implementation of *Agenda 21* in a comprehensive manner remains vitally important and is more urgent now than ever."[3]

Yet given the likely global population of 9.4 billion in 2050, the challenge to humankind to achieve sustainable development in the twenty-first century will be immense.

The definition of sustainable development noted earlier means that it should be possible for a given economic activity to continue indefinitely for an unlimited period of time. This must clearly be taken to be a longer time perspective than current policy planning embraces. It has, indeed, been suggested that, while falling short of evolutionary scale, it should be accepted as comprising a few thousand years – until the next Ice Age.[4] Stretching policy concerns simply into the next generation will be a qualitatively new approach. Such a new philosophical attitude requires both moral and political paradigmatic change, involving new theories of social justice and economic growth.

Socially, it requires an acceptance by all, including the richest nations and individuals on the planet, that all peoples have a right to a minimum standard of living, a right that is not simply theoretical but which will, if necessary, affect the lifestyle of the wealthy. In economic theory, it requires an equally fundamental change. Traditionally it has been held that human and technological resources applied to the natural resource base would produce an unconstrained level of economic output that would match whatever level of demand was imposed by human numbers and values. Prosperity was measured within a national context, both quantitatively and morally, with an exclusionist attitude both to the environment and to other peoples. The environment and the natural resource base were not factored into the economic equation, and there were no perceived limits to growth.

Over the past three decades, this cornucopian approach has been subjected to fundamental revision based on the notion of a limit of some kind on planetary economic growth. That revision has taken two forms. In the 1970s it was posited, in a neo-Malthusian sense, that the planet's resources imposed certain absolute limits to growth, primarily the food supply and the availability of non-renewable resources, however difficult these might be to gauge with the present state of knowledge.[5] This "static" view gave way to the "dynamic" view embraced in the 1980s and retained today. This holds that the limits which humanity will face in the twenty-first century will be the result of elastic, though still powerful, constraints "imposed by the present state of technology and social organization on environmental resources, and by the ability of the biosphere to absorb the effects of human activities".[6] Identifying what those constraints are at the global level, and what consequential constraints each nation-state must face within that global context, is the task ahead.

THE GLOBAL PROBLEM

The problem of global sustainable development is broad-ranging and complex. It focuses essentially on the alleviation of poverty and the satisfaction of basic human needs for all of humanity, primarily food, shelter and health. The world's economic development over the past 50 years has been considerable: by the end of the twentieth century, some 3 to 4 billion people – about 60% of the global population – will have experienced substantial improvements in their standards of living.[7] Global economic growth, moreover, is estimated to have been 2.9% in 1996 and 3.1% in 1997, and is expected to accelerate to 3.5% per annum from 1998 to 2000.[8] Yet some 1.3 billion people, 23% of humanity, live on less than $1 per day. Some 1 billion people, 17% of humanity, live in unacceptable conditions of poverty. About 330 million people, 6% of humanity, still live in "absolute poverty".[9]

Food

At present 14% of the global population, some 840 million people, are malnourished, including 200 million children.[10] Some 15 million hunger-related deaths occur each year – some 40,000 each day. Half of these are children, comprising 50% of the total number of child deaths each year. Yet over the next 30 years some 2.5 billion extra humans will need to be fed as well. World food demand is projected to double between 2000 and 2050.[11]

This will impose severe strain on the productive capacity of the planet's arable land. Yet of the 4.8 billion hectares under crop and pasture, already 6% is strongly degraded, a quarter of this having been damaged by overgrazing and another quarter by improper land management. Nearly 20% more is estimated to be moderately degraded, facing declines in productivity.[12] All told, that is one-quarter of the planet's arable land strongly or moderately degraded.

The international community recognizes the global nature of the problem that ensues from this. In 1996 at the World Food Summit in Rome, nation-states formally stated that

> We express our deep concern over the persistence of hunger which, on such a scale, constitutes a threat both to national societies and, through a variety of ways, to the stability of the international community itself.[13]

Shelter

Despite world economic growth over the last half century, about 1 billion people lack access to safe and healthy shelter.[14] Some 800 million live in sub-standard housing.[15] About 100 million, or 2%, are homeless, of whom 30 million are children without parental protection.

In the first decade of the twenty-first century, humankind will cross a threshold where over 50% of the population live in cities. This is an increase from 30% in 1950 and 43% in 1990. Whereas in 1950, there was only one "megacity" with over 10 million inhabitants, there will be 25 such conglomerations in 2000. The number of cities with over 1 million people will increase from 187 in 1990 to 279 in 2000.[16] Managing human settlements towards sustainability will be a daunting task. The international community, at the Istanbul Summit on Human Settlements (Habitat II) in 1996, expressed concern at the "deteriorating conditions of shelter and human settlements that in most cases, particularly in developing countries, have reached crisis proportions".[17]

Health

Human life expectancy has improved considerably in recent decades, from 48 years in the early 1950s to 64 in the late 1980s. One of the principal reasons is the increased nutrition level consumed today, from 2,300 calories per day in the early 1960s to 2,700 in the mid-1980s. Yet these improvements are predicated on a low base of living standards in those earlier decades. The level of human health on a global scale remains problematic. Some 25% of the global population lack access to safe water, and 35% lack safe sanitation. Some 23% live in urban areas that do not meet WHO standards for airborne dust and smoke,[18] and 18% live in cities that exceed WHO standards for sulphur dioxide emission.[19]

The lack of basic health experienced by such a large proportion of humanity in the 1990s has its consequences. Some 22 million people die each year from parasitic and infectious disorders, and 0.5 million women die each year during pregnancy and childbirth.[20] Some 13 million children under 5 years die each year – 35,000 each day – 60% from the five major diseases: pneumonia, diarrhoea, measles, tetanus and whooping cough.[21] Some 30,000 babies die each year, 120,000 children are born as cretins, and 300 million suffer from lowered mental ability through iodine deficiency, a preventable health problem.[22] A quarter of a million children are blinded each year through Vitamin A deficiency. About 10% of humanity suffers from goitre through iodine deficiency.[23]

The international community has expressed its concern as follows:

> Health and development are intimately connected. Both insufficient development leading to poverty and inappropriate development resulting in overconsumption, coupled with an expanding world population, can result in severe environmental health problems . . . Health ultimately depends on the ability to manage successfully the interaction between the physical, spiritual, biological and economic/social environment . . . The health sector cannot meet basic human needs on its own.[24]

THE GLOBAL OBJECTIVE AND STRATEGY

In response to this fundamental problem, the international community has recently set certain goals. In *Agenda 21*, the international community identified as its goal, through the "global partnership", the "fulfilment of basic needs, improved living standards for all and better protected and managed ecosystems".[25]

Food

The global objective is essentially food security for all.[26] But the target date of 2000 set in previous world food conferences proved unattainable and more realistic goals have since been adopted. The 1996 World Food Summit set a target of reducing by 50% the number of malnourished from 840 million that year to 420 million by 2015, despite the increase in global population.[27] The Rome Declaration affirmed "the right of everyone to have access to safe and nutritional food consistent with the right to adequate food and the fundamental right of everyone to be free from hunger".[28]

The strategy to achieve that objective is both greater productivity and better distribution of product. UN Secretary-General Kofi Annan has noted that the world at present has enough food: "what it lacks is the political will to ensure that all people have access to this bounty, that all people enjoy food security".[29] But the global population growth will strain the capacity of the planet even to ensure sufficient production in the future. In order to feed the world's projected population in 2025, for example, agricultural production must increase by 2% per annum. FAO estimates that the planet must increase global food production by 75% by 2030 to keep pace with population growth.[30] This production increase must come through increased yields rather than increased land since most cultivable land is already utilized, requiring almost a doubling of yields on the existing cultivable land area.[31] Yet that doubling of yield must be achieved in the context of sustainability.

Shelter

The global objective, proclaimed at the 1996 UN Conference on Human Settlements (Habitat II) at Istanbul, is two-fold: adequate shelter for all; and "safer, healthier, and more livable, equitable, sustainable and productive human settlements".[32] No quantitative targets nor any deadline, however, were agreed upon. The *Habitat Agenda* was described as a "global call to action at all levels, and a guide towards the achievement of sustainable development of the world's cities, towns and villages into the first two decades of the next century".[33]

To attain this kind of objective, the Global Strategy for Shelter to the Year 2000, adopted in 1988, had already emphasized the need for an enabling strategy for improved production and delivery of shelter, and revised national housing policies to that end.[34] The 1988 strategy was updated by the 1996 agenda. To achieve adequate shelter for all the world's people by 2020, the *Habitat Agenda* lays down ten goals and principles.[35] They are, however, vague and intrinsically broader even than the strategic objective itself. As such, they are of little use in assisting the international community attain the objective.

One innovation in the Istanbul summit, however, was the increased participation of the global civil society, building upon Rio, Cairo, Copenhagen and Beijing. In the Istanbul Declaration, governments declared that they would increase co-operation with parliamentarians, the private sector, labour unions and non-governmental and other civil society organizations "with due respect for their autonomy".[36] For their part, the parliamentarians called for the strengthening of community involvement in city development and stressed the role which they could play in promoting laws to ensure healthy cities.[37]

The gender dimension to human settlements was also recognized. The *Habitat Agenda* stressed that women have an important role to play in the attainment of sustainable human settlements. But because of the "persistent and increasing burden" of poverty and discrimination against them, women faced particular constraints in obtaining adequate shelter and in fully participating in key decision-making. The empowerment of women and their full and equal participation in political life, and their improvement in health and eradication of poverty were therefore essential to achieving sustainable human settlements.[38]

Health

The stated basic global objective, identified in *Agenda 21* in 1992, is to achieve "health for all by the year 2000".[39] The major global health goals were set out in the Plan of Action for Implementing the World Declaration on the Survival, Protection and Development of Children in the 1990s adopted at the Children's Summit. These goals for 2000, identified in *Agenda 21* and on a baseline of 1984, were to: eliminate measles, polio and Guinea worm; "effectively control" leprosy and river blindness; reduce child diarrhoea by at least 25% and deaths from this by at least 50%; reduce child respiratory deaths by 33% and provide child respiratory care for 90% of the global population; provide 100% coverage for anti-malaria; reduce schistosomiasis by 40% and the incidence of trematode by 25%; and contain any resurgence of tuberculosis.[40]

The strategy for attaining these goals is a vast and loosely integrated undertaking in sustainable development. The specific strategies for each sector – food, shelter and health – are the concern of specialized UN agencies, but the overall strategy is the focus of the Commission on Sustainable Development and the Earth Summits of 1992 and 1997, both attended by a large number of heads of state and government. As Secretary-General Annan observed, their presence was a "welcome demonstration" of political will. The task now, he said, "is to turn that political will into deeds and actions. We must aim . . . to set a sure course for the world community into the new millennium, on this most urgent and vital global issue".[41] At the World Summit for Social Development in Copenhagen in 1995, the international community adopted the Poverty Strategies Initiative, located in UNDP, to support national efforts in poverty reduction strategies and programmes. Part of the initiative involves the "20/20 agreement", which aims to ensure that 20% of ODA and national development budgets are committed to achieving universal access to basic social services.

Estimated costs of basic human needs

The annual costs of meeting these basic needs during the 1990s is estimated in Table 9.1.1. The annual cost of promoting sustainable agriculture and rural development is $32 billion, of which $5 billion would need to come from the international community, basically from the North to the South in the form of bilateral or multilateral ODA. The annual cost of promoting sustainable human settlements is $223 billion, of which $34 billion would need to be concessionary. And the annual cost of attaining "health for all by 2000" is $51 billion, with $6 billion concessionary. For these three basic human needs, the total annual estimated cost is some $306 billion, with $46 billion concessionary.

Table 9.1.1 Estimated annual costs of basic human needs: 1993–2000 ($billion)

	Concessionary assistance	Total costs
(a) Sustainable agriculture and rural development		
Food security	0.45	3.00
Peoples' participation	0.65	4.40
Farm diversification	1.50	10.00
Land resource plans	0.25	1.70
Land conservation	0.80	5.00
Plant genetic resources	0.30	0.60
Animal genetic resources	0.10	0.20
Pest management	0.28	1.90
Plant nutrition	0.47	3.20
Energy transition	0.27	1.80
Sub-total	5.07	31.80
(b) Sustainable human settlements		
Adequate universal shelter	10.00	75.00
Urban management	15.00	100.00
Land-use planning	0.30	3.00
Urban sanitation	0.05	0.05
Urban transport	5.00	5.00
Disaster management	0.05	0.05
Sustainable construction	4.00	40.00
Human resources	0.06	0.06
Sub-total	34.46	223.16
(c) Human health		
Primary health care	5.00	40.00
Disease control	0.90	4.00
Protection of vulnerable groups	0.40	3.70
Urban health	0.02	0.22
Environmental health	0.11	3.00
Sub-total	6.43	50.92
Total	45.96	305.88

Note: Costs of urban transport are taken from *Agenda 21*, Chapter 9, and estimated at one-quarter of the $20 billion cost in paragraph 9.33.
Source: *Agenda 21*, Chapters 6, 7, 14.

PRESCRIBED NATIONAL POLICIES

The Rio Declaration states as one of its principles that all states and all peoples shall co-operate in the essential task of eradicating poverty as an indispensable requirement for sustainable development, in order to decrease the disparities in living standards and better meet the needs of a majority of the people of the world. In order to achieve sustainable development and a higher quality of life for all people, states are enjoined to "reduce and eliminate unsustainable patterns of production and consumption and promote appropriate demographic policies".[42]

Food

These strategies will not be easily implemented. *Agenda 21* observed that the absence of a coherent national policy framework for sustainable agriculture and rural development (SARD) is widespread. The major thrust of food security, it said, is to effect a significant increase in agricultural production in a sustainable way and to achieve a substantial improvement in people's entitlement to adequate food and "culturally appropriate" food supplies.[43] The agenda calls upon governments to carry out national policy reviews related to food security, including adequate levels and stability of food supply and access to food by all households.[44]

In particular, land usage is critical to this goal. *Agenda 21* noted that "inappropriate and uncontrolled land uses" are a major cause of degradation and depletion of the planet's land resources. Present land use often disregards the actual potential, carrying capacity and limitation of such resources. "The need to increase food production to meet the expanding needs of the population will put enormous pressure on all natural resources, including land."[45]

The 1996 Rome Plan of Action is designed to rectify these problems and achieve the 50% reduction in malnutrition by 2015. The action plan has governments commit themselves to seven steps:

(i)   a political, social and economic environment conducive to achieving sustainable food security;
(ii)   national policies for nutritionally adequate and safe food for all at all times;
(iii) participatory and sustainable food and rural development policies, combating pests, drought and desertification;
(iv)   a fair and market-oriented trade system;
(v)   prevention of man-made emergencies and promotion of recovery and rehabilitation;
(vi)   optimal allocation of public and private investment for these goals;
(vii) monitoring the Plan of Action.[46]

In committing to these seven steps, governments recognized that the multifaceted character of food security would necessitate "concerted national action and effective international efforts" to reinforce national action. They were cognizant of the political challenge it posed. In response, they entered an explicit undertaking: "We pledge our political will and our common and national commitment to achieving food security for all and to an on-going effort to eradicate hunger in all countries . . .".[47]

Shelter

Agenda 21 identifies the global objective as to "improve the social, economic and environmental quality of human settlements and the living and working conditions of all people".[48] This serves as the "core" of national settlement strategies which are expected to respond to eight programme areas, namely: providing adequate shelter for all; improving human settlement management; promoting sustainable land-use planning and management; an integrated environmental structure of water, sanitation, drainage and solid waste management; sustainable energy and transport system; special planning in disaster-prone areas; sustainable construction activity; and human resource development.[49]

The *Habitat Agenda* identified seven commitments to attain the goal of adequate shelter for all.[50] They are:

(i)   adequate shelter for all, including an obligation by governments to enable people to obtain shelter and to protect and improve dwellings and neighbourhoods;
(ii)   sustainable human settlements: efficient use of resources within the carrying capacity of ecosystems and taking into account the precautionary principle approach;
(iii) enablement and participation: enabling all key actors in the public, private and community sectors to play an effective role at the national, state/provincial, metropolitan and local levels;
(iv)   gender equality: integrating gender perspectives in housing-related legislation; highlighting the unremunerated work of women; and formulating policies to promote the full and equal participation of women in human settlements planning and decision-making;

(v) financing shelter and human settlements: strengthening of existing financial mechanisms and innovative approaches for financing the implementation of the *Habitat Agenda*, which will mobilize additional resources from various sources of finance – public, private, multilateral and bilateral – at the international, regional, national and local levels;

(vi) international co-operation: enhancement of international co-operation and partnerships for the *Habitat Agenda*;

(vii) assessing progress: monitoring progress towards these goals.

Health

Agenda 21 is quite vague in its recommendations to countries for achieving "health for all by the year 2000". It recommends that governments consider developing a "national health action plan" in national public health, urban health, environmental health, health education, communicable disease control programmes and primary health care, with special focus on infants, youth and women.[51]

LEGITIMATE NATIONAL INTERESTS

Judging the legitimate national interest of each country, North and South, is hazardous. To what extent do those of the North have an obligation to ensure the sustainable development of those in the South? The international community is agreed now, after decades of hesitation, that every human has a right to food security, a right to health and a right to development. That is progress on a theoretical, normative basis, and it took a considerable time. Another norm, non-binding, is the prescription, recommended originally by the independent Pearson Commission in 1970 and endorsed in a UN General Assembly resolution, that countries of the North spend 0.7% of their national GNP on official development assistance. As Table 9.1.2 shows, however, the performance of the North has slipped badly, notwithstanding the undertaking of Rio in 1992 to devote "new and additional resources" for

Table 9.1.2 ODA performance of DAC countries: selected years

| Country | ODA as a percentage of GNP | | | Volume ($million) |
	1996	1986/90	1981/5	1996
Denmark	1.04	0.91	0.77	1,772
Norway	0.85	1.12	1.00	1,311
Sweden	0.84	0.90	0.87	1,999
Netherlands	0.81	0.96	1.00	3,246
France	0.48	0.59	0.57	7,451
Luxembourg	0.44	0.19	0.13	82
Belgium	0.34	0.45	0.58	913
Finland	0.34	0.58	0.33	408
Switzerland	0.34	0.31	0.28	1,026
Germany	0.33	0.41	0.47	7,601
Canada	0.32	0.46	0.46	1,795
Ireland	0.31	0.20	0.22	179
Australia	0.30	0.39	0.48	1,121
UK	0.27	0.30	0.37	3,171
Austria	0.24	0.22	0.32	557
Spain	0.22	0.13	0.10	1,251
New Zealand	0.21	0.25	0.27	122
Portugal	0.21	0.19	0.04	218
Italy	0.20	0.37	0.22	2,416
Japan	0.20	0.31	0.30	9,439
USA	0.12	0.20	0.24	9,377
OECD	0.25	0.33	0.34	55,455

Source: OECD-DAC: Table 6(a). Statistics supplied by e-mail.

global and national sustainable development. In percentage of GNP terms, the performance of the North has dropped by one-quarter since the 1980s, from 0.34% to 0.25% in 1996, the lowest percentage yet recorded. So long as the assistance from the North falls away, it cannot be easily seen how countries of the South can achieve sustainable development, or the vital planetary interest in attaining global sustainability can be met. The "global partnership for sustainable development" has clearly not taken off in any way.

Two countries symbolize the problem of sustainable development more starkly than most. Both Bangladesh and Kenya have national populations that are projected to double over the next three to four decades. Yet both live at or over the edge of national sustainability. The challenge for these two countries to attain sustainable development, particularly as it affects the basic human needs of their national populations in food, shelter and health in the twenty-first century, will be severe. How do they perceive their legitimate national interest, and that of other nations, in the quest for global sustainable development?

NOTES

1. *Agenda 21*, 1.1, 1.3, 1.6, 2.1, 2.4.
2. Rio Declaration, Principles 7, 8.
3. UNDH, 28 June 1997.
4. See A. Jernelöv & S. Jernelöv, "Sustainable development and sustainable consumption" (http://www.mbnet.mb.ca/consume/inst.sd.html; 1 January 1997).
5. D.L. Meadows et al., *The limits to growth* (New York: Universe Books, 1972). The study, in fact, estimated a population figure for the planet's carrying capacity, which was approximately that existing at the time.
6. World Commission on Environment and Development, *Our common future* (Oxford: Oxford University Press, 1987), 16. See also, *inter alia*, J.T. Mathews (ed.), *Preserving the global environment* (New York: W.W. Norton, 1991), 16.
7. UNDP Associate Administrator R. Ahmed, launching 1997 UNDP Human Development Report, UNDH, 12 June 1997.
8. Global Model LINK economic forecasts, reviewed by the UN Ad Hoc Expert Group on Short- and Medium-term Prospects of the World Economy, UNDH, 25 March 1997. The Asian crisis may require some revision.
9. UN secretary-general, statement on International Day for the Eradication of Poverty, UNDH, 17 October 1997; United Nations Conference on Human Settlements (Habitat II) 1996, Programme of Action, *Habitat Agenda*, 53 (hereafter *Habitat Agenda*); UN document A/CONF.165/7, citing IBRD report. (UN press release, "New partnership to meet global shelter crisis focus of UN Conference on Human Settlements"), 3 June 1996. (http://www.un.org:80/Conferences/habitat/eng-pres/3/habit´st1.htm).
10. World Food Summit Plan of Action, 1996, (hereafter WFSPA). "Severe malnourishment" is defined as a daily calorie intake below 1.4 times the established energy requirements in a state of fasting and at complete rest.
11. *Agenda 21*, 14.74.
12. UN document E/CN.17/1995/13, 20 March 1995. "Strongly degraded" is defined as "the large destruction of the original biotic functions of land".
13. Rome Declaration on World Food Security 1996: 6.; WFS 96/3, November 1996 (hereafter RDWFS).
14. *Agenda 21*, 7.6.
15. UN document A/CONF.165/7, citing IBRD report (UN press release, "New partnership to meet global shelter crisis focus of UN Conference on Human Settlements", 3 June 1996). (http://www.un.org:80/Conferences/habitat/eng-pres/3/habit´st1.htm).
16. Ibid.
17. Istanbul Declaration on Human Settlements, 14 June 1996: 4 (hereafter Istanbul Declaration).
18. *Habitat Agenda*, 2.
19. Ibid.
20. *State of the world*, 1994, 17.
21. Ibid., 1.
22. Ibid., 2, 26.
23. Ibid., 94, 26.
24. *Agenda 21*, 6.1.
25. Ibid., 1.1.
26. "Food security" is defined broadly as: "Food security exists when all people, at all times, have economic access to sufficient, safe and nutritious food to meet their dietary needs and food preferences for an active and healthy life" (WFASPA, 1).

27. RDWFS, 2. See also FAO: WFS 96/3, November 1996, and *IHT*, 13 November 1996.
28. RDWFS, 1. See also *IHT*, 18 November 1996.
29. Statement on World Food Day, UNDH, 21 October 1997.
30. *IHT*, 13 November 1996.
31. Ismail Serageldin, Vice President of World Bank, *IHT*, 15 November 1996.
32. Istanbul Declaration, 1.
33. United Nations press release: HAB/IST/25, 15 June 1996, 5.
34. UNGA Resolution 43/181, annex; *Habitat Agenda*, 1.6.
35. *Habitat Agenda*, 22–36. The goals were: equitable human settlements, poverty eradication, sustainable development, spatial characteristics, family strengthening, citizen rights, international partnership, solidarity with vulnerable groups, financial resources and human health.
36. Istanbul Declaration, 12.
37. UN press release, HAB/IST/25, 15 June 1996, 11. (http://www.un.org:80/Conferences/habitat/eng-pres/3/habist25.htm).
38. *Habitat Agenda*, 1, 15.
39. *Agenda 21*, 6.4.
40. Ibid., 6.12.
41. UNDH, 23 June 1997.
42. Rio Declaration, Principles 5 and 8.
43. *Agenda 21*, 14.6.
44. Ibid., 14.9(a).
45. Ibid., 14.34.
46. WFSPA, 13–62.
47. RDWFS, 2.
48. *Agenda 21*, 7.4.
49. Ibid., 7.5.
50. *Habitat Agenda*, 37–52.
51. *Agenda 21*, Ch. 6.

9.2   Bangladesh

Abdul Moyeen Khan

"... forests preceded civilization, deserts followed."

Anon.

There is no country like Bangladesh, anywhere on the planet. No country less understood, less well known, more misperceived. The images of the country carried in the minds of people around the world are scarcely flattering – Kissinger's "basket-case economy" and CNN shots of countless people drowned from floods and cyclones as the sea surges over the low islands of the Ganges–Brahmaputra delta.

Yet without exception in my experience, visitors to Bangladesh fall in love with this beautiful land and the simple people once they are here, and they go back transformed. They never really forget, once they have been here, and many keep coming back as if to their first love. The charm of the country lies in the simplicity of the people's lifestyle, their contentment with "so little" in this materialistic world, and their amazing resilience to emerge again and again from the scourge of natural calamities year after year.

Bangladesh is a microcosm of the challenge of sustainable development for the planet. The problems of development are at their extreme in the national context here. If we can achieve sustainable development in Bangladesh, we can achieve it worldwide. Escapism is not the solution. Nor must continued struggle be our perpetual fate. Sustainability, even if at a bare minimum, is the key to the survival of the teeming millions of Bangladesh. Once this is achieved we shall be able to make the transition to a world of peace, and prosperity can then be accelerated in a natural way.

The problems of Bangladesh are not only daunting but they have become sad and rather perverse. Thirty years ago in Bangladesh, people may have been poor yet nobody starved. They just caught fish. In the 1990s you cannot do that any more. In most places the pond life is not fit for consumption; in others, the fish are simply not there. Sustainable development for a country like Bangladesh will only succeed if human activity becomes reconciled with the natural order. We must not exploit our resources, but use them in a natural way. Humankind must not exploit mother Earth any more. We must change our mindsets. We must harness rather than dominate nature, and sustain life for both humans and all other life forms – beginning with the Royal Bengal Tiger, of which only a few remain. Over the long term, exploitation of nature will mean deprivation for humans. We must live with the planet, not off it, so that both humanity and the planet survive together.

NATIONAL POLICY

Rio's *Agenda 21* called for a "global partnership for sustainable development". It called for the "fulfilment of basic needs, improved living standards for all". The Rome Food Summit envisaged the "right to adequate food and the right of everyone to be free from hunger". The Habitat II agenda spoke of "adequate shelter for all" by 2020. The WHO programme envisages "health for all by the year 2000".

In Bangladesh we have committed ourselves to achieving all these goals in our national policy. We aspire to self-sufficiency in food, appropriate shelter in particular for the urban poor and health for all our citizens, in time for the new millennium.

A few centuries ago, the land of Bengal was a rich country, with a vibrant economic life and quite a lavish lifestyle, more sustainable no doubt than today's "lavish lifestyles" and impressive with its colour and pageantry. It so impressed the Europeans that we were treated to a colonial experience. Our resources, and the fruits of our resources, drained away to a distant land. Our people fell behind, first in their prosperity, then in their most basic development.

Half a century ago, we started again from a clean slate, at least politically if not economically. We inherited new ideals of democracy, ideals which in all fairness had not been known before colonialism. So, we tried to sustain our people for half a century, but it was only a partial success. The demographic explosion had begun and the population began to burgeon. The race between numbers and resources commenced. Our experiment with Western democracy has been only a partial success as well. We have not been able to establish the appropriate linkages between democracy and development.

So Bangladesh is a microcosm of global sustainable development. Let me address the major challenges.

Food

How to feed 120 million in an area half the size of Britain?

Two decades ago we experienced the Green Revolution – a breakthrough in the rice yield and at the same time a significant increase in the use of water, insecticides and pesticides. Productivity increased by a factor of two. It was just as well for this also allowed us to keep pace with the population growth which doubled in this period and yet people did not starve.

Yet our dependency on agro-chemicals continued to grow. And the fact remains that our agricultural productivity is still a quarter of Japan's and one half of South East Asia's. Experts say there is still scope for a four-fold increase in the yield through intensive monoculture. This surely shows enormous elasticity in the concept of national carrying capacity. But new questions arise as to whether it is advisable to stretch it to the end of the tether for the sake of the consumer society, or restrain ourselves and settle for a more realistic sustainable level of lifestyle for the centuries to come. Poor countries like Bangladesh are often forced to do things they do not wish to do. Globally, DDT is illegal but in Bangladesh we still use it. Thirty years and more after Rachel Carson's *Silent spring* frightened the North, the DDT plant in Bangladesh cheerfully produces in full swing. The agricultural extension service has failed to make our rural people aware of the environmental consequences of the use of this material. It is time that the dangers of such negligence are brought into focus and given importance in our policy planning. We know it is harmful and we don't want to use it, yet there seems no choice right now. Meanwhile, the chemicals continue to destroy the micro-nutrients in the soil even at the current rate of use, and they are poisoning the fish in the ponds as well.

Indeed, fertilizers and pesticides are used on the land indiscriminately by our farmers. Not having the education or technical knowledge of the items they are using so frequently, they consider them to be the panacea for all yield problems. Such materials are now distributed mostly in the private sector, leaving very little scope for control of their use. A consequence is the failure to sustain the level of yield as an appropriate proportion of their use over longer time periods. Knowledge of this is widespread in the developed countries but there is an obvious time lag in disseminating this information in our country. And again, the immediate needs take priority over the long-term considerations. It has already prompted people to go for only one crop. The high-yield varieties of rice (HYV) and the monoculture reduced the nutrient balance in the soil. Some of the damage is irreversible, not only to the material order of things but to the psyche of the people living in the area. In future we shall need a better balance, a balance between technology and psychology.

Soil erosion and land degradation are taking place so fast in Bangladesh that soil productivity is reducing in many areas, setting irreversible processes in train. A significant fraction of the 8.3 million hectares of arable land is lost every year due to river bank erosion, industrial use, burial of fresh sediment by major rivers and flash floods, ill-advised agri-planning on slopes and the effects of urbanization. With the population increasing, the stress due to increased agricultural efforts on our soil over the next 30 years will be immense, and may result in serious depletion of micro-nutrients in the soil.

Traditional farming practices in Bangladesh were ecologically compatible with the available natural resources. But population pressure, coupled with increasing demand for a better lifestyle, has led to fast deterioration of this compatibility and an overexploitation of soil. Yet there is no going back to the past. We must now look for an environmentally sound equilibrium at a higher level of technology so that we can also ensure food security for our large population.

"*Machhe Bhate Bangali*", so to say – the people of Bangladesh cannot live without fish and rice. Fish has been consumed over the centuries in the riverine country of Bangladesh, without recourse having been taken to modern methods of fish cultivation, and without any regard for sustainable fisheries management. The consequences are now obvious. A more important conflict has shown up recently. On the one hand, there is a lucrative shrimp culture in the bay areas along the coastlines which is resulting in the depletion of the naturally occurring post-larvae of shrimp. On the other hand, this is resulting in brackish water pools along our southern coasts, thus destroying the more environment-friendly paddy fields and resulting in massive land degradation of coastal areas. Consequently open water as well as marine fishery management systems have to be considered in careful detail with a view to increased productivity and sustainability involving the fish population dynamics.

We can of course look to sister nations for inspiration. Malaysia's income per capita has tripled over 30 years when it was below ours. Admittedly, the population density there is only 60 per square kilometre but the arable land is only 13% of the total land. In Bangladesh, it is 64%, which testifies to the stress to which the land is being subjected in order to ensure "sustainable livelihood" The economies of South East Asia are confronting instabilities right now and the confident growth rate may be a thing of the past. But they have achieved wonders nonetheless, and their problems are those of important economies wrestling with globalization and the associated predations of a modern exploitation.

Water is to become the critical problem for the whole planet in the twenty-first century, and Bangladesh again illustrates the extreme. Our rivers – the holy Ganges, the mighty Brahmaputra and the treacherous Jamuna – all originate in the Himalayan foothills of India and Nepal. India, with its recent nuclear ambitions, has not been beyond violating international law in the past and diverting the Ganges for its own national needs. On our side of the friendly border, silting first made the river unnavigable, then the water completely dried up, parching an otherwise fertile land and making life a torment for millions struggling for subsistence. The Farraka Barrage became internationally known, but no compulsory jurisdiction by the International Court existed to resolve a dispute between a large and a small country. The matter has been resolved recently but the toll over three decades can never be undone. A poor country becomes poorer.

Artesian water has its own problems. There is arsenic poisoning in the ground around the wells and the sub-soil water is drained off to support irrigation for modern agriculture. People dig deeper but the concentration of the arsenic in the water has risen to dangerous levels already resulting in fatal diseases.[1] And in the southwestern part of the country there is a different problem with the soil. We could further develop the Sundarbans, the world's largest mangrove forest in the Ganges delta. Thanks to UNESCO for its belated inclusion in the list of world heritage. But the Sundarbans already suffer from "top-dying" – the leaves at the top of the trees are dying away due to the increased salinity of the soil resulting from massive withdrawal of the water at the upper reaches of the Ganges.

Bangladesh is known fondly as the land of rivers. But the water – rivers, monsoons and floods and tidal waves – all contribute to its environmental problems. While the monsoon flooding continues to disrupt the lives of millions every year, it used to bring in the alluvial soil to cover the agricultural flood plains and add natural fertility to the soil. This led to a concept basic to our livelihood, "living with the floods". More recently, however, some flood control projects have upset the natural balance, in many cases resulting in man-made flash flooding and other ecological imbalances. On top of the surface water system management which had its own shortcomings, a severe depletion of the ground water resource in Bangladesh resulted from irrigation water needs for the HYVs. These two apparently distinct yet interrelated areas of surface water and ground water systems have already seriously impacted on the environmental aspects of Bangladesh.

The Flood Control and Drainage projects have been implemented with a view to their impact on hydrology and morphology. But the socio-economic impact on the people in the area in turn affected their livelihood and the ecosystem in general. Almost 90% of the population in Bangladesh depend on ground water for potable supplies and, during the dry seasons, agriculture is becoming increasingly dependent on irrigation from ground water. But usage already exceeds the annual recharge. In the northern part of the country irrigating tube wells have to be sunk much deeper now than ten years ago, and many are ending up as dry bores.

Shelter

Providing adequate housing was one of the principal elements of the Participatory Perspective Plan 1995–2010 whose formulation I steered in the mid-1990s.[2] Traditional planning, I found, tended to focus on the provision of accommodation for squatter and low-income groups, and for the rehabilitation of houses for those devastated by floods and other natural calamities. This needed, of course, to remain, but a greater priority than in the past needed to be placed on the problem of urbanization – the problems facing the two main cities of Dhaka and Chittagong along with a number of other secondary urban centres had taken acute form. The challenge of human settlements has not only to do with the growth of slums in an urbanizing world; it also involves the associated problems of solid waste disposal, power supply, drinking water, sanitation and mass transit if the real basic needs of the population are to be met. The perspective plan included the improvement of ten "strategic secondary towns" with these goals in mind. And it included the strengthening of municipal capabilities of the main centres for better operation and maintenance of their urban assets. We tried hard in the Planning Commission and made some headway. But it is not easy when the population is set to double in a matter of decades, and when the urban drift is felt, even in a rural country such as Bangladesh. Some say that high-rise buildings are the answer to population growth, since they take less land per person. I do not fully advocate that, but we may be forced into it as the land recedes.

Health

Five years ago, my government put emphasis on creating a "free" maternal child health care centre (MCH) at each of the nearly 4,500 *unions* in the country and a "free" 31-bed hospital with "full emergency operation table facilities for maternity care services" and related x-ray and emergency ambulance service in each of the 469 *thanas* to cover the whole of the countryside occupied by some 100 million rural people.[3] The programme was not simple by any standards. At the same time the government committed itself to supplying at least a simple bamboo or thatched hut for everybody to have a place where they could take shelter during rain and sun. Part of a modest *dal-bhat* (rice and lentil) dream for Bangladesh – both realistic and consistent with the planetary interest.

Other developmental concerns

For any country living "on the edge", population growth is the big concern. Bangladesh has done well with its population planning. The growth rate during the past five years has been brought below that projected by UNFPA – down to 1.8%. Government succeeded in providing services to the rural population better than was expected even by external donors. We realized that although pills and condoms were critical items for family welfare, the more fundamental item is education and in particular girls' education. Women and girls have traditionally been disadvantaged in Bangladesh, in education and many other ways. Yet the role of women is critical to the success of sustainable development. We therefore prevailed on the donor community as to where the real thrust should be. So 45 years after colonial rule had ended and 20 years after independence, we took the bold step of instituting compulsory basic primary education for all and the unprecedented step of providing free girls' education together with scholarships for all rural girls up to the secondary level.

The results have been conspicuous within the short span of five years. There has been an enormous increase in school enrolment, significant decrease in drop-out rates and a significant rise in the literacy rates, particularly for girls. Infrastructural development included building or reconstructing 50,000 primary schools at a cost of $10,000 each and similarly for nearly 10,000 secondary schools and pre-university colleges at an average cost of $20,000 a piece. Now the donors wash their hands of the population programme saying that enough has been done, while the reality is that much remains to be done in population planning. The development partners still need to support us at least during this critical transition period into a level of sustainable population as well as economic growth rate when we would be able to look after ourselves.

A country's development turns critically on its energy situation. Although Bangladesh was considered devoid of any significant natural resources, more recent indications testify in favour of a considerable amount of reserves in natural gas. There is, however, an acute shortage of energy as well as power since we lack the resources to develop them. Meanwhile the first coal mining in the country started just a few years ago, albeit with great difficulty in organizing the investment required. But the dilemma of choosing between fossil fuel and cleaner alternatives continues to baffle our energy planners. The real choice for Bangladesh is between having a sizeable component of fossil fuel in its energy mix or continuing to be energy starved. Over 20 million earthen hearths in rural Bangladeshi homes are fired by fuel from trees and even from wood collected by children in order to prepare two meals every day in the absence of any formal source of energy. The process contributes to the vanishing tree line in the country, gradually leading to an ecological disaster just for the sake of this one compelling activity that people cannot do without. Whether to continue this enormous consumption of bio-mass every day, the lifecycle and hence renewal period for wood being from 20 to 50 years, or take recourse to fossil fuel for a transitional period which itself is not environmentally friendly is a key question. How to strike a balance between our most immediate critical energy requirements and a future ecologically sound energy policy in Bangladesh? Only 15% of the people are being catered for by formal energy sources in the country right now and over two-thirds of our foreign exchange reserves are drained off annually by the importation of oil and oil products. This is hard, I think, for anyone in the North actually to comprehend.

THE LEGITIMATE NATIONAL INTEREST

A simple question. Can we not strive for a minimal quality of life for the millions of the poor while at the same time reversing the current trend of degradation of mother Earth during the next hundred years to come? The answer is not so simple.

Let me dilute the concept of sustainable development of the poor by redefining it in the context of their survival as "sustainable livelihood". It is our legitimate national interest to have the human basic needs – a sustainable livelihood – as the birthright of having been born into the species. And it is this legitimate national interest that I am talking about that is to be synthesized into our novel concept of the planetary interest.

In planetary terms the crux of the problem lies in the global tension between survival of the poor in the South, and the height of over-consumption and arrogance of mindless wastage in the North. Poverty and environmental degradation may have been locked into a vicious circle not so much as a consequence of actions in the South, but in many cases due to reasons very much originating in the rich countries. What we really need to do is move away from the traditional concept of overexploitation of nature that is so prevalent in the North to that of harnessing it through a global approach.

While there is no doubt that the overpopulation of the South continues to be a threat to the planetary interest, few people realize in the North that adding just one new child in their countries amounts to, in consumption terms, an extra hundred new-borns in a country like Bangladesh. The notion of global carrying capacity is no more dependent on technological breakthroughs than on our acceptance of a limit to which we might restrict ourselves in respect of consumption – that is to say, avoiding the squandering of our limited global resources. The resolution of the conflict between the planetary interest and the legitimate national interest of Bangladesh may in fact lie in restricting the consumption pattern to a "realistic level" in countries other than Bangladesh.

Consider, for example, climate change. Bangladesh contributes the least to this global phenomenon but could be affected the most. Even a few degrees of rise in global temperature would result in a quarter of the deltaic flood plain of Bangladesh going under the sea, destroying one-third of the crop and other livelihood of our people. While the principle of "polluter pays" has been accepted in the national context, a key question today is whether the principle should not be extrapolated to the global context at a time when, in the environmental sense, the concept of geographical sovereignties

Figure 9.2.1 "Women and girls", says Abdul Moyeen Khan, "have traditionally been disadvantaged in Bangladesh, in education and many other ways. Yet the role of women is critical to the success of sustainable development." In Dhaka, Bangladeshi women stage a torch-light march in November 1997, on International Protest Day against the Repression of Women. (Courtesy Popperfoto/Reuters)

transcends national boundaries and the security of nations transforms to the security of people. Is it a legitimate national interest of ten countries to emit over 60% of all greenhouse gases into the atmosphere when it is now recognized that a significant part of my crowded country will be lost to the sea? It is a clear violation. The legitimate national interest of Bangladesh demands that this stop.

Thus the challenge of sustainable development of Bangladesh is not confined to the localized parameters inside the country itself. They are only the sub-sets of a much wider global set, and thereby intimately related to the issue of the sustainable development of the planet as a whole. Whether cutting down on the consumption patterns of the North to a "realistic level" is practical in the context of contemporary consumer world trends is a different issue, but the fact remains that the carrying capacity of the planet can only be determined, ultimately, on an objective global basis and not through ideological bravado.

The basic instincts of sustainable livelihood in any part of the world may require decision-makers to take into account the planetary interest as the simplest mechanism for ensuring the survival of homo sapiens on the face of the Earth.

CONCLUSION

The choices over sustainable development are excruciating for policy-makers worldwide. In the short term they face dauntingly tough challenges. If they relent from the harsh discipline of their decision-making for the sake of short-term demands arising out of political exigencies or otherwise, they destroy the long-term base of sustainability for future generations. If they survive the pressure and are courageous enough to make decisions that sometimes sacrifice the short-term interest, they face being voted out. For three years, I had to look after the challenges of development as Associate Minister of Planning in the hardest country to plan for in the world. After an 18-hour day, I would return home in the early hours of the morning to be greeted by constituents who had come to the capital by bus to see me, unannounced. That meant another hour or two's meeting. Then back to the ministry at 8 o'clock in the morning. At present, we are in opposition – the pressure is just as great.

At the 97th Inter-Parliamentary Conference in Seoul in April 1997, UN Secretary-General Kofi Annan urged parliamentarians to continue their "impressive level of commitment, engagement and advocacy" towards sustainable development.[4] I work with many of my parliamentarian colleagues around the world on global issues, and I am truly impressed by their personal commitment to the planetary interest. But why does this not translate into greater ODA levels through governments? Total flows dropped in 1996 to their lowest level ever. The secretary-general, a few months earlier, had told the World Economic Forum that "we must bury the myth that development co-operation is no longer needed in light of private sector flows, trade opportunities, and other benefits of globalization".[5] Private capital flows from North to South have risen from $5 billion to $176 billion in two decades, yet ODA is shrinking and global disparities in wealth are growing. During the preparations for Rio+5, the G-77/China group agreed with the secretary-general: the emphasis on private capital flows, said the spokesman, was a "fallacious argument", since very little of them goes to the countries that need them most. "The lack of aid will mean the collapse of international co-operation, killing the dream of sustainable development."[6] This cannot be allowed to happen. There is a need, I believe, for greater input from parliamentarians into the whole global policy-making process as the twenty-first century opens.

There are no conclusions. The above is simply a glimpse of the contradictions of sustainable development facing Bangladesh in the context of the global scenario. It needs immediate attention both from us and all partner countries in our pursuit of the planetary interest. In right earnest, one cannot really believe that we shall continue on the Earth into the indefinite future in the unrestricted affluent manner we do today. Not if you factor in even the simplest, most basic notion of global equity. The North must concede certain things for Bangladeshis to attain their legitimate national interest. It has always been a moral obligation. Today, it is becoming a political compulsion.

This is our people's way of thinking and not my personal approach. I have always adopted a practical line. In my judgement, right at this point in time it may not be realistic to try to influence the North into a recognition that their consumption patterns must actually fall for the sake of the South, although I presume some form of realization may be coming through. This kind of sacrifice by the North may not happen immediately. People's compassion, ignited by the global television news before dinner, falls away during the local police dramas after dinner. Next morning they go back to work for their family. Apart from the Nordics and the Dutch, the compassion has not yet translated into national politics. We should not be so naïve. The United Nations budget, after all, is less than the amount spent by the citizens of one country on slimming products to counter the effects of over-eating.[7]

To be pragmatic, I would still be satisfied if we can, as the years go by, persuade the North at least to be content with what they have right now, to level off the amount of their current consumption patterns – to stop aspiring to growth for its own sake, to stop believing that the sky is the economic limit. It is not; the ground is the base. They cannot go any further, not in the name of global equity and the holistic planetary interest.

The consumption pattern can almost be measured today in quantitative terms. One American draws down on the planet's resources 100 times more than a Bangladeshi. Population growth in the South, consumption patterns in the North – both are taking their toll but the latter takes the bigger one. The ecological "footprint", as they say, is maybe ten times larger. The conscience of the planet can not let it go on like this.

Effectively, various studies have confirmed that the South is still subsidizing the North. In the sense of global sustainable development, Bangladesh is subsidizing the United States in its profligate consumption pattern. By what factor this is occurring can be measured by our respective "footprints". This compares with the "voluntary simplicity" of the Nordics who choose to lead a lifestyle more in keeping with the dignity of the rest of humanity.

It is a question of values that may need to be cultured around the world. Global values. Olaf Stapleton spoke of "a world beyond poverty, beyond luxury". We must dispel the illusory charisma of the West. There is the American Dream. A large and modern house with all "mod-cons". Two cars. A local golf-course that gobbles land and water. Air travel to Disneyworld for the vacation. Fast food from battery-hens and penned livestock. The world envies it and aspires to emulate it.

Around the other side of the planet there is the Bangladesh Dream. It is less well known, less spectacular. It is much more modest. A simple thatched house. Clean running water. Electricity, sanitation and sewerage. Perhaps it is too modest. But 50 million Bangladeshis do not have it even today. It depends on the kind of technology we wish for and the kind of lifestyle we want. American life is in shame if they do not have a "two-car family". Our contentment is in two square meals. Americans may want to send their every child to university. We would like to send ours at least to primary school. Just as every American wants the best of health insurance, we want to have the basic health services. Some 50 million human beings, 40% of our population, do not have these basic human needs yet.

And there is a Dream of the Earth too. The Reverend Thomas Berry wrote about it in a book with that title. It is of an environment like the one we inherited when we came of age as a species, pristine and natural, untrammelled by the predations of humanity. One where economic theories are not inherently destructive of the planet and its resources. It is the global dream. The Bangladeshi Dream and the Dream of the Earth are one. And they are reconcilable with the American Dream too. For Thomas Berry is an American.

The purpose of this book is to explore new concepts – the planetary interest, the vital planetary interest and the legitimate national interest. They are relevant to the case of my country. The planetary interest lies in sustainable development for all the world's people. We have not yet reached a stage of global ethical development where this is truly entertained by all countries. But we certainly shall and it will be within the next century. Once that is secured, policy-making will intensify, in earnest, over consumption patterns. It will be seen as grotesque, and normatively unacceptable – unfashionable – to engage in excessive consumption. National policies will induce more modest levels of consumption – not compared with what we already have but compared with what the "elasticity" could conceivably provide for the richest. Technology will allow continued improvement in the human condition including for the richest countries. But social norms will induce a degree of self-restraint on the richest for the sake of those attaining basic human needs elsewhere on the planet. Anything beyond that will be seen as exceeding the legitimate national interest of a country.

Meanwhile, may I ask the North, not only the United States, will you address these issues to yourselves today, not 50 years from now; what is a legitimate consumption pattern for yourselves, as Bangladesh struggles to sustain its population at the dawn of a new century and a new millennium?

NOTES

1. A recorded 849 deaths from arsenic poisoning to date, with 16 million people at risk in the 23 southwestern districts alone. See *New Scientist*, 31 May 1997.
2. Planning Commission, Ministry of Planning, *Participatory perspective plan for Bangladesh 1995–2010*, (Dhaka, 1995).
3. A *union* is a combine of about 15 to 20 villages in the rural areas; a *thana* is a combine of 10 unions on the average.
4. UNDH, 14 April 1997.
5. UN press release SG/SM/6153, 1 February 1997.
6. Representative of Tanzania, speaking for Group of 77 developing countries and China, UNDH, 9 April 1997.
7. UNDH, 13 November 1996.

9.3 Kenya

Charity Kaluki Ngilu

> "I offer my presidential candidature to galvanize and translate our majority votes into a government
> . . . Development programmes will be recast to focus on the basic human needs among Kenyans – personal
> security, adequate food, primary health, adequate housing, primary education and employment."
>
> Charity Kaluki Ngilu, "My agenda for Kenya", July 1997

The Kenyan flag is vivid. Black, red and green horizontal stripes, with a shield and crossed arrows in the centre. The black stands for adversity, and freedom from colonial oppression. Red for the blood of the people shed in the struggle. Green for the fertility of the land. The shield and the arrows for the defiance and the vigour of the warrior humans that occupy it – the commitment of the Kenyan people to their sovereignty.

In the course of my political career I have had occasion many times to stand before my country's flag, and when I do it brings home to me the meaning of politics. Politics is about struggle, but that is often misunderstood. The essential struggle is not, as is so often believed, between sectional interests competing for power, although that certainly is an underlying part of the game. The true struggle is a more fundamental one. It is between life and death – a struggle for survival. Humanity, for all its accomplishments, has not put that behind it. Survival is the common goal, and those of us in politics are called upon to act on behalf of the people we serve in the name of promoting our collective chances. That goes for the rich North just as much as for the poor South. In the North they do not recognize it properly yet, but it is so. And when I see the blue flag of the United Nations too, I think of survival – a global survival for humanity. So the two flags, the national and the global, are not unrelated, and the moral call to us politicians both in the North and the South is to help ensure the survival of all our people – humanity.

In my country and perhaps in the world, survival will mean, in the twenty-first century, sustainable development. Past human generations have lived off the bounty of Earth's resources with little thought to conservation, protection or renewal. Hitherto, the planet has proven resilient. But Earth, it is now clear, cannot continue bearing the stress to its environment indefinitely, without a serious crisis for human and other forms of life as we know them today.

Sustainable development is, therefore, the prescription for the planet's restoration to health. Any developmental activity must be able to continue for an unlimited period of time. All nations, including the richest, must henceforth accept that every human dweller on the planet enjoys the right to a minimum standard of living – adequate food and clean drinking water, primary health care and shelter. All children born to this Earth, under whatever circumstances, are entitled to minimum standards of food, health and shelter. On entering adulthood, they have the right to work productively for self-support, and develop a sense of belonging through owning a home they can call their own. Human dignity is made of this kind of thinking. The human rights philosophy, supported and financed today by the United Nations, is truly environment-friendly.

This acceptance of minimum standards of living for all people has far-reaching implications for international relations. It is conditional upon a genuine adoption by the international community of new lifestyles and sharing. It also carries the implication that, if need be, affluent styles of consumption may have to change, if by so doing the world can afford a fairer distribution of its wealth to all and be saved from environmental degradation. The cost implications may be enormous, but the alternative of non-sustainable development would be catastrophic.

Expressed differently, the international community can realize hope for the planet's future only by subjecting excessively selfish interests to the vital planetary interest. This will take care of Earth's environmental integrity as each nation-state, in turn, takes care of its own environmental integrity. Excessively affluent consumption styles to be found in industrialized countries have been, until recently, basically selfish. But the acceptance by the same countries of some system of a just distribution of wealth in the interests of poorer countries is a step forward towards a global environmental conservation. Equally, excessive dependence on over-grazing, deforestation and surface water erosion in the developing countries is environmentally extractive and scarcely survivalist.

NATIONAL POLICY

Kenya is a poor country. The international community perceives five categories of developing countries – least developed, other low-income countries, lower-middle income countries, upper-middle income countries and high-income countries. We are not a least developed country, but we are the next poorest. That means pretty poor. Our GNP is some $10 billion – about $400 per capita.

In population density, we are 50 persons to the sq. km. That is not overcrowded. But it is a question less of space than of resources, of sustainability. Our arable land is only 4% of our territory. And its geographic incidence is skewed. The equator divides my country. The north, above the equator, is semi-desert and only 20% of the people live there. To the south, it is rainy and 80% live there. We are 33 million people. Some 70% of us are in agriculture, but they contribute only 31% to the GNP – much of it is subsistence living. The main crop is maize, and it covers 62% of the cultivated land. The yield is mediocre, with only 1,500 k per hectare. We grow a lot of tea – the second largest producer in the world, per capita. We have substantial livestock – 14 million cattle, 7 million sheep – and we know how to herd them – you will have heard of the *Maasai*. We don't have much in the way of minerals, and hydro-electricity is our only industrial asset. So we don't start with much.

Kenya is a signatory to the UN declarations and action programmes that address the environment and development. It has, however, argued that the North should contribute more towards the costs of rectifying the damage to the planet from air and water pollution. And it has argued that no sustainable development can take place in a world sharply divided into the affluent North and the deprived South.

In line with *Agenda 21*, Kenya's national policies have revolved around the alleviation of poverty, the attainment of high educational standards, modest population growth, health for all including clean drinking water by the year 2000 and, now, industrialization. The National Development Plan, 1997–2001, contains four policy objectives central to sustainable development. In the agricultural sector, budgetary increases will ensure increased productivity, additional storage and processing plants and intensification of extension services in an effort to achieve food security. In population, it contains measures to accelerate the decline in the fertility rate. In health, policies for the alleviation of past constraints of underfunding, low staffing and uneven distribution of personnel by 1999. In shelter, the attainment of adequate housing for all while ensuring sustainable rural settlement and urbanization in Kenya. But look at some of the problems here.

Food

Kenya knows famine. Recorded first in 1884, thereafter in 1928, 1944, 1949, 1981, 1984 and 1997. Each of these years has been severe for our citizens, necessitating the uncertainties and indignity of international food aid. In 1997, close to 5 million tonnes of maize were imported into Kenya. Between 1993 and 1995, maize, wheat, sorghum, millet, rice, beans, beef and milk recorded shortfalls in supply. Although population growth was, and continues to be, an important factor, a scarcity of pest-free storage facilities, the incidence of crop diseases and the vagaries of weather worsened the level of shortages. The trend will not be easy to reverse.

Ireland knew famine. In the 1850s nearly 1 million emigrated to America. That is not open to Kenyans today – they will not let us in, neither will Europe. Nor would we wish to go. We simply want to be able to eat. It would help if the North ate less and used less energy when they did. I know the trade-off is not immediate or direct, but it does exist, over the long term, in a global sense.

Shelter

Kenya is more conscious than most over national housing conditions with the UN's HABITAT head-quarters located in Nairobi. Yet the government's participation in shelter provision has been limited to land grants to individual private developers and to some initial funding for the National Housing Corporation. These two measures have achieved commendable results in the main urban areas. But the existing building codes exclude many Kenyans from obtaining the type of house they can afford. Many low income groups that migrate to cities and towns are forced to live in slums and *majengo* locations.[1] They have to do without piped water and proper sanitation, and they live in horrendously crowded conditions.

National demand for housing is projected to rise by 9% over a four-year period between 1997 and 2001, totalling over a quarter of a million units annually. Can we keep up? The estimated cost will be some $425 million. Government proposed a national "plan of action" at Habitat II in Istanbul in 1996. But no details are available beyond the traditional national plan promises. It is hard to take the plan seriously. In any event, much needs to be done through deregulation and reduced bureaucracy to hasten the pace of surveying, change of user and the granting of certificates of ownership.

The government faces serious land shortages in urban areas due to corrupt "land grabbing". Urban extension will in future most likely spell the end of existing nearby gazetted forests and recreation parks – there are examples of this in Nairobi even within the past two years. Elsewhere, shelter provisions will remain mainly a private sector sphere of operation at strictly commercial prices. This is not likely to hasten the pace at which the rural and urban poor can be housed sustainably in my country. I must say I worry.

Health

Malaria and respiratory diseases are the main causes of morbidity in Kenya. They account for 50% of all reported diagnoses in government health facilities. But the single biggest health challenge is the HIV/AIDS pandemic. It stands to reverse the significant gains made recently, after much national effort, in life expectancy and infant mortality.

The physical health infrastructure translates into approximately 2 beds per 1,000 patients. The ratio of patients to doctor in 1990 was 7,000 to 1. I invite my brothers and sisters in the North to ponder this. Demand for health care greatly outstrips supply. The level of financing has been low. Remuneration for professional personnel has been so unattractive we now have a brain-drain to southern Africa. Quality medical service is not available to all who need it and its availability cannot be guaranteed. Many who need it cannot afford it. Many who might afford it cannot easily access it.

Other developmental concerns

Kenya has one of the highest population growth rates in the world – 3.4% in 1994. Its population is projected to double over 30 years, bringing it to 53 million by 2025.[2] The social and economic implications of this are alarming. The alleviation of poverty, based on the achievement of acceptable standards of living for all, seems an illusion in light of the problems facing future governments in Kenya.

Population density in the high and medium potential land is 200–500 per square kilometre. These figures create a gloomy picture for a country officially known as "agricultural". Urban migration is endemic because of the diminishing farm sizes through sub-division among family members. And they also sell up to pay for school fees. Urban centres in turn have, since 1963, suffered stress from their inability to provide shelter, adequate health and clean drinking water to migrants from the country. Sanitation services have reached breaking-point in Nairobi, placing the lives of the disadvantaged at great health risk.

The alternative outlet for the growing population would be extended settlement into the ecologically fragile arid and semi-arid lands. But the rain pattern there does not allow for year-round cultivation. Although these lands could absorb some 20% of the total population, the cost of effecting this would be prohibitively high. It would involve, *inter alia*, research into soil productivity, water retention capacity, vegetation cover and micro-drainage patterns; dam construction and catchment area afforestation; agricultural extension services and protective legislation for wood fuel energy conservation.

Kenya's arid and semi-arid lands are currently undergoing serious degradation through overstocking and tree felling for wood fuel and charcoal. National demand for this, having risen from 19 million tonnes in 1980 to 39 million tonnes in 1995, is projected to reach 47.1 million tonnes in 2000 – a threat even to the gazetted forests. In 1980, annual supply was equal to demand; by 1995, it was 41%. Even using the backlog, total supply was only 69%.[3] The estimated supply shortfall in 2000 is 31 million tonnes. At the present rate of consumption and without clear afforestation policies, Kenya could experience an energy crisis by 2020. Most people cannot afford the high prices of electricity, gas or solar energy even when it is available.

Fuel wood means little to people in the North. They find it quaint or simply do not comprehend it. But to my people it means survival. In France, 70% of the energy is nuclear. Imagine closing all the power plants there over 10 or 20 years. Imagine how the French would react.

Under the present development plans, infrastructure and research will benefit from the budgetary increases to boost *Jua Kali* operations. *Jua Kali* is a new phenomenon. It is Kiswahili for "hot sun". In this context it means any small or informal manufacturing or retail activity carried out in the open, or in simple sheds to provide shade and keep out the rain. *Jua Kali* was born in the early 1980s when unemployment was undermining the economy and the very process of governance. The aim is to produce goods and services that the poorer people can afford, using skills imparted at secondary level or in the youth polytechnics. Instead of depending on raw materials which are scarce, it utilizes scrap such as discarded wooden crates, oil drums and metal, and uses hand tools and simple electric drills, saws and hammers. That way, it economizes on capital. It straddles many sectors of activity and participates in trade, commerce, transport and distribution, construction, agro-business, and repair and maintenance. A good example is the basket industry; others are gift-making and tourist carving. In manufacturing alone, it employed 0.6 million people in 1995. All told, it employs today some 2.2 million Kenyans, up 80% since 1992. In terms of poverty alleviation, this "informal sector" can play a crucial role in curbing environmental degradation through strengthening employment, especially of the young. At first, the initiative was simply tolerated by the government. But more recently it has provided relatively unsecured credit, and the World Bank too has supported training schemes in the area. It is, in my view, an excellent example of grass-roots initiative in promoting national sustainable development, directly in line with *Agenda 21*.

What is the carrying capacity of Kenya? No-one has accurately estimated. It would not be an exaggeration to say that the term "sustainable development" has limited currency in Kenya. Much that passes for development here amounts to replication of Western structures in the form of buildings and infrastructural installations that are of doubtful economic value. There are many such cases. The construction of an expensive third international airport at Eldoret for instance, without clear need in the agriculture or tourism sectors has been publicly questioned. The recent construction of the expensive power dam and plant on the Turkwel River is unlikely to yield the projected power because the high rate of local atmospheric evaporation will never allow the dam to fill up. The prestigious Kenyatta International Conference Centre, built at great cost some twenty years ago, is approaching the relic stage. Why is this? Because the term "care and maintenance" is foreign to the language of any one of Kenya's 46 tribes. So is "sustainability". And yet the entire concept of environmental conservation for sustainable development rests squarely on the Western budgetary culture of care and maintenance.

Recently, $180 million of public funds were stolen from under the noses of top public affairs managers through a businessman's dabbling in shady deals of non-existent mineral exports. Some ten years ago, a potentially productive cotton irrigation scheme came to grief because a public engineer preferred mechanical diesel pumping power to gravity-fed irrigation from the nearby Tana River. The once famous Bura irrigation scheme is now dead, leaving thousands of new settlers poorer than they were prior to migrating from their traditional homes.

These ill-planned and wasteful "development" projects are a far cry from the Western culture in which development is viewed as the process whereby technology may be used to harness nature as cheaply as possible, for the express purpose of making human life simpler, more comfortable and more satisfying than yesterday.

To be a manager in Kenya is synonymous with securing an opportunity "to eat" (to be corrupt) in order to be rich. To be a policy-maker is to have the freedom to benefit one's ethnic group from public funds. To develop is to spend public funds to construct white elephants, infrastructures which give Kenya a touch of metropolitan Europe – not a touch of metropolitan wealth. Kenya has the deplorable distinction of having the second most unequal income in the world. We have a few billionaires and millions of paupers. This is unacceptable. It also constrains our economic growth. Such socio-economic mismanagement has been mainly responsible for its continuing poverty and apparent stagnation in its effort to industrialize. Poverty, in turn, leads to the adoption of "extractive" lifestyles and resource depletion is the consequence. Kenya does not score very highly on these and many facets of democratic governance.

THE LEGITIMATE NATIONAL INTEREST

Two political concepts have for many centuries determined the course of action nations will take in international affairs – legitimacy and sovereignty. Nationalism has, of course, had a lot to do with whatever final action was taken, and quite often was taken as legitimate in the mind of the nationalist. But the world has become a different place since the creation of the United Nations. Nation-states have learnt to tame their extreme nationalism and to compromise on what before that would have been seen as legitimate. Nations have now committed themselves to resolutions and declarations of the UN General Assembly, UN specialized agencies and the Security Council, in those matters which enhance sustainable development.

Since the creation of UNEP an unprecedented concern for the integrity and health of the environment has been supported by the world community. Agreement to co-operate in the implementation of UN resolutions on the environment is an implicit admission of certain inevitable future developments. As a politician, I see these in terms of political principles. Let me put them in my own words:

- not even vital national interests can override the planetary interest;
- a "threatened" planet calls for a common strategic approach to save humanity – "the planetary interest";
- the "planetary interest" cannot be served through an environmentally perverse division of the world between the affluent rich North and the deprived poor South. A "dead" Earth is no respecter of poverty, affluence or civilization;
- the primary "planetary interest" of humanity as a whole – to protect Earth in order to preserve the source of humanity's basic needs – is as much a "planetary interest" as it is a "legitimate national interest";
- the manufacture of weapons of mass destruction is neither a planetary nor a legitimate national interest, because of its very potential for destroying the world.

The legitimate national interest which obeys the above propositions would cover the following areas among others:

- the protection, conservation and renewal of the environment;[4]
- the alleviation of poverty and eventual assurance of adequate standards of living for all, through sustainable agricultural management methods; sustainable population sizes; relevant education and literacy, delivery, accessibility and affordability of health services, food security and the provision of shelter;
- fighting internationally for fairer international trade including debt repayment relief and easier access to affordable and relevant technology;[5]
- persuading the rich nations not to withhold their dues to the United Nations. The UN has about $4.6 billion annually to spend on economic and social development for the entire world population. New York State University spends more than this amount.[6]

It is perhaps no accident that hard-line communism is now a thing of the past and the market economy the system of the future. This has come at a time when some of the world's largest multinational corporations have annual turnovers far in excess of the GDP of some nation-states.[7] But this has only intensified the fact that the corporate world is the most direct beneficiary of Earth's natural resources. Governments are secondary beneficiaries through taxation and other duties. There is a strong case for the private sector, therefore, as an organized "world interest" to contribute to UN policy on environmental protection, undertake such protection within their own industries and be entitled to any available UN funding especially for research designated for such protection. Monitoring services could then be provided by the UN through national governments.

In our struggle for sustainable development, what help do we get from the rest of the world? Assistance from the international community to Kenya is bedevilled by our politics, whose shortcomings I have pointed out. The donor community doesn't like the Moi version of "democracy". Governmental aid (ODA) has tumbled, as Table 9.3.1 illustrates.

Table 9.3.1   Kenya: official development assistance: 1984–96 ($million)

Country	1986	1988	1990	1992	1994	1995	Total*
Japan	49.8	144.7	93.2	128.7	128.9	198.4	1,447.3
Germany	43.0	55.9	143.1	68.0	46.7	52.3	699.1
United States	29.0	52.0	95.0	56.0	29.0	36.0	626.0
United Kingdom	34.9	75.1	67.3	47.3	44.3	34.8	586.0
Netherlands	44.4	56.7	67.0	54.2	42.0	36.4	565.3
France	32.1	32.2	58.6	40.0	16.1	13.2	355.6
Denmark	25.9	35.4	36.8	18.8	21.4	21.5	336.1
Italy	31.7	37.6	53.5	20.3	22.1	16.9	304.8
Sweden	14.5	27.3	31.2	28.4	17.4	19.8	297.3
Canada	25.3	24.0	19.5	14.1	7.8	6.5	223.3
Finland	9.0	27.7	30.2	20.6	6.0	6.1	211.0
Norway	31.7	31.3	22.5	2.6	2.9	2.2	202.4
Other	11.5	10.0	17.3	20.7	15.9	14.6	198.7
Sub-total	382.8	609.9	735.2	519.7	400.5	458.7	6,052.9
IDA	28.2	95.0	230.0	85.2	88.9	149.6	1,433.4
EU	11.1	73.5	39.5	91.7	36.3	61.8	502.8
IMF	−10.6	27.4	134.3	0	18.5	−39.1	278.3
WFP	3.7	5.2	3.5	71.8	48.7	9.7	276.9
UNHCR	2.2	2.7	2.0	65.0	41.6	23.4	219.4
AFDF	9.4	5.4	12.0	25.1	15.5	45.2	184.7
UNDP	6.3	5.6	12.6	12.2	10.8	4.5	99.6
Other	11.8	11.3	18.2	15.7	15.7	17.9	227.8
Total	444.9	836.0	1,187.3	886.4	676.5	731.7	9,275.8

* Totals include data for the entire period 1984–96.
Source: OECD Reporting Systems Division: e-mail information, 10 October 1997.

Over the past decade, our aid receipts have grown and declined according to the country's unpredictable politics. In 1986 when the Cold War continued and the West thought Daniel arap Moi indispensable, our ODA receipts were $445 million. In 1988, even with the single-party system still prevailing, they had doubled to $838 million. In 1990 it reached a peak of $1,187 million. Then, in the new post-Cold War world, with the wave of democracy influencing Western policy, the international community became disillusioned with Mr Moi's cynical treatment of his country's political system and abuse of the citizenry. Aid flows dropped to $886 million in 1992, the last presidential election year. And again to $676 million in 1994, 57% of the peak year. It remains around that level today.

For their part, donors face the agonizing choice of "political conditionality" – between cutting off aid as an expression of disapproval of the political situation in Kenya or continuing to try to improve the lot of the Kenyan citizen. And it is not only aid donors. In 1997, the International Monetary Fund withheld funds allocated for Kenya's Structural Adjustment Programmes on grounds of endemic corruption, non-accountability and non-transparency in governance. The underlying philosophy in sustainable development embraces the capacity of a national government to produce realistic plans, to economize on resource utilization and to distribute the fruits of economic growth so that poverty is seen to diminish by degrees. For our part, we opposition politicians understand that. What is the "legitimate national interest" of Kenya in that situation? What is the "legitimate national interest" of the aid donor, faced with the exhortation of the Rio Declaration and Action Programme to help the poorer countries attain sustainable national development? The answers are not easy.

Figure 9.3.1   "And so in 1997 . . . I decided . . . to run for the presidency" says Charity Kaluki Ngilu. "If we can introduce a true, stable democracy, then the basis for sustainable development will be laid. Then, and only then, can we expect the international community to fully respond, with assistance, in the planetary interest." Riot police break up a political rally in Kamukunji, Kenya, October 1997. (Courtesy Popperfoto/Reuters)

CONCLUSION

I have not been in politics very long. My story is a rather strange one. I used to be in business, running quite a successful food factory. One evening in 1991 I attended a women's rally. Women's issues were big in Kenya in the early 1990s. I sat at the back of the room, expecting an enjoyable if unchallenging evening. Near the end the guest speaker challenged us to go into politics, to change the country. She spoke to me directly, challenging me to enter. It was the first time the thought had entered my head, and it had been placed there by someone else. I resisted, but others challenged me as well. Several days later, I found myself registering as a candidate in my home district, challenging a sitting cabinet minister. I suffered pressure, intimidation and threats over the ensuing months during the 1992 campaign. But I am a fighter and that only steeled my resolve. Against the odds, I won, and entered parliament.

In parliament, the more I learned the more concerned I became. I became concerned over the inadequate policies on sustainable development. But even more, I became alarmed at the government's undermining of the principles of democracy as I understood it. For in Kenya the problem is more political than economic. Democracy is a prerequisite for sustainable development. You cannot have development for the people unless it is development of the people, by the people. They happen to know best whether the local environment is degrading. They know their developmental needs better than a planner or even a political leader back in the capital city. Their only shortcoming is an ignorance, borne of a lack of education, over the long-term effects of their livelihood practices. That is where the political leaders come in, both in the short term and the long term.

So, in the course of my parliamentary work, I found myself increasingly in conflict with the present government, and first, and most especially, over issues of democracy. I would go to places where the government did not wish me to go, exercising my human rights that I knew were in the UN covenants if not in national policy. On more than a few occasions I was physically assaulted and injured. My life has once or twice been on the line. But a woman in politics must keep going. My stand attracted public attention.

And so, in 1997, with the government reneging further on basic human rights, and the opposition continuing to be divided, I decided, having been empowered by the experience of political struggle, to run for the presidency. This was an unheard of thing to do. A woman had never stood for the presidency before. And that of course was a very good reason to do so. The result of the election was contested by me and other opposition candidates. But the main thing was to stand, and stand as an alternative to the status quo.

Whether I win or lose in future elections, I stand for something new. I stand for a gender balance in Kenyan politics, in line with the UN Declaration at Beijing. I stand for a new openness in restoring democracy to Kenya, in line with the call of the UN for democracy to be a goal of every society. Democracy according to the Kenyan model, but not the current government model – rather a true democracy that the rest of the world will find compatible with the universal ideal. And I stand for sustainable development that has eluded Kenya to date. A national sustainable development that is a part of global sustainable development. If we can introduce a true, stable democracy, then the basis for sustainable development will be laid. Then, and only then, will we be serving the legitimate national interest. Then, and only then, can we expect the international community fully to respond, with assistance, in the planetary interest.

The legitimate national interest of Kenya. Compatible with the vital planetary interest of the world. That is what I stand for.

NOTES

1. *Majengo* in Kiswahili means the housing in a town or city in a location exempt from the expensive building regulations. *Majengo* are a grade higher than slums.
2. The 1994 estimate was 26.5 million (New York: UNDP Human Development Report, 1997), 195.
3. National Development Plan estimates, 1989–93.
4. Kenya's best example of renewal is at Bamburi, Mombasa, where cement material excavation is succeeded by the best man-made forest and wildlife sanctuary in Africa.
5. Effective debt relief to the 20 worst-affected countries would cost between $5.5 billion and $7 billion, less than the cost of one Stealth bomber, and equivalent to the cost of building the EuroDisney theme park in France (New York: United Nations, UNDP Human Development Report, 1997), 93.
6. Ibid.
7. In 1994, General Motors had a GDP of $168.8 billion, Royal Dutch Shell $109.8 billion, while Nigeria had $30.4 billion, Pakistan $57.1 billion. The top five corporations had $8,711.4 billion, while the whole of sub-Saharan Africa had $246.8 billion (*Fortune Magazine*, 1996).

The author gratefully acknowledges the assistance of Mr Habel Nyamu in the preparation of this chapter.

CHAPTER TEN

Forest management

10.1 Introduction

Perhaps the best example of the challenge of sustainability for the planet's health concerns forest management. Forests are a critical source of economic development, biodiversity, medicinal potential, human habitat, and climate regulation. They therefore symbolize and are a microcosm of the planet's sustainability challenge. Forest management is chosen here essentially as a case study of global sustainable development and consumption.

THE GLOBAL PROBLEM

The planet has in recent centuries been stripped of a large fraction of its original forest cover. Some 10,000 years ago, forests covered 34% of the planet's land surface.[1] About 2,500 years ago, the depletion starts in southern Europe. About 1,000 years ago, it spreads across the rest of Europe, and into South and East Asia and Central America. One century ago, the depletion occurs across North America. But the global coverage remains high – at 32% of the planet's land. In the past half-century, that global coverage has diminished to 26% of the land surface. Only 12% remains as an intact original forest ecosystem.

In 1995, the global forest cover (both natural forest and plantations) stood at 3.454 billion hectares. The annual rate of deforestation was 15.5 million hectares in the 1980s, reduced to 13.7 million in the first half of the 1990s.[2] Thus, the annual rate of depletion is 0.4%. At this rate, the planet would be completely denuded of its tree cover in 252 years.

In the words of the United Nations, "both the growing size and increasing urbanization of the world's population have had, and will continue to have, major impacts on forest cover and condition, demand for wood and non-wood forest products, and the ability of forests to fulfil essential environmental functions".[3] As Table 10.1.1 shows, forest cover declined by 2% during the 1980s while roundwood production increased by 17%.

Table 10.1.1 Forest coverage and roundwood production 1980–89

	World*	Africa	North America	South America	Asia	Europe	Oceania
Forests (m. ha)							
1980	4,112	696	683	943	546	155	151
1989	4,049	683	687	896	524	157	156
% change	98%	98%	101%	95%	96%	101%	103%
Roundwood production (m. cu. m.)							
1980	2,934	390	629	281	908	334	35
1989	3,431	488	773	325	1,048	364	40
% change	117%	125%	123%	116%	115%	109%	114%

* World total is more than the sum of the regions shown.
Source: *World statistics in brief* (United Nations, 1992), 88–100.

The most serious depletion of forest has occurred in South America (4%) and Asia (3%). The increase in forest in North America, Europe and Oceania, however, is due to net reforestation, with original forest cover being depleted. Thus, the various non-timber resources, including especially biodiversity and medicinal ingredients, are lost.

The problem has been recognized by the international community, most particularly at the Rio Earth Summit in 1992. Forests, agreed the nation-states, are "essential to economic development and the maintenance of all forms of life".[4] All types of forest embody complex and unique ecological processes which are the basis for their present and potential capacity to provide resources to satisfy human needs as well as environmental values.[5]

In the coming decades, concludes the UN, pressures for increased food production are expected to lead to continued conversion of forest land to agriculture. This is likely to be especially critical in Latin America and Africa where other options for meeting food needs are limited. And while the world's forest area has been steadily decreasing, there has been a continued increase in demand for wood products – a 36% increase between 1970 and 1994. Demand for fuelwood, the main source of energy for 40% of the global population, continues to grow by 1.2% per year.[6]

THE GLOBAL OBJECTIVE AND STRATEGY

Agenda 21 identifies the global objective as maintaining existing forests through conservation and management, and sustaining and expanding areas under forest and tree cover with a view to maintaining or restoring the ecological balance and expanding the contribution of forests to human needs and welfare.[7]

The international community, however, was unable to agree on any legally binding document at Rio; simply a non-binding statement of principles. These principles, said the document, reflect a "first global consensus on forests". The "guiding objective" of the principles was to contribute to the management, conservation and sustainable development of forests and to provide for their multiple and complementary functions and uses.[8]

The principles themselves are broad in the extreme. Forestry issues and opportunities, they assert, should be examined in a holistic and balanced manner within the overall context of environment and development. They need to take into consideration the multiple functions and uses of forests, including traditional uses, and the likely economic and social stress when these are constrained, as well as their potential for development that sustainable forest management can offer. The vital role of all types of forest in maintaining the ecological processes and balance at the local, national, regional and global levels needed to be recognized.[9] Efforts should be undertaken towards the "greening of the world": all countries, notably developed countries, should take positive and transparent action towards reforestation, afforestation and forest conservation.[10]

The question of a legally binding treaty on sustainable forestry has proven controversial. The Inter-Governmental Panel on Forestry (IPF), set up after the 1992 Earth Summit, was tasked with following up the conference's recommendations and encouraging international consensus on key forestry issues, including "appropriate legal mechanisms".[11] After five sessions over 1996–7, the IPF submitted its final report to the UN Commission on Sustainable Development without agreement over a treaty. Some countries (the European Union, Canada and Malaysia) advocated a treaty, while others (Brazil, India, United States) opposed the idea. At the second Earth Summit in June 1997, agreement was reached to establish a new Inter-Governmental Forum on Forests with a view to considering the issue afresh in 2000.

PRESCRIBED NATIONAL POLICIES

The national policies required to implement a global forestry strategy, such as it is, have proved to be a highly sensitive matter. The final outcome of some acrimonious debate was the following two principles:

> States have, in accordance with the Charter of the United Nations and the principles of international law, the sovereign right to exploit their own resources pursuant to their own environmental policies and have

the responsibility to ensure that activities within their jurisdiction or control do not cause damage to the environment of other States or of areas beyond the limits of national jurisdiction.

States have the sovereign and inalienable right to utilise, manage and develop their forests in accordance with their development needs and level of socio-economic development and on the basis of national policies consistent with sustainable development and legislation including the conversion of such areas for other uses within the overall socio-economic development plans and based on rational land-use policies.[12]

The North is called upon to assist. Principle 9 of the Statement on Forest Principles states that the efforts of developing countries to strengthen the management, conservation and sustainable development of their forest resources should be supported by the international community. Principle 10 states that new and additional resources should be provided to developing countries to enable them sustainably to manage, conserve and develop their forest resources, including through afforestation, reforestation and combating deforestation and forest and land degradation.[13] The assistance of the North to forest-rich countries of the South is a critical factor in determining the legitimate national interest of countries in sustainable forestry.

Agenda 21 estimated the cost of the forestry component of all activities at $31 billion, of which some $6 billion would come in aid from the North, as illustrated in Table 10.1.2

Table 10.1.2   Sustainable forests: the annual global cost: 1993–2000 ($billion)

Programme	Cost	ODA assistance	%
1. Multiple forest functions	2.50	0.86	34
2. Afforestation and reforestation	10.00	3.70	37
3. Utilization efficiency	18.00	0.88	5
4. Planning and assessments	0.75	0.23	31
Total programme cost: forestry	31.25	5.67	18

Source: *Agenda 21*, 11.6, 11.16, 11.25, 11.34.

LEGITIMATE NATIONAL INTERESTS

Two countries that attract special global attention in sustainable forestry are Brazil and Indonesia. Brazil, with 551 million hectares, has the second-largest forest area in the world, with 16% of the global coverage. Indonesia, with 110 million hectares, has the sixth largest with 3% of the global coverage.[14] Brazil and Indonesia have the largest, and second-largest, tropical forests in the world, respectively. Both are populous developing countries, dependent on utilizing their natural resource base to provide for their people, and determined to do so. Both are vocal in international fora over their sovereign right to exploit their national resources. But both publicly acknowledge their responsibility to avoid unsustainable forestry or transnational pollution. Both governments have difficulty controlling their private sectors.

How do these two countries see the balance of those rights and interests on the one hand, and responsibilities on the other hand, in the vital planetary interest?

NOTES

1. *State of the world 1994*, 22.
2. *State of the world's forests 1997: executive summary* (Rome: Food and Agriculture Organization, 1997), (hereafter SOFO:ES).
3. Ibid.
4. Non-legally binding authoritative statement of principles for a global consensus on the management, conservation and sustainable development of all types of forests, preambular para. g. (hereafter *Forest principles*) in *Agenda 21*, p. 291.
5. Ibid., preambular para. f.
6. SOFO:ES.

7. *Agenda 21*: 11.12(a).
8. *Forest principles*, preambular paras d and b.
9. Ibid., 4.
10. Ibid., preambular para. c, 4, 8(a).
11. UN Inter-Governmental Forum on Forests, Commission on Sustainable Development (www.un.org; 17 November 1997).
12. *Forest principles*, 1(a) and 2(a).
13. Ibid., 9 and 10.
14. The seven largest forested countries comprise 61% of the global forest coverage. The statistics are as follows (billion hectares):

	Temperate and boreal zones	Tropical zone	% of global total	% of territory
Russia	0.764		22	45
Brazil		0.551	16	65
Canada	0.245		7	27
United States	0.213		6	23
China	0.133		4	14
Indonesia		0.110	3	61
Zaire		0.109	3	48
Earth		3.454	100	27

Source: SOFO, 182–5.

The global distribution of forests is skewed, with 52% in the tropical zone (0 to 25 degrees N and S), 18% in the temperate zone (25 to 50 degrees N and S), and 30% in the boreal zone (50 to 75 degrees N and S). Temperate and boreal forests are currently estimated to be a net carbon sink of about 0.7 billion tonnes (range = 0.2 bill. tnne), since there is effectively no net deforestation and the forests are composed of relatively young classes with high rates of growth and therefore of carbon sequestration. Tropical forests, on the other hand, are estimated to be a net carbon source of 1.65 bill. tnne (range = 0.4 bill. tnne) because of the high rate of deforestation in the tropical zone. There is uncertainty over the extent to which, if at all, forests are currently contributing to climate change. But it is expected that, since temperate and boreal forests will contribute less to carbon sequestration as they approach maturity during the 21st century, the world's forests will contribute to climate change if current rates of tropical deforestation and degradation continue. See S. Brown, "Present and potential roles of forests in the global climate change debate", in *Unasylva* **185**, Vol. 47 (1996), 3–10.

10.2 Indonesia

Theo Sambuaga

> States have . . . the sovereign right to exploit their own resources pursuant to their own environmental and developmental policies, and have the responsibility to ensure that activities within their jurisdiction or control do not cause damage to the environment of other States or of areas beyond the limits of national jurisdiction.
>
> Rio Declaration on Environment and Development (1992), Principle 1a

Earth, humanity and civilization are a unity of integral life in a functional relationship. Human life will be threatened and civilization will deteriorate if they are not supported by appropriate natural resources. The alternative is a planet which will turn barren and be incapable of supporting human life if that civilization is governed by people who are not environmentally aware.

It is this environmental awareness that, among other factors, encourages humans to keep population growth at a level where natural resources are able to support the needs of that population with a viable quality of life. The growth rate of the human population has been successfully reduced in the last two decades. But the projected global population of nearly 10 billion by the middle of the twenty-first century is a major cause for concern for Earth's carrying capacity.

Of course the population is not evenly distributed among the 200 sovereign states. And those states possess or control varied natural resources. They also share different levels of educational, social and economic attainment. This has driven each country to seek various ways of independently exploiting our planet and its natural resources in the interest of their national welfare.

Our unique and irreplaceable Earth shares one common interest for all humankind. It is an overarching interest for us all to ensure that human life proceeds and civilization develops by maintaining Earth's carrying capacity. Such an interest is interlinked with all others. But the most central and decisive of all the factors is humanity itself. It is we humans who play an active and dynamic role in the functional relationship. It is we humans who have the most important influence whether or not civilization shall be formed, developed, stagnate or even disappear. It is we who determine whether or not Earth's support capacity shall decline, completely disappear, or be properly sustained or even developed.

One of Earth's vital natural resources is forests. To a developing country, forests are a prized commodity, capable of earning foreign exchange quickly and easily. They are also a source of biological life containing food and medicinal ingredients. They contain basic genetic diversity capable of enriching food plants as well as benefiting animal husbandry. And the wide variety of natural resources inherent in forestry also contributes to the development of culture and science. The ecological functions of forests are beyond doubt: they protect water resources, prevent erosion which otherwise leads to floods, and play a decisive role in controlling the weather.

The functions of forests are diverse and their impact on human life so vital that their continued existence and wellbeing have become indispensable to our common future. What humans do or do not do to Earth's forests will have a negative or positive impact on the species far beyond the geographical boundaries of the forest locations.

Like all other natural resources, forests are exploited and utilized by humankind in its own self-interest. Even though forests are among the few natural resources which can be renewed, the fast rate of population growth and consequent development of human needs makes it difficult to renew forest resources as fast as the demand grows. Forest exploitation is very often followed by pollution and even destruction in spite of conscious efforts to conserve the resource.

At present there are many societies that utilize forests to help free themselves from poverty. Generally speaking, these people are in the South. But an equally dangerous risk of pollution from mismanaged forestry comes from more affluent societies of the North as a result of their uneconomic lifestyles and excessive patterns of consumption.

The *Forest principles* adopted at Rio called for the sustainable management and development of the world's forests. The "vital role" of forests in maintaining the global balance needed to be recognized. States had the sovereign right to utilize their forests according to their development needs and based on rational land-use policies, but also with responsibility to avoid transnational environmental damage.[1]

NATIONAL POLICY

"... It is our responsibility for those directly involved in the forest and forestry sector to realise sustainable forest management as soon as possible, at least by the year 2000. It is not only to fulfil international agreement, but moreover, for national interest."

Djamaludin, Minister of Forestry, December 1995

There is a need for international co-operation to make it possible for developing nations to reach an adequate level of economic growth. Yet, on the other hand, there is a need for self-control by the advanced countries to generate a commendable lifestyle which would economize on the use of natural resources. It is true that international co-operation is urgently required to maintain Earth's carrying capacity in the interest of humankind. Such co-operation must be based on the perception that natural resources are a vital human inheritance from Earth in the interest of present and future generations. These vital natural resources must be considered to belong to all humankind and the utilization and safeguarding of these shall be the common responsibility of everybody.

Indonesia has an abundant tropical forest region – with 110 million hectares, the second largest in the world. It covers about 61% of our national territory. There is a diversity of forest territory – tropical lowland and highland rain forest, peat swamp, freshwater swamp and mangrove forests. In socio-cultural terms, forests sustain the development of the interior communities. In economic terms, the forest's natural resources have made an important contribution to Indonesia's wealth for development and improvement of its people's welfare.

In 1970 when Indonesia started a more methodical and systematic development with the First Five Year Development Plan, the value of exported forest products was some $30 million. At that time Indonesia's population of 117 million had a per capita income of about $70 per year. Twenty-five years later, Indonesia's population had increased to 195 million. Yet its per capita income was $1,000 per year. Its production of forest products had developed to an export value of $8 billion, ranking it as the most important export commodity after oil and natural gas, comprising 18% of Indonesia's total exports in 1995.

The contribution of forestry to development has been apparent not only by its share in generating public revenue but also by its share in the results of development itself. These are not merely the measurement of increased per capita income. In the past 25 years the portion of Indonesia's population living below the subsistence level has decreased from 60% in 1970 to 12% in 1995. The overall improvement of people's welfare, particularly the effort to free them from poverty, has included people who settled and work around the forestry areas.

It is simple. Our people would not have climbed out of the poverty which colonialism bequeathed us without the exploitation of our forest resources.

The riches of Indonesia's forests are utilized and enjoyed not only by Indonesia but by the international community as a whole. Most of Indonesia's forest products are consumed in other countries. Direct proceeds of the forestry industry have improved employment opportunities, economic added value and industrial development. All of this has benefited the international community resulting from the capital invested in managing the forests and its production processing industries which have originated from the business investment interests of various countries.

So that is the upside. The world, of course, is acutely aware of the downside.

In exploiting its natural forest resources, Indonesia has also suffered some bitter experiences. Excessive forest exploitation has been motivated by the high profit figures at the hands of the business sector, by a lack of corporate and governmental control, by the lack of people's awareness of the functions of forest sustainability and by the inadequate quality of human resources. Each of these factors has had a negative impact on forest conservation in Indonesia. According to *Bappenas,* the Indonesian National Planning and Development Agency, the rate of deforestation has now reached 1 million hectares per year.

What underlying pressures caused this reduction of forests and the pressure on forest resources? First, the uneven growth and distribution of population. Secondly, the conversion of forest to plantations and mining developments. Thirdly, transmigration programmes, industrial and agricultural pollution, excessive exploitation of special woods and other products and damage to mangrove areas. So it is partly business motive but more particularly the interests of sectoral development, a lack of co-ordination, and different perceptions of forest sustainability.

Reacting to these experiences and heeding the lessons learnt from them, Indonesia has taken various correctional measures. In the late 1980s a campaign was launched for sustainable forest management. Regreening and reforestation programmes have been intensified by means of a fund originating from the business sector. Tree cutting has been allowed only on the basis of rigid criteria and strictly limited to certain species. From 1990 to 1995, over 5.5 million hectares of reforestation was carried out and this is increasing each year. Following the introduction of the laws of foreign investment in 1967 and domestic investment in 1968, forestry business began to grow rapidly. Private companies were given Forest Concession Rights. Under these rights they are obliged to apply the Indonesian Selective Cutting System whose aim is forest sustainability. In 1970, there were 64 FCR holders working on 7.7 million hectares of forest. By 1979, 462 units were working 45.0 million hectares; and by 1989, 565 units were working 57.7 million hectares.[2] And a reafforestation fund has been set up, standing at $660 million in 1994 in order to develop timber estates.

Out of Indonesia's total forest area, about 45% is categorized as production forest. This is the area managed for utilization on condition that the holder of the right to forest exploitation is required to pay a contribution intended for replanting programmes or forest rehabilitation. Of the forest area, 20% is to be protected forests which are tightly maintained and controlled for conservation. Of the remaining area, 20% is to be conversion forest and 15% maintained for tourism and conservation purposes.

In line with the global *Agenda 21,* Indonesia's 1993 Guidelines of State Policy further prescribe that forest development should be directed towards providing the maximum benefit to the people's prosperity. This is to be achieved by maintaining the conservation and continuation of forest functions with priority placed on sustaining natural resources and the environmental function. An environmental impact analysis is an integral part of every development project, whether in business or for public service. Similarly, eco-labelling was introduced as a condition for every environmentally related product.

The government does what it can. It has legislated, but enforcement is weak and in some areas virtually non-existent.

THE LEGITIMATE NATIONAL INTEREST

> "The thick smoke not only hurts our own community but also people from neighbouring countries."
> President Soeharto, October 1997

Is Indonesia doing enough in the planetary interest? Is it pursuing a legitimate national interest in pursuit of global sustainable forest management?

As the twenty-first century approaches, effort must be intensified to achieve sustainable forest management. The first thing to be done is to develop integrated sustainable forest production. Ways of producing timber wood as a business with the quickest yield must be worked out on the principle of national sustainability. Forest management that concentrates only on wood production will jeopardize sustainability. Business circles and the consumer public have to date tended to see non-wood products such as rattan, herbal woods and foodstuffs command less commercial value. This needs to be changed. The principle of integrated and sustainable development of forest production must be emphasized.

Forest rehabilitation, protection and regeneration must also be intensified. The present level of reforestation has to be increased to catch up with the speed of tree cutting. Greater attention must be paid to rehabilitation of non-wood forest resources including fauna. The wellbeing of the people who have settled in and around the forest areas must be given special attention. They should be given an adequate role and effective involvement in every aspect of forest management resulting in positive benefit to their welfare. Otherwise the forest-dwelling communities will be increasingly isolated to a marginal position and this can encourage the emergence of unlawful conduct leading to environmental damage.

All such efforts will be meaningless if they are not backed up by law enforcement, institutional capacity and quality human resources. The certainty of legal provisions will be essential in view of the fact that forest products will be increasingly in demand. In addition the free trade agreement will soon take effect, resulting in a greater need for legal certainty and law enforcement. Such measures are necessary to ensure optimal conservation of forest resources, together with a climate conducive to the development of business as well as the interests of consumers and of manpower in the forestry sector.

In this respect the existing regulations on eco-labelling need to be intensified and applied more consistently. Eco-labelling will strengthen the efforts to maintain forest resources and in turn ensure the use of forest products in accordance with approved principles of sustainable forest management. In addition, this regulation must maintain and develop scientific resources and biodiversity as well as ensure access for the participation of settlers around the forest areas.

An environment-oriented national development programme must therefore be part of the national agenda. International support and co-operation must be increased on the basis of a global awareness that the interests of our planet Earth is the interest of everyone – that is to say, the sustainability of Earth's carrying capacity, the betterment of human life and the development of civilization. Damage to this capacity anywhere on Earth will have a damaging impact on humanity as a whole. Continued poverty suffered by sections of society in other parts of the world will influence and decrease the living standard of the people who inherit the world as a whole.

Improvement in people's welfare and a nation's carrying capacity, however, can only be achieved within the competence of a national government. International co-operation is a system that functions to recognize common interests, and to provide supervision and control. Here lies the important role of international bodies such as UNCED with its Statement of Forest Principles, the ITTO (International Tropical Timber Organization) with its Tropical Forestry Action Plan as well as other institutions and bodies which regulate international co-operation in the field of forestry.

Through international institutions and bodies, the different national interests of states may be accommodated and conflicts avoided. Such international arrangement and co-operation should include the provision of incentives and the application of sanctions, but without linking these to any political interests. Other institutions such as the United Nations should be left to deal with political interests as part of the international political network. It is my view that we should avoid the risk of being dragged into the issue of global government. Instead, the mechanism and the forms of international co-operation, based on specific issues, will be valuable in developing a common perception of the planetary interest. Our efforts to safeguard the planetary interest in respect of forest resources will be in the interest of better human life and civilization for present and future generations.

The fires of 1997: a "planetary disaster"

> "Why should we burn the forests. We need the raw materials. It doesn't make sense."
>
> Mohamed Hasan

Like no other phenomenon before it, the forest fires of September and October 1997 have concentrated the world's mind on the critical question of the planetary interest in preserving Indonesia's forests.

Official estimates are that some 0.51 million hectares in Sumatra, Kalimantan, Sulawesi and Irian Jaya were burnt. In total, WWF estimates that between 0.5 million hectares and 1 million hectares have been burnt in 1997. The resulting forest haze over South East Asia became a phenomenon on global television for months, and was accurately described by WWF as a "planetary disaster". In addition to Indonesia, our regional neighbours, especially Singapore and Malaysia, suffered badly: in Sarawak, the Air Pollutant Index reached the "extremely hazardous" level of 530 in mid-September – anything above 301 is considered dangerous. Some 22,000 people were hospitalized in Indonesia and 140,000 throughout South East Asia. Health hazards from the haze involve the lungs and heart, reduce fertility, and damage the nervous system, blood cells and kidneys. Experts predict that cancer and leukaemia will increase in 20 to 30 years as a result. The lack of sunlight inhibits photosynthesis with poorer fruit resulting. Visibility was at zero point, i.e., less than 100 metres, in Jambi and Palembang in Sumatra and Nangapinoh and Balikpapan in Kalimantan. In many other areas it was down to 500 metres. The haze caused the death of 28 people when two ships collided and sank, and 234 people in the crash of a Garuda flight over Sumatra. Some 2,000 flights were cancelled throughout the region.

Beyond the immediate devastation to the country and the region, the fires have destroyed an essential natural element in absorbing greenhouse carbon gases. Perniciously, they have in fact exacerbated the climate change problem by adding, in some expert opinions, up to 5% extra CO_2 into the atmosphere – more than all the emissions of Western Europe in one year.

Yet, to gain a perspective on the damage that has been done to the planet over recent decades, it is worth recalling that in 1982–3, a forest clearance fire wiped out over 3.6 million hectares of Indonesian rain forest – larger than this year's destruction by a factor of seven. Similar clearance fires happened in 1991 and 1994. That last time, ASEAN countries agreed upon the ASEAN Co-operation Plan on Trans-boundary Pollution, with agreement to share technology and information to prevent exactly this kind of thing.

The disaster was of such proportions that President Soeharto was obliged to offer a public apology to our neighbouring countries – in September at the ASEAN Environmental Ministerial meeting, and again in October. It is one of the clearest examples of the transnational impact of a nation's actions in the modern world. The government proclaimed a State of Emergency in response to the calamity. I doubt there is a better example of a vital national interest judgement being made by a government than declaring a state of emergency for a country as a whole. Yet the interests of neighbouring states were equally vital. The world has changed. Instead of going to war to defend the vital national interest, nation-states today co-operate to protect the vital national interest in common. Indonesia's thanks go to Australia, Singapore and the United States for the provision of water-bombing aircraft, to Malaysia for 1,000 fire-fighters, and to Canada, France, Japan and Korea for money and technical assistance.

Why is this kind of thing still happening, five years after Rio? Several reasons are behind it. It is estimated that 80% of the fires were caused by big forestry and plantation companies, and the remaining 20% by small "slash-and-burn" farmers. "If you do land-clearing in pioneer areas, where no roads are established", says A.F.S. Budiman, Executive Director of the Rubber Association of Indonesia, "the only practical way to get rid of the debris is to burn it."[3] So there is the economic imperative. Palm oil, for example, is a major export resource in our region. Malaysia is the world's largest exporter and Indonesia has plans to emulate it. In 1996, our exports exceeded $1 billion, in response to a 32% growth in global demand from 1991–6. The government is encouraging this with plans for the production of 7.2 million tons of crude palm oil by 2000. To effect this, the plantation area is expected to double to 5.5 million hectares by that year – up from 0.6 million hectares in 1985 and 2.2 million hectares in 1995. In addition to palm oil, industrial pulpwood and timber plantations are projected to grow from 1.8 million hectares to 2.3 million hectares by 2000. But it is not just palm oil; the rubber companies are responsible for the fires as well.

All told, some 170 companies have been named by the minister of forests as having some degree of responsibility. They were given a month or so to advance proof that they were not guilty of flouting the 1995 official ban on burning forest to clear land. Failure to meet the deadline was to result in revocation of licences and possible prosecution. After the deadline had expired, some 150 licences held by 29 companies were revoked.

There are some ironies to all this. The United States runs what they call the US Initiative on Joint Implementation, an inter-agency project designed to reduce greenhouse gas emissions. In April 1997, the award went to an Indonesian project for reduced impact logging. The project is sited in Kalimantan, and the aim is to reduce greenhouse gas emissions. It was initiated by Mohamed Hasan, one of Indonesia's leading businessmen and environmental reformers. The same month, Mr Hasan received a prestigious award from the World Forestry Center for his deep commitment to forest stewardship. Indonesia, he said on the occasion of the US award, "has shown that preserving our precious tropical forests, meeting the needs of our citizens, and growing our economy are not mutually exclusive goals. They are, in fact, interdependent. No society can build a prosperous economic future for tomorrow unless it values and protects its natural history".[4]

What is the international community doing to help us? Since 1980, we received some $45 million in all, an average of $3 million per year – not a lot of money when we recognize the importance of Indonesia in the planetary interest of global sustainable forestry. Japan has extended ODA commitments of $20 million, and the United Kingdom $15 million. A few other nations have also helped – Finland with $6.5 million, Netherlands with $3 million, and smaller amounts from Canada, Italy, Switzerland and Australia. The United States has given nothing. Rio's Forest Principles 9 and 10 called on the North to assist the forest-rich countries of the South with "new and additional resources". In fact, our aid receipts have significantly declined since Rio – $7 million in 1989, $9 million in 1990, $10 million in 1991 and $9 million in 1992; and then an average of $1.7 million in the three years since Rio. It makes a mockery of the sincerity of the North when they call for sustainable forestry in the South.

Figure 10.2.1 "I doubt", says Theo Sambuaga, "there is a better example of a 'vital national interest' judgement being made than a government declaring a state of emergency . . . The world has changed. Instead of going to war to defend the vital national interest, nation-states today co-operate to protect the vital national interest in common." A Malaysian fire-fighter battles the Indonesian forest fires of October 1997, along with Indonesian servicemen. (Courtesy Popperfoto/Reuters)

CONCLUSION

It is my belief that by the year 2000, all forest products must come from sustainable forest areas in realization of our overall responsibility towards humankind as consumers and towards planet Earth's carrying capacity as a whole.

Forests are a gift of God which must be utilized in the best possible manner for the betterment of human life. Indonesia, which is blessed in terms of its vast forest areas, must, as an imperative, henceforth utilize its forest riches responsibly in order to ensure prosperity for its people. To allow settlements and settlers around forest areas to be paralysed by poverty is not only uncivilized but also dangerous to the continued life of the forest areas. In this context, the measures taken by national governments to manage and utilize forests in the best interests of people's welfare through the principles of environmental concern need to be encouraged by the international community. The success and resultant prosperity for forest communities will also bring benefit to planet Earth and the international community.

I often attend international conferences where people from other countries imply that a global responsibility lies on the shoulders of Indonesia. We possess, they say, the lungs of the planet. There is an irony in countries of the South being told by sister nations of the North to halt the exploitation of the very same forests from which they, as colonial rulers, became wealthy through earlier exploitation. Six centuries ago, they destroyed their own forests. A century ago, they took much of ours. Now, we are told that what remains is subject to new and restrictive global constraints.

I agree. The planetary interest demands such constraints. But the planetary interest is temporal as well as spatial. It does not forget. It looks back as well as forward. The planetary interest requires, as an integral package, constraints on consumption in the North along with greater assistance to the South. Otherwise, the planetary interest is not implemented. Not only is there a moral dimension to this, but there is a practical, rational dimension as well. Those who demand Indonesia halt deforestation immediately might equally demand an immediate halt to automobile production in the United States and coal production in China. There is a certain momentum to the economic imperative of humanity. The challenge is not to stop the train in its tracks but to divert it on to an ecological track. You cannot selectively choose from within the concept of the planetary interest for that is to exceed your legitimate national interest. The planetary interest *is*. It exists in the totality of its conceptual content, all of which must be applied or it is not applied at all.

NOTES

1. *Forest principles,* preamble C, 4, 1(a) 2(a).
2. Ministry of Forestry, *Progress towards sustainable management of tropical forests* (Jakarta: Ministry of Forestry, 1996), 12.
3. *Far Eastern Economic Review*, 2 October 1996, 28.
4. Indonesia Forestry Community, 28 April 1997. (http://forests.org/gopher/indonesia/indowina.txt).

EDITOR'S POSTSCRIPT

This chapter was completed by the contributor in the beginning of 1998, during the economic crisis that was afflicting Indonesia but before the political crisis that resulted in the resignation of President Soeharto. The change of leadership has opened the way for democratic reforms and has accordingly changed the national political landscape in the country. But in the more underlying sense of national and planetary survival, the issues remain the same, namely, the imperative of sustainable forestry in Indonesia, and everywhere on Earth.

10.3   Brazil

Fabio Feldmann

> The Earth we abuse and the living things we kill will, in the end, take their revenge; for in exploiting their presence we are diminishing our future.
>
> Marya Mannes, *More in unger*

One must look back at the recent past and notice the great cultural transformation and behavioural changes that are now allowing a discussion of the concept of the planetary interest in our times.

The first efforts towards a global approach to environmental matters were consolidated at the Stockholm conference of 1972. The first UN conference on environment placed the relationship between man and nature at the centre of the debate on preservation. In 1980, the World Strategy for the Conservation of Nature, prepared by the World Conservation Union and the World Wildlife Fund, stressed the basic environmental themes, emphasizing the interdependency of preservation and development and introducing, for the first time, the concept of sustainability in the field of conservation. This concept has become the foundation on which the current international environmental protection system is now being built.

The term "development" has been in use since the mid-twentieth century when the concept of economic growth was consolidated. Further elaboration of this concept required the consideration of long-term issues, which was accomplished with the addition of the word "sustainable", implying a guarantee of natural resource availability for future generations, and equity in the distribution of the benefits.

The Brundtland Report of 1987 stressed that the quality of development should experience change with a view to decreasing the demand for raw materials and preventing its effects on the environment. It introduced the conflict between short- and long-term goals as a challenge to sustainability. And it concluded that a persistence of the current economic models would impede future generations from having access to the resources necessary for survival. The report's conclusions constitute the basis for contemporary discussion.

The Rio conference of 1992 was crucial in improving consciousness about environmental problems. The general public became aware of issues never before discussed in such a wide and open manner. Media coverage of environmental issues reached its climax. The planning process for Rio was as important as the conference itself. The Preparatory Committee introduced new procedures pertinent to official international meetings by marrying political and technical discussions on the proposed agreements. This allows official delegations and representatives of different sectors of society, as well as independent scientists, to participate together for the first time in a great political debate. And the conference itself was a success, too, introducing a pragmatic approach to the idea of sustainability through fundamental agreements with Agenda 21, the Biodiversity Convention, the Forest Principles, the Climate Change Convention and the Declaration of Rio de Janeiro.

But the five years since 1992, assessed at the "Rio+5" UN Conference in 1997, concluded that the results to date have fallen short of expectations. The absence of effective procedures and measures has led to a demobilization of effort and a sense of frustration.

NATIONAL POLICY

Let me now focus on the main question facing my society: the concept of sustainable forestry. I stress from the outset that forestry cannot be considered separately from other major environmental questions. Two parallel issues must be addressed together: forest management and sustainable transport. These are the major challenges, not just to Brazil, but to the global society

Sustainable transport

Along with forest burning, motor vehicles are one of the major sources of greenhouse gases that cause global climate change. In spite of this imminent risk, production by the world car industry will possibly reach 80 million units by the year 2000. Ironically, cars are symbols of high living standards. In the twentieth century, human society everywhere has been marked by increasing mobility: never before have people been able to come and go at such a pace.

The car is known around the world as a symbol of social status, safety and freedom. This notion has been strongly reinforced by the marketing of the product. Does anyone recall having seen a car commercial where an avenue is jammed? The appeal is directed instead to a free paradisiacal highway with a beautiful woman, hair flowing in the wind, set against a magnificent sunset. An invitation to a fictional freedom.

Before long car commercials may have to feature a message such as "warning: indiscriminate use of this product may cause damage to health and global climate". Technological improvements cannot offset the noxious effects of the chronic dependence of today's society on motor vehicles. It is very likely that cars will soon be considered environmentally unfriendly products and undergo the same pressure that occurs today against smoking.

Yet it is difficult to persuade society not to use the product after a consumer pattern has been established, regardless of the impacts on the environment. It takes time to create awareness, to convince, and thereafter establish compensating measures for a citizen to surrender a habit. Meanwhile, demand tends to persist.

On the supply side, forecasts indicate a surplus global production of about 20 million cars in the year 2000. Considering that Europe and America are slow growing markets, this surplus production will be directed to Asia and Latin America which have had high growth rates. Today, the greatest investment in the car industry is occurring in Brazil where, according to car manufacturers, planned investment until 2000 is $17 billion.

Aside from that, governments in the South tend to encourage car industry investments, since this industry is regarded as a vector of economic growth. In Brazil, it answers for 12% of GNP, employs 102,000 people, generates 5 million indirect jobs and contributes significantly to tax revenue – tax on vehicles ranges from 20% to 35%. The Brazilian car industry was greatly promoted by the recent currency stabilization which caused a significant increase in the purchasing power of the population. Production growth rates increased from 1% in 1992, to 3% in 1993 and 4% in 1994. The Greater São Paulo metropolitan area's fleet grew from 3.8 million in 1990 to 5.7 million in 1996, with an occupancy rate of 1.5 persons per car.

But cities such as São Paulo, Mexico City, Bangkok and their metropolitan areas are simply unable to absorb a greater amount of cars. Every day 3 million cars fill the streets of São Paulo. There has been a frightening increase in traffic jams that sometimes stretch to 240 km in length. This increase in the number of vehicles has aggravated the concentration of pollutants, posing risks to public health. In the Greater São Paulo metropolitan area, cars are responsible for the emission of 98% of carbon monoxide, 97% of hydrocarbons, 97% of NOx, 85% of SOx and 41% of particulate matter. The situation is aggravated by the general preference for individual instead of public transport, an attitude that is encouraged by local governments which choose to invest in roads rather than public transportation routes. For electoral purposes, public officials tend to focus on voter demands which are short-term oriented.

Thus the individual citizen must be the driving force in changing the current scenario into a sustainable one in the future. The facts noted above need to be brought to public discussion in an attempt to promote awareness and pave the way for change in deeply rooted lifestyles. The challenge resides in offsetting the undeniable independence, pleasure and mobility a car can offer, taking into account its importance in the economy of the twentieth century and the next millennium.

Experience with restrictions on the use of vehicles such as those implemented in São Paulo in the last three years have succeeded in introducing a public concern about air pollution and its health effects, the quality of public transport and transportation alternatives. This may constitute the basis for the establishment of urban planning, traffic, public and cargo transportation, energy, health and pollution control policies.

In sum, then, it is my contention that discussion of global themes such as climate change must henceforth address the fundamental role of the world car industry at local, national and international levels.

Sustainable forestry

Implementation of sustainable transport policies implies dramatic change in human behaviour. Similar measures are necessary when proposing sustainable forestry policies.

There is general consensus about the importance of preserving forests, however difficult this may be. The problem is to define how to implement the necessary changes and aggregate the idea of sustainability in decisions made by society. Again, the key to success is individual awareness.

The first obstacle to overcome is the lack of a correct perception with regard to the real dimension of forests. Opinion-makers, notably those in the North, tend not to have the correct idea of the gigantic territorial scale of tropical forests. They adopt what I call the "narrow-minded mythical approach".

The Amazon forest, for instance, is spread along the territories of eight countries in the northern part of South America. Close to 62% of it is situated within Brazilian territory. Brazil's forest coverage is 5.5 million sq km, which comprises 65% of its national territory. Of this, the Brazilian Amazon encompasses 3.7 million sq km, about 42% of national territory. That is larger than India, by 12%. Larger than Indonesia, by 83%. Fifteen times larger than the United Kingdom. The Brazilian Amazon would cover 48% of Australia, and 40% of the United States. It is a vast forest.

Yet in spite of this continental scale, tropical forests tend to be regarded as small areas, simply managed.

The Amazon is the American forest that most attracts worldwide attention, notwithstanding that other rain forests are subject to greater threats and devastation. It is the case of the Brazilian Atlantic Forest, one of the most devastated biomes of the planet. Originally, this forest used to cover a practically continuous area of about 1.3 million sq km along the Brazilian coast, from north to south. Today, only 9% of the original forest remains (95,000 sq km). The Brazilian Atlantic Rainforest is considered one of the richest forests of the planet, with expressive biodiversity, affording shelter to a great number of endangered flora and fauna species, including species not yet catalogued by science.

This negative reductionist vision of the forests is further exacerbated by a mythical view of tropical forests that still persists in the collective imagination – the untouched Eden, the Hollywood-like conception of a jungle inhabited by Tarzan and Jane, native Indian people along the lines of Rousseau's "noble savage". The real dimension of forests, in fact, makes the development and implementation of sustainable forestry models extremely complex. There are no examples yet of successful mechanisms, nor of financial instruments, aimed at fostering production cycles that could last from 30 to 50 years.

The Brazilian Amazon experienced prosperity during the rubber cycle, when foreign companies were established in the region to extract latex. The population increased, rubber exports reached the same level as coffee, and the economy quickly developed at the end of the nineteenth century. Manaus, the capital of the state of Amazonas, became a European-like metropolis – it was the second Brazilian city to have electricity. This development stage, however, did not last long. From 1910 to 1920, the Amazon rubber lost its market to Asian competition and the regional economy rapidly declined. Today, activities such as extensive cattle raising, agriculture in unsuited soils, irrational exploitation of both forest and mineral resources, as well as predatory fishing in the Amazon have provoked high levels of deforestation with great loss of biological diversity. Other impacts are air pollution caused by forest burning, chemical pollution of rivers caused by mining activities and the flooding of large areas for hydroelectric power plants.

Figure 10.3.1 "What might be the path of sustainability?" asks Fabio Feldmann. "First, a philosophical shift needs to occur on the part of humanity. Forests must be preserved for themselves – for their own sake . . . There is a long way ahead before this ideal is accepted by society . . . from local to global is the only way to achieve a sincere commitment by citizens and their real engagement in promoting the planetary interest." The result of a clearing fire in the Amazon region, Brazil, 1988. (Courtesy Popperfoto/Reuters)

None of the activities implemented in the Brazilian Atlantic Forest has led to sustainable development. Successive exploration cycles brought economic prosperity at the cost of severe environmental degradation. First, the extraction of brazilwood (*Pau-Brasil*) and timber for charcoal. Then, the colonization of the interior, mining activities and export-driven monocultures in successive cycles – sugar cane, coffee, bananas, tea – all of which were abandoned due to the loss of competitive advantage. Today, pressures on the Atlantic Forest derive mainly from a growing urbanization in coastal regions and the predatory extraction of wood and other forest products such as the heart of palm.

Difficulties in implementing sustainable forestry principles are being experienced throughout the world. The lack of successful forestry models eases the way for the predatory exploitation of forest resources that takes place not only in tropical countries, but also in the temperate forests of Canada and the United States.

Beyond the commercial exploitation, the global heritage of forests carries a special significance for local communities. In many places, the exploitation of natural resources can be the only possible means for local groups to earn their living. To date, no methods have been developed to compensate the populations that live in these areas of global heritage.

Take, as an example, the Vale do Ribeira (valley of the Ribeira do Iguape River), a region in the state of São Paulo where the largest area of continuous Atlantic rainforest is located. Vale do Ribeira has the lowest social economic rates in the state. More than half of the 280,000 inhabitants do not participate in the formal economic sector. The illiteracy and schooling truancy rates are very high. About 20% of this territory is composed of parks, ecological reserves and environmental protection areas and more than 60% of the region is subject to restriction at different levels. But despite the restrictions provided for in legal instruments, the region is constantly vulnerable to degradation of its natural heritage. This is due mainly to the lack of public policies capable of guiding economic activities so as to guarantee revenue sources to generate income for the local population and the preservation of its natural resources. For decades, the inhabitants of the region extracted the *juçara* heart of palm from the Atlantic Forest, a highly appreciated culinary speciality. But in the last few years the exploitation of the *juçara* has become the population's main income source. This caused large habitats to be destroyed since the exploitation has become predatory. The *juçara* heart of palm is extracted from the tree's only trunk. Its extraction destroys the tree, and other plants as well, since tracks have to be opened in the forest in order to reach the remote areas where such palm trees can be found. Almost 600 tons of heart of palm are illegally taken from the forest every year. No successful sustainable management of heart of palm on a large economic scale has been implemented to date.

In spite of such extraction being illegal, those who do this cannot really be considered criminals. It is difficult to convince these people, who have no other source of subsistence, of the need to preserve the forest resources and biodiversity and maintain the climate of the planet. At the same time, local governments tend to choose short-term alternatives in the search for development patterns for the region. In the specific case of the heart of palm, one of the alternatives is to promote sustainable extraction through plantation or management of existing stock, permitting this activity to be legal and introducing it into the formal market so as to guarantee a reliable and permanent source of revenue for the population. As a fundamental action, consumers must be encouraged to buy heart of palm extracted in a sustainable manner.

There is an additional factor to consider with sustainable forestry. Not many of us today, citizens or policy-makers, recognize the power of the consumer. But consumer power is the key to the implementation of a healthy and sustainable living standard in the world. Influencing market demand for heart of palm by imposing discrimination on its origin through identification of the container jars, and promoting educational campaigns about sound consumption, are the most effective ways to banish predatory exploitation practices. A similar rationale can be applied to the predatory exploitation of mahogany timber in the Amazon. Mahogany is a tropical hardwood obtained by rainforest logging. It has a warm red colour and high polish. The species is under threat due to its popularity for use in the manufacture of musical instruments, furniture and veneers. Mahogany demand comes mainly from the North and consumers are probably unaware of the environmental damage caused by its unsustainable extraction. There are attempts to make mahogany the first hardwood tree listed under the CITES Convention, thus establishing an international market mechanism to control the origin of mahogany imports. Significantly, however, Brazil did not support this initiative in the last meeting of the parties in Harare.

The association of sustainable forest management with sustainable transport measures is key to the solution of global climate change and other related matters. Forest and fossil fuel burning are the major contributors, and only a change in consumer and production patterns in these two areas can improve the situation. Consumers can ride buses instead of driving their own cars. They can drive less, buy cars that pollute less, and avoid purchasing products that hasten the destruction of forest habitats. Consumers can say no to mahogany or buy an electric car where available. They can switch to solar panels and refuse to buy meat from cattle raised in the rain forest. Numerous measures are within the reach of common citizens. Consumers are the sleeping bears in this matter who can roar once awakened.

THE LEGITIMATE NATIONAL INTEREST

Is Brazil meeting the standard of the legitimate national interest in respect to its national forestry management?

Fallacious perception of the opinion-makers together with the lack of sustainable management models impairs the success of international negotiations for forest preservation. Since Rio 92, nation-states have tried to find ways to protect their own forest resources. The Forest Principles, the Biodiversity Convention, the UN Forest Panel, all these covenants and the UN discussion forum reflect a true planetary concern with this problem.

The initial idea of Rio was to produce a binding treaty for forests similar to the Biodiversity Convention. But the governments failed to reach an agreement and the final product was the non-binding declaration of principles, still to be consolidated.

The issue of sovereignty is crucial when considering the conservation of forests. In countries that hold significant portions of forested areas, regarded as a global heritage, the notion of forests as depositories of biodiversity and a fundamental factor for global climate equilibrium is a sensitive issue. Foreign conspiracy, nationalism and a fear of territorial occupation by foreign countries become common arguments against forest preservation.

Can states solely decide on the destiny of their natural resources, their biodiversity, and also carry out polluting activities that affect others? Principle 2 of the Declaration of Rio is by now well known – the sovereign right to exploit, the responsibility to avoid damage. The main challenge for sustainable management of forest resources relies on finding ways to preserve the global heritage and, at the same time, ensure that local people will be able to benefit from the sustainable use of those resources. It has not yet been possible, however, to build an international framework that can provide compensatory mechanisms for countries that hold significant portions of the global heritage.

What, then, is to be done? What might be the path of sustainability? First, a philosophical shift needs to occur on the part of humanity. Forests must be preserved for themselves – for their own sake – as the Convention on Biodiversity establishes. There is a long way ahead, however, before this ideal is accepted by society. Traditionally, global themes are realized through national and local policies. But, in fact, the opposite approach, from local to global, is the only way to achieve a sincere commitment by citizens and their real engagement in promoting the planetary interest.

Negotiations for the preservation of forests must involve governments and the societies of all countries. Decision-making processes must include a greater participation by society. Many agreements that decide the fate of the planet are still entered into only by governments, not by citizens. On the other hand, society has to do its part and demand the right to participate. The legal agreements of Rio are proof that a consensus was reached as to the importance of the conservation of forests and reduction of air pollution that leads to global climate change. Implementing these agreements is the major challenge we face nowadays, in the context of "common but differentiated responsibilities".

Has the international community helped with Brazil's sustainable forestry? Since 1980, we have received some $110 million – $49 million from Germany, $32 million from Japan, $17 million from the United Kingdom, $8 million from Canada and $4 million from the United States. Has the international community responded to the call of Rio? Not appreciably in the case of Brazil: $13 million in 1990, $10 million in 1991, $20 million in 1992; and then $19 million, $1 million, $4 million, $25 million and $11 million respectively in 1993–7. That is to say, an annual average of $14 million in the three years before Rio and $12 million in the five years since. It could not be said that the world has rushed to provide the major forest nations with additional financial resources in response to the Earth Summit.

CONCLUSION

As one who has been and remains deeply involved in Brazil's environmental and developmental challenge, and conscious of its global implications, I am less than happy with the way things have developed. Fulfilment of the commitments of Rio '92, especially those in *Agenda 21*, has been impaired by issues involving governance which were not adequately addressed. The international agreements of 1992 established relevant goals and recognized the importance of public participation and democracy. But little attention has been paid to a crucial issue: countries have different institutional designs. In countries with presidential regimes such as Brazil, international agreements are signed by the executive and are subject to ratification by parliament which can raise difficulties depending on political interests prevailing at different times. This was the case of Brazil with regard to the ratification of the Biodiversity Convention. In Brazil, as in many other countries, biodiversity, climate change and forests are recognized as themes of great importance, but are not adequately contemplated in the national agenda. My personal experience as a congressman elected on an environmentalist platform demonstrates how difficult it is to insert these themes into the parliament's agenda. A great number of projects that I submitted did not receive the deserved attention.

A politician's work is quite a delicate task; and environmental politics in Brazil especially so. The expansion of the economic frontier in the Amazon region was promoted by the military government in order to guarantee national sovereignty, disregarding the environmental costs involved. During the Rio '92 conference, Brazilian congressmen participating in the meeting were urged to testify on the "internationalization of the Amazon" before a legislative committee. Given such an opportunity, as a congressman elected by São Paulo, a cosmopolitan and industrialized state, but concerned with the problems of the Amazon region, I had to defend myself against accusations of serving the national interests of other countries.

The introduction of global themes in local agendas is not easy. This is due mainly to the complexity of issues such as lifestyle and consumption patterns in modern society that favour individual interests and satisfaction of immediate demands while disregarding collective interests and future needs. It is quite a political feat to introduce the idea of sustainability into citizens' everyday lives – for example to convince anyone to renounce any comfort such as a car for the sake of the global climate equilibrium.

Now that the Kyoto conference has thrown down the gauntlet to the North, discussions over drastic change will be underway behind the scenes – involving restrictions on motor vehicle production, reduction of emissions generated by industrial activities, revision of energy generation models and production processes, as well as improvement of mechanisms for the conservation of forests. The global economy will be greatly affected by any of these measures, which will imply dramatic behavioural change. That is why the Kyoto conference was so critical. Only when its provisions are consolidated and prompt such change on the part of both governments and citizens shall we know what progress will be made towards guaranteeing the rights of future generations and, consequently, the consolidation of the planetary interest.

CHAPTER ELEVEN

Consumption

11.1   Introduction

Sustainable consumption has been defined as the use of goods and services that respond to basic needs and bring a better quality of life, while minimizing the use of natural resources, toxic materials and emissions of waste and pollutants over the lifecycle, so as not to jeopardize the needs of future generations.[1] The term is essentially an umbrella concept that links a number of key issues: meeting basic human needs; enhancing the quality of life; improving resource efficiency; increasing the use of renewable energy resources; minimizing waste and avoiding toxic emissions; and taking a lifecycle perspective and keeping international and intergenerational equity in mind in consumer behaviour.

THE GLOBAL PROBLEM

The essence of the problem of sustainable consumption was captured in *Agenda 21*:

> Although consumption patterns are very high in certain parts of the world, the basic consumer needs of a large section of humanity are not being met. This results in excessive demands and unsustainable lifestyles among the richer segments, which place immense stress on the environment. The poorer segments, mean-while, are unable to meet food, health care, and shelter and educational needs.[2]

It is increasingly recognized that rectifying "global unsustainability" will take decades, in terms of both consumption and production. Many unsustainable patterns of consumption are deeply rooted in cultural habits. And despite a growing environmental awareness worldwide, recent experience in promoting sustainable consumption in a number of countries suggests that the majority of consumers still have little knowledge of the environmental impact of their consumption habits and lifestyles. While an increasing number express their readiness to purchase environmentally friendly products and even to pay a "green premium", they may be unable to tell which producers make such products or where to find them. On the production side the situation is equally difficult: current capital stocks of physical infrastructure, for example in housing, energy, transportation and waste management, can lock societies into unsustainable patterns of consumption over which consumers have little influence.

THE GLOBAL OBJECTIVE AND STRATEGY

The official statement of objective by the international community was made at the Cairo conference in 1994:

> To achieve sustainable development and a higher quality of life for all people, Governments should reduce and eliminate unsustainable patterns of production and consumption . . . Developed countries should take the lead in achieving sustainable consumption patterns and effective waste management.[3]

As the secretary-general of the United Nations has pointed out, the success in changing consumption and production patterns may well determine whether sustainable development can be put into operation and practised.[4] And as one researcher has put it: "our challenge is to find a way to balance human consumption and nature's limited productivity in order to ensure that our commitments are sustainable locally, regionally and globally. We don't have a choice about whether to do this, but we can choose how we do it."[5]

The global strategy was identified in *Agenda 21* as

(a)   to promote patterns of consumption and production that will reduce environmental stress and meet the basic needs of humanity;

(b)   to develop a better understanding of the role of consumption and how to bring about more sustainable consumption patterns.[6]

This is to be achieved through "appropriate economic, legislative and administrative measures with a view to fostering sustainable resource use and preventing environmental degradation".[7]

At its 1994 session, the UN Commission on Sustainable Development called for the elaboration of elements of a possible work programme in the area of sustainable consumption and production. The UN secretary-general has developed a "possible work programme" on sustainable consumption and production patterns. It proposes three main areas:

(a)   identifying the policy implications of projected trends in consumption and production patterns;

(b)   assessing the impact on the South of changes in the North;

(c)   evaluating the effectiveness of policy measures intended to change consumption and production patterns such as command-and-control, economic and social instruments, and governmental procurement policies and guidelines.

The commission should, the secretary-general proposed, "consider the periodic preparation of reports containing long-term projections of the world economy with a time horizon of up to 40 years".[8]

The consideration of sustainability issues leading up to the 1992 Rio conference was marked by considerable North–South differences of perception. The South tended to view "sustainable development" as synonymous with, and replaceable by, "sustainable growth". Tension was evident in the negotiations at Rio over the *Agenda 21* chapter "Changing consumption patterns". Since then, however, this has given way to a more pragmatic debate in which the planetary interest of humankind and the "shared but differentiated responsibilities" of all nations are increasingly accepted.[9]

Within the North itself, there has also been progress, with a more positive recognition by both governments and business that changes can be made to consumption and production patterns in ways that can sustain preferred living standards and yet enhance competitiveness and economic performance.[10]

PRESCRIBED NATIONAL POLICIES

National policies to achieve the global strategy are set out in both the Rio and Cairo Programmes of Action. Changing consumption patterns, says *Agenda 21*, will require a multipronged strategy focusing on demand, meeting the basic needs of the poor and reducing wastage and the use of finite resources in the production process. All countries should strive to promote sustainable consumption patterns. Developed countries should take the lead in achieving sustainable consumption patterns. In order to support this broad strategy, governments should make a concerted effort to identify balanced patterns of consumption worldwide which the Earth can support in the long term. They should strive to develop a domestic policy framework that will encourage a shift to more sustainable patterns of production and consumption.[11]

This was echoed at Cairo two years later. States, said the global population programme, should reduce and eliminate unsustainable patterns of production and consumption and promote appropriate policies, including population-related policies, in order to meet the needs of current generations without compromising the ability of future generations to meet their needs. To achieve sustainable development and a higher quality of life for all people, governments should reduce and eliminate unsustainable patterns of production and consumption and promote appropriate demographic policies. Developed countries should take the lead in achieving sustainable consumption patterns and effective waste management.[12]

Without the necessary data on trends in the environment and ecosystems, however, policy-making in this new area of focus will be impaired. At its 2nd Session, the UN Commission on Sustainable Development called on governments to intensify and expand their efforts to collect relevant data at the national and sub-national levels. In recent years, many governments have initiated or intensified efforts in this direction, and especially in four areas: environmental monitoring, environmental resource accounting, sustainable development indicators, and consumer information.[13]

LEGITIMATE NATIONAL INTERESTS

In no area of human activity is the world divided more than in consumption levels, and this division must itself be seen as part of the global problem. The North, consisting of some 40 countries and comprising 20% of the global population, lives at an artificially high and globally unsustainable consumption level. The South, consisting of 150 countries and comprising 80% of humanity, lives at low consumption levels which are nonetheless ecologically inefficient and damaging to the planet. And it is striving to reach the same level of consumption as the North. The "global divide" is illustrated in Table 11.1.1.

Table 11.1.1   Consumption and consumption-related levels: the North–South divide

Product	Year	Unit	North	South
Fossil fuels	1986–90	Gigajoules/person	60.06	17.28
Metal recycling			25–50%	2–40%
Food supply	1988–90	Calories/person/day	3,410	2,470
Chronic malnutrition	1988–90	No. persons (m.)	0	781
		(% population)	(0%)	(20%)
Beef and veal	1986–90	Kg/person	27.17	4.29
Pesticides	1990		80%	20%
Roundwood	1986–90	Cu. m/person	1.29	0.48
Paper	1990	Kg/p.c./p.a.	150	10
Road vehicle usage (% population)			80%	20%

Source: Changing Consumption and Production Patterns: Report of the Secretary-General (New York: United Nations, 1995), (UN document E/CN. 17/1995/13) Tables 3–6.

The challenge will be to ensure that the rising production levels in the South are achieved on the basis of ecologically efficient and benign methods. As Norway's minister of the environment put it in an address to the UN Commission on Sustainable Development:

> The unsustainable lifestyles of the rich – both between and within countries – must be harnessed. Our consumption patterns – and our efforts to multiply them worldwide – will undermine the environmental resource base even if we were to introduce the best available technology worldwide.[14]

In specific country terms, the link between consumption and population is well illustrated by Table 11.1.2. As the table indicates, the "effective population" of these five countries, in terms of their draw-down on the planet's natural resources is much greater than the actual population. Adjusted in this way, the United States is over twice as large as China and over five times as large as India.

Table 11.1.2   Consumption-adjusted population: selected countries, 1990

Country	Population (billions)	Adjusted population (billions)
United States	0.249	22.993
former Soviet Union	0.289	16.828
China	1.139	9.329
India	0.853	3.907
Canada	0.027	3.159

Source: Earth Council, San José: *The other side of population for development*, paper presented to the International Conference on Population and Development, September 1994. In *Our global neighbourhood*, 145.

Within the North itself there are significant differences. The waste generated by individual countries for example, is illustrated in Table 11.1.3. In the course of the twenty-first century the North is going to have to answer to the South. In contrast to Kenya and Bangladesh stand Sweden and the United States – two of the "wealthier" countries of the world. But even within the North, wastefulness varies by a factor of four with municipal waste and a factor of twenty with industrial waste. It might legitimately be asked: why should the United States throw away over twice as much municipal waste per person as Sweden? And generate five times as much industrial waste per person? What is the legitimate national interest of the US and Sweden as they reassess their national lifestyles in the planetary interest?

Table 11.1.3   Waste generated by the North: late 1980s

Municipal waste			Industrial waste		
	P.c. (Kg)	Tons (000)		Per unit/GDP	Tons (000)
United States	864	200,800	Portugal	292	6,620
Australia	681	10,000	Japan	235	312,300
New Zealand	662	2,110	Finland	221	12,700
Canada	632	16,400	Austria	211	13,260
Finland	608	3,000	United States	186	760,000
Norway	475	2,000	Canada	155	61,000
Denmark	469	2,400	Australia	146	20,000
Netherlands	467	6,900	United Kingdom	146	50,000
Switzerland	427	2,850	Greece	123	4,300
Japan	394	48,300	Belgium	104	8,000
UK	353	17,700	Germany (FR)	95	61,400
Germany (FR)	331	20,230	Italy	94	43,700
Spain	332	12,550	France	89	50,000
Sweden	317	2,650	Ireland	87	1,580
Greece	314	3,150	Netherlands	50	6,690
Belgium	313	3,080	Denmark	41	2,400
Ireland	311	1,100	Sweden	37	4,000
France	304	17,000	Norway	35	2,190
Italy	301	17,300	Spain	27	5,110
Portugal	231	2,350	New Zealand	15	300
Austria	228	1,730	Switzerland	–	–
North	513	420,000	North	146	1,430,000

Source: Changing Consumption and Production Patterns: Report of the Secretary-General (New York; United Nations, 1995), (UN document E/CN.17/1995/13) Table 2.

NOTES

1. Oslo Roundtable on Sustainable Production and Consumption, 1994: 1 (http://www.iisd.ca/linkages/consume/oslo004.html).
2. *Agenda 21*, 4.3.
3. ICPD, 3.9.
4. *Changing production and consumption patterns: report of the secretary-general.* UN doc. E/CN.17/1995/13, 20 March 1995, para. 84.
5. M. Wackernagel, *How big is our ecological footprint? Using the concept of appropriated carrying capacity for measuring sustainability*, paper on Internet (http:/www.iisd.ca/linkages/consume/mwfoot.html), 2.
6. *Agenda 21*, 4.7

7. E/CN.17/1995/13, 20 March 1995, para. 86.
8. Ibid., paras 114–15.
9. OECD-MIT Experts Seminar (http://www.iisd.ca/linkages/consume/mit.html), para. 3.
10. Ibid., para. 3.
11. *Agenda 21*, 4.3, 4.8, 4.10(e), 4.17.
12. ICPD: Ch. II, Principle 6; 3.9.
13. E/CN.17/1995/13, 20 March 1995, paras 39, 40.
14. See: http://www.iisd.ca/linkages/consume/forword.html; 17 January 1997.

11.2 United States

Claudine Schneider

> I know of no safe depository of the ultimate powers of society but the people themselves; and if we think them not enlightened enough to exercise their control with a wholesome discretion, the remedy is not to take it from them, but to inform their discretion by education.
>
> Thomas Jefferson

The United States comprises 5% of Earth's population and consumes 25% of its resources.

It is deeply painful, as an American, to state this. Yet these are the facts. Americans use twice as much water as someone from a developing country. Americans use twice as much energy as someone from Germany, France or the United Kingdom; 50 times that of a Guatemalan, 100 times that of a Vietnamese and 500 times that of a person living in Chad. With 5% of the global population, we consume 25% of the planet's fossil fuels each year, emitting 20% of its greenhouse gases. City dwellers in the US generate twice the amount of trash as their counterparts in Spain, Italy or Germany. The US produces ten times the amount of hazardous waste as the next largest producer. When we speak of transportation in America, we are speaking primarily of the automobile. Only 8% of all of the people on Earth own a car. In the United States 89% have at least one car. Working people spend nine hours a week behind the wheel – almost one-tenth of our waking moments – emitting carbon monoxide into the atmosphere. No people use air travel more than Americans, and plane travel consumes over six times more energy than travelling by car. Food production and consumption places enormous stress on the human as well as the planetary system. A typical American dinner travels over 1,000 miles from farm to table. The processing and packaging add substantial costs to the food (4% of our per capita expenditure on all consumer goods goes for packaging – $225 per person a year). A can of corn has used ten times the amount of energy that fresh corn in season has used. Meat is perhaps the most energy-consumptive food: it takes 5 kg of grain and the energy equivalent of 2 litres of gasoline to produce 1 kg of steak. About 28% of Americans are classified as "obese" – the criterion being more than 25% above the median weight. In the last 200 years we have lost 50% of our wetlands, 90% of our old growth forests, 99% of the tall grass prairie and as many as 490 species of native plant and animal species. Every day we turn 23 sq. km of rural land into developed areas.

I could illustrate indefinitely the extraordinary consumption patterns of the United States, but countless books have been written about the impact of the excessive American lifestyle. It is not only the rapid depletion of our natural resources that results, but also the broadening of the gap between the rich and the poor, both nationally and globally. I would rather address the solutions, beginning with the role of the government and others in moving our citizenry towards a sustainable lifestyle. Despite our signing of various international agreements, we have made only marginal progress, given the urgency and scope of the challenges.

NATIONAL POLICY

To meet these challenges, there are essentially six paths of potential leadership; the federal government (the president, his administration and the Congress), state and local governments, the business community, non-governmental organizations, religions and the media. The active participation of each of these sectors is required to achieve progress towards sustainable consumption.

Federal government

One could not accurately say that the US government as a whole supports the concept of the planetary interest, or the principle of sustainable development. The executive yes, the legislature no. The government also includes the legislature – Congress. The president understands the "planetary interest" but the Congress, responding mostly to the short-term interests of a two-year electoral cycle, does not. Thus he is limited in his ability to implement change. Yet my country, and indeed the world, expects so much from the office. The reality is that, due to the constitutional constraint which creates a "balance of power", it is actually within the realm of Congress to implement either the president's vision or its own. We have a well-known saying in Washington, "the President proposes, and the Congress disposes". As a former member of the US Congress from 1980 to 1990, I can personally attest to the fact that there is substantial opportunity for leadership in achieving sustainable goals as a congressperson. But I do not hold out much hope for the present Congress. Consider the evidence as it pertains to the government, at least at the federal level.

President Clinton and his administration do, I believe, support sustainable development. He has appointed a Council on Sustainable Development made up of his cabinet members, business and non-profit representatives. The action plan has been developed through consensus. Now, for the implementation, which will require strong leadership by the president, each member of the president's council, and an education campaign and co-operation of the members of Congress, since many of the remedies are legislatively driven.

The president proposed eliminating many resource subsidies and increasing fees for various federal services in 1993. Subsidies have been defined as government actions that enable producers to avoid the full burden of the economic costs of production. A subsidy is almost universally accepted as appropriate when there is some private market failure or to further the public interest. The government has used subsidies to settle the West, advance research and development, and further education and public welfare. But most of the vast resource subsidies today are based on decisions made in the late nineteenth or early twentieth centuries. The mining, grazing and land settlement subsidies were all established to encourage settlement in the West.

Interest free loans for water projects, free access to mineral lands and low cost grazing fees can no longer be justified today, given altered national priorities, increased management costs, shrinking federal budgets and, perhaps most important, our current knowledge of the value and fragility of natural resources.

Times have changed. There is no frontier any more, not only across the United States, but around the planet. Yet despite this, there is an absence of courage to make a case and take on the well-entrenched special interests in the United States. Some examples:

- Fisheries: In 1993, 6.3 billion lb of seafood, valued at $1.8 billion was harvested offshore in federal waters. The fees paid by fishermen totalled $0.9 million and yet the Congress allocated $102 million to manage and enforce the programme. The president proposed that fees be based on the cost of issuing permits, implementing management regimes and the value of the fish taken. In other words, he suggested "full-cost accounting" measures that valued and managed this precious natural resource. In addition his proposal would have allowed the use of fees to reduce harvesting in overfished areas. Both the House and Senate gave the measure perfunctory attention but to date no legislation has been passed.
- Water Reclamation: Since early in the twentieth century, the government has built and operated large water projects throughout the West. The costs were to be repaid by the irrigators over a ten-year period. Instead, repayment typically has spanned 40 years and has often not covered the full cost of delivering irrigated water. In 1990 water contract rates ranged from $0.22 to $16.99 per acre/foot. "Full-cost" agricultural water ranged from $4 to $251 per acre/foot. Less than 1% of government-supplied irrigation water was delivered at full cost. In 1993 the president proposed a surcharge as part of his 1994 budget request. A similar surcharge was passed in the House, but was deleted in conference with the Senate and was not enacted.

Other issues such as timber fees, recreation fees for use of our national forests and parks, mining fees – all have been addressed by the president. Regrettably, leadership on the part of policy-makers has been ineffectual. If there is no willingness on the part of "the representatives of the people" even to dispose of subsidies that have outlived their usefulness and do not bear the costs, then how can we expect them to take the next proactive step? Actually, there are many next steps. Legislation that I introduced into Congress nearly ten years ago called for economic incentives to recycle and re-use hazardous waste rather than pouring them into our streams and rivers. It passed both Houses, but in conference a Texan chairman eliminated my bill because it would be most costly to the oil industry due to their usual disposal method of deep-well injection. Because we have no technological remedies for this procedure, deep-well injection would be most heavily fined. My Global Warming Prevention Act in the late 1980s included numerous provisions which addressed a variety of market imperfections and institutional barriers that inhibit an efficient use of resources. It also addressed the planetary interest with its policies for increasing family planning funds as well as technology transfer of gas turbines through the Agency for International Development to developing countries. The gas turbines could cost-effectively meet the steam processing needs of the sugar cane factories located in 70 developing countries while also co-generating an estimated 50,000 megawatts of excess electricity. This is equal to a quarter of all electricity currently generated in these countries.

Another step would be tax shifting. At present we tax or punish those things we should encourage like work and enterprise, and reward the wasting of resources and pollution. Instead of taxing the creation of wealth, we could tax the depletion of it. Recently 2,300 economists, including five Nobel laureates, suggested such remedies to address the Framework Convention on Climate Change signed in 1992. But Congress has turned a deaf ear here too.

In addition to "full cost" accounting, removal of antiquated and environmentally damaging subsidies, improved governmental procurement practices and tax shifting from payroll and capital gains to pollution taxes, there is also a need to reconfigure the Gross Domestic Product (GDP). It is the primary indicator of economic wellbeing. The reality, however, is that the essential social and environmental elements that truly spell "quality of life" for the American people are overlooked. So, although the GDP has risen steadily, the Genuine Progress Indicator (developed by an NGO, Redefining Progress) which more accurately reflects the quality of life, clearly indicates a decline in economic wellbeing since the early 1970s. It appears to some of us that the costs of our current economic path have begun to outweigh the benefits.

Our official national policy is addressed not only by the president and Congress, but also by the federal agencies such as the Environmental Protection Agency, the Department of the Interior and the Department of Energy. They have been the unsung heroes of reducing consumption of energy, water, industrial and municipal wastes as well as addressing some of the more daunting challenges such as transportation.

The Climatewise Programme of the Department of Energy is a voluntary project directed towards corporations to reduce energy, water and resource use. It is a clearinghouse of information on technical assistance and financing opportunities. It has received commitments from 270 major companies to reduce over 3 million metric tons of CO_2 by the year 2000. The potential for energy savings for our nation is somewhere between 12% and 38%. The Climatewise Programme was created in response to the Climate Change Action Plan resulting from our commitments to the 1992 Framework Convention. The overall goal is to bring annual greenhouse gas emissions in 2000 back to 1990 levels. In addition, the Energy Star Buildings and Rebuild America programmes assist with voluntary comprehensive upgrades of building systems. "Green Lights" focuses on installing energy-efficient lighting in industrial and commercial facilities.

These are just a few of the voluntary efforts by the federal government to reduce waste. Despite the cost effectiveness of these programmes, they have been under constant attack in Congress. The programmes are exceptional, but because they are voluntary the rate of change is much slower than it would otherwise be if regulatory, legislative or true market costs of energy, water or resources were substituted.

Voter confidence in the elected officials is in a state of malaise. Polling data indicate that with the passage of the most recent budget and tax bill, 82% of those polled said they believed that members of the US Congress acted in their own self-interest, while a small minority felt they acted in the best interest of the country. Because of this frustration and distrust between officials and those who elect them, only 41% of the eligible voters participated in the last presidential election. For a country so committed to democracy, we demonstrate very little willingness to participate in the most basic responsibility and opportunity of choosing our leaders. Will this trend change? Not until the process of campaigns and the role of the media change and until the gap between words and deeds is eliminated.

State and local government

State and local governments are miles ahead of the federal government. Chicago, San Francisco, Seattle, and Boulder among others are redesigning entire cities as well as transportation systems. They are stimulating industries and individuals to save energy, water and precious natural environments, implementing new forest and urban park set-asides, changing building codes for greater energy efficiency and helping the poor and homeless at the same time.

The state of Minnesota is considering a sustainable tax proposal that would cut $1.5 billion from various personal and corporate taxes and to assess a $50 per ton carbon tax, with a tax also on nuclear energy equivalent to the average rate of electricity. Renewable energy (solar, wind, biomass, etc.) would not be taxed. The impact on net tax revenue would be neutral. In addition, there would be $50 million for a revolving loan fund for industrial efficiency investments, $20 million for low-income housing weatherization, $20 million for low-income energy assistance, $16 million in transit expenditure and $14 million in bridge repairs for rural areas.

Cities are in the forefront. The Sustainable City Project in San Jose, California has implemented several integrated programmes on water reclamation, integrated waste management, energy management, air quality and water conservation. These measures have contributed, for example, to local air quality improvements and reduced CO_2 emissions by 50,000 tons per year. Newark, New Jersey uses loans, grants, tax benefits and other advantages to encourage the establishment or expansion of recycling businesses. More than 80 recycling firms, employing over 1,000 people, have been established. Businesses are involved in collecting, shipping and processing paper, metals, plastics and chemical solvents. Seattle, Washington created a partnership of 863 local retailers, manufacturers, consumers and government officials to stimulate increased sales of recycled-content products instead of their virgin material counterparts. Sales of recycled products increased between 40% and 140% for the retailers involved in the campaign. Portland, Oregon provides a one-stop shop of technical and financial assistance for owners to upgrade their home's efficiency. To date 55 programmes have been created which have resulted in 14,300 apartment units being weatherized and 46,500 units now recycling. These programmes have resulted in annual energy savings of 26% and a one-third reduction in the amount of garbage being disposed.

Finally, a four-state private and public partnership is working to conserve natural, cultural, historical and agricultural resources of the blufflands along the Upper Mississippi and St Croix Rivers. So it is clear that local communities have a much greater sense of responsibility towards their environment and their fellow man than do the federal policy-makers.

Business

"We Europeans", said one leading businessman recently, "find it incredible to hear that a nation capable of landing a robot on Mars does not believe it can master the technological challenge of protecting the environment."[1] In my view, we are up to that challenge. Sustainable development cannot be achieved by one sector alone, but progressive, farsighted businesses are leading the charge. Many have astute chairmen who know that blazing the sustainability path is creating win/win scenarios for their companies. Some examples.

Utilities:　Due to the recent deregulation of the utilities, we are seeing a rapid reconsideration of energy efficiency and renewables as a result of consumer preference. This is coming from an industry that, for the most part, has been doing business as usual. Now creativity and community service are becoming much more typical. For example, Osage Municipal Utilities in Iowa have been a model of energy efficiency. Over 85% of all of the homes are well insulated. Many received free infra-red scanning, free appliance efficiency testing, furnace tune-ups and compact fluorescent lighting rebates.

Because of these efforts since 1974, the town now saves $1 million per year in energy bills. The Southern California Gas Company has developed a demonstration sustainable building that exceeds California building standards (the strongest in the country) by 24%, by relying on recycled materials, energy efficiency and resource design.

3M: In the 1970s, 3M started a wave across this country by independently initiating their "three Ps" Programme (Pollution Prevention Pays). It called for recycling and reusing their wastes, thereby saving billions of dollars in the manufacturing process. They and others have become increasingly more sophisticated in their efforts towards closed-loop manufacturing, or turning their wastes into feedstock.

Blandin Paper: This company undertook a steam reduction project that saved them $1.8 million annually, saved our environment from 37,000 tons of CO_2 emissions annually and saved 2.3 million kWh annually in energy usage. An additional benefit was improved employee morale and increased company recognition.

Patagonia: This outdoor clothing and equipment company has taken every step imaginable to reduce pollution and, in addition, took a more unusual course in 1995. Its managing director, led by the Buddhist dictum, "do no harm", chose to forego the cheaper cotton, produced in an environmentally damaging way, and to substitute organically grown cotton in all of his clothes. He also blazed a trail in manufacturing fleece jackets using recycled plastic beverage containers. Patagonia is a $154 million company that consistently donates 1% of its profits to environmental organizations.

Hewlett Packard: Hewlett Packard has taken the most progressive step to date by agreeing to do an in-house case study on the impact of shifting from payroll taxes to pollution taxes. This will enable it, upon completion, to act as a "responsible citizen" and credible spokesperson on the tax shifting issue.

The Natural Step: Begun in Sweden by Dr Karl Hendrick Robert, this is a growing movement now in the United States, as is the Business Ecology Network (BEN), founded by two former mavericks from the Environmental Protection Agency and the Department of Energy and a communications expert. This network of consultants blends the wisdom of natural systems with industrial ecology, ecological economics, total quality management, profitability and stakeholder relations. Not only are numerous consulting services developing as a result of the corporate movement towards sustainability, but so are new non-profit organizations such as Businesses for Social Responsibility and the Business Council for Sustainable Energy. New magazines and journals are also fulfilling the demand for more answers on how to do more with less.

The business community in the US remains competitive by being able to read trends and forecast possible scenarios. Global trade patterns have made it clear to the US that if the Japanese manufacture cleaner and more energy efficient cars, as they did in the 1980s, American car companies lose out. Germany's parliament has approved a new system of vehicle taxation aimed at penalizing polluting cars. Electrolux of Sweden, the world's leading appliance manufacturer, has a line of kitchen ovens that consume 60% less energy than comparable products.

Multinational corporations are observing the global trends towards reducing consumption of our precious resources, and many are rising to the occasion. Businesses, large and small, have begun the effort towards ending wasteful resource consumption. For their leadership, I hold the greatest hope. Regardless of whether they have been motivated by increased profit or a sense of corporate responsibility to act in the community and planetary interest, they are clearly the current driving force towards sustainable development and consumption. The role of business in the US is far more progressive than that of Congress, which at this point isn't even aware of these international trends. But business alone cannot take us the enormous distance we need to go in implementing *Agenda 21*. The governments must set agreed upon framework conditions.

Non-governmental organizations

The power and influence of the national NGOs that once were the driving force in the 1970s and 1980s, have been declining. Their confrontational and advocacy approach has been replaced by smaller state and local NGOs that emphasize partnerships and education. One national exception is the Green Scissors Campaign, a coalition of several national environmental and taxpayer groups dedicated to saving taxpayers billions of dollars, end inadvisable subsidies and leave the environment enhanced.

They single out wasteful projects for elimination by the Congress, and lobby them on their economic and environmental impact.

Perhaps one of the most impressive campaigns is the GAP (Global Action Plan for the Earth). It is a national community-based campaign empowering and educating citizens to live environmentally sustainable lives. They organize neighbourhood eco-teams that help change lifestyle habits and reduce resource use.

In an effort to save the forests, the first US magazine printed on 100% recycled paper has been initiated by the Earth Island Institute. They have undertaken a national campaign demonstrating that sustainable bleaching and pulping processes, as well as plant fibres such as kenaf, hemp and straw rather than wood pulp from trees, provide a sustainable alternative.

An environmental education and demonstration facility teaches consumers how to save 50% to 80% in energy and resources. Over 3,100 members of the public have toured the facility and seen how this home reuses materials – tyres as carpet padding, plastic soda bottles as carpeting, and newspapers as insulation. Earthways, in Missouri, developed this programme as a model.

The US's first successful scheme for the combination of rural affordable housing with farmland preservation (preserving 4,275 acres through 42 projects) was implemented within 12 towns by the Franklin Land Trust in western Massachusetts. They also formed a farm products promotion association to improve the local agricultural economy and save the land from development.

The Lighthouse Farm Network in California sets up model farms, which demonstrate alternative and organic farming methods, and emphasizes the economic and ecological benefits of such an initiative. This farmer-to-farmer approach has been very effective.

There are thousands of community-based efforts underway throughout the United States, but one of the most successful in reducing consumption levels is the New Road Map Foundation. It uses a variety of tools including lifestyle assessment questionnaires that emphasize how our patterns of consumption affect our personal lives, those of other contemporary human beings, as well as generations to come, and also the environment. People who follow the nine-step programme find that within a year their expenses decline by 25% and their quality of life usually goes up. Doing more with less. Though questions are asked about every aspect of our lives, including what we feel about the relationship between our spiritual or religious beliefs and our lifestyle choices, this clearly is a valid area for enquiry, one that leads to the fifth avenue of leadership opportunity.

Religions

Organized religion can be a powerful force all around the world, a "wake-up call" that reminds us of a few things: we are charged with being responsible stewards of all creation; that we are, in fact, "our brother's keeper". "What we consume beyond need, is greed", said the Buddha. There is growing concern about our preoccupation with materialism, something that many denominations are studying in order to design an appropriate response. But discussion of eco-justice and developmental foreign aid, as well as the relationship between the rich and the poor, has been a part of the ecumenical movement for the last 30 years. Here, too, the impact has not risen to the full potential of the religious communities. With the current hunger among the American people for purpose and connection, the religious leaders clearly have an opening. The Old Testament taught that the abundance of the rich was a form of thievery, so long as others suffered from starvation and homelessness. Our ethic is to "love thy neighbour". Religions have millions of followers to whom they can provide the inspiration to guide us in the practical ways in which we can turn these beliefs into responsible lifestyles. The National Religious Partnership for the Environment and the North American Coalition on Religion and Ecology are two coalitions committed to stimulating leadership from the religious communities.

The media

When I single out the media as one of the critical avenues of leadership, the reporters and pundits run for cover with disclaimers of non-engagement. They are merely the "observers" of the American

Figure 11.2.1 One American, says Claudine Schneider, uses twice as much energy as a German, 100 times that of a Vietnamese. "The reality is that our planet cannot endure the excesses of the US and we must accept that our way of life must change. Other nations cannot and should not emulate the American lifestyle." The lights of New York's World Trade Center burn through the night, using more electricity than an Asian village would in a year. But she is confident that Americans, who are a "generous and fair-minded people", are capable of rising to the occasion and leading the world to a more sustainable existence. (Courtesy Archive Photos/Lambert)

Dream, not the perpetrators of it. From the sit-com directors to the advertisers, from the news anchors to the talk show hosts, there is one message: more is better.

But fundamental change is possible. It will require both personal change as well as systemic change. It will require many messengers and many leaders to move the agenda forward more rapidly. Short of a revolution or similar crisis, there is one way to accelerate the dissemination of the message: through the medium of television. In American life, there are few conduits more effective or omni-present than television. The average American will spend one entire year of his or her life watching TV commercials.

If the richness of talent in the media and advertising world were to be redirected toward rais-ing awareness of the impact of our consumer lifestyle on the environment, our neighbours and future generations, then the shift toward sustainable consumption would occur much more rapidly. The media could play a critical role in informing Americans about the breadth and depth of our consumptive ways and their impact on our global family. In addition, they could shine the spotlight on the inactive, yet critical role that Congress can embrace. The media could lead the enquiry into the American Dream. Is it becoming a nightmare?

THE LEGITIMATE NATIONAL INTEREST

Nobody outside and not too many inside would, I believe, disagree that the US is grossly exceeding the legitimate national interest in overconsuming the planet's resources. Our estimated "ecological footprint" is 10.3 hectares per person, the largest in the world and almost seven times above the available earthshare per person. *Agenda 21* calls for all countries to move rapidly towards national sustainable consumption. That is clearly in the vital planetary interest. But the US is not doing this. It does not make me proud. But it does make me determined. And since leaving the US Congress, I have realized that such determination is shared by many other Americans. We all should, I believe, play to our strength, and America's strength is its energy, openness, ingenuity and ability to change.

As the international community gathered in Kyoto in December 1997 to address the issue of climate change, the *New York Times* ran a poll on American public opinion. Of those surveyed, 65% said that the US should take steps now to cut its own GHG emissions, regardless of what other countries do. Only 15% counselled delay until international agreement were reached. Moreover, 61% favoured environmental protection even at the cost of local employment; and 57% said environmental improvement must be made regardless of cost. Only 13% thought that climate change would have no serious effect while 43% thought it would. And a majority were or would be willing to spend more on efficient appliances in order to cut GHG emissions, with only 20% unwilling.[2] So I believe there is a mandate out there for our national leaders to make that sea-change in policy that is so needed towards sustainable consumption patterns in the United States.

CONCLUSION

For ten years I served as a national policy-maker in the US Congress – a mixture of satisfaction and frustration. For seven years, I have been a private consultant committed to ecologically sustainable living. In both spheres of life, what keeps coming home to me is the question of what kind of lifestyle Americans fundamentally want, or should have.

Recently I convened a series of informal focus groups into how people define the American Dream. The responses fell into four areas. People often think of acquiring a home, a car and a TV. Others think of "life, liberty and the pursuit of happiness". Thirdly, many relate to the opportunities of being an American, to rise from poverty to wealth, from obscurity to fame, to reach any goal with either luck or hard work. And, finally, there is a strong belief that each generation will be "better off" (more educated, more prosperous, more secure) than their parents. When I query non-Americans about the American Dream it is their enthusiasm for the material wealth that attracts them. Whether it is in the communes of China or the jungles of the Amazon, everyone seems to want a TV, a car and a big home.

The reality is that our planet cannot endure the excesses of the US, and we must accept that our way of life must change considerably. But also that other nations cannot and should not strive to emulate the American lifestyle. Even though the reasons for that are not evident to people, a recent survey conducted by a US foundation on the views of Americans on consumption, materialism and the environment make it clear that more is not always seen as better. The conclusions are revealing. There were four key messages. Americans believe that our priorities are out of balance and that materialism dominates our lives and crowds out our more meaningful values that centre around family, responsibility and community. We are alarmed about the future, and anticipate greater struggles for our children if we do not steer away from our consumptive course. We are ambivalent about what to do. And although we see a link between consumption and the environment, Americans have not thought deeply about the ecological implications of our lifestyle.[3]

There is nothing more empowering than experiencing models of sustainability, many of which I've highlighted here – the success stories, the savings, the self-satisfaction in changing from a course that is out of control to one that is exemplary to the occasion. Media and thus public pressure would ultimately move Congress to at least respond to the people. The president, too, could be more aggressively engaged in building the bridge to sustainable consumption in the twenty-first century. It is a matter of national security in the near term and one of historic proportions for the future. He has the potential to be remembered as the world leader who provided impetus to the transformation from an industrial world of "haves and have nots" to a new age of knowing and acting as though we were one family. Global trade, communication, finance and travel are weaving our world ever closer together. I am confident that if the Americans, who are a generous and fair-minded people, were to be called into action by the president, our creativity and ingenuity could lead all nations towards a more sustainable existence. He need only declare that achieving sustainability is a mission equivalent to sending a man to the moon and, I am sure, in our search for connection and a common purpose, we would rise to the occasion.

NOTES

1.   *IHT*, 15 December 1997.
2.   Ibid., 1 December 1997.
3.   *Yearning for balance: views of Americans on consumption, materialism and the environment*, Harwood group, for Merck Family Fund (Tacoma, Maryland), July 1995.

11.3 Sweden

Lena Klevenås

> "I would like to make Sweden into a model country for ecologically sustainable development. We will rebuild the country step by step. Building 'a sustainable Sweden' means reviewing our values, what we think is most important in life. An existential dimension, which affects our view of what is sacred and indispensable."
>
> Göran Persson, 1996

There is a Swedish word *lagom*. Legend says it comes from our ancestors, the Vikings. They would sit around a table, drinking from one big common cup. They passed the cup around as they talked and everyone had to drink, but no more than required, for something to be left for the last man. Sustainable consumption might be like that – not taking more than your fair share, so there will be something left for every human being living in the world, even in the future.

Sweden is known for its sensible and sane policies of consumption – its tradition of equality and sharing. Perhaps it is so. We in Sweden do not think we have it perfect. There is still a way to go. But when the mayor of your capital city can drink the water from the lake outside City Hall, when the local people can swim and fish from the waters outside your parliamentary office, it can't be all bad.

Rio's Programme of Action urged every nation-state to attain sustainable consumption, and urged developed countries to take the lead. If that is the planetary interest, that is fine with me. It is, in my view, absolutely clearly in my country's national interest to do so.

NATIONAL POLICY

Changing consumption patterns, said Rio, will require a multipronged strategy focusing on demand, meeting the basic needs of the poor, and reducing wastage and the use of finite resources. That is what Sweden is trying to do.

In the Swedish election of 1991, I entered parliament at the same time as my Social Democratic Party lost power and we entered the opposition. I was assigned to the Agricultural Committee where most of the environmental legislation is discussed. My colleague, Göran Persson, was appointed chairman. In 1996 he became prime minister. He is currently not popular because of the austerity programme, but he is a committed environmentalist. And he is a leader.

A Swedish parliamentary committee meets three days a week. We worked hard, wrote many proposals. One motion I initiated asked for research into the relationship between the economy and ecology. We tried to make our politics "greener". It was difficult sometimes because our party is a labour one which loves traditional industry and economic growth. That is why I asked.

In 1992 Göran Persson led the Swedish delegation to the UN Earth Summit in Rio. I saw his serious concern about climate change and ozone depletion. I also saw his increasing interest in spiritual values. As newly elected party leader and prime minister, in March 1996, Persson declared:

> Now at the threshold of a new century, we witness a new spring for solidarity, for humanism and for compassion. Consider the young generation. Many of them have wonderful ideas. They struggle for a better environment, for peace, for refugees and for immigrants. Some of them lead a very simple life from a material point of view, and they place a higher value on community and culture than they do on owning

things. I believe that these young people are more in tune with what development requires than was the case with the values which dominated the 1980s. We face a tremendous and beautiful challenge.[1]

I believe that the Swedish government has the will to reduce the gap between poor and rich people, both in Sweden and between the countries of the world, through a policy of sustainable consumption, both nationally and globally. Sweden is well aware that there is a planetary interest, that we are all interdependent and have to find common solutions to global problems.

At the national level we had a political breakthrough when Göran Persson also declared:

> I would like to make Sweden into a model country for ecologically sustainable development. We will rebuild the country step by step. Building "a sustainable Sweden" means reviewing our values, what we think is most important in life. An existential dimension, which affects our view of what is sacred and indispensable. The vision of a sustainable Sweden has all the opportunities for combining what is best in the traditions of the labour movement with the new challenges which we face; a view of the whole together with the reformist strategy of small steps at a time, justice and internationalism; jobs and the struggle for our life environment on the planet Earth.[2]

Similarly, the government's policy declaration of September 1996 states that Sweden "shall be" a leading force and an example to other countries in its efforts to create an ecological, sustainably developed country. Prosperity shall be built on more efficient use of natural resources – energy, water and raw materials. And in the national follow-up report to the second Earth Summit in 1997, the government declared:

> Consumption and production patterns are very important in the context of sustainable development. Estimates indicate that the households are responsible for a considerable part of emissions to air and water. During the 1990s, consumption in Sweden has to a large extent been redirected towards more environmentally friendly products, mainly as a result of consumers demanding environmentally adapted and eco-labelled products. Many producers have rapidly adjusted to these changes in demand. In addition, some actors in the financial market have started to formulate environmental requirements for investments and credits.[3]

The prime minister has appointed a body of ministers for the promotion of ecologically sustainable development. In March 1997, the body presented its first report and proposed to develop a common platform for the different sectors of society, a structure comprising both environmental targets and means of implementation. The delegation also proposed to develop the first stages of a broad-based, long-term investment programme for ecological sustainability and employment. Over three years that is likely to come to about $3.5 billion, comprising investment in municipalities, an ecocycle programme, alternative energy, public transport, "green agriculture" and nature conservation.

So, what are we doing in practical terms to deliver on these undertakings? Three sectors can be seen as having been active: government, business and civil society. I briefly explain each.

Government

Both the parliament and the executive have been active in promoting sustainable consumption in Sweden. Swedish environmental legislation is expanding and a revision of all legislation is under way. A draft Environmental Policy Act is before the *Riksdag* – essentially a codification of the Rio principles. It will also include stricter rules concerning criminality and penalties for environmental abuses. For its part, government policy focuses on a variety of measures: economic instruments, environmental accounting, energy policy, eco-labelling and public awareness.

Economic instruments

During the 1990s, the use of economic instruments in the environmental sector has substantially increased. Sweden now has more environmental taxes and charges than almost any other country in the world. Fears of impairing the competitive capacity of national industry can, however, deter a country from "going it alone" with economic instruments. Revenue from environment- and energy-related taxes in 1994 equalled 3% of GDP and is expected to be 3.7% in 1998.

Figure 11.3.1 Clean water in the city centre. Mayor Mats Hulth drinks a glass of water from Lake Mälaren, outside City Hall, Stockholm. Ten years ago, the water was polluted. Today, citizens swim and fish in the lake and the Baltic. But Sweden still has the 13th largest ecological footprint of nations surveyed to date. "We in Sweden do not think we have it perfect", says Lena Klevenås. "There is still a way to go." (Courtesy Helena Närä)

The biggest items of revenue include the energy tax on fuels and electricity and the carbon dioxide tax. Environmentally differentiated taxes include, for example, sulphur tax on fuels, carbon dioxide tax, energy tax on fuels for motor vehicles and vehicle tax. As of July 1997, 1 litre of gasoline cost about 8 Swedish kroner ($1.05), of which 75% was tax (energy tax of 45% and carbon dioxide tax of 10%, plus an add-on sales tax). People still drive. There is a decision to increase the tax by 0.1 kroner annually over 20 years to make consumers change. The Swedish National Road Administration, *Vägverket*, has just decided not to permit official cars that use more than 8.6 litres per 100 km. The Swedish car industry is furious but the environment minister keeps cool and says that there has been a long-lasting debate and that they have had time to adapt.

Also encouraging are the sales figures for bicycles in Sweden for the first nine months of 1997, up 12% while gasoline sales were down 2%. Sweden has 9 million inhabitants and 3.7 million cars, but 43% of Swedes walk, bicycle or take the bus to work, compared with 10% in the United States.

Related to governmental action of course is legislative action by the parliament. One recent example is the proposal before it to ban the use of any chemical that accumulates in the environment, whether it is toxic or not. The recommendation from the relevant committee is that by 2007, all products on the market should be "free from substances that are persistent and liable to accumulate", and that by 2002 manufacturers must label products with information about the chemicals they contain. Products should be free from anything known to have "serious or irreversible effects" on human health or the environment. The chemical industry is strongly opposed, but the committee rests its judgement on the precautionary principle and indeed proposes that the European Union adopt the same measure.

Environmental accounting

Governmental departments and research agencies are working on developing an economic model for use of environmental accounting. The model will be designed for analyzing environmental policy as well as ordinary economic analyses. So far the accounts have been classified in 16 industries, governmental services and private consumption. Work is going on to compile data for about 100 industries. The physical data included in the accounts so far cover emissions of carbon dioxide, sulphur dioxide, nitrous oxide and other hazardous chemicals. In January 1997 data were published for the first time, for 1989, 1991 and 1993. Energy data are presented in physical as well as monetary terms.

At present, waste data are included in the accounts for waste generation, and there has been a survey of the waste coming from extraction and manufacturing industries. In resource use accounting, the previous pilot study on carbon in wood material is being followed up by an inventory of data on iron and steel, aluminium, copper, food, building material and chemicals. Work with natural resource accounting has started for forests.

We are not at a stage, however, where such "integrated environmental accounts" are being assimilated by policy-makers or the public in a manner that is affecting decision-making. In November 1997 I asked in parliament when it would be possible for Sweden to have national accounts showing the costs of environmental damage as a deficit. The finance minister was unable to say "exactly when" this would happen; environmental accounts had been completed for sulphur and nitrogen, but more work was required before any complete environmental account could be presented. Indeed, the minister thought that environmental accounts will always be a complement rather than a substitute for conventional accounts. They probably never would be complete in the sense of all environmental effects being identified and valued correctly. Yet the government regarded such accounts as "very important", and a "crucial step" leading Sweden towards ecological sustainability.

Energy policy

In 1991 the Swedish parliament adopted a programme for the more efficient use of energy with the objective of ensuring that the full potential for more efficient use was exploited and financially reasonable. Seven public authorities co-operate. The main methods of working are technology procurement, incentive agreements and performance requirements.

Technology procurement is a means of helping new technology over a market threshold. It gathers representatives of a number of large potential purchasers of the product, specifying performance requirements in respect of improved efficiency and other aspects such as price, reduced pollution and ease of operation. Manufacturers are then invited to compete, with the performance specification setting out the minimum requirements to be fulfilled by the new product. The prize is often in the form of guaranteed larger orders, together with the publicity resulting from information dissemination.

Sweden's nuclear power policy has occasioned considerable attention since the 1980s. A referendum on nuclear power was held in 1980 after the Three Mile Island disaster in the United States. Although the wording of the referendum was rather ambiguous, the public chose to end Sweden's reliance on nuclear power. After a long delay, the parliament acted. An energy bill was approved in December 1997 that included the closure of two nuclear power stations. A new energy system built on highly effective use of energy and reliant to a greater extent on renewable fuel is a precondition for a sustainable Sweden. We don't want to continue to produce nuclear waste that is not congruent with an ecocycle society. We will keep the nuclear waste that we have already produced within our national borders, even though we have not yet found the place or the method to keep it safely during the thousands of years that is needed. We will close our plants over a gradual time-period. We don't want to be put in a situation of being forced to close them rapidly, which might be the case after a future accident. That is why we start now. We will try to compensate for the energy loss from the closure of the nuclear plants through greater energy efficiency and more renewable energy. One example is exhaust air ventilation fans for apartment buildings. They are available today with considerably higher efficiency than those commonly used at present, and investment grants can be obtained for up to 25% of the capital cost.

We do not intend to increase our emissions of greenhouse gases. Half the electricity from our nuclear plants is now used for home heating and we are committed to changing the kind of energy used for heating away from electricity to some kind of renewable energy. You may, for example, replace direct electric heating in your house now with some kind of water-borne heating system – there are also subsidies for this kind of thing.

We don't think there is one big solution to the energy issue. Rather, a lot of small solutions that together will solve the big problem. The challenge is to find the most effective solution in every situation.

Eco-labelling

One instrument to encourage industry to enhance their production environmentally is eco-labelling schemes. Currently, there are two organizations that grant licences for eco-labels: one is the Nordic eco-labelling system which operates with standardized licensing criteria among all Scandinavian countries; the second was set up by a Swedish NGO. There is also a popular labelling of "chemical-free products", and ecologically-produced food of every type is available under the KRAV certification system. A campaign, called the 10% campaign, supported by a decision in parliament, aims at "ecological farming" on 10% of Sweden's cultivated land by 2000. This means no pesticides, no fertilisers and cattle-rearing in a low-intensive way where the animals keep their natural behaviour and are fed "chemical-free" foodstuffs. There is a growing demand for these kinds of products despite the need for a separate infrastructure for distribution.

Public awareness

Sustainable consumption depends on public awareness. Sweden has a long experience of environmental education. I can still remember a tremendous day of study for teachers 30 years ago with the title "Shall the teachers save the world?" that gave us a strong feeling of responsibility for bringing up the next generation to care for the environment. And Swedish teachers and students have demonstrated a strong commitment to the environment in recent decades. At universities there is a wide curriculum of environmental subjects. They offer courses to ordinary students but also to companies and elderly people. Work has begun on the formulation of cognitive targets to confer a greater understanding of the connection between lifestyles and environmental problems.

Business

Around the world, business is "greening". Sweden is, I think, among the leaders in this. A good environmental image is an advantage in the eyes of the customers – they demand it. We still have our problem areas but we are working on them. There is, for example, "statutory producer responsibility" for many products, the intention being to influence product design so as to minimize the environmental impact when products are discarded. Citizens have to pre-separate and hand in discarded products. Even before producer responsibility was introduced, collection systems existed in certain areas – for packaging, tyres and newspapers since 1994, furniture and building waste, batteries and electronic products since 1997, cars in 1998. There is no question but that producer responsibility is an imposition. Yet it is a call to the relevant branches of economic activity to assume direct responsibility. Sometimes impending producer responsibility has been replaced with a voluntary undertaking from the industry, as for example when the construction industry pledged itself to reduce the quantity of builder's waste sent for landfill disposal.

Another side of producer responsibility is the pledge by Sweden's petroleum companies to reinstate contaminated soil around abandoned petrol stations, at a cost of $200 million over a 15-year period. And the oil companies have started to sell a special type of gasoline in the city of Gothenburg, where they have substituted methanol up to 10% of volume. Sweden has no oil but a lot of biomass from forests that we like to use in order to reduce our carbon dioxide emissions. It is possible to use this new type of fuel only for cars later than 1993 models, but it is a promising start. If it works out it will be possible to buy it all over the country. In Gothenburg you can also recharge the batteries of your electric car.

Further measures to change consumption patterns are, however, needed. The "Factor 10" approach, originally launched by the Wuppertal Institute in Germany, calls for a ten-fold increase in resource and energy productivity within 50 years. And the Swedish Natural Step is an organization that trains companies and municipalities to make the change to environmentally better behaviour. Their first challenge was to build up a network of scientists who agreed that any substance which continues to accumulate in nature will inevitably bring irreversible damage and that thousands of substances are rising in concentration around us. That prompted the legislation I described earlier. They also agreed that our linear economy converts resources to waste faster than nature can cope. Their four "system conditions" are that substances from the Earth's crust must not be extracted at a rate faster than they can naturally regenerate; that substances produced by society must not systematically increase in nature; that the physical basis for the productivity and diversity of nature must not be systematically diminished; and the just and efficient use of energy and other resources. The Natural Step has trained several major international groups such as IKEA and Electrolux but also the Swedish Rail company, Swedish MacDonald's, Scandic Hotel and the Federation of Swedish Farmers. The Natural Step organizations have been springing up in the US, Australia, the UK and the Netherlands. The consensus spreads.

Civil society

Sweden has a culture of caring and maintenance. Perhaps it is due to our cold climate during the winter. Today we have nice and comfortable houses and buildings which we repair regularly. But it was not long ago when Sweden was a poor country. We all remember.

It was easy for modern Swedes to adopt the new concept of "reduce, reuse and recirculate". It started with composting and separating waste at home. And something happened in people's minds – they started to think not just of the waste mountain but also from where the products came. The waste bins were almost empty. The lorry removing the waste didn't need to come as often as before. We saved money. We reduced emissions. We became aware of what we brought back from the supermarkets. We didn't like big boxes and unnecessary packing anymore. Now almost every family separates its waste and brings back to special collecting places used paper packages, hard and soft plastic packages, metal packages, batteries and hazardous waste. Lorries continue to collect newspapers every month and large waste items such as furniture every half year. There is also large-scale treatment of biological household waste at municipality level, putrefaction in order to produce biogas to replace electricity.

Environmental thinking is integrated in everything. Radio and TV stations provide information. Study circles gather to discuss and learn. Municipal energy boards make policy plans to help their customers reduce their energy use. They don't just deliver electricity but they revise the energy use of hospitals, restaurants and stores and advise them how they can use energy more effectively.

In order to change consumption patterns, the role of consumers must be strengthened. In Sweden this is done by dissemination of information by state agencies, municipalities, non-governmental organizations, the media, industry and local consumer groups. There is, strangely enough, no major consumer organization in Sweden, but individual consumers have an increasing awareness of their power.

As a customer of Stockholm Energy you can choose from which resource you want your electricity to come. The result was that even though electricity from wind plants is more expensive, many people choose it. Some 13% choose wind energy, 47% water, 20% nuclear and 17% choose energy from combined power and heating plants.

The companies are well aware of the consumers' demand. Seven out of ten Swedish consumers have a private "black list" of companies they don't like and whose products they refuse to buy. Reasons given include "unserious methods", inhuman behaviour, "stupid advertising", low environmental consciousness, and a lack of public engagement.

A good example of the co-operative relationship between government and the public concerns the use of paper. Chlorine-free paper pulp constitutes only 5% to 10% of all pulp manufactured in the world. In the 1980s, the Swedish industry's annual production of chlorine (absorbable organic halide, AOX) totalled 30,000 tonnes. Environmental groups began a campaign of consumer awareness and initiated agreement with 17 companies over "Panda labelling" of environmentally friendly paper. In 1988 the *Riksdag* decided to support the government's proposed measures for reducing emissions of organic chlorine compounds to 1.5 kg per tonne of pulp by 1992.[4] Emissions stand now at only 1,500 tonnes. Consumers effectively forced the paper mills to redesign their processes.

There is a saying in Sweden, "there is so little you can do, so do the little you can". Swedish consumers are really discovering the big potential of their purchasing power. After the French nuclear testing in 1993, a national boycott of French wine saw sales drop 40% in one year. It was very encouraging for Swedish buyers but not for French farmers who had to talk to their president. It made a big impact and the number of tests was reduced. I'm not sure if that helped sustainability in Sweden, but it certainly was in the planetary interest.

THE LEGITIMATE NATIONAL INTEREST

It is hard to determine whether one's own country is acting in the legitimate national interest, especially on an issue as broad and complex as sustainable consumption. Certainly, in terms of the North, Sweden is quite virtuous in its consumption habits. Yet, in a global context, I am not so sure. The work on "ecological footprints" described earlier in this book is pretty sobering for us all, not least for Sweden – we have, according to the preliminary estimates, the 13th largest footprint on Earth. As time goes by, and this analytical work improves, the ecological footprint will be the ultimate test. I think our personal efforts make a bit of a difference, but it is the economic system that counts.

In the future, two objective tests will be needed for judging comparative national sustainability: the ecological footprint and environmental accounting. Then we shall be able to compare our various countries for the legitimate national interest. There is nothing wrong with comparing countries for sustainability in the future. I could envisage, for example, a "challenge comparison" between countries over sustainability – all in the planetary interest. But until then, we must simply do what we can in our own countries. There is enough to be done.

It will be a challenge to relate the national interest to the planetary interest over consumption patterns. Sweden, for example, is consciously trying to mesh the new goal of sustainability with the old, traditional goals of government. In a way, it can be described as solving two problems with one solution. There is a new aspiration in Sweden concerning the two huge problems we confront – environmental degradation and unemployment. We have an increasingly optimistic feeling that they are each other's solution. By rebuilding Sweden into an ecologically sustainable society we will need a lot of workers to do all the jobs. We will also need new technology, the best available environmentally friendly technology for our production. And we are confident that the environmental adaptation of Swedish enterprises should lead to a competitive advantage.

In striving to ensure that Sweden answers to the legitimate national interest, we face both strengths and weaknesses in our habits and beliefs. I see four strengths in Sweden today. There is a strong environmental consciousness and a changing mentality towards materialism, especially among young people. There are strong popular movements, a democratic tradition, and strong support for the United Nations system. The government is committed to building an ecologically sustainable society and has support from the local and regional governments. And we have good experience of environmental regulations also in order to strengthen industrial capacity and competitiveness.

And then I see three fundamental problems in the national policy that makes it difficult to be optimistic about Sweden's contribution to sustainable consumption. There is the lingering belief in eternal economic growth. There is a strong dependence on our car industry for creating jobs. And there is a lack of overview and interest in the planet and humanity as a whole.

The most challenging aspect of the GNP figure is when we compare different countries' economic development without taking notice of their starting-point. Swedish economists often say we are lagging behind as measured by the GNP. But how can we obtain a more fair distribution without stopping the growth at the top? How can the gap be smaller if the developed countries don't let the developing ones catch up. Even though there is progress in creating environmentally adjusted economic accounts, it is tragic that this "economic growth" thinking still has such impact on policy-making.

I see a severe problem in our dependence on the two car manufacturers, Saab and Volvo. We want them to be successful but they are not in the forefront of creating a car that uses a minimum of gasoline. On the contrary. Energy and transport are the sectors where Sweden has the biggest problems. The transport sector accounts for 20% of Sweden's total energy use, and 90% of this energy is derived from fossil fuels. Transport in Sweden is one of the biggest sources of emissions of environmentally harmful substances such as greenhouse gases and substances causing acidification, eutrophication of soil and water and damage to vegetation. Catalytic conversion has been compulsory for new motor vehicles in Sweden since 1989. Technical progress has created a potential for cleaner vehicles, but this is being partly thwarted by the introduction of heavier and faster vehicles using larger amounts of fuel. Vehicular emissions of nitrogen oxides, hydrocarbons, lead and particulate matter have been substantially reduced by the introduction of better engines and exhaust purification, and the quality of air in big Swedish cities is fairly good. But total traffic volume continues to increase and carbon dioxide emissions have not declined. And the traffic system impacts on the environment by claiming substantial areas of land, especially in urban areas, where green spaces are limited.

Developments in the transport sector today are not compatible with sustainable consumption. Some 70% of the road transport is personal and not caused by trade. This is a kind of trap. Ivan Illich noted in 1974 that if we count the time we spend on earning money to buy the car, pay for the insurance, the gasoline, the parking and the washing, plus the time you spend in your car queuing, the average speed is 8 km per hour. That is about the speed you walk.

The car industry is too big for the world. This is a big political problem for any country with a car industry. It is the same problem with military aircraft. We need the jobs in the short run but we also need to save the peace and environment. It is difficult for one single country to go ahead. It is even difficult for the big European Union. What we need is a global decision-making mechanism that can regulate and restrict the use of fossil fuel – an economic policy for the world as a whole. I welcome the idea of an economic security council within the UN. But we also need to scrutinize the political concepts and myths on which we build our political practice.

CONCLUSION

To become a politician is a long journey. The first thing you need is a strong will to change something and a belief that it is worth trying. Choosing a party, or creating a new one, is not the main point. All parties are tools and you can use them. No change will be completed without political decisions.

You need some solemn declarations to rely upon when pushing your issue forward. You also need a personal political declaration not to get lost in the daily political life. My political ambition is to decrease the gap between poor and rich people, both in Sweden and the world as a whole. It may sound pathetic but I don't hesitate to tell my voters, whatever my political fate.

Sweden is, just as other countries, a fragmented society. Most people are specialists, not generalists. If you want to make a career, it is important to be good in the employment market, have deep knowledge about specific things, be really good at something. Few people are confident enough or have enough time to care about the planet as a whole.

The most important issue is to see to it that every human being on Earth has clean drinking water and food. In my constituency I was "international leader" over a ten-year period. I initiated a successful project for providing drinking water in a small town, Ocotal in Nicaragua. I am happy to have the experience that my constituency, "despite" my preference for global issues, has so far elected me to represent them in parliament. Perhaps it will not be forever. Not all of them are happy, especially not those who work in the car and the military industries which have big enterprises, Saab and Volvo aerospace in Trollhättan, in my district.

I have tried for a long time to discuss the concept of "economic growth". It has been very difficult. My party's philosophy is based on the industrialized society and all the reforms we could introduce in our welfare system thanks to the economic growth during the twentieth century. We have been happy to become richer with every new generation.

I believe that people feel there is something fundamentally wrong with ordinary economic thinking today. I also believe that many Swedes are fed up with all the material goods they have gathered. Many people feel shame seeing starving people on TV every night. Some people have stopped reading newspapers, fed up with the bad news. People need to know that other people also have food, health care and schools, and somewhere to live peacefully, to feel happy. The feeling for solidarity is not buried. I would like to see a global debate on how the concept of indefinite economic growth, even in the richest countries, will solve the problem of feeding the hungry and starving people in the world. I would also like a debate about free trade, another of those concepts that we use very carelessly. How can those 1.3 billion people who live on less than one dollar a day act as consumers in the world market?

My experience, having been born a Swede, in a society with a fairly small gap between rich and poor, makes me sure that this is good for the society as a whole. The basic human concept of every human being's equality is the guiding star for Swedish society. It is hard for most Swedes to see the situation of the poorest billion in the world. We long believed that it was possible to lift them up to our level of material standard. Now we slowly realize that this will never happen – at least not to the same level. The footprint would be too large for the planet.

We who belong to the richest billion leave ecological footprints that are too big. The question is whether we can keep our standard of living just by using energy and other resources more effectively or if we also have to reduce our consumption in some important aspect. And the biggest challenge is how we will handle the car industry. How can we go on growing economically and at the same time reduce the gap between us and the poorest billion? How can we keep our GNP growing, comparing it with a poor country? Should they never be allowed to catch up? What about keeping our position in the world economy? We are too much addicted to competition and growth. Now we must work harder with co-operation and sharing.

I am sure that we have to, at the political level, if we want to keep the people's confidence – to put a real strength behind the planetary interest in the common good.

NOTES

1. Address by Prime Minister Göran Persson, Swedish Social Democratic Party Congress, Stockholm, 16 March 1996.
2. Ibid.
3. Report of the Government of Sweden to the United Nations Special Assembly of the General Assembly, *From environmental protection to sustainable development*, 1997
4. Government Bill 1987/88:85.

PART THREE

The vital planetary interest and legitimate global power

In Part III, the question of legitimate global power is addressed. The fundamental proposition, developed from Part I, is that global power, including enforcement power, is likely to be taken as legitimate by the peoples of the world only in those strictly circumscribed areas where the vital planetary interest is at stake. If that vital interest is not at stake, nation-states should be free to pursue their interests as they see fit, including in a peaceful competitive manner and even where national interests might conflict. But where the common survival of humanity is concerned, including over the long term, nation-states must be prepared, in the twenty-first century, to accept the legitimacy of the planetary interest in formulating their policies and determining their behaviour. They must, in short, obey the common interest.

As the world is transformed by the information revolution, the role of the nation-state is likely to diminish in relative importance while yet remaining the principal agent for legitimate political behaviour. Sovereignty is likely to be "stretched in both directions" with some narrowly defined issues requiring legitimate power at the global level, others at the regional level, and yet others below the national jurisdiction at the provincial or municipal level. In the fast-changing world of the twenty-first century, the jurisdictional relationships between the various levels of authority will become complex. It is important that, in the course of this process, the proper norms of established moral and political behaviour be observed. It is critical that they be observed especially at the global level, where power will be most potent.

Part III therefore addresses the relationship between established national power and the changes in global, regional and municipal power, in response to the needs and demands of humanity as it confronts the global problems that threaten the vital planetary interest.

CHAPTER TWELVE

Global powers: Earth's planetary interest

Shridath Ramphal

> "The empires of the future are the empires of the mind."
>
> Sir Winston Churchill

It was over half a century ago when Churchill offered his keen observation. The leading statesman of the time was speaking before a Harvard audience after receiving an honorary degree for his prodigious accomplishments spearheading civilization's defence against barbarism. Well enough did he know what was required of the future. The problems ahead were daunting. "We have learned from hard experience", he told his young audience, "that stronger, more efficient, more rigorous world institutions must be created to preserve peace and to forestall the causes of future wars." The main challenge would be, he thought, to devise the form which a "system of world security" might take. That included recognizing and accepting "derogations . . . from national sovereignty for the sake of a larger synthesis". The empires of the future, he said, were "the empires of the mind".[1]

That larger synthesis is what the world has been groping towards ever since. It was captured with eloquence and political courage by Hammarskjöld in the 1960s. It was laid out with eloquence and scientific insight by Ward and Dubos in the 1970s. It was freed from ideological suffocation and brought into the post-Cold War world by Gorbachev in the 1980s. It has underpinned the global conferences of the 1990s. It is, in a phrase, the "planetary interest". It will lead us into the twenty-first century.

The tension between stronger world institutions and national sovereignty is the hallmark of the age of transition through which we now pass. The UN Charter proposes harmonizing the actions of nations for the common ends, but it acknowledges the sovereign equality of nation-states and the sanctity of their domestic jurisdiction at the same time. The synthesis between these two seeming contradictions in the larger interest is the challenge before us, requiring all the creative talent which we can collectively contribute.

When humanity faces a critical juncture in its path, the contradictions it confronts generally prove to be more apparent than real, and largely the product of its own making. I believe this to be the case here. So often do we look back upon historic tensions of the past, and find them to have been irrelevant to the real issues before people of the time, distractions from the true solutions. The number of angels that can dance on the point of a pin no longer preoccupies our waking moments. Nor will the number of sovereign states that can squeeze inside the UN, and pose on the stage with nominally equal powers, mesmerize the decision-makers of the future.

Indeed, the demystification of national sovereignty is already underway. Something has happened on the way to the twenty-first century. Many of the elements of the nation-state system, of hallowed proportion during the hinge of the twentieth, have become less creedal, less assertive, less defining. Even the two-thirds of humankind who defend national sovereignty with such verve do so because they cherish the concept as the symbol of a newly won liberation from past exploitation, and the instrumental saviour from future predation. They proclaim it not in the name of a profligate freedom but of a tempered justice. Once a "system of world security" is devised, one that guarantees true global justice for all peoples, the instrument of national sovereignty will fade in the night. I know this to be true – as foreign minister of one of the more impoverished nations on Earth, I was, at the time, insistent on this point in my country's foreign policy. But it was not an unbridled sovereignty over the rest of humanity we craved; it was, and remains, a joining with them in true brotherhood that delivers our basic human needs – that meets the legitimate national interest of all our countries.

This modern historical conundrum takes form in a certain angst over the notion of world government. There are those who do espouse some form of world government, but they are a small minority. They sit at the other end of the spectrum of public opinion from the ultra-nationalists. They are less numerous today, and they are less dangerous too – no Oklahoma-style bombings occur in their name. Between these two extremes, at the centre of world opinion, is to be found the steady growth of global co-operation which, with the passage of time and the strengthening of trust, will lead to a true global governance – the "new supranational restructuring of the globe", as Eric Hobsbawm has put it.

THE PLANETARY INTEREST AND GLOBAL GOVERNANCE

The notion of global governance, in fact, was the focus of the most recent independent commission in a series over the last two decades which pursued the planetary interest without employing that term.[2] What the commission had in mind was a balance between these extremes, one that is likely to enjoy fruition, barring cataclysm. Global governance, we stressed, is not global government. We are not proposing movement towards world government, we said, for were we to travel in that direction we could find ourselves in an even less democratic world than we have – one more accommodating to power, more hospitable to hegemonic ambition, and more reinforcing of the role of states and governments than the rights of people.[3] The challenge, rather, is to merge the present with the future in such a way that the management of global affairs is responsive to the interests of all people in a sustainable world, that is guided by basic human values and that makes global organization conform to the reality of global diversity. The strongest message we could convey, we felt, is that humanity can agree on a better way to manage human affairs, and give hope to the present and future generations.

The alternative, of course, is unacceptable. As the commission put it, it would be a struggle for primacy – in which each nation-state sees virtue in the advancement of national self-interest, with states and people pitted against each other.[4] In such an environment, there can be no winners.

That alternative, however, will not eventuate. The development of global governance is part of the evolution of human efforts to organize life on the planet. The world is moving on from the designs evolved over centuries past and given new form in the establishment of the United Nations some 50 years ago. We are at a time that demands freshness and innovation in political thinking. We must move forward to a new era of security that responds to law and collective will, and a sense of common responsibility, one that places the security of people and of the planet at the centre.

There is no single model or form of global governance, nor is there a single structure or set of structures. There is no mystical significance to the term. In a sense, global governance has already arrived; but it is imperfect and inadequate to the needs of our time. Global governance is a process, a broad, dynamic, complex process of interactive decision-making that is constantly evolving and responding to changing circumstances. So the option is constantly open for the international community to refine it. And the need exists. There must, henceforth, be an agreed global framework for actions and policies to be carried out at appropriate levels. And a multifaceted strategy for getting there.

The cardinal principle of any future global governance is democratic legitimacy. In the commission's view:

> As at the national level, so in the global neighbourhood: the democratic principle must be ascendant. The need for greater democracy arises out of the close linkage between legitimacy and effectiveness. Institutions that lack legitimacy are seldom effective over the long run. Hence, as the role of international institutions in global governance grows, the need to ensure that they are democratic also increases.[5]

No such legitimacy can occur without a basis of shared ethics and values. The quality of global governance, said the commission, will be determined by several factors. High among them is the broad acceptance of a global ethic to guide actions within the global neighbourhood. Without such an ethic, the frictions and tensions of living in an increasingly intimate world will multiply. Action to improve global governance to cope with contemporary challenges will be greatly helped by a common commitment to a set of core values that can unite people of all cultural and religious backgrounds. Such "global values" must be appropriate to the needs of a crowded and diverse planet. I believe humanity must, for example, uphold the core values of respect for life, liberty, justice and equity, mutual respect, caring and integrity. These values would provide a foundation for transforming a world based on economic exchange and improved communications into a universal moral community in which people are bound together by more than proximity or identity. As Jean-Paul Sartre once observed, "when one day our human kind becomes full grown, it will not define itself as the sum total of the whole world's inhabitants, but as the infinite unity of their mutual needs".[6]

Once that base of global values is secured, nation-states will fundamentally alter their perception of international affairs, and their own national conduct will change. Although governments tend to act as if it is so, the United Nations is not a thing apart from the nation-states or from the peoples in whose name the UN Charter opens. It is made and maintained by its members. It is "us" because its systems, its policies, its practices are those that its member states have ordained. Its decisions are the decisions taken, or declined, by its members. The greatest failings of the UN have been the failings of the nation-states that collectively form the entity. When governments speak of reform of the UN, or improving the management of global affairs more generally, they are really addressing a process of change that must begin with their own national behaviour. It is what goes on in the corridors of capitals more than those of New York that determines our future. National behaviour is a product of national perception of the world, of international co-operation and its relevance to the national interest. That perception informs national decision-making and shapes national policy. It is here, on the threshold of values, that enhancing global security through strengthening the United Nations must begin.

The concept underpinning such a qualitative change in human outlook is a rather stark one – survival. The fact of demonstrable threats to our collective survival, and a species-responsibility for securing it, is new. Perhaps that is why the notion of survival, with its eschatological connotations, tends to invite dismissal by some as hyperbole. In the commission, we saw it differently. Unprecedented increases in human activity and human numbers, we observed, have reached the point where their impacts are impinging on the basic conditions on which life depends.[7] We do not have to be speaking of the apocalypse to concentrate the human mind on "survival". We mean rather the remorseless degradation of the planet, until an irrevocable stage has been reached and passed, after which the fate of humankind will resound, not with a bang but with a whimper. It was not diplomatic excess that prompted the Earth Summit in 1992 to enshrine the precautionary principle into the lexicon of global management. Those who frame our future must face up to the most vital issue of our time – humanity's most clear and present danger, and the prospects of those who follow us – the innocent, unborn generations of the future.

The fundamental concept running through this book – the "vital planetary interest" – captures this notion of survival exceedingly well. Whatever is in the vital planetary interest, it has been contended in earlier chapters, warrants legitimate global power. With the proviso that such legitimacy is based on a proper consent of all peoples of the world, speaking transparently through a global civil society and thereby directing their governments, I agree. The dictate of collective survival will distinguish, in the future, what is in the vital planetary interest, and what legitimate global powers need to be recognized.

Institutional reform at the global level will follow. It is no accident that this is a matter of intense preoccupation around the world at present. The institutional realities reflect the values and beliefs underlying them. As the world changes, the intangibles change ahead of the tangible. As the institutions increasingly reflect the reality of a bygone age, tensions enter. Efforts are made to adapt them to keep pace. The unknown is always the inherent adaptability of the constitutional base that links the intangible to the tangible. If it can be reinterpreted, it survives. If not, it must be amended or replaced.

The framers of the UN Charter knew this better than their successors. They frequently refer in the document to the "present Charter", and they provided, too, for its self-renewal and regeneration. It is open, under the charter, for a general conference to review it upon a two-thirds vote of the General Assembly and any nine members of the Security Council. If such a conference were not held by the 10th General Assembly session, that is to say by 1955, the matter "shall be placed" on the assembly's agenda and would be decided by a simple majority of the assembly and seven members of the council. This has, of course, not occurred, despite the legal obligation obtaining after the first ten years – another example of the nation-states failing to meet their own proclaimed standards through the United Nations.

The reason for such a failure is a reluctance to open the charter to the "floodgates of change". Certainly, stability of norms and institutions in a turbulent world is a necessary thing. But we must be careful to avoid masking self-interest in false virtue and wisdom. Forces for the status quo often rest their argumentation on grounds of the proclaimed broader interest while in reality such reasoning rests on a more sectional narrow interest. Those nation-states that framed the charter and possess positions of relative power and privilege under it are less inclined to wish to see it altered. But the framers knew, even those from the very same nations, that the passage of time would inexorably build a momentum for change. This has occurred and cannot now be resisted. I am not talking here simply about additions to the Security Council. I am talking about a new overview of the whole institutional system of global governance – one that reflects the broader dimensions of human security today, in ways that could not have been conceived by the framers 50 years ago. They knew this too, which is why they entered constitutional scope for its revision. It is left to our contemporary leaders to display the same insight and conviction and act upon that invitation.

LEGITIMATE GLOBAL POWER

In earlier chapters the vital planetary interest is identified as encompassing those issues that threaten the integrity of the planet and the survival of the species. This is, I believe, an adequate taxonomy for the immediate purpose. The three issues identified earlier, strategic security, environmental integrity and sustainability, are indeed the contemporary global imperatives. These three meet the criterion of "survival". They can only be resolved through global solutions that are backed by legitimate global powers. Those, I repeat, are not the powers of a world government – but rather the authority of a strengthened global co-operation.

It was on this understanding that the Commission on Global Governance put forward a number of proposals in 1995, which I believe will remain relevant into the twenty-first century. Let me enumerate the most fundamental ones.

Global strategic security

Despite the end of the Cold War and a number of achievements in arms reductions in recent years, the planet remains threatened by our own hand. As long as some nation-states retain weapons of mass destruction and insist on perceiving them as legitimate instruments of national defence, that threat will remain. The commission saw three areas of reform for the strengthening of global governance in peace and security.

First, the existence of weapons of mass destruction themselves, most specifically nuclear weapons, the last in the category yet to be proscribed. It is imperative that all nations, including the existing nuclear powers, accept the principle of the elimination of nuclear weapons within a prescribed timeframe. As the commission put it, the international community should "reaffirm its commitment to eliminate nuclear and other weapons of mass destruction progressively from all nations, and should initiate a ten-to-fifteen year programme to achieve this goal ... Work towards nuclear disarmament should involve action on ... the initiation of talks among all declared nuclear powers to establish a process to reduce and eventually eliminate all nuclear arsenals".[8]

Secondly, the Security Council itself is in need of reform, as is widely accepted. The commission proposed a reform process in two stages:

(i)   Over the next ten years, a new class of five "standing members", which would retain membership until the second stage of the reform process, would be established. They would be selected by the General Assembly and would comprise two from industrial countries and one each from Africa, Asia, and Latin America. The number of non-permanent members should be raised from ten to thirteen, and the number of votes required for a decision of the Council raised from nine to fourteen. The veto is now an unacceptable anachronism and must be phased out. To facilitate this, the permanent members should enter into a concordat agreeing to forego its use save in circumstances they consider to be of an exceptional and overriding nature.

(ii) The second stage should be a review of the membership of the Council, including these arrangements, around 2005. The veto would be phased out; the position of the permanent members would then also be reviewed, and account taken of new circumstances – including the growing strength of regional bodies.[9]

Thirdly, the principle of humanitarian intervention needs to be more formally recognized – preserving the rights and interests of the international community in situations within individual states in which the security of a whole people is extensively endangered. The commission proposed a charter amendment to permit such intervention but restricting it to cases which, in the judgement of a reformed Security Council, constitute a violation of the security of people so extreme that it requires an international response on humanitarian grounds.[10]

Global environmental integrity

The most direct challenge to global governance in the environmental field, the commission observed, is that presented by the "tragedy of the commons" – the overuse of common environmental assets because of the absence of an effective system of co-operative management. The pollution of the global atmosphere and the depletion of ocean fisheries, just as with the destruction of local common grazing land, stem from inadequacies of governance when there are neither secure property rights nor collective responsibilities to govern a shared resource.

That collective responsibility has already been embodied in the concept of the "common heritage of humankind", which found early expression in the Law of the Sea Convention and the Moon Treaty. It will increasingly affect the manner in which the international community determines its stewardship of Earth in the future. The International Court of Justice has already determined that in cases of violation of certain absolutely basic duties, obligations *erga omnes*, one nation-state may assert the right to represent the interests of the international community, without the need to prove damage to its own nationals or its national interest as traditionally perceived. Such obligations by their very nature are, the court asserted, the concern of all states. In view of the rights involved, all states can be held to have a legal interest in their protection. The court identified such obligations: the avoidance of aggression, genocide, slavery and racial discrimination.

It is the view of a number of eminent jurists that, similarly, certain standards of environmental conservation may come to be regarded as norms binding *erga omnes*.[11] New juridical views of property law and property rights are developing as the degradation of the global commons continues to accelerate through the use of private or nationally owned resources. As one jurist puts it, sovereignty signals no longer a simple legal basis for exclusion, but has become the legal basis for inclusion, or of a commitment to co-operate for the good of the international community at large. Sovereign rights are, in fact, shared powers, shared between the holder of the power and the community of states, in which regard for the interests of other states and of all states is the essence.[12] This notion, of course, is captured in the second principle of the Rio Declaration, that states have the sovereign right to exploit their resources but also the responsibility to avoid damage to the environment beyond their national jurisdiction.

How that right is to be exercised and that responsibility enforced is of critical moment. A consensus is gathering that an institution with greater authority is required on global environmental issues. The remarkable meeting of heads of government at The Hague in 1989, when the full dimensions of ozone depletion and climate change were beginning to be realized within the political establishment, was one of the first and most far-reaching expressions of such concern. Signed by 24 heads of government, the declaration entered a true statement of vision for the future. Action to protect the world's climate, it said, is "vital, urgent and global". The leaders called for "the development of new principles of international law including new and more effective decision-making and enforcement mechanisms". A new institutional authority needed to be established within the UN framework, empowered with "such decision-making procedures as may be effective even if, on occasion, unanimous agreement has not been reached".[13]

In the commission's view the main problem is the lack of any consistent approach and oversight of the global commons. It believed that one body should exercise overall responsibility, acting on behalf of all nation-states. The commission proposed a way in which this could be achieved. The Trusteeship Council, which has effectively completed its job of administering former colonial territories, should be given a new mandate over the global commons in the context of concern for the security of the planet.[14]

Global sustainability

What model of decision-making, the commission asked, should an emerging system of global economic governance adopt? At present, the international community has no satisfactory way of considering global economic problems and their link to social, environmental and security issues. The Group of Seven is the nearest the world comes to having an apex body concerned with the global economy. That is palpably inadequate, simply on grounds of basic equity. The G-7 represents 12% of humankind – any such body purporting to decide on behalf of the world reveals a total deficit in global legitimacy. It is the UN system working with the Bretton Woods bodies which, with all its flaws, can claim a better mandate. Yet for their part, the Bretton Woods institutions have historically shunned any close operational relationship with the United Nations. In the commission's view, the time is overdue for the creation of a global forum that can provide leadership in economic, social and environmental fields. Such a body would need to be more broadly based than the G-7 or Bretton Woods bodies, and more effective than the UN's Economic and Social Council.

We therefore proposed the establishment of an Economic Security Council, in lieu of the present ECOSOC. The new council would meet at high political level, though it would have deliberative functions only. Its main tasks would be multifaceted: to assess the overall state of the world economy and the interaction between major policy areas; to provide a long-term strategic policy framework in order to promote stable, balanced and sustainable development; and to secure consistency between the policy goals of the major international organizations, particularly the Bretton Woods institutions and the World Trade Organization (WTO).[15] While not having the authority to make binding decisions, the council would gain influence through competence and relevance, and acquire the standing in relation to global economic matters that the Security Council has in peace and security matters.

These three issues, then, strategic security, global environment and sustainability, all lay claim to legitimate global powers in the "vital planetary interest". New or reformed authoritative bodies are needed to reflect these new realities. But what does this mean for the extent of enforcement power at the global level? How are the "architects of the future" to provide convincing reassurance to those justifiably concerned at the implications such global authority might have for democracy and fundamental freedoms?

The question is a valid one, but it can be validly turned around. How, obversely, might those architects reassure those concerned over the implications for a democratic world if legitimate powers reflecting an input from all peoples are not in place, leaving comparable powers, by default, in the hands of a small group of powerful nation-states? Power will be exercised at the global level in the twenty-first century. That much must be recognized as a given. What is unknown is the degree of global legitimacy that will have been built to sanction it. As the president of the 1997 UN General Assembly put it recently, the UN will have to transform itself from an organization serving the interests of states to an organization serving the interests of people living in an interdependent and global society.[16]

Of the three issues identified, far-reaching enforcement power is already enshrined in the present UN Charter in one area – the maintenance of peace and security. The decision of the Security Council that the further proliferation of weapons of mass destruction constitutes a threat to the peace has accorded, if not arrogated, enforcement power to that body to deprive in the 1990s one nation-state, Iraq, of all weapons of mass destruction. It will not happen immediately, but it will happen, that all nation-states surrender that right. When that occurs, the onus will be upon the same body to regulate the conduct of all its members, in the name of the same freedom, freedom from all weapons of mass destruction. It will be, one day, a legitimate power of the Security Council to enforce the absence of weapons of mass destruction from the national arsenals of every nation-state, as prescribed in the Non-Proliferation Treaty.

The Declaration of The Hague made it clear that a new body for global environmental matters should have binding authority and enforcement power. I agree. This does not, of course, mean military action when a state's environmental conduct violates a global norm. But it does mean enforcement through other means. Economic incentives and disincentives, such as those incorporated in the new World Trade Organization, together with the overwhelming opprobrium of world opinion, should suffice to turn around any country whose polluting actions will harm the national interests of all.

Sustainability, however, is a more complex issue and the question of power less clear. There can, in fact, be no enforcement power over sustainable development. The authority of proscription accorded to any body can apply only to actions violating a norm, not to the omission of prescribed, lawful actions. That is why we envisaged purely deliberative powers for the new Economic Security Council. But that does not necessarily render it less effective as a result. What is required in this area is co-operation and co-ordination, not enforcement. Whether excessive consumption patterns might be seen as violating a global norm is probably for the future to decide.

These varying levels of global power – enforcement, influence and co-operation – will all prove to be legitimate in the face of the different global problems humanity will increasingly face in the early twenty-first century.

Underpinning these institutional and juridical reforms, two factors must be addressed for legitimate global power to be realized in the future. The emerging global civil society must be empowered, and make a proper input into global deliberations and decision-making. And nation-states must abide by the rule of law.

To strengthen the civil society at the global level, the commission proposed two innovations. There should be a new "right of petition" for non-state actors to bring situations massively endangering the security of people within states to the attention of the Security Council. This would, in turn, require the formation of a Council of Petitions – a high-level panel of five to seven persons, independent of governments, to entertain petitions. Its recommendations would go as appropriate to the secretary-general or the General Assembly, and allow for action under the UN Charter.[17]

Secondly, we proposed an annual Forum of Civil Society consisting of representatives of organizations to be accredited to the General Assembly as "civil society organizations". The forum should be convened in the General Assembly Hall sometime before the annual session of the assembly. International civil society should itself be involved in determining the character and functions of the forum.[18]

To strengthen the rule of law at the global level, a number of goals were envisaged. An international criminal court had to be established quickly with independent prosecutors of the highest calibre and experience. Secondly, a number of reform measures to strengthen the International Court are easily envisaged. Member states of the UN which have not already done so must forthwith accept the compulsory jurisdiction of the court. The chamber procedure of that court should be modified to enhance its appeal to states and to avoid damage to the court's integrity. Judges should be appointed for one ten-year term only. The UN secretary-general should have the right to refer the legal aspects of international issues to the court for advice, particularly in the early stages of emerging disputes. The Security Council should appoint a distinguished legal person to provide advice at all relevant stages on the international legal aspects of issues before it. It should also make greater use of the court as a source of advisory opinions, to avoid being itself the judge of international law in particular cases. Failing voluntary compliance, Security Council enforcement of court decisions and other international legal obligations should be pursued under Article 94 of the charter.[19]

These were our proposals for institutional reform. Yet whatever the extent of reform undertaken, no effective global governance will develop without a proper funding base. Notwithstanding an accurate perception of the threat, an accurate appreciation of the planetary interest, an agreed global objective and strategy to meet it, and prescribed national policies to implement it, nothing will be achieved if the resources for implementation are lacking. At the global institutional level, the world is basically bankrupt.

The estimated total worldwide expenditure through the UN system in 1992 as a whole was $10.5 billion. That is one two-thousandth of the world's gross domestic product (GDP). Those worried about being taken over by world government need have no fear. The true worry is that, in absence of greater global public expenditure, there will be no habitable world for humans to "govern". Relative to other areas of public expenditure, the funding of the UN is abysmally insignificant. Consider a few comparisons. The budget of the UN is less than the money spent in the United States each year on cut flowers. The amount spent each year on alcohol in Britain, by 1% of the global population, is three and a half times as great as that spent on the UN system. The UN's peacekeeping budget is less than the combined budgets of New York City's Fire and Police Departments. We are happy to drink and send one another flowers but not collectively save the world from the abyss. We risk conflagration, not at the municipal level, but at the planetary level.

Figure 12.1   The UN Security Council at its historic summit meeting in January 1992. The council decided that day that the proliferation of weapons of mass destruction constitutes a threat to the peace. "One day", says Sir Shridath Ramphal, "it will be a legitimate power of the Security Council to enforce the absence of weapons of mass destruction from the national arsenal of every nation-state, as prescribed in the Non-Proliferation Treaty." (Courtesy UN Photo)

The complexities of global interdependence may demand, in the words of one recent study, a "strategic quantum leap", including the recognition that the time may have come for global activities to be financed not by governments alone.[20] Some other global funding mechanism is now necessary. Not only will this release new funds but it will also make programmes to implement agreed global policies less vulnerable to the vagaries of national budgetary provision. Governments are not lining up to support any proposal of this nature. But its time will come.

One of the main problems at present in global financing is the lack of a global needs assessment and a priority list. At present, no comprehensive study exists of the world's overall financial needs. There is no global treasurer with facts and policies readily to hand. The UN secretary-general, it has been suggested, should compile a detailed inventory of internationally agreed programmes and related cost estimates. Until that inventory is compiled, governments should refrain from adopting new programmes in international fora entailing additional financial commitments unless existing ones can be fulfilled.

It will be a complex undertaking. The estimated annual cost of global sustainable development, for example, as estimated in *Agenda 21*, is some $600 billion, of which $125 billion is to come through assistance from the North to the South. The annual global housing programme is some $15 billion, the AIDS prevention and treatment programme $7 billion, the population planning programme $5 billion, the nuclear weapon dismantling programme, and associated clean-up and reactor retrofitting activities, some $5 billion.

Where is this money to come from? Current international development assistance totals $50 billion, only 0.25% of the North's combined GNP, about one-third the target of 0.7% which those countries set for themselves in 1970.[21] What is required is innovative thinking on new sources of funding. There are, in fact, a number of "global taxation" proposals that have been put forward: charges on foreign currency transactions, government securities and corporate bonds; or fees for the use of the global commons such as air travel, ocean maritime transport, geostationary satellite parking, Antarctic resources, and the electromagnetic spectrum; or a tax on arms transfers. One study has shown that a minuscule charge of 0.1% on foreign currency transactions, government security trading in the North, OTC interest-rate swaps and Eurobond turnovers, could raise some $120 billion.[22] It is clear that something along these lines must be adopted in the future.

Much is in the perception of the notion of "global taxation". It should be seen, not as an extra source of financial burden, but as an alternative means of funding a global imperative, through normal activities rather than through governmental channels.[23] A global convention has been proposed to create a new international authority that would administer and apportion the funds raised through international generating instruments. The funds would be raised nationally and remitted to an international repository, from which the new international authority would authorize disbursements. Decision-making would involve four groups of parties: governments; the private and banking sectors; international organizations and financing institutions; and representatives of the civil society including parliamentarians, NGOs and trade unions.[24]

CONCLUSION

The Report of the Commission on Global Governance was issued in 1995, the 50th anniversary of the United Nations. We recommended that the General Assembly hold a world conference and that decisions taken at the conference take effect by 2000. We urged governments to set in motion a process of change that can give hope to people everywhere, and especially to the young.[25]

Following its release, a group of 16 governments did in fact take up the commission's report before the General Assembly. The Group of Sixteen Heads of State and Government, as it has come to be known, has made several appeals before the international community and been active at the United Nations in galvanizing support for reforms.

The accumulating pressure of global opinion, spawned from the commission's and other proposals and the views of many member states, is having the needed effect. In March 1997, UNGA President Razali Ismail put forward a paper on Security Council reform with proposals closely reflecting those of the commission. The proposals, he said, were based on "the need to enhance the representativeness, the credibility, the legitimacy and authority of the Security Council". A "qualitative change" was needed in all its aspects. The proposal for new membership was broadly similar to the commission's. It was recommended that new permanent members not possess the veto, and current permanent members were urged to limit its use to Chapter VII of the UN Charter. Such a linkage, it was noted, would be a first concrete step towards making the veto on other matters "progressively and politically untenable". The functions of permanent membership had to begin to evolve so that it becomes decoupled from, or no longer equated with, the possession of veto power.

Subsequently, in July 1997, Secretary-General Kofi Annan presented to a Special Session of the General Assembly the long-awaited "reform package". Administrative reform proposals include a senior management group, a strategic planning unit, four executive committees and a deputy secretary-general. Recommendations for streamlining the UN system include a no-growth budget, elimination of 1,000 posts, administrative cost cutting of 30% and the establishment of a revolving credit fund. Two broader proposals, however, were of particular interest since they mirror the commission's report. First, the Trusteeship Council, said the secretary-general, should be "reconstituted as the forum through which member states exercise their collective trusteeship for the integrity of the global environment and common areas such as the oceans, atmosphere and outer space". Freed of its original responsibilities now, the council should be given "the mandate of exercising trusteeship over the global commons". Secondly, the General Assembly should, in the year 2000, be convened as a special Millennium Assembly with a summit for heads of government to develop a common vision for the UN in the twenty-first century.

I hope that there will be strong support from governments for the secretary-general's suggestions. Heads of government must respond to the challenge. For the experience of the Commission on Global Governance was that the peoples of the world are ready for fundamental change of this kind, and that they will, with the passing of time, demand it from their governments. I believe such a day is closer than some governments realize. And it will spell the beginning of true change that will raise the prospects for a safer and saner planet than that which we have known in our time. It is a question of attitude – a question of mind – the "empire of the mind".

NOTES

1. Quoted in S. Ramphal, *Our country, the planet* (Washington, DC: Island Press, 1992), 242.
2. *Our global neighbourhood.* Preceding commissions with their publications were *North–South: a programme for survival*, Independent Commission on International Development Issues (known as the Brandt Commission) (London: Pan, 1980); *Common security: a blueprint for survival*, Independent Commission on Disarmament and Security Issues (Palme Commission) (Simon & Schuster, New York; 1982); *Our common future*, World Commission on Environment and Development (Brundtland Commission) (Oxford: Oxford University Press, 1987); and *The challenge to the South*, South Commission (Oxford: Oxford University Press, 1990). As a member of each, I was able to trace the thread of thinking that was common to them, and which reached culmination in *Our global neighbourhood*.
3. *Our global neighbourhood*, xvi.
4. Ibid., 356.
5. Ibid., 66.
6. Jean-Paul Sartre's preface to *The wretched of the Earth* by Franz Fanon, in S. Ramphal, "Global governance: the second global security lecture", Cambridge University, 5 June 1995, 1.
7. *Our global neighbourhood*, 82.
8. Ibid., 340–1.
9. Ibid., 344–5.
10. Ibid., 339.
11. Professors Ian Brownlie and Kevin Gray, quoted in K. Gray, "The ambivalence of property" in G. Prins (ed.), *Threats without enemies: facing environmental insecurity* (London: Earthscan, 1993), 151.
12. Günter Handl, in P.J. Allott, "Power sharing in the law of the sea", *American Journal of International Law* 77, 1983, 1, 27 (quoted in Gray, op. cit., 169).
13. Quoted in J.J. Mathews, *Preserving the global environment* (New York: W.W. Norton, 1991), 18.
14. *Our global neigbourhood*, 345.
15. Ibid., 342.
16. Razali Ismail, "The United Nations in the twenty-first century: prospects for reform", Erskine Childers Memorial Lecture, London, 30 June 1997.
17. *Our global neighbourhood*, 339, 345–6.
18. Ibid., 345.
19. Ibid., 347–8.
20. D. Najman & H. d'Orville, *Towards a new multilateralism: funding global priorities* (Paris: Independent Commission on Population and Quality of Life, 1995), 18.
21. UN General Assembly resolution 2626 (XXV), 24 October 1970, para. 2.
22. Najman & d'Orville, *Towards a new multilateralism*, 4, 43.

23.   As the Najman & d'Orville study puts it,

> efforts to raise funds through international instruments and modalities should principally not be motivated by taxing sin or vice or by pursuing general economic policy goals. Rather, they should be based on a different rationale: as a corollary to the diminishing ability of nation-states to exercise control and to solve a growing number of problems unilaterally in globalised markets and an ever more interdependent world, the revenue for financing internationally-agreed objectives and programmes should be raised through international means by tapping activities in the global markets (ibid., 1).

24.   Ibid., 8.
25.   *Our global neighbourhood*, 352.

CHAPTER THIRTEEN

Global and regional powers: Europe's regional interest

Emma Bonino

> "The first, indispensable principle of [the European Coal and Steel Community] is the renunciation of national sovereignty in a limited but decisive field."
>
> Jean Monnet

My contribution to this book will be political, not academic. This is no snub to those scholars of world affairs whose work I use as often as I can in carrying out my political responsibilities. Indeed, I wish my attitude were more common among my fellow office-holders. One of the tragedies of our time is the lack of communication between experts and decision-makers. So my choice of approach is, rather, an act of humility. I have been involved in politics ever since becoming a young adult, but I have never been an academic. Politics is the only terrain on which I can step with some confidence in the hope of being useful to my fellow citizens at home and around the planet.

The first political judgement I have to offer is an element of caution. The authors, and most of the readers, of this book, I expect, probably share the view offered in the preface, namely that "certain problems of a global nature are beyond the capacity of any country, no matter how large and powerful, to solve alone". But the public at large, and certainly most of their leaders, are far from this realization. Our decision-makers are still elected, if they are elected at all, on the basis of national concerns. International, not to mention planetary, issues play scant role in most political contests. As the saying goes, "elections are won or lost at home". Our first priority, therefore, at both an intellectual and a political level, should be how to overcome this state of affairs. Since planetary problems call, in my opinion, for planetary constituencies, we should try to see how we can develop these constituencies.

The idea developed in this chapter is that regional groupings can go some way in this respect. First, they can provide the initial impulse to move us from the level that is the least adequate to tackle our planetary challenges, that is, the nation-state. Secondly, they can guarantee a better and more balanced representation of the interests shared by the world population than the present system based on nation-states. The ongoing process of European integration through the European Community/European Union can be critically yet positively reviewed in this light as a useful model for other regions to follow.

In the parlance of current international relations, the regional dimension sounds like the natural intermediate level between what is global or "planetary" and what is national. Yet the fact that the nation-state remains the basic unit of account is *per se* implied by the term international relations.

Of these three dimensions, the regional one seems the most impervious to immediate comprehension. Almost none of the terms commonly used to define a given region implies definite boundaries or a discrete number of countries. What exactly is the Asia-Pacific region? Or the Middle East? Even Europe is a case in point: which "Europe" are we talking about? A security zone that encompasses North America and the former Soviet Union as defined by the OSCE? A cultural entity, that then regroups most of the above plus most of whatever we mean by the Middle East? A geographical concept, then, stretching "from the Atlantic to the Urals"? Or, as is the case in this chapter, the Europe of 15 – the European Union?

THE PLANETARY INTEREST AND THE REGIONAL INTEREST

In a world of nation-states, the basic difference between national and planetary interests on the one hand, and regional interests on the other, is that with the latter the definition of the interests comes first. It is they, a set of interests shared by a certain number of nations lying more or less in geographical proximity, that define a region.[1]

Which interests, then, define the EU as a region?

The first and foremost, especially when seen in an historical perspective, is peace. In the first half of the twentieth century, the continent had experienced two devastating wars. Responsible statesmen felt, correctly, that peace was an absolute precondition for the reconstruction and development of their nations. One way to achieve peace, it was judged, was to pool the resources that were then at the roots of the industrialized economies. Thus, in 1951 the European Coal and Steel Community (ECSC) and, six years later, Euratom and the European Economic Community (EEC) were created. The latter established a customs union and also the basis for a common trade policy. Although the relevant treaties remained well within the boundaries of the economic sphere, those responsible statesmen recalled above saw more in them than mere economic co-operation. As Jean Monnet, one of the true statesmen of the century put it: "the first, indispensable principle of (the European Coal and Steel Community) is the renunciation of national sovereignty in a limited but decisive field". And German Chancellor Konrad Adenauer declared to the *Bundestag* in June 1950 that "the importance of the project is mainly political, not economic".

As the twentieth century comes to a close, the least that can be said is that the primary objective, the very basic interest, of peace among the nations which belong to the community has been achieved. Back in 1985, another of Europe's founding fathers, Altiero Spinelli, observed that "for centuries, neighbouring countries saw each other as potential enemies against whom it was necessary to keep up the guard and be ready to fight. Now, these neighbours are perceived as friendly nations which share a common destiny". But the tension between a Europe as an ever-growing area of free trade and economic co-operation on the one hand, and a Europe as a political entity, the "United States of Europe", on the other, is still with us. This author, this politician, stands firmly in the latter camp.

With all its shortcomings, and taking into account that this process of European integration and enlargement is still open-ended, the fact remains that a number of nation-states in Europe have come peacefully to recognize that some problems are by their nature transnational and cannot effectively be tackled at the national level. These go beyond the economic domain to include some which are closer to the focus of this book – energy, the environment and even some global security problems. Despite being still largely a matter of intergovernmental co-operation, it is nonetheless a success that the European Union is now an actor in its own right in several global fora that attempt to address some "vital" planetary interests. This has been the case, for example, in 1995 with the renewal of the nuclear Non-Proliferation Treaty; and also with the Kyoto conference on global warming, where the EU tabled a proposal that called for a reduction of 15% of greenhouse emissions by 2010.

It is also and increasingly the case with a host of normative planetary interests, defined in Chapter 1 as the universal improvement in the human condition in terms of basic human needs and fundamental human rights. The European Union (the community plus its member states) is nowadays the world's leading donor of both development and humanitarian aid – in the latter case providing some two-thirds of the global total. The EU speaks with one voice at the UN Committee on Human Rights. And finally, human rights clauses are now an integral part of the many partnership and co-operation agreements that link the European Union with third countries, thus adding an important political touch to its external relations, initially conceived mainly in commercial terms. Again, I do not want to paint too rosy a picture; oftentimes the 15 fail to define a common approach *vis-à-vis* some specific country where human rights abuses take place, from the Democratic Republic of Congo to China. But at least they systematically try through constant consultation to arrive at a common stance.

Even a critic of European integration, one who is inclined to point the finger at what remains to be done rather than at what has been done so far, has nonetheless to recognize that this is a considerable simplification of world affairs. The assertion may be proven *a contrario*: try to imagine what the world would be like today had the confederates won the American Civil War.

Fortunately, other parts of the world are also engaged in a similar process of region-building. It is significant how in most of these cases it all started on the basis of the shared perception of one or more "interests", with the attendant tendency for those to spill over into others. Thus, the Association of South East Asian Nations (ASEAN) was borne mainly out of security concerns, whereas in Latin America the creation of Mercosur reflects mainly trade and competition concerns, much like the EC at its origins.

In sum, the world stands to gain much by as widespread a process as possible of regionalization, meaning the peaceful and consensual coming together of nation-states in different areas of the world by means of institution-building around a set of shared interests and values. Planetary interests would be more easily identifiable by a limited number of regions having already undergone the process of identifying their own regional interests, and planetary problems would be more effectively tackled by a few regions than by some 200 nation-states. By the same token, turning the planetary body *par excellence*, the United Nations, into the "United Regions" would immensely simplify its decision-making process and also eliminate many thorny problems of fair representation, beginning with the composition of the Security Council.

Unfortunately, the prevailing tendency thus far pulls in exactly the opposite direction, despite being sold in the name of, in fact, regionalization. Creating permanent seats for nation-states lying in regions currently not covered by the permanent five (Britain, China, France, Russia and the United States) does not move the UN one inch from its state-centred nature. Moreover, this approach is proving, if anything, more divisive than coalescent on the regions concerned for the simple reason that there is, in any given region, inevitably more than one nation-state having legitimate claims on the title of regional leader. Also unfortunate is the European attitude on this matter: as one proposal for the UN Security Council reform has it, a permanent seat would be bestowed on Germany. This proposal seems to enjoy the support of the majority of EU member states, despite the fact that its acceptance would actually increase the number of European nations with a permanent seat and in a sense further nationalize the EU representation at the United Nations. A far more sensible approach for the EU would indeed be to renounce the individual states' seats it now has in favour of one and only one EU seat in the council. One can clearly touch here the limits of the process of European integration so far.

The scheme I have been advocating here clearly leaves out the problem of a democratic representation of the planetary interests – a problem I raised earlier by saying that planetary problems call for planetary constituencies. We would instead have several regional constituencies where, hopefully, politicians would strive to get elected on regional platforms – akin to what happens, or should be happening, with the European Parliament.[2] But again, following the EU model of institution-building around shared interests, some thought could be given to the creation of specific institutions combining a dedicated executive body akin to the European Commission, balanced by a body of regional governments and by a directly elected assembly, charged in fact with the administration of our "planetary interests" as defined in this book. The more politicians are *not* elected on a national platform, the more the world population becomes accustomed to the idea that a host of problems cannot be effectively solved at the national level. Regional and planetary parliaments would, if nothing else, serve this purpose. I note, *en passant*, that I have always been disturbed less by the lack of democracy of the UN Security Council, with its two-tier structure of permanent members with veto power and non-permanent members, than by the democratic deficit of the General Assembly where the executive branches of governments sit, including unelected governments, rather than a country's directly elected representatives – as the term "assembly" would lead one to expect.

LEGITIMATE GLOBAL POWER AND EUROPE

The relationship between regional and global power remains in the 1990s indeterminate, not least because the eventual outcome of "Europe's game" is still open. Despite its shortcomings, the 1992 Treaty of Maastricht did create the European Union. It did this by adding two other pillars – intergovernmental co-operation on foreign and security matters, as well as on internal and judicial affairs – to the earlier treaties. The reforms agreed in Amsterdam in June 1997 pushed this process a few

Figure 13.1   Sky-diving over Europe. "The European Union", says Emma Bonino, "is now an actor in its own right in several global fora that attempt to address some vital planetary interests." Examples are nuclear non-proliferation and climate change. "It seems to me that the UN and the EU, with all their conspicuous imperfections, are there to testify to a clear quest for broader jurisdiction." (Courtesy EC Audio-Visual Library)

steps further along the road to political union, albeit too few in my own view. But the EU can, nonetheless, be defined as a region in which three factors obtain:

- a sharp perception of the commonality of some interests, to the point of largely surrendering national sovereignty on them to the community's institutions (trade, competition, agriculture, and soon monetary policy);
- a less sharp perception of some others, in which sovereignty is shared between the community's institutions and member states (transport, culture, consumer protection, industry, the environment and development co-operation); and
- a rather dim perception of the commonality of yet other interests, largely left in the hands of member states' governments with some provisions for loose co-operation (the second and third pillars in the EU's treaty).

Yet, so defined, the European Union is undergoing a process of enlargement. Ten Central and Eastern European countries (Estonia, Latvia, Lithuania, Poland, the Czech Republic, Hungary, Slovakia, Slovenia, Romania and Bulgaria) plus Cyprus are candidate members.[3] According to the commission, six of these have a good prospect of joining the union early in the twenty-first century. But the final word on when and with which countries to proceed with enlargement negotiations rests with the council, that is, the governments of the current members of the EU. So, the union is indeed enlarging but without a sufficient parallel deepening of its political identity. Nation-states in Europe, as elsewhere, remain reluctant to transfer their key sovereignty to a larger jurisdiction.

One notable exception is the proposed Economic and Monetary Union, with the *de facto* loss of national autonomy in monetary matters and the sharing of one currency, the Euro. But this will not apply to new members for many years to come. As things stand, whichever country joins the union is not asked to surrender any of its key prerogatives as a nation-state: printing money, possessing armed forces and one's own diplomatic service, not to mention the judicial system. It will, moreover, keep a veto power on any substantial decision it deems inimical to its national interests. EU trade and competition rules to which new and old members must conform are basically in the best interest of whichever state is keen to give its economy a chance to compete globally. And newcomers are granted not only financial support but also transitional periods before fully adhering to those rules and obligations. It is no wonder that everybody wants to join.

Thus there is surfacing today a rather weird debate on where Europe stops, on what are the boundaries of Europe – which leads us once again to our original question of how to define a given region. I use the term "weird" advisedly because there are several countries in Europe that may become candidates for membership of the union and once they have satisfied the basic criteria for admission (democracy and human rights, the existence of market rules), there are no other grounds on which the door may be closed. In other words I find inadmissible, and slightly tainted with racism, any reasoning based on culture and/or religion. By the same token, and to offer specific examples, it is unacceptable to say, as some do, that Russia and Turkey should be excluded from the EU not only on cultural and religious grounds but also because of their sheer size in terms of population and geography – the latter in both cases overlapping with Asia.

Ideally, the burden of proof should be placed on the applicants' shoulders. If joining the union entailed not only the right to a veto power and a package of benefits with relatively few obligations outside the trade and competition fields, but also the renunciation of substantial elements of national sovereignty, then capitals such as Moscow and Ankara would think twice before applying to join.

The principle of having several democratic institutions at different levels – of having more than one polis from the local or sub-national to the transnational and global dealing with different questions of societal life – is in fact explicitly mentioned in the Maastricht Treaty on the European Union under the term "subsidiarity". Article 3.b of the treaty reads:

> The Community shall act within the limits of the powers conferred upon it by this Treaty and of the objectives assigned to it herein. In areas which do not fall within its exclusive competence, the Community shall take action, in accordance with the principle of subsidiarity, only if and in so far as the objectives of the proposed action cannot be sufficiently achieved by the Member States and can therefore, by reason of the scale or effects of the proposed action, be better achieved by the Community.

Albeit conceived in the spirit of preserving as much power as possible to local and national institutions, the principle of subsidiarity cuts both ways, since it recognizes that some objectives cannot be "sufficiently achieved" by the nation-state. It deserves, therefore, wider, more global application. This is, in essence, the case for legitimate global power in the twenty-first century, and it can be found, by extension, in this forward-looking regional instrument.

CONCLUSION

The staunchly realist scholar of international affairs would certainly see the approach put forward in this chapter as simply utopian. But, still with respect, the staunchly realist scholar does not fight in the trenches for a normative vision of a better world. Much depends on how one reads contemporary world events: it seems to me that the UN and the EU, with all their conspicuous imperfections, testify to a clear quest for broader jurisdictions. The much-touted globalization of the world economy works in the same direction. Even in the most impervious areas, such as justice, things are changing fast, such as the creation of the International Criminal Court, a body that springs out of the recognition that crimes against humanity call for humanity-wide jurisdiction.

In the end, the slowest wagons in this march toward globalization appear, ironically, to be political parties – precisely those organizations whose stated goal is to mediate between citizens and their democratic institutions. They still insist on being firmly anchored to their local and national constituencies and are fast becoming more an obstacle than an engine of change. As always, though, there is one exception, the Radical Party, of which I was privileged to be a leader. "Radical" means here "reform" in English, as in the reform movement of nineteenth-century Britain. In 1989, that party, reflecting the vision of a post-Cold War world and the advent of the twenty-first century, decided to change its name to the Transnational Radical Party, shift all its activities to a transnational level and cease to present its own lists in national elections. Alone among political parties, it truly reflects the planetary interest. Others may catch a glimpse, but this one embodies the vision in its make-up, in its very nature.

If there is anything I find myself proud of in my political life, it is this.

NOTES

1. Nations too are, of course, borne out of a set of interests shared by a given population. But the 200 or so of them that already exist represent an unambiguous unit of analysis: defining their interests is of relative importance, and all that is needed is to take for granted that nations promote their own interests. In contrast, the concept of planet Earth is self-explanatory and so are its vital interests, i.e., its survival.
2. In reality, whatever legislative power the European Parliament has is shared with the European Commission and the council, i.e., member states' governments. However imperfect, it is nevertheless, and to the best of my knowledge, the only directly elected regional assembly in the world today.
3. Malta and Turkey should also be included in this category. The former, though, has unilaterally suspended its application, while the latter raises a host of specific problems, primarily its treatment of minorities and human rights policy, that make its accession unlikely in the medium term.

CHAPTER FOURTEEN

Global and national powers: Britain's national interest

Michael Marshall

> "I emphasize[d] the role that parliamentarians must play, among other players on the international scene. For you are the vital channels for public opinion . . . we must all work to give our national institutions and our international organizations still greater legitimacy and to make them still more democratic."
>
> Boutros Boutros Ghali, UN Secretary-General, 1995

I am pleased to have the opportunity to contribute a view on global and national powers, and the British national interest. The principal theme of this book, the planetary interest, and its relationship to the national interest of nation-states, adumbrates the issue of power and thus the relationship between global and national power. The issue is complex and difficult, and not without national sensitivities. But it is important that it be addressed.

One of the basic premises of this book, as I take it, is that global enforcement power is justified and must be seen as legitimate when the "vital planetary interest" is at stake. I am prepared to give this notion serious consideration. Whether such an idea is accepted early in the twenty-first century or later, its time will no doubt come. But what might this mean for the United Kingdom, and what effect might it have on the relationship between the planetary interest and the British national interest?

THE PLANETARY INTEREST AND THE NATIONAL INTEREST

As a parliamentarian serving in the House of Commons for almost a quarter of a century until 1997, I have been required on countless occasions to have regard for the British national interest. Politicians rarely employ theoretical terminology in the cut and thrust of debate, whether in the chamber or on the hustings. We are expected to be practical people who can cut to the quick and offer solutions without delay or fanfare. But the conceptual perceptions and distinctions exist nonetheless, and in a world that is changing so rapidly and uncertainly, the task of grasping the national interest of one's country and assessing it against a higher notion of the interests of humanity and the planet is increasingly before us. In that respect the concept of the "legitimate national interest" holds promise, as I shall seek to show.

My own country was among the earliest to embrace the concept of the national interest. In the sixteenth century, England began using the term as a replacement to the "will of the prince" and an alternative to the "divine reason of the Pope". There were no think-tanks as such in Elizabethan times, but Raleigh with his bowls and the messenger rushing with word of the approaching Armada had no need of such intellectual support to know what to do. The protection of a people who by then saw themselves as one was the first national interest, and it came instinctively to the heart first, and only later to the mind. Today, even with the changing relationships between the four home unions, Britain can look to Spain and other European states as partners in regional co-operation. Whatever the angst in my country over the pace and direction of Europe and however heated the argumentation over the "Euro" currency and diminishing sovereignty, setting forth with sail and canon is no longer the preferred option for finishing the debate. So that much is progress, and it will not stop there.

Yet even as Europe integrates, the national interest remains the criterion for judgement of the direction and pace of the process. It was Prime Minister Blair, upon returning from the Amsterdam summit, who proclaimed that his first principal objective was to maintain "vital British interests" as Europe expanded.[1] In an age of rapid change, the same applies at the global level.

What is the British national interest on the eve of the third millennium? Over half a century ago, it was the clear-eyed and rock-hard conviction of the need to defend the beaches against tyranny and aggression – a national interest that was, perhaps ironically, as close to a prototype planetary interest as one could expect in the nation-state era. But the nation, and the world, have moved on, beyond the Churchillian strength and eloquence of a single-minded need, and the political environment is more complex in defining and pursuing the legitimate national interest.

The new British government seems mindful of the fundamental nature of this change and the pace at which it is proceeding. A recent mission statement formally asserts that its foreign policy is "to promote the national interests of the United Kingdom and to contribute to a strong world community". No incompatibility perceived there. The statement identifies four "benefits" to be secured for Britain through a "global foreign policy" with five "strategic aims". Those benefits – as explicit and rational an exposition of Britain's current all-party consensus of our national interest as I have seen before – are security, prosperity, quality of life and mutual respect. We shall, it is said, "ensure the security of the UK and the Dependent Territories, and peace for our people by promoting international stability, fostering our defence alliances and promoting arms control activity". Prosperity is to be realized by promoting trade abroad and boosting jobs at home. The quality of life will be enhanced by protecting the world's environment, and countering the menace of drugs, terrorism and crime. And mutual respect will be strengthened by spreading the values of human rights, civil liberties and democracy.[2]

The British national interest in global environmental integrity is equal to none. I recall quite vividly the policy change on the ozone issue undertaken by the UK on the initiative of Prime Minister Thatcher, which changed the country's policy from follower to leader in developing global norms and compliance through the Montreal Protocol. On climate change, the UK also proposed binding commitments for national emission cuts.[3] Half a decade later it is projected to cut its global emissions by 94% over the 1990s, recording after Spain and Germany the most positive trend of OECD countries. And I remember Britain's positive participation in the 1989 summit meeting in The Hague in which 24 leaders called for binding global powers over nation-states in global environmental matters.

The global carrying capacity is a most complex phenomenon and too new, in my view, to investigate the issue of global powers. But it is without question that the national interest of Britain, along with all nations, lies in a sound global population policy through the Cairo Programme of Action, stabilization of global forestry resources and sustainable development and consumption by all countries.

When we turn to the relationship between the environment and arms control, there is clearly scope for a major debate on the threat to the global ecosystem posed by weapons of mass destruction. The views of those who see this as central in the development of the planetary interest are, I know, expressed elsewhere in this book. From the standpoint of the British national interest at this stage, I can only reflect the political realities which seem certain to keep my country for the next decade, and perhaps beyond, more concerned with conventional than nuclear disarmament. But this should not blind us to the progress of recent years. It was former Prime Minister Major who took the initiative to convene the Security Council summit in 1992 which sought to seize upon the new opportunities for securing a "safer, more equitable and more humane world" as the declaration put it. The need for all member states to prevent the proliferation of weapons of mass destruction in "all its aspects" – thus not only horizontal but vertical proliferation as well – has direct relevance for the country which convened the meeting. Britain was an early ratifier of both the 1972 Biological Weapons Convention and the 1993 Chemical Weapons Convention.

Its nuclear power status, however, remains a different thing, underpinning deterrence which still secures the global strategic order in the continuing age of nation-states. The threat of traditional aggression against Britain hardly emanates today from other nation-states, but are the major powers about to agree to forfeit the retention of weapons of mass destruction as a deterrent against other major powers in the event of an extreme crisis? The strengthening of global security is something that Britain strives to attain as sincerely as any nation, and there is a powerful British as well as planetary interest in strengthening the international non-proliferation regime. At the heart of this regime is a bargain between nuclear and non-nuclear states: the latter forego the nuclear option on the basis that the former are serious and sincere about working for ultimate elimination. The logic of the original NPT and its 1995 extension is that the UK should demonstrate good intent and be proactive in working to reduce stockpiles worldwide. At the same time, it is not striving to outpace the Russians and the Americans in the race for a nuclear-free world. British citizens have made it clear that they would not countenance unilateral nuclear disarmament and the party currently forming the government was obliged to drop that policy before its chances of being elected could become serious. National power appears of bedrock solidity in this respect. Global control over weapons of mass destruction is razor thin.

The accusation of discrimination is often advanced over the situation where nuclear powers retain such weapons while Iraq is deprived of them through a binding Security Council decision. I see no contradiction here between the national and the planetary interest – indeed I have argued that in parliamentary debate in Britain.[4] If it is a question of legitimacy, let us remember that Britain acquired nuclear weapons at a time when it had helped to secure the world from nation-state aggression and faced the prospect of another version of the same thing in the 1950s. A majority of the British people supported that. The world has changed since and the nuclear debate is pursued now in a new and different light in which the national and planetary interest can be more clearly related. Let us pursue that debate with a new insight, but let us not engage in a revisionism of what were proper judgements taken at a different time.

The propensity of the major powers for further nuclear reductions is related to the stability of the world situation, and thus to the effectiveness of the Security Council. Reform of the council, to make it more "equitable" in representation and more effective in practice, is under intensive debate. The Security Council has been criticized in recent years on two grounds: that some permanent members misuse their privileged position in excessive pursuit of their national interests; and that the composition of the council is not adequately representative of the international community.

Power and equity relate uneasily at the global level. Member states of the UN are of vastly disparate size and influence. The right of veto that belongs to the existing five permanent members – the concurring vote on non-procedural matters under Article 27(3) – is a legacy of a proud past and one which many in my country see as a privilege earned by sacrifice for the common good. Britain, with 1% of the global population and no longer a world power, remains one of the five. The continuance of that privilege evokes concern by some other member states and not least those whose economic growth has made them recently more powerful. Should a state that is no longer a "superpower" such as Britain or France still possess the right of veto? Should any state? It is a plausible claim that only one true "superpower" with a full global reach in military might exists on the planet today. It is a credible query whether, *prima facie*, any single nation-state should have veto power in the world organization when a true global society emerges.

Britain, as any state, perceives a national interest in retaining whatever power and influence in the world it has, and retaining whatever mechanism it possesses to that end, even as its relative importance declines – "punching above its weight" as it is often said. No other state would be different in this respect, as one of my colleagues in government once pointed out.[5] But it also has a strong sense of honour and fair play, and it recognizes that the world will be vastly different in 2000 than in 1945. What is the correct policy to square this circle? The issue of the veto has not been specifically discussed in parliament and I rather doubt it will be apart from some passing comment.[6] But it was the view of the House Foreign Affairs Committee in 1993, having noted the government's policy that it was "not keen" to lose the veto power, that "we do not believe that it is practical to expect the permanent members of the Security Council as presently constituted to give up their right of veto".[7]

What is surely required is an element of common sense in which the permanent states do not abuse or overuse the veto, where they are prepared to engage in a policy dialogue over its future use, where certain customary practices develop in which they undertake not to use it in circumstances other than when, to borrow from arms control language, extraordinary events jeopardize their supreme national interests. This way, a balance, once again, can be struck as we enter the twenty-first century between change and stability, between the national interests of the major powers and the planetary interest of giving due voice to all the peoples of the world as articulated through their nation-states.

The composition of the council has been one of the major issues under the UN reform item on the General Assembly agenda, and a working group has been studying proposals for expansion of permanent membership. There has been some discussion of this matter in the British parliament, and retention of its own permanent seat has total bipartisan support.[8] But Germany, which pays 9% of the budget, and Japan, which pays 12%, compared with Britain's 5%, are claiming such a right, as are leading regional states such as India, Brazil, Nigeria and South Africa. The House Foreign Affairs Committee focused on this matter, without drawing a conclusion. It heard from the government, however, that there was "no natural correlation" between economic weight and permanent council membership, and that the UK was, in any event, sensitive to the views of other EU member states, discussed matters with them and represented their views on the council.[9] I scarcely think that this policy could be defended as a "legitimate national interest". But the matter is not a simple one, and it is fraught with political sensitivities. The US proposal of July 1997 for Germany and Japan plus one from Africa, Asia and Latin America as permanent members at least addresses the question, although it raises as many problems as it solves. No universally acceptable formula has been found to date. There may be a planetary interest here but I do not pretend to know what it is. Except that India and Pakistan's nuclear capacities do not automatically qualify them – on the contrary.

In increasing the effectiveness of the Security Council, one issue that often arises concerns the ability of the Security Council to react quickly in a crisis. This raises the question of a permanent United Nations force of some kind   perhaps small, well trained and equipped, and able to move quickly into an area as an "advance guard" for peace. Such an innovation, however, immediately raises the issue of the relationship between global and national power, since it would accord greater scope for action by the United Nations as an organization as opposed to the member states acting through it. Although it elicited some support in parliament,[10] Britain did not support the idea of even a small force as proposed in "Agenda for Peace".

The propensity of nation-states agreeing to strengthened global powers in the maintenance of peace and security turns on the extent to which each perceives the world as one unit and is prepared to undergo sacrifice to ensure its stability. The ultimate test of commitment is the willingness to sacrifice, and the test of a nation's commitment to stability is its willingness to risk the lives of its nationals. Britain's commitment in this respect is clear. We lost 24 personnel in the Gulf and 29 in Bosnia. The debates in the British parliament reflect an agonizing series of argumentation over this judgement. In particular, I recall the debate over Bosnia in May 1995, when some of our forces serving in UNPROFOR had been taken hostage by the Bosnian Serbs. The special debate convened in the House that day evoked all the conflicting interests a nation must face in a time of crisis, providing a glimpse of the intensity of political decision-making in a situation where lives are at risk, and the critical role of the concept of the national interest.[11] I cite it here because it is a microcosm of the issue at stake as we consider the planetary interest as a concept for the twenty-first century.

In carrying this concept forward, we are constantly brought back to the need to sustain the United Nations. In that process, I believe we must embrace fully the opportunities and demands placed upon us in creating the global information society. As a long-time enthusiast for information technology, I see great scope for taking advantage of the process by which personal computers will be available in ever-increasing numbers in libraries, schools, universities, and indeed through converging television technology, in the great majority of our homes – in the South as well as the North. The opportunities for presenting the case for the planetary interest via the UN Web and other sites is self-evident. It is by this kind of grass-roots appeal that the United Nations, national governments and parliaments can demonstrate the courage and vision required to make this concept a reality.

LEGITIMATE GLOBAL POWER AND THE UNITED KINGDOM

Having declared a personal global interest, I must consider whether the growth of such power is in the British national interest and whether Britain is pursuing a legitimate national interest in its activities towards that growth.

In addressing these questions, one must recognize the real difficulty in defining such interests. In his memoir of eight years in Downing Street as foreign policy adviser to Margaret Thatcher and John Major, Sir Percy Cradock refers to "that besetting weakness of British foreign policy, the expectation that foreign governments would, or should, feel and reason as we do".[12] While this criticism can no doubt be extended to many other countries, it is hard in the British case to ignore Edmund Burke's dictum, "Nothing is so fatal to a nation as an extreme of self-partiality".

The vital planetary interest, it has been advanced elsewhere in this book, concerns strategic international stability at minimum levels of weaponry, the integrity of the planet's environment and an optimal relationship between the global population and the planet's carrying capacity. In those areas, it is contended, global enforcement powers are justified. This is certainly a rational enough approach to our common survival as a species. Whether we show the level of rationality required, as a species, to implement such an approach is another thing.

In all its future functions, the key concept that will link national with global powers in the twenty-first century is legitimacy – the "informed consent of the people", to use Gwyn Prins' phrase. The United Nations must be able to act with the "informed consent" of the people of the world. We, the peoples of the United Nations, as the Charter puts it, must be satisfied that the legal–political mix underpinning the power structure of the organization is perceived worldwide as fair and worthy of popular support. Without that, dissent from member states will intensify and the application of power, especially on the part of the Security Council, will be loosened from the bedrock of legitimacy. For that legitimacy to be secured, two fundamental things must occur. States must have genuine intent in their application of the Charter. And the peoples of the United Nations must have adequate direct knowledge of the global issues at stake, and some reasonable mechanism for making an input into its deliberations.

There exists, in my view, one underrecognized instrument to that end – the principle of good faith identified in Chapter 3. This principle goes a long way to ensuring that the legitimacy of the United Nations is preserved and indeed strengthened, that the legitimate national interest of states is sanctioned, and that permanent members of the Security Council act in a manner that is not to the detriment of the United Nations and the emerging global society. It was noted earlier that this principle applies most pertinently to Article 24 concerning the "primary responsibility" of the Security Council for maintaining international peace and security, and that in carrying out its duties under this responsibility the council acts on behalf of all member states. The permanent members, possessing the veto power in recognition of their historical military might, carry a special national responsibility in that regard. They must recognize and accept that, in all their actions in the council, not least in the exercise of their veto power, they are acting, not only on their own behalf and in their own interests, but on behalf of and in the interests of all other member states of the United Nations. There must be no "willful obstruction of the operations of the Security Council", to cite the San Francisco Declaration. Only when rights and obligations are properly balanced, and that balance properly observed, can a permanent member of the council retain its claim to legitimate authority. Here, the legitimate national interest and the planetary interest must be recognized as inseparably linked.

There can be no double standards in this respect – no compromising of the principle of good faith. There can be no excessive national interest pursued. There must be an unquestioned acceptance by all members that the permanent members of the Security Council are truly acting in the interests of the world organization. Only in this way can the privilege of the veto continue to be acceptable to others, and only in this way can the United Nations preserve and strengthen its credibility and its legitimacy.

Any student of the United Nations can cite contentious cases that bring this principle into question. Since the beginning of the UN, nearly 300 vetos have been cast, nearly 80% of them during the Cold War. Of the 232 cast between 1945 and 1989, 114 were entered by the USSR (49 of these on membership applications), 67 by the United States, 30 by the UK, 18 by France and 3 by China. And the threat of veto precludes issues being submitted. Possession of the veto imposes a special responsibility on permanent members to pursue only a legitimate national interest.

If the principle of good faith is applied and properly honoured by all permanent members of the council, the veto will not be abused and the legitimacy of the council and the UN will be sanctified.

The second key to legitimate global power is popular involvement. The ready availability of UN documentation through Internet today allows the public around the world, albeit those at present in the more technologically advanced countries, to follow UN issues quite closely. This is a very recent phenomenon and promises to have a revolutionary effect on the ability of the individual citizen to remain apprised of the activities and the emerging norms of international life and the global issues of our day.

Figure 14.1   "If", says Sir Michael Marshall, "we are to give our international organizations 'still greater legitimacy' through more democratic norms and procedures, we must ensure that our countries recognize the planetary interest and do not exceed the legitimate national interest in all matters." Former British Foreign Secretary Malcolm Rifkind leads his national delegation in discussing global issues during the 51st Session of the General Assembly, 1996. (Courtesy UN Photo)

CONCLUSION

It is a common misconception of conservative politicians that they fear change. We do not. Rather, we insist on due regard for and a safeguarding of the values and principles that have been built up, generally as a result of painstaking effort and sacrifice, by those who have gone before. We do not need to be historians to recognize the richness and importance of the past. The history of my own country is replete with the twists and turns of nation-building, a conservative respect for which comes naturally to many as a consequence. But that philosophical predisposition can lead us forward in two ways. It can result in a resistance to change or it can temper excess and shape one's judgement over such change with a judicious appreciation of the opportunities and risks involved. I prefer the latter, and believe that in doing so one can strike the correct balance between the planetary and the national interests.

In the twenty-first century that balance will turn on the degree of legitimacy we shall have secured in the United Nations. Increasingly, legitimacy will depend on a direct input by the people themselves into UN deliberations. Hitherto the public has had little opportunity to become involved. The "peoples of the United Nations", having identified the four fundamental aims of the organization and resolved to combine their efforts to accomplish them, immediately delegated authority to their governments to agree to the terms of the Charter and establish the organization of which nation-states are the constituent members. The governments of the member states, through the executive branches including their diplomatic arms, act before the UN on behalf of the people. This they do with varying degrees of domestic democratic integrity. So the question of legitimacy arises in two ways – not only in relation to the sovereign equality of states of disparate size but also the extent to which the government of each member state can genuinely claim to represent its own people.

In both cases the involvement of parliamentarians will prove to be of increasing importance. My own experience, as chairman of the British Group of the IPU, and later as president of the IPU International Council, has shown that there is a practical opportunity in increasing understanding and reducing mistrust through what President Gorbachev called "parliamentary diplomacy". For example, between 1982 and 1989 British involvement in parliamentary exchanges with Argentina and Eastern Europe demonstrated beyond doubt that these channels can play a significant part in the improvement of international relations, ending bilateral disputes and wider threats from the Cold War. With Argentina, these changes helped build mutual confidence after the Falklands/Malvinas conflict in a period when there were no formal diplomatic relations between our two countries. On the wider world stage, the role of parliamentarians in support of global governance was highlighted by the UN secretary-general at the IPU 's Special Session in August 1995, convened in New York for the 50th anniversary of the United Nations. The very phrase "We the peoples of the United Nations", said Dr Boutros-Ghali, "is a constant invitation to promote increasing democratization of international life". His comments pertaining to the role of parliamentarians and the IPU in this respect are worthy of recall, and I cite excerpts from them in the Box.

For this author, there is a need and an opportunity for parliamentarians and policy-makers around the world to act on behalf of international public opinion as we develop the global society. If we are to give our international organizations "still greater legitimacy" through more democratic norms and procedures, we must ensure that our countries recognize the planetary interest and do not exceed the legitimate national interest in all matters. Only in this way can we ensure that national and global powers are optimally related and the national interest is legitimately pursued in the next stage of our political evolution on this planet.

Let us indeed never forget that the United Nations was born, 50 years ago, out of the will of a small number of individuals to view the world as a whole, to mobilise the international community in the service of the great objectives of progress and peace, and to disseminate democratic ideals world-wide. In this respect, the Inter-Parliamentary Union is certainly the most advanced institutional forum of international democratic co-operation . . . in a sense it is undoubtedly the first institution to have introduced the democratic imperative into the international legal order. Quite naturally, therefore, the Inter-Parliamentary Union is today in the front line of the struggle being waged by international institutions to meet this new aspiration to freedom and democracy that is rising up from so many peoples and so many nations. As such, you are the privileged partners of the United Nations . . .

We are all aware that any process of democratisation requires an effort of will on the part of the government concerned and also on the part of its citizens. Citizens should have the opportunity to participate fully, freely and democratically in the process of political and social decision-making . . .

I know that, as parliamentarians, you are particularly sensitive to the importance of these activities . . . Your wealth of experience, as individuals and parliamentarians, at the institutional level and as an international organization, seems to me to be an indispensable resource of which the entire international community ought to take advantage . . . Democracy is the political expression of our common heritage; as such it possesses a universal dimension . . . I emphasise[d] the role that parliamentarians must play, among other players on the international scene. For you are the vital channels for public opinion. As members of the Inter-Parliamentary Union you are among the privileged voices through which public opinion can be heard on the international stage . . . without the support of public opinion the United Nations is nothing; its effectiveness diminishes, its very legitimacy fades . . .

. . . you will understand how much more closely I wish to see the Inter-Parliamentary Union associated with the United Nations action . . . For you are a vital element in the representation of the world, and it is therefore important that you play your full part within the world Organization . . . We are all of us aware, today, that we have indisputably entered the era of the global society. International political opinion and States are fully persuaded that the key problems of the future of mankind are essentially transnational problems. International society is no longer merely interstatal, but will henceforth be one great inter-dependent family . . . It is this interpretation that I place in your presence here today in this world Organ-ization. For we must all work to give our national institutions and our international organizations still greater legitimacy and to make them still more democratic ("Democratization is essential tool for strengthen-ing of activities of United Nations", secretary-general tells parliamentarians. UN DPI press release SG/SM/5711, 29 August 1995).

NOTES

1. BBC World Service News broadcast, 18 June 1997.
2. Foreign and Commonwealth Office, *Mission statement* (London: Foreign and Commonwealth Office, 12 May 1997).
3. Minister of State, Foreign and Commonwealth Office, Mrs Lynda Chalker:

> The global environment, the natural world in which we live, is changing fast. We do not yet know enough about phenomena such as ozone depletion and global warming, but we already appreciate that they could be as significant for the future of this planet and thousands of millions of people, as anything now happening on the political scene , , , we called for an international convention of global climate change, which would commit signatories to reduce activities that contribute to global warming . . . We do not want a grey approach . . . The message is simple and clear – at a time of great opportunity, Britain is at the forefront in helping to shape events. In Europe, as in other regions of the world, and in areas of truly global concern, we are managing that change constructively (*House of Commons*: 1246–7, 14 July 1989 (hereafter *HoC*)).

4. Sir Michael Marshall (Arundel):

> One exciting factor of the way that the United Nations has been involved in Iraq is that it has sought, through the power and support of the international community, to dismantle the nuclear capacity of Saddam Hussein. It was one of the most vital breakthroughs in the concept of a United Nations role (*HoC*: 151, 25 September 1992).

5. Mr Douglas Hogg (Minister of State, Foreign and Commonwealth Office):

> Hon. Members must realise that the Security Council of the United Nations is in a sense an aggregate of independent states which will certainly determine where their national interests lie when deciding how they will vote in the Security Council. That is inevitable and right (*HoC*: 739, 13 September 1993).

6. Mr Peter Archer (Warley, West):

> Already national sovereignty in the absolute terms envisaged in the 19th century has been reduced to safer proportions . . . A legal system is like currency – its acceptance is almost wholly proportionate to the confidence that people have in it. That requires progress in a number of fronts. First, the United Nations needs to operate in a crisis decisively and quickly, and that will require Governments to lay on the line a little more of their sovereignty. It may mean considering abolishing the veto in the Security Council (*HoC*: 1164, 28 September 1991).

7. London: House of Commons, Session 1992–3, Foreign Affairs Committee Third Report. "The expanding rôle of the United Nations and its implications for United Kingdom policy", Vol. 1, xlix.
8. Secretary of State for Foreign and Commonwealth Affairs, Mr Douglas Hurd:

> The debate is not about giving up the British seat but about whether there should be additions to the permanent membership to reflect changes in the world since 1945. We have neither the will nor the power to stifle such debate, but some words of caution are perhaps in order . . . I cannot imagine a solution that would satisfy all aspirations to the extent necessary for the reform of the charter, which needs unanimity among the permanent members and a two-thirds majority in the General Assembly (*HoC*: 784, 23 February 1993).

Cyril D. Townsend (Bexleyheath):

> It will not be easy for the United Kingdom permanently to defend the fact that, because the United Nations was set up at the end of the war, the United Kingdom, which has a comparatively low per capita income compared with that of other countries and a small defence force, should maintain a permanent seat (*HoC*: 502, 4 December 1992).

The Minister of State, Foreign and Commonwealth Office, Mr Douglas Hogg:

> The Government are not seeking to change the composition of the Security Council, not least because it would require a change in the Charter, which we do not want at the moment. I should be surprised – I speak now as a politician rather than as a world statesman – if it were in the interests of France or the United Kingdom to promote such a change. It is probably not in the interests of anybody else either, because for about the first time since the war the Security Council is working harmoniously together and the five permanent members have been constructive about the way in which the Council has been using its power. We should not interrupt that which is going well (*HoC*: 560–1, 4 December 1992).

Mr Hogg:

> There has been much discussion, again rightly, about the reform of the Security Council. If my hon. Friend will forgive me, I do not agree with his basic proposition – which he admitted was heretical – to the effect that the United Kingdom should cede its permanency (*HoC*: 854, 23 February 1993).

9. Foreign Affairs Committee, Third Report, vol. 1, xlviii.
10. Sir David Steel (Tweeddale, Ettrick and Lauderdale):

> The Secretary-General was right to argue in his document "An Agenda for Peace" that, even if the political concurrence of the five permanent members of the Security Council is necessary, the UN should have a standby capacity of its own for the purpose of enforcement. If such a force were created – to which we among others would have to assign troops – the organisation would be able to react at even shorter notice. Such a capacity would also fulfil a preventive function by giving added seriousness to the resolutions and positions from time to time by the Security Council. As the Secretary-General proposed in his report, those forces could be set up by agreements mentioned in article 43 of chapter VII of the Charter. I hope that Her Majesty's Government will give high priority to that (*HoC*: 797, 23 February 1993).

Mr Tony Banks (Newham, North-West):

> I believe that there should be a United Nations army under the control of the Security Council. I believe that Britain should pledge its full defence resources to the United Nations and should put them at the disposal of the United Nations . . . On the basis of unanimity within the Security Council, the United Nations should have the power and be prepared to intervene in the domestic affairs of other countries. I know that there are dangers in that respect, but there are even greater dangers for the people who are on the receiving end of political leaders around the world (*HoC*: 535, 4 December 1992).

11. The Prime Minister, Mr John Major:

> If it is in our national interest to avert a greater calamity in Bosnia and the Balkans, so it is for other members of NATO and the European Union. The strategic case and the humanitarian case were the twin reasons that I thought it right to commit British troops in 1992 (*HoC*: 999, 31 May 1995);

Mr Andrew Robathan (Blaby):

> I volunteered to go to the Gulf because that too was an international emergency, and I could see the national and international interest – and, indeed, I went. . . . It is difficult for us to see a clear national interest for us [in Bosnia], or a clear aim. . . . There is no obvious British national interest, so why are our troops in the area? (*HoC*: 1077–9, 31 May 1995);

The Secretary of State for Defence, Mr Malcom Rifkind:

> Is Britain the sort of country that can stand and watch but do nothing while tens of thousands are being slaughtered in a not-far away country of which we know quite a lot? . . . Is it being suggested that British troops could withdraw from Bosnia even if French, Dutch, Canadian and other forces stay? Would that be either honourable or in our national interest? (*HoC*: 1096, 31 May 1995);

The Prime Minister, Mr John Major:

> . . . the troops on the ground in Bosnia now need more protection, and the safety of those troops is, as I said, of vital national interest . . . Within hours of the capture of the British troops, we took steps to make it clear, directly and unequivocally, to the Bosnian Serb leadership that the safety of our troops in Bosnia was of vital British interest . . . They are defending British interests and international security (*HoC*: 1002, 1003, 1007, 31 May 1995);

Mr Tony Blair:

> Naturally today, the House unites in its support for our troops and its demand that the hostages, so wickedly seized, should be returned. That is our vital national interest and we shall protect it. Britain has always been a country willing to lift its eyes to the far horizon and judge its actions by their immediate impact not only on ourselves but on world events and history. The decisions that we take are of momentous import for the world and its order and stability. Let us ensure that those decisions are the right ones, for we shall live with their consequences (*HoC*: 1009, 1012, 31 May 1995);

Sir Peter Tapsell (East Lindsey):

> What will the attitude of the British people who sent us here be when, as may only too possibly happen in future weeks and months, considerable numbers of British troops are sent home in body bags for burial? . . . the British people were prepared to fight for the Falkland Islands. I know that my constituents are prepared to fight for the union of Northern Ireland and the rest of Britain and, as a Unionist, I am passionately committed to that. However, I have represented my constituents for over 30 years and I have lived in my constituency for all that time, and I doubt whether they will be prepared to see their sons die to protect the people of Bosnia (*HoC*: 1050, 1053, 31 May 1995).

12. P. Cradock, *In pursuit of British interests* (London: John Murray, 1997).

CHAPTER FIFTEEN

Global and local powers: Rome's municipal interest

Francesco Rutelli

> "It is clear that the world of the 21st century will be predominantly urban and that the transition to global sustainability will largely depend on the success in ensuring the sustainable development of our cities and towns."
>
> Kofi Annan, UN Secretary-General, 1997

As the political evolution of our world continues, global power is emerging. In the age of the city, city powers prevailed. In the age of the nation, national powers. As the global age strengthens and deepens, global powers will grow and consolidate. I lead a city – one of the great cities of the world – but I am a citizen of the planet as well. I and my colleagues face the phenomenon of the "global city" – certain metropolises which have attained global reach, not by virtue of population size but rather through their dynamism, their concentration of talent and what they contribute to the world as a whole. Each "global city" relates to the planet today as much as to the nation in which it resides.[1] As John Eade has observed, "the significance of nation-state boundaries and institutions declines as global and local social relations interweave and world-wide social relations intensify".[2]

So I endorse the growth of global powers, where it is appropriate and where it is legitimate. I endorse a spread of sovereignty across all jurisdictional levels – global and regional, national and municipal. But that is resulting in a more complex set of political relationships around the world at different levels of jurisdiction. The responsibility of political leaders increases as a result, including accountability when economic forces look to a world market rather than local economic and social needs. "Think globally, act locally", has become the slogan of the age. Like most good slogans, it captures the mood of the times. It is exactly what I try to do in my job.

That, in fact, is what I was elected to do. I did not come into office without a reputation, without a past. In earlier days, I was a committed "green" political activist. Elected to the national parliament in my twenties in an age of pollution, I stood firmly for environmental politics in the hurly-burly of Italian political life. Then sensing the challenge of the city, I stood for the mayoralty of Rome. The voters got what they saw when they elected me. They did it with their eyes open, and they enjoyed what was the first direct election for the office in the city's history. That was 1993. By voting me in, they opted for an environmental programme.

Then came the hard part – four years of governing a major metropolis, a city of 3 million people. In Cicero's time, there were 300,000 within the city walls, the same size as the Greek city states. In the Middle Ages it was a tenth of that. Even in 1870 when Rome became capital of the new Kingdom of Italy, there were only 200,000. It is only in the last half-century that the city burgeoned, especially in the 1960s with Italy's "economic miracle". Running a city of 3 million is a qualitatively different thing from the past. Size itself is half the issue – not only in problems created but solutions implemented. I have done, in my first term, what I could. In 1997 I turned, again, to face the voters. My re-election reinforces the conviction that a global approach to municipal politics, and the "sustainable city" concept, is what the people want today.

THE PLANETARY INTEREST AND THE MUNICIPAL INTEREST

We are, today, more than we often tend to realize, one collective political body existing on this planet. If there is one thing that has been brought home to me in the course of my work as mayor of Rome, it is the commonality of interest among our fellow humans all around the world. Even where the specific problems of nations and cities might differ, the interest is held in common. We all aspire to a similar life, health and environmental harmony, adequate prosperity, peace and stability. There is no reason why we cannot, as a species, act together in the common interest. That has been called the "planetary interest" here. I know of no better term. The planetary interest and the municipal interest are one and the same; they are simply pursued at different levels of magnitude. Global peace and sustainability will not be attained unless the cities are safe and sustainable themselves. Municipal interests can scarcely be served if the global environment on which they depend is degraded.

The transformation of the world is, at bottom, an urban transformation, and so the planetary interest and the municipal interest intimately interweave. What is happening in the world at present is a revolution comparable, probably, to the Neolithic Revolution 10,000 years ago, when humans turned from continuous migration to settle in one place and farm. For millennia the hinterland retained most of the people, and the city was an island of human concentration. A rural numerical dominance continued until the twentieth century, indeed until today. The urban–rural hinge, the point when the numerical curves cross, is very soon. In 1997, city inhabitants around the world accounted for 46% of the global population. In 2006, it will be 50%. That is the year when the curves meet – 50% in the cities, 50% in the countryside. It will be quite an historic moment. And in 2030, it will be 60%.[3] Along with it, the mega-cities will come: concentrations of humanity of astounding magnitude – 20 million today, perhaps 30 million or 40 million in the twenty-first century. The challenges of the future will dwarf those of our time.

Cities pollute. They pollute locally, in the rivers and harbours and in the air above the buildings. And they pollute globally. This is where the juxtaposition of global and local interests and powers comes in. For city dwellers tend to think of local pollution and wish to see that cleared away first. The stratosphere is further away than the troposphere and out of people's minds. The local city ozone that hurts the eyes hangs closer than the global ozone whose depletion burns the skin. And the latter is certainly less irksome if it is on the other side of the planet. Yet it will threaten us too one day, and the global conferences of the 1990s remind us that the city is causally connected to the global problem. So global power, such as it is, must gently require the city to think globally, as it acts locally. The planetary interest.

The problems of the planet are the problems of the city and vice versa. Environment, housing, food security, sanitation and health, physical security. They are adequately summed up by Rio and Istanbul, in a word, sustainability. As Rio put it:

> Because so many of the problems and solutions have their roots in local activities, the participation and co-operation of local authorities will be a determining factor in fulfilling [these] objectives. Local authorities construct, operate and maintain economic, social and environmental infrastructure, oversee planning processes, establish local environmental policies and regulations, and assist in implementing national and subregional environmental policies. As the level of governance closest to the people, they play a vital role in educating, mobilising and responding to the public to promote sustainable development.[4]

Four years later, Habitat II sounded a special alarm. We have considered with a sense of urgency, said the nation-states in the Istanbul Declaration, the continuing deterioration of conditions of shelter and human settlements. At the same time, we recognize cities and towns as centres of civilization, generating economic development and social, cultural, spiritual and scientific advancement.[5]

How do cities reflect these problems that are now perceived on such a global scale? Cities, it is clear, differ in their make-up and their problems. So the solutions and strategies they need to meet the challenges identified at Rio and Istanbul will themselves differ. One of the problems, as usual, is that the world lacks reliable comparative data. But the United Nations is moving to rectify this: its Commission on Human Settlements (Habitat) has recently developed a Global Indicators Database (GID) to provide governments and urban planners with a series of key urban indicators. The database already has some 40 indicators reflecting general, urban and housing conditions. It will allow a worldwide City Development Index (CDI) to be constructed. This will serve as an important benchmark for countries and cities to compare their future performance in meeting the planetary interest through the various global strategies of action. At Istanbul, governments were urged to collect the key indicators for one or more of their cities, as well as at the national level.[6]

The GID already throws light on city conditions around the world, and the picture is not pretty. Urban population density varies from 70 people per hectare in the rich countries of the North to some 240 in, for example, Asian cities. Household size ranges from 2.5 in the North to 6.5 in the South. The poverty gap is huge. The "city product" per person of the poorest fifth of all cities in the world surveyed is 1% of that of the richest fifth. Even the next poorest fifth produce only 16% of the richest. Locally defined poverty in the cities of the South captures 42% of the people; in the North, 12%. In the cities of the least-developed countries, only 33% of the citizens have electricity, 26% have water connected. Only 7% have telephones, only 5% have sewerage. The children are 25 times more likely to die than in cities of the North. Some 15% die under 5 years of age. Car ownership is 18 times higher in the cities of the North. Car commuting is 80% of all transport in Auckland and Melbourne, 90% in Des Moines. In the smaller cities of India and Nepal, it is 2%. So pollution, it can be seen, comes in two forms – underconsumption and overconsumption. The pollution of the poor, the pollution of the rich.

The CDI includes data on child mortality and city product, but otherwise only investment in infrastructural facilities such as potable water, sewerage, electricity, telephones, waste-water treatment, garbage collection, open dumping, primary classrooms, secondary classrooms and hospital beds. It does not as yet include such "livability" measures as income inequality, poverty, congestion, crime or pollution. But it offers insights even at this early stage. Phase I of the first report ranks 236 cities worldwide according to their CDIs for each data variable. Table 15.1 shows the regional totals for cities with high, medium and low City Development Indexes. It is clear that a strong correlation exists between city development and level of national development.

Table 15.1 City development index: ranking for 236 cities (number of cities, totals by region)

	Africa	Arab region	Asia/Pacific	High-income states	Latin Amer./Carib.	Transitional states	Earth
High CDI	1	1	0	34	2	19	57
Medium CDI	5	6	16	0	27	12	66
Low CDI	81	3	26	0	3	0	113
Total	87	10	42	34	32	31	236

Source: HS/C/16/INF.8 Table 2.

Rome, of course, is a "high income state" city. Basically, its city problems are those of the rich, with an added dash from its historical antiquity. So it is not Mexico, or Beijing, or Lagos. It is Rome. There must be Roman solutions to our problems.

How to solve the problems of the cities? Through the 1990s, the world has laboured, quite intensively, to develop a strategic response at all levels of jurisdiction. My focus here is on the planetary and municipal interests, and the global and city strategies to achieve them.

The planetary interest; the global strategy

If humanity is to think globally and act locally in a truly effective way, then we need to *meet* globally first, before we can agree on how to act. This we are doing. The world has met at Rio, Cairo, Copenhagen, Beijing, Istanbul. Global strategies have been devised. Some are better than others. All are necessary. In every one, the cities of the world have a central and critical role to play. Let me explain the relationship, in this context, not between the city and nation but between the city and the planet. Because it is, as Rio said, crucial to the survival of humanity. The global objective – the planetary interest – is set out clearly enough. In the words of the Istanbul Declaration:

> Everyone has the right to an adequate standard of living for themselves and their families, including adequate food, clothing, housing, water and sanitation, and to the continuous improvement of living conditions.[7]

The global strategy for this is essentially Rio's *Agenda 21* – a "new global partnership for sustainable development".[8] More specifically, the Global Strategy for Shelter to the Year 2000 of 1988 called for improved production and delivery of shelter, and for revised national housing for the realization of adequate shelter for all in the twenty-first century. Environmental issues, said the Rio Declaration, are best handled with the participation of all concerned citizens, at the relevant level.[9]

At the regional level, the European Charter of Local Self-Government has been developed. It can be used as a basis for developing a global charter that would set out the key principles underlying a sound constitutional or legal framework for a democratic local government system.[10]

The global strategy for sustainable development adopted at Rio prescribes certain measures for local authorities: new consultative processes between local authorities by 1994; a consultative process between local authorities and their populations resulting in a *Local Agenda 21* by 1996; the decentralization of authority by national governments to "democratic local authorities"; increased financial support for local authority programmes through partnerships fostered among relevant international organizations such as the UN and World Bank, and international local authorities (Union of Local Authorities, World Association of Major Metropolises, United Towns Organization, and the Summit of Great Cities of the World); greater empowerment of women in the municipal level of government; and a closer partnership and dialogue among parliamentarians and local government leaders in pursuit of a "global charter".[11]

The municipal interest; the city strategy

In addition to the "global strategy for local authorities", the local authorities themselves took their own initiative for a collective redemption. They developed, simultaneously with the global conferences, city strategies for commensurate action to improve their sustainability. Three, in particular, are relevant to our work as mayors henceforth: the Declaration on Social Development and Sustainable Human Settlements of 1994; the Final Declaration of the World Assembly of Cities and Local Authorities (WACLA) of 1996; and the Istanbul Manifesto on Implementing the Urban Environment Agenda the same year. In addition, a steering group, led by the mayors of Barcelona, Bologna and Manchester, launched the Inter-Cities Solidarity Fund to facilitate the participation of local authorities in national, regional and global preparations for Habitat II at Istanbul.

During Habitat II, the World Assembly of Cities and Local Authorities, comprising over 400 mayors from around the world, drew up a Global Charter for Local Self-Governance. The assembly was organized by the G4+, comprising the four major international associations of municipal governments (International Union of Local Authorities, Metropolis, Summit, and United Towns Organization). The WACLA Declaration as it is also known, was handed to the UN secretary-general. It focuses on four areas: sustainable development, democratization, decentralization and local empowerment. It is based on the premise that governmental decisions should be taken at the level closest to the citizens, with other levels of government undertaking only those matters which local governments cannot carry out alone.[12]

The Istanbul Manifesto, Implementing the Urban Environment Agenda, was adopted in June 1996 by 200 participants from over 70 cities on the eve of the City Summit. The manifesto noted the "impressive range of initiatives and accomplishments in local urban environment management worldwide, and the resources and expertise which have been mobilised".

Five years after Rio, what progress has been made by local authorities in implementing the strategies laid down at the global and local levels? I have been mayor of Rome for about the same period of time. I have devoted myself totally to the task. But the problems of a major modern city with infrastructure that dates back over two millennia are not insignificant. They are not resolved in half a decade.

What are the major problems facing Rome in the late 1990s? It is difficult to give them a precise ranking. But an interrelated package of problems has to be addressed: transportation with its associated noise and air pollution, waste management, energy supply, water management, urban regeneration, land conservation and the protection and valuation of historical and cultural artefacts. What can we do about these?

First, the traffic. Anyone who has visited Rome carries lifelong memories of the city's glorious chaos of cars and mopeds. We are seeking to deprive tourists of this pleasure, and we shall do it by restoring a new balance in what we call the "modal split" in the city's transport. This involves improvements to public transport, especially rail, trams and the underground; a new priority extended to cyclists and pedestrians; and better traffic management. Stronger and more strictly implemented traffic and parking regulations, and new controls over traffic circulation are also aimed at mitigating the adverse impact which the city's transportation activity has on human health, especially of course on its residents.

Secondly, waste management. We have municipal policies now to minimize the generation of waste, and we are improving both the infrastructure and the logistics of collection. We are developing a specialized collection system, and applying various technological processes to the treatment and disposal systems. I remember Victor Ciorbea, when he was just elected mayor of Bucharest, striving to clean up the extraordinary mess lying about his city through innovative deals with the private garbage trucking companies. It worked well enough. And then, as prime minister, he sought to ensure that sufficient funds were channelled in the right direction for a new level of sanitation, not only for the capital but for other Romanian cities and towns. I know the problem he had. Rome is capital of one of the richest countries on Earth, yet I encounter problems of financing as well.

Thirdly, energy supply. Rome's City Energy Plan is essentially an organic municipal energy policy that incorporates the criterion of sustainability. Various initiatives have been put in place in recent years that respond to certain strategic goals of energy saving, mainly through incentives for renewable sources at the urban level.

Water management is a problem. We are continuing with our efforts to reorganize the supply system for the city, through modernization of certain aspects and a general rationalizing and strengthening of the system. And we are widening the system's purification capacity rather than seeking to increase the efficiency of the existing plants.

Housing has always been a challenge for Rome. We do not have the horrendous problem of homelessness of the scale one can find in Calcutta or New York, but we do have our housing problems. At Habitat II, nation-states promised to work to expand the supply of affordable housing by enabling markets to perform "efficiently and in a socially and environmentally responsible manner".[13] We were all to enhance access to land and credit and assist those who are unable to participate in the housing markets. The housing market in Rome, I have to say, does not completely perform "efficiently and in an environmentally responsible manner". One of the reasons is the inelasticity of supply. Another is the urban planning regulations which have traditionally made it difficult to modify the building type. So we are trying to rectify this. With the Certainties Plan adopted by the town council in May 1997, a new mechanism for simplifying rules and procedures has been introduced, involving the renovation, or the demolition and reconstruction, of buildings which do not hold particular interest from an historical or architectural point of view. And we can subdivide existing housing units so that young couples and singles can move in. It is now possible, for example, to demolish an old building and rebuild to a maximum volume of 7 cubic metres per square metre. Forgive the technicality, but this is the level of local detail we must act upon – to think globally.

Regeneration of the urban environment is a major component of my strategic vision of the future Rome. Our Certainties Plan identified three areas of the city for efficient urban planning. The "consolidated town" comprises the urban areas that are already well developed with extensive road networks. The "out-of-town" area, comprising the network of large parks and also the *Agro Romano* will be preserved. And the "town-to-be-completed" area, basically alternating full and empty urban space, will be improved with new residential units. These last two areas, comprising about 70% of the total municipal land, are now territorially defined and new normative instruments apply. Policies for the consolidated area will be the focus of subsequent town planning.

It may come as a surprise that, despite its antiquity and modern growth, Rome has a vast green belt running through it. Some 63% of the city's municipal land is protected, and the *Agro Romano* has been recognized by UNESCO as a "Reserve of the Biosphere". Land conservation and biodiversity are both close to my heart, and I shall ensure that they are respected by locals and visitors alike.

In all of these policies, the aim is to combine an overall macro-strategy for the protection of our historical and cultural heritage – at once the heritage of Rome and of the world – reflecting due regard for a more micro-level economic and architectural planning in specific areas of the city.

Responding to the challenge of Rio, Rome is drawing up its own *Local Agenda 21*. This is essentially the formalization of a process that has been going on since Rio itself. Consultation with the urban community has been continuing informally through numerous public meetings focusing on current environmental policies and their weaknesses, and proposing ways of strengthening them. The citizens of my town are not without ideas. In response, my officials have developed a few basic tools to promote the process. The State of the Environment Report identifies the current state of the urban environment and the gaps to be filled. The City's Environmental Observatory is collecting data from public bodies and universities. All the citizenry, specialist and generalist, have been drawn into the participatory process. Proposals for improvement will be agreed upon between administrative and scientific circles and set out in the Environmental Action Plan. This paper allows a global perspective on the environmental problems of Rome, the actions and choices made hitherto, and the problems that lie ahead. The plan sets the general goal of sustainability, and seeks to establish a mechanism for determining the degree of success in its attainment. It explains the process my administration envisages, involving essentially a forum where specialized technical discussions can take place. It then identifies the particular environmental problems the city faces, with proposed goals and policies, and finally outlines the actions already underway by the administration. It does not, however, presume to define priorities or any time-frame for action: that will be agreed upon in the forum.

Figure 15.1   "Anyone who has visited Rome", says Francesco Rutelli, "carries lifelong memories of the city's glorious chaos of cars and mopeds. We are seeking to deprive them of this pleasure." New public transport, priority to cyclists and pedestrians, stronger parking regulations and better traffic circulation will be tried. Twenty-first-century politics, says the mayor, will reflect a "more complex web of vertical and horizontal lines of authority as the world grapples with the problems that, at one and the same time, concern the city, the nation, the region and the planet". (Courtesy Comune di Roma)

In November 1997 I presented the final report to the citizens of Rome. The central message was of some improvement and some continuing problems. Air quality has improved – over the past three years, the increased use of catalytic converters and the new restrictions on city traffic have helped. But noise pollution was up 20% in 1996 over the previous year, mainly because of the scooters.[14]

Success in galvanizing public action will depend on public involvement, and for this various incentives and models are important. At the global level, Habitat runs what is known as a Best Practices and Local Leadership Programme, which gives examples of good initiatives around the world in sustainability. Examples in Europe alone include traffic-calm zones in Amsterdam, a waste control programme in Cordoba, house heating in Glasgow, wind energy in Gotland, urban renewal in Madrid, and old-city restoration in Barcelona. At the national level, we have done a similar thing in Italy. The Agency for the Sustainable Development of the Mediterranean (ECOMED) was created by Rome some time back. ECOMED proposed through Italian administration and environmental associations the establishment of an Italian Best Practices award series. Activities are centred on Padua where exchanges of experience are facilitated. An inventory of 50 "best practices" in sustainable urban planning in Italy has been entered in Habitat's list.

LEGITIMATE GLOBAL POWER AND ROME

A conceptual message of this book concerns "legitimate global power" in the face of certain critical global problems that threaten humanity and the planet. This, I believe, is self-evidently necessary. What does it mean for the city?

Hitherto, the main relationship in authority and power has been between the national and local levels – between the nation-state and the city. But the world is changing fast, and a dynamic transformation is underway. As Europe unites, links spring up between the regional and local levels. As the world develops a global consciousness, links are established between the global and local levels. This carries far-reaching implications, not least for funding. For over a century now, the battle of the purse was between the *Piazza del Campidoglio* and the *Camera dei Deputati,* an especially Italian dialogue for Italians by Italians, within Rome. In recent decades, that has been supplemented by a new dialogue between the *Piazza* and Strasbourg. In the future, it will increasingly be between the *Piazza* and New York. The simple and straightforward lines of communication and command that we have all known in politics in the twentieth century will metamorphose into a more complex web of vertical and horizontal lines of authority as the world grapples with problems that, at one and the same time, concern the city, the nation, the region and the planet. The Commission on Global Governance got it right. The city, it said, is a vital subject of all levels of governance. Global governance has an important contribution to make in tackling causes of excessively rapid population growth and urbanization and in strengthening regional, state and local capacities to cope with their consequences.[15]

But this does not mean, necessarily, coercive power. Authority is at its best when its touch is pleasant to the skin. There is no reason why global powers cannot rest on rational thought and consensual decision-making. The "legitimate global power" I wish to see in the twenty-first century is a power that perceives, plans, explains and assists. In a practical sense it is a matter, I believe, of reaching out to others, reaching out in a multidimensional way. As a municipal leader, I must reach out, at the local level, to the citizenry of the city and involve them more. That applies most especially to women who are not as involved in Rome's political decision-making as they should be, despite a fair presence on the citizens' committees. We need to "feminize" politics more, starting with the cities. At the national level, I must reach out to Italian parliamentarians. At the regional level, to my fellow Europeans, not only in Brussels but in all cities across our soft and beautiful continent. And at the global level, I must reach out to global leaders, not least my municipal colleagues in the major cities around the world.

The initiatives I have outlined above show what we are doing with the people of Rome. At the national level, we have increased co-operation with representatives in the parliament, engaged in a most important process of constitutional reform. This process will strengthen the powers and the autonomy of Italian regions and cities.

At the regional level, Rome is working in close co-operation with Europe. For the first time, in fact, the city has obtained funding from European programmes on sustainable urban development. Several come to mind. One is URBAN, a programme devoted to the regeneration of the most degraded urban areas on the outskirts of big cities in Europe, low-income areas with unemployment, infrastructural and social problems. In Rome, this support has gone to *Tor Bella Monaca* and *Torre Angela*, districts of Rome where people may not know a lot about global warming but a great deal about certain other aspects of human survival. Another is the MEDURBS-NOUN Programme in which natural technologies of water purification through reticulation are being introduced. A third is the Low Technology for Urban Waste Management Programme. All are having effect. Once Rome governed Europe. Now Europe is helping to govern Rome.

At the global level, Rome has also participated in the Cities' Charter, which recognizes a "strategic priority" in action for the urban environment, and notifies of any delays in policy implementation, and of any decay in the artistic heritage of the "world's most beautiful cities". We sent the charter to the Habitat II Conference, and in it the local authorities undertook a range of commitments to fulfil before 2010. In 1995 I hosted an international meeting in the Capitol which produced the Aalborg Charter on Sustainable Cities. The same year I organized the Mediterranean Local Agenda 21 Conference in collaboration with the International Council for Local Environmental Initiatives. And I was heavily involved in the United Nations Habitat II Conference in Istanbul in 1996, and the European Conference on Sustainable Cities the same year. In 1996 in fact, I acted as consultant to UN Secretary-General Boutros-Ghali for the Istanbul Habitat Conference. I made sure time was available to attend Istanbul in 1996, and the Special Session of the General Assembly in 1997 – "Rio+5". This is not simply to show the flag – it is to learn from others, and hopefully contribute to the common global cause.

As president of the Commission on Urban Policies of the Committee of the Regions, I associate with numerous other municipal leaders when we collectively address the issues of the environment and sustainable development. Both nationally and globally. Within the country, Rome twins with other Italian cities through the ANCI network. Regionally, it links with the Eurocities network. And globally, Rome leads with Padua and Genoa in what is known as the Forum for Decentralized Co-operation with Mozambique. These reinforce my conviction that the "global neighbourhood", as Sir Shridath Ramphal says, can only be developed through building links through the civil society, from city to city, town to town, from one professional association to another. One of the closest professional relationships I have in this respect is with my colleague from Barcelona, Pasqual Maragall, who led the global drive for sustainable cities with flair and commitment. These relationships bond into the personal level when they are steeled in the fires of public scrutiny for a common end. Pasqual has recently retired from the local arena, but we shall hear more of him in the global cause of sustainable nations and cities as time passes.

Rio urged international assistance to cities to assist them in implementation. Have we been assisted by the international community? Up to a point, yes. The city has received new and additional resources for urban planning since Rio, at both regional and national levels. Do the cities need more to properly complete the job? Well, yes.

CONCLUSION

At the outset I referred to the concept of the "sustainable city". Some have queried whether "sustainable city" is not an oxymoron.[16] A concentrated group of 10 million humans and more, surrounded by concrete and glass, cannot sustain themselves. So what we really mean is the sustainability of the city and its local hinterland. And the urban–rural relationship has its own conundrum: the faster we cure the problems of the city, the faster is the rural–urban migration. I have heard it said that the place to cure the problems of the cities is in the villages. This may hold for Dhaka more than for Rome, but it holds for Rome as well. And it is not simple or clear-cut: it is not just the local hinterland that sustains Rome; it is the global hinterland. So we are back to the triangular municipal–national–global relationship of power. There is a way to go in refining this.

I confess to a mix of inspiration and apprehension when I meet with the other municipal leaders at conferences and we discuss issues of sustainability and the question of jurisdictional competence at the various levels. They are so committed, so full of ideas and what I suppose is best termed "lateral thinking". So I conclude that we shall rescue the planet and the city from the problems of the present and the hazards of the future. But then I also see the scale and severity of some of the problems, and the limited scope we have as individuals to direct matters. And the apprehension arises.

Inspiration and apprehension are two sides of the same coin. It is the coin of humanity, flipped in the air. For, ultimately, the problems of the planet and the problems of the city are people problems. It is we who are causing the damage to Earth. It is people who decide to build new coal plants that consume dirty coal. People who decide, sometimes knowingly, to use aerosols with CFCs still. People who decide to migrate to the city, driven by the instinct of survival that drove their ancestors to settle in the Neolithic villages and towns before them – in *Catal Hüyük* – and later on the Palatine. No democratic municipal leader can direct the people. They can only influence them, encourage them, urge them, offer incentives and disincentives. But the people must decide, individually and collectively. It is they who must decide.

NOTES

1. For an insightful treatment of this new phenomenon, see: S. Sassen, *The global city* (Princeton, NJ: Princeton University Press, 1991).
2. J. Eade, *Living the global city: globalization as a local process* (London: Routledge, 1997), 3.
3. *World urbanisation prospects, 1996 revision* (New York: United Nations, 1997). UNDH, 2 May 1997.
4. *Agenda 21*, 28.1.
5. Istanbul Declaration, 2.
6. HS/C/16/INF.8, 22 April 1997.
7. *Habitat Agenda*, 11.
8. *Agenda 21*, 1.6.
9. Rio Declaration, Principle 10.
10. Istanbul: *Report of Committee II. Chairperson's summary*, 23.
11. *Agenda 21*, 28.1–28.7.
12. Extract from *Forum* (Sept.–Oct. 1996)
13. *Habitat Agenda*, para. 9.
14. My report was commented upon in the global media: see *IHT*, 5 November 1997.
15. *Our global neighbourhood*, 28.
16. See, for example, W. Rees, "Is 'sustainable city' an oxymoron?", *Local Environment*, 31 March 1997; W. Rees & M. Wackernagel, "Urban ecological footprints: why cities cannot be sustainable – and why they are a key to sustainability", *Environmental Impact Assessment Review* **16**, 223–48, 1996. Also:

    > Cities are among the brightest stars in the constellation of human achievement. At the same time, ecological footprint analysis shows that they act as entropic black holes, sweeping up the output of whole regions of the ecosphere vastly larger than themselves (*Getting efficient: Report of BCSD First Antwerp Eco-Efficiency Workshop* (Geneva: Business Council for Sustainable Development, 1993)).

PART FOUR

Conclusion

Part IV offers some concluding thoughts on the planetary interest drawn from the contributions from the various authors to the book.

The conclusion does not purport to find the answers to the problems that confront humanity today. The concept of the planetary interest is not the substance of any reasoning in identifying interest, objective, strategy and policies. It is simply a conceptual tool, a mechanism for facilitating the reasoning process. Individuals will continue to differ and hold opposite views on political issues, not least and perhaps the most on issues that are of global scale and yet threatening. The slow and general coalescence of values and interests among our various political societies is only just beginning to be felt at the global level. The planetary interest, it is concluded from the foregoing chapters, will be a critical concept for facilitating this process, both for policy-makers and citizens around the world.

CHAPTER SIXTEEN

The planetary interest: thoughts for the future

Kennedy Graham

> Our loyalties are to the species and the planet. *We* speak for Earth.
>
> Carl Sagan, *Cosmos*, 345

In this book, 20 eminent politicians have contributed their thoughts to the challenges before humanity on the cusp of the new millennium.

These challenges are formidable and daunting. We stand ready, still, to ignite a conflagration involving weapons of mass destruction that can devastate the planet. We are emitting gases into the atmosphere at a rate that is altering Earth's climate. We have unwittingly been producing chemicals which have dangerously depleted the planet's ozone layer whose recovery will take half a century. We are consuming the planet's resources at an unsustainable rate, causing an ecological "overshoot" of Earth's carrying capacity, unconscionably subsidizing ourselves at the cost of the next generation whose fundamental wellbeing will be jeopardized. We are, in short, placing the planet at risk and living on borrowed time, drawing on credit from our children and theirs.

How much time we have left to attain a civilized state of being at the global level and restore a natural equilibrium for the planet is difficult to judge. But the "precautionary principle" enshrined in the recent global conferences requires us – that is to say humanity – to act now and not tomorrow. This is a judgement which the international community has formally made, acting through the governments of nation-states in the exercise of their sovereign discretion and powers. It is therefore binding upon us, as nations, as leaders, as citizens.

It is only recently that humanity has begun to think and act as one. In the twentieth century, international organizations took form and began to range alongside the nation-state as a vehicle for political perceptions, values and decisions. Sovereign power, however, remained with the latter. In the 1990s, with a more clearly focused recognition of the existence of global problems and an increasing alarm over the severity of the threats they pose, the world has begun to think, politically, as one. We have begun, through the global conferences though not confined to them, to grope our way towards an identification of the planetary interest in respect of those problems of the global scale we face. It is in our interest as a species that we avoid mass destruction of ourselves and our fellow life-forms, that we stabilize the climate, protect the ozone layer and live sustainably within the carrying capacity of Earth. Intellectually, it is a relatively straightforward task to identify the planetary interest. Politically, it is only recently that we have begun to attempt this in any formal way. That is a quantum step forward in the political evolution of the species.

Acting upon that identification is another matter. Implementing the strategies agreed upon, or even agreeing upon them in the first place, is more difficult than identifying the planetary interest. Putting a concept of this kind into effect requires political power. While the corporate reach is strongly influencing nation-states through its effect on the global economy, political power remains, on balance, confined to the nation-state, even in the 1990s. National interest therefore remains the guiding concept. The programmes of action, deriving from the global conferences, can only serve in today's world as prescriptions for the ills of the planet. There is no single sovereign power of enforcement at the global level to ensure implementation. So the question then becomes, to what extent can the citizens and leaders of a country pursue a national interest that is compatible with the larger interests of the planet and humanity? This is where we are currently failing the next generation.

In the matter of weapons of mass destruction, it has been shown that the world is agreed that the planetary interest requires the total elimination of weapons of mass destruction at some stage. But it remains bifurcated between those who believe that global strategic stability requires the selective retention of such weapons into the indefinite future, and those who believe that the strategic imperative does not preclude total elimination within 20 years. Those who adhere to the former view are hard-pressed to persuade others of the rationale, and certainly the justification, for the thesis that some nation-states are more responsible than others and are the only ones which humanity can trust to be in command of such weapons. A chorus is beginning to mount that dismisses this view as antithetical to the notion of the emerging unity of humankind. As Sir Shridath Ramphal observes, we must be careful to avoid masking self-interest in a false virtue and wisdom. The day will come, he concludes, when the Security Council will enforce the absence of weapons of mass destruction from the national arsenals of every nation-state. The fact that we do not yet understand how that will occur does not preclude its inevitability. The will develops, and after it, the way.

By the same token, making the transition from national reliance on weapons of mass destruction through a reliance on their planetary control to a world entirely free of them remains almost as elusive in the 1990s as in earlier decades. As David Lange and Andrei Kozyrev observe, that dilemma may continue "well into the twenty-first century". The dilemma takes dual form: their relinquishment by the major powers that are used to governing the world through force, and the non-deployment by regional middle-power adversaries. The nuclear testing in South Asia, along with possible weapon deployment, increases the risk of regional, and to a lesser extent global, nuclear conflict. But it does not alter in any way the underlying dilemma that confronts humanity – the ownership of nuclear military power by nation-states with no discernible movement beyond the threshold of national nuclear deterrence and into an era of collective ownership or control of the weapons leading to their elimination. The South Asian states are simply holding the mirror of logic up to the major powers. In a short-term tactical sense, everything has changed since May 1998. In a long-term strategic sense, nothing has changed. Similarly, the agony of the Middle East underlines the difficulty of progressing towards the planetary interest when to do so might, even temporarily, place the national interest at risk. The point here, it would seem, is not how to reconcile the national with the planetary interests, but how to take the actual steps towards such a reconciliation in a dangerous world. Israel's "security paradox" as explained by Naomi Chazan suggests that there is still, in the more intractable cases, an "unbridgeable chasm" separating the national interest from the planetary in the real world. Even if we can perceive and accept the latter in theory, it is difficult to find the way of getting there without courting serious risk in the process. And, indeed, what the vital planetary interest is perceived to be depends to a degree on one's level of angst over who is running today's semi-anarchic world, as Toujan Faisal is concerned to point out.

Global environmental integrity is less divisive for humanity. We are one in wishing fervently to avoid fundamental disruption to the global climate and ozone layer. The vital planetary interest lies in ozone protection and climate stabilization. In the former case, the global strategy of phasing out the ozone-depleting substances at a relatively fast rate is being achieved as Koji Kakizawa observes, although as Dante Caputo maintains the phase-out and financial assistance to those in need could be faster and larger than it has been. A degree of danger and discomfort would have been avoided – still could be avoided. But here at least, humanity is acting together within a broad context. With regard to climate change, however, the experience has revealed inertia rather than bifurcation – the difficulty of turning the ships of state around in time to avoid disaster. As Qian Yi says, many problems remain to be solved, "step by step", for China to achieve sustainable development; and the problems ahead for her country, especially those relating to climate change, are also ahead for the world at large. But Kyoto has flung down the gauntlet: the lifestyle of the North will need to adjust significantly for the problem to be solved.

The same dilemma attends the question of global sustainability. Environment and development are interwoven. Are the nation-states moving fast enough to compress the demographic transition and curtail the rate of population growth? The late 1990s is critical, determining by some decimal points of a percentage in growth rate an exponential consequence in global population size half a century later. Are those of us who are able to do so contributing enough to those in need since Cairo, in 1994, so that the global strategy for population planning can be implemented? It does not seem so, concludes Margaret Alva. Are the less populated countries prepared to open their doors more to others? Not yet, notes Margaret Reynolds. Can the world double its agricultural yield on essentially the same amount of land to feed twice the present population? Can the South, in particular, break from the vicious circle imposed by the contemporary global economic order? Not unless there is a change of mindset on the part of all peoples on the planet, says Abdul Moyeen Khan, sufficient for the South to meet basic human needs – attain "sustainable livelihood". Is the North prepared to curtail its consumption pattern for the sake of humanity? There is, say Claudine Schneider and Lena Klevenås, a long way to go. Will our global ecological overshoot change in time? Will the concepts of economic growth and sustainable growth be reconciled? Where is the "new global partnership" to restore the integrity of Earth, proclaimed at Rio?

As Francesco Rutelli, re-elected in 1997 for another five-year term as mayor of Rome says, there are moments of inspiration and apprehension in contemplating the problems of the city and nation, region and planet. Inspiration draws from the ideas and creativity of committed people. Apprehension comes from a recognition of the sheer magnitude and complexity of the problems we now face, and the limited political and institutional means we have developed in the twentieth century for dealing with them. But, he concludes, leaders operate within the context of public opinion. The effect may be indirect and time-lagged, but it is we, the people, who decide our fate. Emma Bonino agrees: our decision-makers, she says, are still elected on the basis of national concerns and elections are won or lost at home. Fabio Feldmann of Brazil turns the point around: the individual citizen will be the driving force in changing the present scenario of excessive automobile use into a sustainable pattern of behaviour – and Theo Sambuaga of Indonesia when he calls for a global awareness that the interest of planet Earth is the interest of everyone. Sir Michael Marshall completes the reasoning process when he calls for parliamentarians and policy-makers around the world to act on behalf of "international public opinion" in developing the global society. Here are the practical politicians of the world, our representatives, effectively telling us that they want to move on the planetary interest but are reliant on public opinion to give them the "mandate by extension" to develop national policies that reflect a legitimate national interest.

What kind of a planet, then, what kind of world society does humanity want for the middle of the twenty-first century? Use of the "planetary interest" concept lights the way ahead in the search for answers, but it does not provide any answer itself. A conceptual instrument is not the substance of an issue. The question summons thoughts of a fundamental philosophical nature. We want a world that is stable and safe. How to obtain this in a world of aggressive human behaviour? Humanity emerged from prehistory as the Darwinian victor through its Faustian qualities of intelligence and aggression. Almost alone among the species, it has turned that aggression in upon itself. Instability and aggression have an inflationary push on weapon accumulation – both numbers and destructive power. How to break from this vicious circle – "God's riddle"?

Military security in today's world, it is generally accepted, derives from the broader notion of human security. If humans have their basic needs met, their sense of security rises commensurately, their societies become more stable and aggression diminishes. So the planetary interest can be seen as interrelated in all its aspects. Two fundamental issues are at stake: a recognition of the planet's constraints and fragility on the one hand, and an appreciation of a common human justice on the other. If we succeed in curbing both population growth and consumption patterns around the world, and manage at the same time to effect the change from finite to renewable energy resources faster than we currently are, then we shall have come a long way to living within the planet's carrying capacity. And the resources of Earth must be shared more equitably than hitherto. This does not mean an enforced classless uniformity of a nineteenth-century ideological kind. People live within the same nation-state today with vastly different levels of wealth. But they recognize nonetheless a societal responsibility for their compatriots. In the twenty-first century, that responsibility should become global – there will be standards of dignity and material wellbeing below which the world society will not tolerate its human members falling. It is a matter of degree. These considerations, however, are prescriptive. In reality, is that prescription beginning to happen? No – the discrepancy in wealth both between and among nations is actually widening. Yet, the information age is imposing a new consciousness upon us, not least upon our very young children – the leaders not of 2025 but of 2050. Social values are destined to change in the first half of the twenty-first century from those of the late twentieth. The trend toward a "self-conscious culture of global society" is already underway. It will accelerate – the culture will take stronger hold – with each generation.

Can these ideals of world society be quantified? Not easily, and with some risk at this early stage of our global consciousness. Certainly, the international community has prescribed a global population of some 9 billion by 2050, a stable world free of weapons of mass destruction by 2020 or an indeterminable date thereafter, a fully restored ozone layer by 2045, a stable albeit changed climate in the course of the twenty-first century and a sustainable global lifestyle at some unspecified time in the future. At present, the least resolved of these, and perhaps the most dangerous if left unresolved, is climate stability and its underlying factor of sustainable development and consumption. Unlike the other issues, the trend in human behaviour here has not yet turned the corner.

In determining that behaviour, citizens and governments must henceforth ask themselves whether their country is pursing a legitimate national interest. If they are not, the planet is suffering, and so is humanity. In the world of today, there is no accountability, in legal terms, for such excess or violation of such a norm. There is, however, already a moral accountability. Most people today know full well they are consuming too much when they see images of malnutrition and starvation on their screens from time to time – it no longer matters from where on the globe that image comes. They know they should not use tropical hardwood for coffins or cement casings that are devoted to a futile purpose. They know they are overusing the automobile when the car-pool lanes on the commuter highway are empty, the buses are half-full and the single-driver lanes are clogged. So the moral awareness exists. Between morality and law lies the grey area of politics – political prescription. That is where the legitimate national interest lies too, where citizens must hold their leaders to account – municipal, national and regional. In tomorrow's world, the individual will relate to the planet as much as to the city, the nation and the region, because individual wellbeing and survival will depend on it. That is what Charity Kaluki Ngilu means when she says that the national flag of her country and the blue flag of the United Nations both make her think of survival – survival of her people and of humanity.

Politics, says Gwyn Prins, is about legitimated power, and in the twenty-first century this will be predicated at the global level. For the planetary interest to be not only identified but implemented, a degree of legitimate global power will be unavoidable. As Ibrahim Hussain Zaki says, the voice not only of Darwin but of Hobbes can be heard over the centuries: when there is no other rational choice for common survival, humans will group together. The twentieth century opened with the birth of international organization. The twenty-first will open with its early maturation. It is a sensitive issue and rightly so – power has coalesced before today to malign effect through undue haste or wilful deceit, so we must proceed with caution and circumspection. But proceed we must. As Sir Shridath puts it, as the role of international institutions in global governance grows, the need to ensure that they are democratic also increases. But, as he says, those worried about world government need have no fear, given the impoverishment and political limitations of the current institutions. The true worry is that, without greater global public expenditure, there will be no decent habitable world for humans to govern.

None of this is to counsel despair. The human predicament continues to be a mixture of security and vulnerability, of confidence and apprehension, uncertainty and conviction. It will always be thus, not least when we move out into space seriously as a species, having made our first tentative steps. Space exploration will no doubt bring the world together above all else. The drama of the Mir space station and the co-operation forged between Russian and American crews both in orbit and on the ground brought this home in 1997. In November of that year, the president of the UN General Assembly welcomed the successful launch of space shuttle *Columbia* carrying American, Japanese and Ukrainian astronauts. It demonstrated, he said, the "vital role of international co-operation" in the peaceful uses of outer space – as indeed will the future international space station. Such global co-operation will only intensify in the twenty-first century.

There is, finally, a spiritual dimension to the human predicament, ages old and qualitatively modern at the same time. In recent decades, theologians and politicians have come together to re-examine the "human–Earth" relationship in light of both traditional religious insight and contemporary cosmological thought. Work is underway to intensify the dialogue that has been ongoing, albeit in hesitant manner, among our major religious faiths with a view to achieving a greater mutual understanding and common insight in elevating the plane of human existence. New areas of enquiry are also invigorating the quest for a common spiritual and temporal redemption. Together, these enlightened endeavours are beginning to have a renewed influence on our daily lifestyles, affecting our consumption patterns and our relationship to Nature and to our fellow human. And it is adumbrating our politics – some fear for the worse, others believe for the better. In the greater unity of human knowledge nothing is unrelated, and our spiritual enquiry can only inform our secular behaviour – our politics. We should not be afraid. We must step out, as a species, and in the course of the new century and the millennium unite our strength. As Carl Sagan put it in his final thoughts that formed the answer to his question, Who speaks for Earth?: "Our loyalties are to the species and the planet. *We* speak for Earth."

To speak for Earth as a species, however, we need to identify and pursue the planetary interest, ensuring that our national interests and policies are compatible and our global power confined to what is legitimate. Only then shall we succeed in managing the problems that lie ahead and secure our common human destiny.

Figure 16.1

BIBLIOGRAPHY

Abrams, I. (ed.), *The words of peace, selections from the speeches of the winners of the Nobel Peace Prize.* (New York, Newmarket Press, 1990).

Allot, P., *Eunomia, new order for a new world* (Oxford, Oxford University Press, 1990).

Alvazzi del Fraet, A. & J. Norberry (eds), *Environmental crime, sanctioning strategies and sustainable development* (Rome, UN Interregional Crime and Justice Research Institute, 1993).

Balasuriya, T., *Planetary theology* (Maryknoll, N.Y., Orbis, 1984).

Beard, C.A., *The idea of national interest* (New York, Macmillan 1934).

Beetham, D., *The legitimation of power* (Atlantic Highlands, N.J., Humanities Press, 1991).

Benedick, R., *Ozone diplomacy, new directions in safeguarding the planet* (Cambridge, Mass., Harvard University Press, 1991).

Bertsch, G.K. (ed.), *Global policy studies* (Beverley Hills, Sage Publications, 1982).

Bok, S.A., *A strategy for peace, human values and the threat of war* (New York, Random House, 1990).

Boutros-Ghali, B., *The disarmament agenda of the international community and beyond, statements of the Secretary-General* (New York, United Nations, 1994).

Brock, W. & R. Hormats (eds), *The global economy* (New York, W.W. Norton, 1990).

Brown, L.R. & H. Kane, *Full house, reassessing the Earth's population carrying capacity* (New York, W.W. Norton, 1994).

Brown, L.R. (ed.), *The worldwatch reader on global environmental issues* (New York, W.W. Norton, 1991).

Brown, L.R., C. Flavin, S. Postel, *Saving the planet, how to shape an environmentally sustainable global economy* (New York, W.W. Norton, 1991).

Brown, L.R., et al., *State of the world* (New York, W.W. Norton, 1984–97).

Brown, L.R., M. Renner, C. Flavin, *Vital signs* (New York, W.W. Norton, 1992–97).

Brown, N. (ed.), *Ethics & Agenda 21, moral implications of a global consensus* (New York, UN Publications, 1994).

Buzan, B., *People, states and fear, the national security problem in international relations* (Brighton, Wheatsheaf, 1983).

Cahill, K.M. (ed.), *A framework for survival* (New York, Harper Collins, 1993).

Carlson, D. & C. Comstock (eds), *Securing our planet* (Los Angeles, Tarcher, 1986).

Childers, E. with B. Urquhart, *Renewing the United Nations system* (Uppsala, Dag Hammarskjöld Foundation, 1994).

Clark, R. & M. Sann, *The case against the bomb* (Camden, NJ, Rutgers University School of Law, 1996).

Clements, K. (ed.), *Peace and security in the Asia-Pacific region* (Tokyo, United Nations University Press, 1993).

Cohen, J., *How many people can the Earth support?* (New York, W.W. Norton, 1995).

Cortright, D. & G. A. Lopez (eds), *Economic sanctions, panacea or peace-building in a post-cold war world?* (Boulder, Westview, 1995).

Cradock, P., *In pursuit of British interests* (London, John Murray, 1997).

Eade, J., *Living the global city, globalization as a local process* (London, Routledge, 1997).

Easterbrook, G., *A moment on Earth, the coming age of environmental optimism* (New York, Penguin, 1995).

Elgar, E., *Measuring sustainable development* (London, UCL Press/World Bank, 1997).

Evans, G., *Co-operating for peace, the global agenda for the 1990s and beyond* (St. Leonards, NSW, Allen and Unwin, 1993).

Feather, F. & R. Mayur (eds), *Optimistic outlooks* (Toronto, Global Futures Network, 1982).

Feiveson, H.A. (ed.), *Science and global security, the technical basis for arms control and environmental policy initiatives* (New York, Gordon and Breach, 1989).

Finmore, M., *National interests in international society* (Ithaca, Cornell University Press, 1996).

Frankel, J., *National interest.* (London, Pall Mall, 1970).

Galbraith, J.K., *Economics and public purpose* (London, Vance Packard, 1974).

——, *The hidden persuaders* (Harmondsworth, Penguin, 1981).

Gellner, E., *Conditions of liberty, civil society and its rivals* (Harmondsworth, Penguin, 1996).

Gore, A., *Earth in the balance, ecology and the human spirit* (New York, Plume, 1993).

Graham, K., *National security concepts of states, New Zealand* (New York, Taylor & Francis, 1989).

Guéhenno, J.-M., *The end of the nation-state* (Minneapolis, University of Minnesota Press Tr. V. Elliot, 1995).

Hamilton, E.K. (ed.), *America's global interests, a new agenda* (New York, W.W. Norton, 1989).

Hardin, G., *Living within limits, ecology, economics and population taboos* (Oxford, Oxford University Press, 1995).

Hodgson, M.G.S., *Rethinking world history, essays on Europe, Islam and world history* (Cambridge, Cambridge University Press, 1993).

Johnson, S., *World population, turning the tide* (London, Graham & Trotman, 1994).

Keane, J., *Reflections on violence* (London, Verso, 1996).

Kelsen, H., *The law of the United Nations* (London, Stevens & Sons, 1951).

Kennedy, P., *The rise and fall of the great powers* (New York, Random House, 1987).

——, *Preparing for the twenty-first century* (New York, Random House, 1993).

Kidder, R.M., *Reinventing the future, global goals for the 21st century* (Massachusetts, MIT Press, 1989).

——, *An agenda for the 21st century, interviews from the Christian Science Monitor* (Massachusetts, MIT Press, 1988).

——, *Shared values for a troubled world, conversations with men and women of conscience* (San Francisco, Jossey-Bass, 1994).

Kissinger, K., *Diplomacy* (New York, Simon & Schuster, 1994).

Ku, K. & T. Weiss (eds), *Toward understanding global governance* (Providence, RI, Academic Council on the United Nations, 1998).

Kung, H. & K. Kuschel (eds), *A global ethic, the declaration of the parliament of the world's religions* (New York, Continuum, 1993).

Kung, K., *Global responsibility, in search of a new world ethic* (New York, Continuum, 1993).

Lange, D., *Nuclear free, the New Zealand way* (Auckland, Penguin, 1990).

Lovelock, J.E., *Gaia* (Oxford, Oxford University Press, 1979).

——, *The ages of Gaia, a biography of our living Earth* (New York, Bantam, 1990).

Mathews, J.T. (ed.), *Preserving the global environment, the challenge of shared leadership* (New York, W.W. Norton, 1991).

Maynes, C.W. & R.S. Williamson (eds), *US foreign policy and the United Nations system* (New York, Norton, 1996).

McGurn, M., *Global spirituality, planetary consciousness* (Ardsley-on-Hudson, NY, World Happiness and Co-operation, 1984).

McLoughlin, C. & G. Davidson, *Spiritual politics, changing the world from the inside out* (New York, Ballantine Books, 1994).

McMichael, A.J., *Planetary overload* (Cambridge, Cambridge University Press, 1993).

Meadows, D.L. et al., *The limits to growth* (New York, Universe Books, 1972).

Milbrath, L.W., *Envisioning a sustainable society, learning our way out* (Albany, SUNY Press, 1989).

Morgenthau, H.J., *In defense of the national interest, a critical examination of American foreign policy* (New York, Knopf, 1951).

Muller, R. & D. Roche, *Safe passage into the twenty-first century* (New York, Continuum, 1995).

Muller, R., *New genesis, shaping a global spirituality* (New York, Doubleday, 1984).

Najman, D. & H. d'Orville, *Towards a new multilateralism, funding global priorities* (Paris, Independent Commission on Population and Quality of Life, 1995).

Nuechterlein, D.E., *United States national interests in a changing world* (Lexington, Ky, University Press of Kentucky 1973).

Nye, J., *Nuclear ethics* (New York, Free Press, 1986).

Pedler, K., *The quest for Gaia* (London, Granada, 1979).

Porter, G. & J.W. Brown, *Global environmental politics* (Boulder, Westview, 1991).

Prins, G. (ed.), *Threats without enemies, facing environmental insecurity* (London, Earthscan, 1993).

Ramphal, S.S., *Our country, the planet* (Washington, DC, Island Press, 1992).

Rawls, J., *The theory of justice* (Oxford, Oxford University Press, 1973).

Reich, R.B., *The work of nations* (New York, Alfred A. Knopf, 1991).

Sagan, C., *Cosmos* (London, MacDonald, 1980).

Said, E., *Culture and imperialism* (New York, Alfred A. Knopf, 1994).

Sardar, Z., *The touch of Midas, knowledge and environment in Islam and the West* (Manchester, Manchester University Press, 1982).

Sassen, S., *The global city* (Princeton, NJ, Princeton University Press, 1991).

Schmoockler, A.B., *The parable of the tribes, the problem of power in social evolution* (Boston, Houghton Mifflin, 1984).

Sheldrake, R., *The rebirth of nature, The greening of science and God* (New York, Batam, 1991).

Siedlecky, S. & D. Wyndham, *Populate or perish, Australian women's fight for birth control* (Sydney, Allen & Unwin, 1990).

Simma, B. (ed.), *The charter of the United Nations, a commentary* (Oxford, Oxford University Press, 1995).

Soros, G., *Opening the Soviet system* (London, Weidenfeld & Nicholson, 1990).

Stanley, C.M., *Managing global problems, a guide to survival* (Muscatine, Iowa, Stanley Foundation, 1979).

Stone, C., *The gnat is older than man* (Princeton, NJ, Princeton University Press, 1993).

Tehranian, K. & M. Tehranian, *Restructuring for world peace, on the threshold of the twenty-first century* (Cresskill, Hampton Press, 1992).

Tolba, M.K., *Saving our planet, challenges and hopes* (London, Chapman & Hall, 1992).

Tucker, M.E. & J.A. Grim (eds), *Worldviews and ecology, religion, philosophy, and the environment* (Maryknoll, NY, Orbis, 1994).

Urquhart, B. & E. Childers, *Towards a more effective United Nations* (Uppsala, Dag Hammarskjöld Foundation, 1992).

——, *A world in need of leadership, tomorrow's United Nations* (Uppsala, Dag Hammarskjöld Foundation, 1996).

Van Dyke, J.M., D. Zaelke, G. Hewison (eds), *Freedom for the seas in the 21st century* (Washington, Island Press, 1993).

Varea, C. & A. Maestro (eds), *Guerra y sanciones a Irak, Naciones Unidas y el 'nuevo orden mundial* (Madrid, La Catarata, 1997).

Wackernagel, M. & W. Rees, *Our ecological footprint, reducing human impact on the Earth* (Gabriola Island, BC, New Society Publishers, 1996).

Ward, B. & R. Dubos, *Only one Earth, the care and maintenance of a small planet* (New York, Penguin, 1972).

Ward, B., *Spaceship Earth* (London, Hamish Hamilton, 1966).

——, *Progress for a small planet* (New York, W.W. Norton, 1979).

Waterlow, C., *The hinge of history* (London, One World Trust, 1995).

Weiss, T.G. (ed.), *Beyond UN subcontracting, task-sharing with regional security arrangements and service-providing NGOs* (New York, St. Martin's Press, 1998).

INTERNATIONAL ORGANIZATIONS

United Nations

United Nations, *Renewing the United Nations, a programme for reform, report of the Secretary-General* (New York, United Nations, 1997).

United Nations, *The blue helmets, a review of United Nations peacekeeping* (New York, United Nations, 1990).

United Nations Daily Highlights.

United Nations, *Final document, first special session of the general assembly on disarmament* (New York, United Nations, 1978).

United Nations General Assembly. *Official Records.*

United Nations General Assembly. *Annual Reports of the Secretary-General on the Work of the Organization.*

United Nations, *Study on the climatic and other global effects of nuclear war, report of the UN Secretary-General*, 1988.

United Nations, *Agenda 21 – The United Nations programme of action for sustainable development*, 1992.

United Nations, *Inter-governmental panel on climate change, second assessment report*, 1995.

UNDP, *Human development report*, 1997.

United Nations, *Programme of action of the international conference on population and development*, 1995.

United Nations, *Revision of UN population estimates & projections*, 1996.

United Nations, *Population handbook, population reference bureau.*

United Nations Fund for Population Activities, *State of the world population report, the right to choose, reproductive rights and reproductive health*, 1997.

United Nations, *Global outlook 2000, An economic, social and environmental perspective*, 1990.

United Nations, *World food summit plan of action*, 1996.

United Nations, *Rome declaration on world food security*, 1996.

United Nations, *Istanbul declaration on human settlements*, 1996.

United Nations, *Habitat agenda*, 1996.

United Nations, *World urbanisation prospects, 1996 revision*, 1997.

United Nations, *World statistics in brief 1992*, 14th edition.

United Nations, *Non-legally binding authoritative statement of principles for a global consensus on the management, conservation and sustainable development of all types of forests*, 1992.

Conference on Disarmament

Conference on Disarmament *Official records.*

Organisation for Economic Co-operation and Development

Development Co-operation, Efforts and Policies of the Members of the Development Assistance Committee 1992 Report

Food and Agricultural Organization,

Food and Agriculture Organization, *State of the world's forests, Executive Summary*, 1997.

Food and Agriculture Organization. *Country Briefs.*

Food and Agriculture Organization, *Land, food and people*, 1984.

International Bank for Reconstruction and Development (World Bank),

IBRD *Country Reports, Executive Summary.* World Bank.

IBRD *Making sustainable development, the World Bank and the environment, 1994.*

International Court of Justice

ICJ, *Advisory opinion on the illegality of nuclear weapons*, 1996.

ICJ *Yearbooks.*

INDEPENDENT COMMISSIONS

Canberra Commission on the Elimination of Nuclear Weapons (Canberra, Department of Foreign Affairs and Trade, 1996).

Commission on America's National Interests, *America's national interests* (Kennedy School of Government, Nixon Center for Peace & Freedom, The Rand Corporation, 1996).

Commission on Global Governance, *Our global neighbourhood* (Oxford, Oxford University Press, 1995).

Council on Foreign Relations, *American national interest and the United Nations* (New York, Council on Foreign Relations, 1996).

Independent Commission on Disarmament and Security Issues, *Common security, a blueprint for survival* (New York, Simon & Schuster, 1982).

Independent Commission on International Development Issues, *North–South, a programme for survival* (London, Pan, 1982).

Independent Commission on the Quality of Life, *Caring for the future, report of the Independent Commission on Population and the Quality of Life* (Oxford, Oxford University Press, 1996).

International Commission on Peace and Food, *Uncommon opportunities, an agenda for peace and equitable development* (London, Zed Books, 1998).

The South Commission, *The challenge to the South* (Oxford, Oxford University Press, 1990).

World Commission on Environment and Development, *Our common future* (Oxford, Oxford University Press, 1987).

JOURNALS & PERIODICALS

Alternatives
American Journal of International Law
American Psychological Review
British Journal of International Studies
Environment
Environ Impact Assessment Rev
Foreign Affairs
Foreign Policy
Fortune Magazine
Global Governance
International Affairs
International Organization
Journal of Social Issues
Mezhdunarodnya Zhizn
New Scientist
Orbis
Southern California Law Review
The National Interest
United Nations Chronicle
World Politics

ANNUAL PUBLICATIONS

Greenglobe yearbook. Oxford, Oxford University Press
The Military Balance. London, Brasseys

REFERENCE BOOKS

Atlaseco World Economic Atlas Paris, EOC, 1994
Encyclopaedia of Social Sciences

Encyclopaedia Britannica
Facts on File
Keesings Archives

MONOGRAPHS & RESEARCH PAPERS

Allison, G., O.R. Coté, R.A. Falkenrath, S.E. Miller, *Avoiding nuclear anarchy, containing the threat of loose Russian weapons and fissile material* (Cambridge, Mass; Centre for Science & International Affairs, Harvard University, CSIA Study #12, MIT Press, 1995).

Asmus, R.D., *The New US Strategic Debate* (Rand Corporation, Santa Monica, 1994).

Buchan, G.C., *US Nuclear Strategy for the Post-Cold War Era* (Rand Corporation, Santa Monica, 1994).

Carter, A.B., W.J. Perry, J.D. Steinbrunner, *A New Concept of Cooperative Security* (Brookings Occasional Papers, Brookings Institution, Washington, DC, 1992).

De Andreis, M. & F. Calagero, *The Soviet nuclear weapon legacy.* SIPRI Research Report No. 10 (Oxford, Oxford University Press, 1995).

Graham, K., *The planetary interest*, Occasional Paper No. 7 (Cambridge, Cambridge University, 1995).

Hammarskjöld, D., *Today's world and the United Nations, four addresses by Secretary-General Dag Hammarskjöld* (New York, United Nations, 1960).

Levin, N.D. (ed.), *Prisms and policy, US security strategy after the Cold War* (Rand Corporation, Santa Monica, 1994).

Ramphal, S.S., *Global governance.* The Second Global Security Lecture (Cambridge, Cambridge University, 1995).

Roberts, A. & B. Kingsbury, *Presiding over a divided world, changing UN roles, 1945–93.* Occasional Paper Series (New York, International Peace Academy, 1994).

Tanham, G.K., *Indian Strategic Thought, An Interpretative Essay* (Rand Corporation, Santa Monica. 1992).

Wackernagel, M. et al., *Ecological footprints of nations* (San José, Earth Council, 1997).

Zonnefeld, L. (ed.), *Humanity's Quest for Unity, A United Nations Teilhard Colloquium* (Wassenaar, Mirananda, 1985).

GOVERNMENTAL PUBLICATIONS

Australia:

Australian Agency for International Development, *About Australia's aid program.* Canberra, AUSAID Public Affairs Division, 1996.

Department of Foreign Affairs & Trade, *In the national interest, foreign and trade policy white paper*, 1997.

Australia, National report on population for the United Nations International Conference on Population and Development, 1994.

Australia and the ICPD, Australia's position against the Program of Action of the United Nations International Conference on Population and Development, 1994.

Bangladesh:

Planning Commission, Ministry of Planning, *Participatory perspective plan for Bangladesh 1995–2010*, 1995.

New Zealand:

New Zealand Ministry of Foreign Affairs. *Press statements.*

New Zealand Ministry of Foreign Affairs, *United Nations handbook*, 1997.

Sweden:

Report of the Government of Sweden to the United Nations Special Assembly of the General Assembly, *From environmental protection to sustainable development*, 1997.

United Kingdom:

UK Parliamentary Brief, December 1997.

Foreign and Commonwealth Office, *Mission statement*. London, Foreign and Commonwealth Office, 1997.
London, House of Commons, Session 1992–93, Foreign Affairs Committee Third Report. *The expanding rôle of the United Nations and its implications for United Kingdom policy.*
Department of International Development, *Eliminating world poverty, a challenge for the twenty-first century*. London, Department of International Development, 1997.
United Kingdom House of Commons. *Parliamentary debates (Hansard)*.
United States:
Department of Defense, *Annual report to Congress, Secretary of Defense Caspar Weinberger, F/Y 1985*, 1985.
United States GPO, *US fiscal year 1988 arms control impact statements*, 1998.
United States daily bulletin, Geneva.

NON-GOVERNMENTAL ORGANIZATIONS

Business Council for Sustainable Development, *Getting efficient, report of BCSD first Antwerp Eco-Efficiency Workshop*. Geneva, 1993.
Canadian Broadcasting Corporation, *Balance and biosphere, the environmental crisis*. Toronto, CBC, 1971.
International Forum on Population in the Twenty-First Century, *Amsterdam declaration on a better life for future generations*. Amsterdam, 1989.
Parliamentarians for Global Action, *Annual report*. NY, PGA, 1993.

NEWSPAPERS & RADIO

BBC World
Far Eastern Economic Review
Guardian Weekly
International Herald Tribune
La Stampa
The Guardian
Wall Street Journal
Wall Street Journal Europe
Washington Post

Index

ABM Treaty 58
abortion 141, 142
absolute poverty 160
action, legitimacy and 15, 16, 21
Action Programme of 1978 Final document 3, 32, 34, 35, 39, 40, 46–7, 64
advisory opinion *see* International Court of Justice
Agency for the Sustainable Development of the Mediterranean (ECOMED) 263
Agenda 21 88, 161, 168
  in China 125
  and climate change 117
  and consumption 203, 204, 215
  and forestry 186, 187, 196, 201
  and global sustainability 130–1, 132–3, 159, 164, 168, 237, 258, 260
  and health 161, 162, 165
  and population 141
  see also Habitat Agenda
agriculture 164, 169
  use of chemicals in 100
aid *see* official development assistance
air-fuel explosive weapons 31
Air Pollutant Index 193
Alliance of Small Island States (AOSIS) 113, 117–18, 120
Allott, P. 15, 16
Alva, M. 271
Amazon Forest 198
American Dream 175, 213–14, 215
Amsterdam Declaration on a Better Life for Future Generations 141
Annan, K. xxiii, 111, 161, 162, 174, 238, 257
Annex I countries 108, 109, 118
Antarctic Treaty 1959 7, 43n.
Antarctica 92, 100
  and ozone hole 100, 101, 102
Arab interest, and security 68–71
Arctic, ozone levels 102
Argentina 59, 68, 253
  and ozone depletion 90, 92–8
Article 2 countries 96
Article 5 countries 96

ASEAN (Association of South East Asian Nations) 113, 243
  Co-operation Plan on Trans-boundary Pollution 193
Assessment Report *see* climate change, Assessment Report
Atlantic Forest (Brazil) 198–200
AUSAID 155
Australia 90, 92, 110, 111, 112, 135–6, 194
  ecological footprint 133, 135
  national interest 12n., 152
  nuclear policy 41, 50
  population stabilization 142, 148, 149, 151–7
Austria 97, 110, 112

Balladur, E. 22
ballistic missiles 58
Bangladesh 112, 117, 120, 133, 135–6, 166, 168–75
Barbados Declaration on Sustainable Development of Small Island States 117
Barnett, M. 27n.
basic human needs 129, 161, 166, 172, 175
Beijing Declaration on Women 183
Belarus 54, 56
Berlin Mandate 109, 118
Berry, T. 175
Best Practices and Local Leadership Programme 263
Bhopal disaster 81
Biodiversity Convention 196, 200, 201
biological weapons 31, 32, 63, 71, 75, 79
Biological Weapons Convention 34, 35, 63–4, 65, 75, 248
Blair, T. 247
Bonino, E. 20, 271
Bosnia 69
Boutros-Ghali, B. 7, 8, 247, 253, 264
Brandt Report 3, 22, 24
Brazil 59, 68, 84, 92, 111, 112, 113, 128, 134, 135–6, 250
  forestry in 187, 196–202
Bretton Woods bodies 234
Britain *see* United Kingdom
Brundtland Commission 6, 81, 82
  Report of 130, 132, 196
Budiman, A. 193

Bulgaria 110, 112, 244
business, and sustainability 211–12, 221–2
Business Ecology Network 212

Cairo Conference *see* UN International Conference
    on Population and Development
Cairo Programme of Action 140–1, 144, 147–8, 152,
    153, 203, 204, 248
Cambodia 69
Canada 84, 92, 110, 111, 112, 126, 133, 186, 193, 194,
    201
Caputo, D. 270
car industry 197, 208, 219, 224
carbon budget 105, 106
carbon dioxide 105, 106–7, 109, 111, 112, 220
Carlsson-Ramphal Commission *see* Commission on
    Global Governance
carrying capacity 129, 130, 132, 145, 153, 164, 172,
    173, 179, 189, 192, 195, 248, 269
Carson, R. 169
cause, legitimacy and 15, 16, 21
CFCs (chlorofluorocarbons) 94, 96, 100–1, 102
Chad 208
Chazan, N. 270
chemical weapons 31, 32, 63, 71, 75
    in Gulf War 69, 79
Chemical Weapons Convention 34, 35, 59, 64, 65, 248
    Israel and 75, 77
    USA and 57
chemicals, use of 82, 100
Chernobyl disaster 81
Chile 84, 90, 93
China 31, 54, 58, 63, 65, 92, 97, 134, 155
    and climate change 111, 112, 113, 119, 122–8
    nuclear weapons policy 41
    and population 144
Churchill, Sir W. 229
Ciorbea, V. 261
cities 161, 257–9, 260–3
Cities Charter 264
citizen activism 17–18
    and ozone layer 101–2
City Development Index 258, 259
civil society 15, 16, 24
    global power and 235
    sustainability and 222–3
Clark, R. 69
climate change 82, 105–13, 172–3, 272
    Assessment Report of IPCC 108
    in China 122–8
    in the Maldives 115–21
    UK and 248
Climate Change Convention 17, 83, 108, 123, 196
Climatewise Programme (USA) 210
Clinton, Bill 209, 215–16
collective responsibility 233
Colombia 134
Commission on Global Governance 6, 36, 230, 232–4,
    237, 238, 263

Commission on Sustainable Development *see* UN
    Commission on Sustainable Development
Committee on Disarmament 34
common but differentiated responsibilities 96, 108,
    109, 118, 141, 159, 201
"common heritage of humankind" 233
common interest 6–7
common security 33
Comprehensive Test Ban Treaty 41, 59
Conference on Disarmament 41, 69
Conferences of the Parties to the Climate Change
    Convention 118
consensus 25–6
consumer power 18, 200, 222–3
Costa Rica 134
Council of Petitions 235
counter-proliferation 56
Covenant of the League of Nations *see* League of
    Nations
Cox, R. 6
Cradock, Sir Percy 250
culture of civility 16
Czech Republic 59, 110, 112, 133, 244

DDT 169
Daimuna reactor 68
Darwin, C. 120, 271, 272
decalogue 34
Declaration of The Hague 233, 235, 248
Declaration on Social Development and Sustainable
    Human Settlements 1994 260
delegated authority 17
democracy 183
democratic deficit 243
demographic transition 140, 144
Denmark 84, 97, 110, 112, 133
deterrence *see* nuclear deterrence
development 135, 159–66
    environment and 96, 123, 159, 196, 270
dictatorship 17, 28n.
differentiation principle 109, 118, 141
direct mandate 17–18
disarmament 32–4, 39–43, 49
    general and complete 33–4
Dubos, R. 229

Eade, J. 257
Earth Summit *see* Rio Earth Summit
earthshare 131
ECHO (European Community Humanitarian Office) 20
eco-labelling 191, 192, 221
ecological footprints 131–2, 133–4, 174
    Sweden 223
    USA 215
ECOMED (Agency for the Sustainable Development of
    the Mediterranean) 263
Economic and Monetary Union 244
economic growth 130, 132, 160, 224, 225
Economic Security Council 234, 235

education on the environment 213, 221
Egypt 65, 76, 77, 112, 120, 134
energy consumption 112, 124
  in Bangladesh 172
  in China 124, 125–7, 179
energy efficiency 211, 220–1, 222
Energy Saving Law 125–6
energy tax 219
environment 3
  see also climate change; ozone protection
environmental accounting 220, 223
environmental education 213, 221
Ethiopia 134
Estonia 54, 110, 112, 134
eunomia 16
Euratom 242
European Charter of Local Self-Government 260
European Coal and Steel Community (ECSC) 242
European Community 20, 241
European Economic Community (EEC) 242
European Parliament 243
European Union 17, 20, 25, 111, 113, 241
  and global power 242–3, 243–5

"Factor 10" approach 222
Faisal, T. 270
Falkland Islands *see* Malvinas
family planning 141, 142, 145–7, 155
Fangataufa atoll 52
FAO *see* UN Food and Agricultural Organization
Farraka Barrage 170
Feldman, F. 271
female infanticide 147
Final document 32, 33, 39, 40, 55
Finland 54, 84, 110, 112, 133, 194
fishery management 170, 209
food 160, 161–2
  national policies on 164, 168, 169–71, 177–8
food security 161, 164, 166n.
forest management 185–202
forest principles 187, 190, 192, 196, 200
Forum for the Future 18
Forum of Civil Society 235
fossil fuel economy 113, 119, 126, 172
"Founding Act" 59–60
Framework Convention on Climate Change *see*
  Climate Change Convention
Framework Convention for the Protection of the
  Ozone Layer *see* Vienna Framework
  Convention
France 48, 54, 58, 65, 97, 110, 112, 133, 179, 193, 208
 nuclear testing 52–3
funding for global governance 235–7

Galbraith, J. 18
Gandhi, I. 145
Gandhi, R. 145
Gayoom, M.A. 115, 116, 117, 118, 120
Gaza strip 69

Gellner, E. 15, 16
general and complete disarmament *see* disarmament
General Assembly 4, 6, 7, 9, 11, 25, 32, 33, 39, 41, 48,
  57, 67, 238
general will 17–18
Germany 65, 84, 97, 110, 111, 112, 119, 128, 133, 148,
  201, 208, 248, 250
Global Action Plan for the Earth 213
Global Charter for Local Self-Governance 260
global commons 23, 103
Global Environment Facility 127
global environmental integrity 10, 30, 81–4, 233–4,
  270
  UK and 248
  see also climate change; ozone protection
global governance 230–2
  funding for 235–7
Global Indicators Database 258, 259
global objectives 11, 26, 30, 259–60
  in environment 82–3, 88, 108
  in security 32–5, 39, 63–4
  in sustainability 130–2, 140–1, 161–3, 186, 203–4
Global Ozone Observing System 88
global partnership 159, 166, 168
global powers 229–38, 249–50, 257
  Europe and 241–6
  see also legitimate global power
global problems 3, 9–10, 11
  of environment 81–2, 87, 105–7
  of security 32, 39, 63
  of sustainability 81–2, 129–30, 139–40, 160–1,
    185–6, 203
  see also risks
global security 19, 33, 35, 41, 49, 54, 55, 59, 60, 66, 75,
  83, 231, 242, 248
global strategic security 10, 30, 31–6, 232–3, 248–9,
  270
  see also nuclear weapons
global strategy 11, 26, 30
  for the environment 88, 108
  for security 32–5, 39, 40–1, 64
  for sustainability 130–1, 140–1, 161, 162, 186, 204
Global Strategy for Shelter to the Year 2000 162,
  260
global sustainable development 10, 30, 129–37, 166,
  234, 270–1
  see also consumption; development; forest
    management; population stabilization
global taxation 237
global threats 11, 21, 26
global values 230–1
global warming 102, 103, 105, 107
  effects of 107, 115, 120, 122–3
Gorbachev, M. 5, 57, 229, 253
Gore, A. 81
Graham, K. 8, 19
Gray, K. 18
Greece 110
Green Futures 18

Green Revolution 129, 169
Green Scissors Campaign 212–13
greenhouse gases 105, 106, 109
    emission of 110–12, 124, 193
    reduction of 125, 127
Group of Eighteen 46
Group of Seven 57, 234
Group of Sixteen 7, 9, 237
Guatemala 208
Gulf War or conflict 68, 69, 79
Günter, S. 69

Habitat Agenda 162, 164–5, 168, 259
Habitat II *see* Istanbul Summit on Human
    Settlements
Hammarskjöld, D. 6, 22, 24, 229
Hanson, P. 155
Hernandez, S. xviii, 7, 8
Hasan, M. 194
health 161, 162, 168
    in Bangladesh 169
    national policies for 165, 171, 178
heart of palm extraction 200
Hiroshima 42, 69
Hobbes, T. 120, 272
Hobsbawn, E. 230
housing, in Rome 261
    see also shelter
Hulth, M. 219
human needs 9, 10, 129–30, 172, 225
    costs of 163
    see also food; health; shelter
human rights 9, 10, 242
Hungary 59, 84, 110, 111, 244
Huntingdon, S. 54
hydrofluorocarbons 96–7

Iceland 110, 111, 112, 133
immigration policy, in Australia 154–5
Improved Limb Atmospheric Spectrometer 100
India 63, 65, 84, 92, 97, 111, 112, 128, 250
    assistance to 148–9, 156
    ecological footprint 134–6
    nuclear weapons policy 34, 35, 41, 59
    population stabilization 142, 144–50
indirect mandate 18–19
Indonesia 111, 128, 134–6
    assistance to 155, 194
    forest fires in 1997 192–4
    forestry in 187, 189–95
informed choice 141
informed consent 18–19, 24, 251
institutional reform 231–2, 232–3, 235
Inter-Governmental Panel on Climate Change 19, 22,
    107, 108, 109
Inter-Governmental Panel on Forestry 186, 200
International Court of Justice 39, 40, 42, 50, 233, 235
International Criminal Court 235, 245
International Development Agency 148

International Monetary Fund 182
International Tropical Timber Organization 192
Inter-Parliamentary Union (IPU) 253
Iran 54, 58, 63, 65, 68, 79
    missile capabilities 76, 77
Iraq 31, 34, 65, 66, 69, 79
    missile capabilities 76, 77
Ireland 84, 110, 112, 133, 177
Ismail, R. 7, 14n., 207, 237
Israel 36, 68, 134, 270
    chemical and biological weapons 63, 65, 66, 71,
        74–80
    nuclear weapons policy 35, 41, 68, 71, 75–7
Istanbul Manifesto 260
Istanbul Summit on Human Settlements 1996
        (Habitat II) 161, 258, 259, 269
Italy 97, 110, 112, 133, 194, 208

Japan 31, 54, 70, 84, 133, 148, 193, 194, 201, 250
    and climate change 110, 112, 113, 119, 128
    and nuclear policy 41
    and ozone depletion 90, 92, 97, 99–103
Jiang, Z. 126
Jordan 76, 134
    chemical and biological weapons 65, 66, 67–72
Jua Kali 179
jurisdictional competence 25

Kakizawa, K. 270
Kazakhstan 54, 56, 58
Keane, J. 16
Kenya 72, 136, 166
    developmental concerns 176–83
Kerala 147
Khameini, A. 77
Khan, A. 271
Kiribati 112, 120
Kissinger, H. 168
Klevenås, L. 119, 271
Korea, South 193
Kozyrev, A. 51, 270
Kuwait 69, 70
Kyoto Protocol 1997 19, 83, 103, 108, 109, 111, 113,
        117, 118, 128, 202, 212, 242, 270

land degradation 169, 179, 199–200
Lange, D. 270
Latvia 54, 110, 112, 244
Law of the Sea Convention 1982 7, 23
League of Nations 24–5, 74
Lebanon 68, 69
legitimacy 16–20, 21, 67
    and global governance 230–2, 251–2
    three factors of 15–16
    UN and 252–3
legitimate global power 21, 23–6, 82, 272
    and Europe 243–5
    and global environmental integrity 233–4
    and global strategic security 232–3

and global sustainability 234–7
  Rome and 263–4
  United Kingdom and 250–1
legitimate national interests 21, 22–3, 26, 30, 53, 67,
    175, 272, 273
  in consumption 205–6, 215, 223–4
  and the environment 82, 83–4, 90, 96–7, 101–3,
    111–13, 118–19, 128
  and security 36, 42–3, 51–2, 58–60, 65–6, 68–71,
    78–9
  and sustainability 133–6, 142, 146–9, 156–7, 165–6,
    172–3, 180–2, 191–4, 200–1
Libya 63, 65, 76
Lie, T. 6
Liechtenstein 110
life expectancy 161
Lithuania 244
Local Agenda 21, Rome 262
local authorities, and sustainability 211, 260
local powers 257–65
Luxembourg 110, 112

Maastricht Treaty 243–4, 245
mahogany 200
Major, J. 248, 250
Malaysia 134, 186, 193
Maldives, and climate change 112, 113, 115–21
Male Declaration on Global Warming and Sea-Level
    Rise 116
Malthus 144, 160
Malvinas 92, 253
mandate by extension 19–20, 271
mandates 17–20, 21
Maragall, P. 264
Marshall, M. 271
Marshall Islands 112, 120
media, and sustainable development 213–14, 215
MEDURBS-NOUN Programme 264
Mercosur 243
methane 105, 106, 124
Mexico 92, 93, 111, 134
Middle East 270
  security in 65–6, 79–80
Millennium Assembly 238
minimum standard of living 10, 160, 172, 176
Minnesota 211
Moi, D. arap 181
Mollin, R. 69
Mongolia 54
Monnet, J. 242
Montreal Protocol 83, 88, 90, 93, 96, 97, 99, 103, 248
Morganthau, H. 5
Moon Treaty 1979 7
Multilateral Fund (for the Protection of the Ozone
    Layer) 88, 89, 96, 97, 101
municipal interest 4
  and city strategies 260–3
  and planetary interest 27, 257–9
Mururoa atoll 52

Nagasaki 42, 69
nation-states xxv, 6–7, 31, 36, 231
  and national interest 4–6
  and planetary interest 21
  sovereignty of 3, 229–30
National Co-ordination Panel on Climate Change
    (China) 124
national interest xxiii, 4–6, 12n., 13n., 16, 193
  and planetary interest 7, 21, 22–3, 27, 74–5, 159,
    247–50, 270
  and sustainable development 10, 152, 156–7,
    159–60, 180
  see also legitimate national interest; vital national
    interest
national policies
  on the environment 83, 88–90, 108–11
    Argentina 92–5
    China 123–7
    Japan 99–101
    Maldives 116–18
  objective assessment of 22–3
  for sustainability 132–3, 141–2, 163–5, 186–7, 204–5
    Australia 152–6
    Bangladesh 168–72
    Brazil 197–200
    India 144–6
    Indonesia 190–1
    Kenya 177–80
    Sweden 217–23
    USA 208–14
  on weapons of mass destruction 35, 39–42, 64–5
    Israel 75–9
    New Zealand 49–50
    Russia 55–8
national security 4, 11, 19, 33, 36, 42, 50, 54, 55, 56,
    57, 59, 63, 65, 66, 74, 75, 79, 83, 92, 215
nationalism 180
NATO (North Atlantic Treaty Organization) 41, 50, 57,
    59
Natural Step 212, 222
Nepal 113
Netherlands 97, 110, 112, 113, 120, 133, 194
New Delhi Declaration 1997 117
New Road Map Foundation 213
New Zealand 36, 90, 110, 111, 112, 133
  nuclear weapons policy 43, 48–53
Ngilu, C. 272
Nigeria 112, 134, 250
nitrous oxide 105, 106, 220
Non-Proliferation Treaty 34, 36, 41, 55, 64, 68, 242,
    249
normal national interest 5–6
normative planetary interest 9, 10, 67, 69
North Korea 63
Norway 50, 54, 84, 110, 111, 112, 133, 148
nuclear deterrence 41, 49, 51, 53, 55
nuclear disarmament 39–43, 49
nuclear-free zone 49
nuclear power 220–1

nuclear weapons 3, 31, 32, 39–43, 48, 55, 59
  convention 41
  first-strike policy 59
  no first-use policy 57
  non-targeting agreement 59
  proliferation of 49, 56–7
  reduction of 35, 50, 52, 56, 232
  Russia and 55–6
  testing of 34–5, 52–3, 270
  UK and 248–9
  USA and 41, 51, 55–6, 57, 58
nuclear winter 40
Nye, J. 14n.

objectivity 22–3
obligations erga omnes 233
official development assistance 157, 162, 165–6, 174,
    181–2
  from Australia 155
  to Brazil 201
  to India 148–9, 156
  to Indonesia 155, 194
  to Kenya 181–2
opinion polls 215
  on nuclear weapons 42
  on state of the planet 83–4
Oslo Accords 79
Organization for Prohibition of Chemical Weapons
    64, 65
Outer Space Treaty 1967 7, 58
ozone protection 82, 87–103

Pakistan 63, 65, 112, 134, 250
  nuclear testing 34, 41
  nuclear weapons policy 35, 59
Palme Commission 6, 33, 35
Papua New Guinea 155
Parliamentarians for Global Action xviii, 7, 13n.
Pearson Commission 165
Peres, S. 74, 79
Perez de Cuellar, J. 6
Persson, G. 217–18
Peru 134
Philippines 134, 155
planetary interest
  definition of 7
  global governance and 230–2
  levels of 9–11
Poland 59, 111, 112, 134, 244
political culture, legitimacy and 15, 16, 21
popular participation 24, 251
population control 125, 141
  in Bangladesh 171–2
  in India 145
population growth 81, 171, 189
  in Australia 153–4
  food and 161, 170, 177
  in Kenya 178
population stabilization 135, 139–42

Portugal 84, 110, 112, 123, 134
poverty 190, 259
  absolute 130, 160
  population and 146
Poverty Strategies Initiative 162
precautionary principle 90, 115, 220, 231, 269
Primakov, Y. 59
principle of good faith 23, 251
principle of informed choice 141
principle of polluter pays 172
principle of subsidiarity 245
Prins, G. 21, 30, 251, 272
producer responsibility 221–2
production, and sustainable development 203, 204
Programme of Action of the International Conference
    on Population and Development, Cairo 1994
    see Cairo Programme of Action
Project Excel 155
pro-natalism 153
public awareness 157, 214, 215, 221
public fear 17

Qian, Y. 270
Qur'an 72

Radical Party *see* Transnational Radical Party
radiological weapons 31
Ramos, F. 157
Ramphal, Shridath 117, 264, 270, 272
Rawls, J. 15
recycling waste 211, 212, 221–2
reforestation 191, 192
refrigeration technology 96–7, 101
regional interest 4, 241
  and planetary interest 27, 242–3
regional powers 241–6
religion, and sustainability 213
reproductive rights 141
responsible states
  for global warming 111–12, 113, 118, 172–3
  for ozone depletion 90
Retroreflector in Space 100
Reynolds, M. 271
Rio Declaration on Environment and Development
    23, 159, 163, 182, 196, 201, 233
Rio Earth Summit 1992 *see* UN Conference on
    Environment and Development
    see also Agenda 21
Rio + 5 Conference 159, 186, 196, 264
risk 16, 21, 71–2
  to environment 81–2, 87, 105–7
  to sustainability 129–30, 139–40, 160–1, 185–6,
    203
  from weapons 32, 39
Robert, K. 212
Rocard, M. 48
Rodionov 59
Romania 244
Rome 257, 259, 260–4

Rome Declaration on World Food Security 160
Rome Plan of Action 164
Rome Summit 1996 *see* World Food Summit
Ruddock, P. 154
rule of law 235
Russia 36, 63, 65, 110, 111, 112, 123, 133, 245
   nuclear weapons policy 41, 42, 51, 54–61
Rutelli, F. 271

Sachs, B. 69
Sagan, C. v, xxvi, 269, 273
SALT II 41
Sambuaga, T. 271
São Paulo 197–8
Sartre, J.-P. 231
Saudi Arabia 65, 76
Save the Ozone Network 101–2
Schneider, C. 119, 271
sea-level rises 107, 116, 120, 123, 172
Security Council 23, 25, 27n., 67, 232–3, 235, 249–50,
   254–5n.
   permanent membership of 243, 250, 251
   right of veto 237, 243, 249, 251
   and weapons of mass destruction 34–5, 48, 55, 65,
     71, 234, 249, 270
shelter 160–1, 162
   national policies for 164, 171, 178
Sinai 68
single negotiating vision 22
Slovakia 110, 112, 244
Slovenia 244
Soros, G. 18
South Africa 134, 250
South Asian Association for Regional Co-operation
   (SAARC) 117
sovereignty 3–4, 11, 12n., 24, 31–2, 233
   forestry and 201
   national 3, 83, 201, 228, 229–30
   UN and 25
space exploration 272
Spain 110, 112, 208, 247, 248
Spinelli, A. 242
Stalingrad 54
stakeholder approach 18–19
Stapleton, O. 175
START 56, 59, 60
Stone, C. 14n.
subsidiarity 25, 245
subsidies 209–10
sulphur dioxide 220
supreme national internet 13n.
survival 9, 231
sustainability deficit 131, 132
sustainable consumption 135, 174, 203–25, 272
sustainable development 10, 82, 130, 176, 196, 201,
   258, 260
   enforcement power over 235
   see global sustainable development
sustainable livelihood 170, 172, 173

sustainable transport 197–8, 224
Sweden 110, 112, 148, 206
   consumption patterns in 217–25
   ecological footprint 135
Switzerland 26, 84, 97, 110, 111, 112, 194
Syria 65, 76, 77

taxation 219, 237
terrorism 42, 49, 51, 57, 58, 59, 70
Thailand 155
Thatcher, M. 248, 250
Three Gorges Dam 126
Tonga 26, 120
traffic 261
tragedy of the commons 233
Transnational Radical Party 245–6
transport 197–8, 224
treason 4
Trusteeship Council 234, 238
Tunisia 68
Turkey 134, 245
Tuvalu 120
20/20 agreement 162

U Thant 6
Ukraine 54, 56, 111
United Kingdom 20, 25, 58, 65, 84, 97, 110, 111, 112,
   119, 134, 144, 148, 149, 151, 194, 201, 208
   global power and 250–1
   nuclear weapons policy 44n., 248–9
   and planetary interest 247–50
United Nations xxiii, 4, 7, 9, 22, 25, 27n., 231, 243,
   253
   Charter xxiii, 7, 23, 25, 36, 53, 55, 58, 72, 74, 75,
     229, 231–2
   Economic and Security Council (ECOSOC) 234
   funding of 236
   and global governance 6–7, 25, 237–8
   General Assembly *see* General Assembly
   legitimacy of 25
   peace force 33
   reform 237–8, 249
   Secretary-General 34, 53, 235, 237
   Security Council *see* Security Council
   Special Session on Disarmament 3, 11, 32, 33, 35
   Trusteeship Council 234, 238
UN Commission for Conventional Armaments 31
UN Commission on Sustainable Development 162,
   186, 204, 205
UN Committee on Disarmament 34, 41, 44n., 251
UN Conference on Environment and Development
   17, 82, 113, 116, 123, 130, 159, 163, 186
   and forestry 196, 201, 202
UN Conference on Human Settlements, Istanbul 1996
   see Habitat Agenda
UN Environment Programme 87, 89, 102, 180
UN Food and Agricultural Organization 161
UN Framework Convention on Climate Change
   108–9, 110, 116, 124, 210

UN Global Conference on Sustainable Development of Small Island States 117
UN International Conference on Population and Development 140, 145, 151, 203
UN Panel on Forestry *see* Inter-Governmental Panel on Forestry
United States of America 31, 63, 65, 84, 92, 101, 133, 135–6, 149, 151, 175, 194, 201, 206
  and Arab interests 69
  consumption in 208–16
  and global warming 110, 111, 112, 118–19
  and Israeli policy 77
  national interest 5, 67–8
  nuclear weapons policy 41, 50, 51, 55–6, 57, 58
  and ozone depletion 97, 101
  policy on sustainable development 209–11
  and UN 12n., 67
URBAN 264
Ushuaia (Argentina) 92
USSR, national interest 5
  see also Russia

Venezuela 92, 93
veto *see* Security Council
viability 9
victim states
  of global warming 112–13
  of ozone depletion 90, 92, 96
Vidal, J. 18
Vienna Framework Convention for the Protection of the Ozone Layer 83, 87, 93, 97
Vietnam 112, 155, 208

vital national interest 5, 180, 248
vital planetary interest 8–11, 82, 232–7, 251

Ward, B. 6, 229
Ward-Dubos Report 3
Warsaw Pact 58
waste 206, 208, 210, 220, 261
  recycling 211, 212, 221–2
water management 170–1, 261
weapons of mass destruction 31–2, 48, 75, 232, 248, 270
  Arab world and 69, 70, 71
  see also biological weapons; chemical weapons; nuclear weapons
White Australia Policy 154
Wirth, T. 151
Wolfensohn, J. 123
women, empowerment of 147, 150, 171
World Assembly of Cities and Local Authorities 260
World Domestic Product 133, 235
World Economic Forum 174
World Food Summit 1996 160, 161, 168
world government 230
World Meteorological Organization 107
World Strategy for the Conservation of Nature 196
World Summit for Social Development Copenhagen 1995 162
World Trade Organization 101, 234, 235

Yeltsin, Boris 59

Zaki, I. 272